What's New in This Edition?

With every release of Visual Basic, Microsoft has added new functionality to ... applications that can be created. Visual Basic 6 took the first real step toward a client/server development tool that could create robust Windows applications. This newest release of Visual Basic, titled Visual Basic .NET, makes the jump from a mostly Windows-based application system to a truly dynamic development environment that allows you to design both Windows and Web-centric applications. The previous *Sams Teach Yourself More Visual Basic in 21 Days* covered many of the more advanced features of the Visual Basic language.

You are probably w   k?" The answer is simple: M   anced Web development and la   g the .NET Framework as th

In addition, every   will see that many of you   vironment have changed to   es, func- tions, and contro   nformative and useful as a re   l good luck!

vell Mauer

in 21 Days

Lowell Mauer

SAMS
Teach Yourself

More Visual Basic .NET

in 21 Days

SAMS

201 West 103rd St., Indianapolis, Indiana, 46290 USA

Sams Teach Yourself More Visual Basic .NET in 21 Days

Copyright ©2002 by Sams Publishing

International Standard Book Number: 0-672-32271-4

Library of Congress Catalog Number: 2001093573

Printed in the United States of America

First Printing: December 2001

05   04   03   02   4   3   2   1

Trademarks

Warning and Disclaimer

ASSOCIATE PUBLISHER
Linda Engelman

MANAGING EDITOR
Charlotte Clapp

ACQUISITIONS EDITOR
Sondra Scott

DEVELOPMENT EDITOR
Susan Shaw Dunn

PROJECT EDITOR
Anthony Reitz

COPY EDITOR
Rachel Lopez

INDEXER
Ginny Bess

PROOFREADER
Suzanne Thomas

TECHNICAL EDITORS
Simon Mordzynski
Deon Schaffer

TEAM COORDINATOR
Lynne Williams

MEDIA DEVELOPER
Dan Scherf

INTERIOR DESIGNER
Gary Adair

COVER DESIGNER
Aren Howell

PAGE LAYOUT
Julie Swenson

Contents at a Glance

Contents

Appendix

About the Author

LOWELL MAUER has worked in the field of data processing for more than 22 years as a programmer, instructor, and consultant. He has taught programming at Brooklyn College in New York City and Montclair State College in New Jersey, and has developed and marketed several Visual Basic applications, including a SQL Server–based reservation system for a private golf course. As a manager he has attended and presented training sessions in several countries and is an expert is more than six computer languages, including Visual Basic and Transact-SQL. He currently is a senior consultant in New York City.

Dedication

I would normally dedicate this book to my wife, Patti, and my dog, Divott.
However, during the course of writing this book, we were blessed with a healthy baby girl.
So, I would like to dedicate this book to my daughter, Katelyn Michelle, who has brought joy into my life,
and to Patti, for allowing me the time to research the material and to work on this book.
And to Divott, my Scottish terrier, who kept me company while I worked.
I love you all.

Tell Us What You Think!

As the reader of this book, *you* are our most important critic and commentator. We value your opinion and want to know what we're doing right, what we could do better, what areas you'd like to see us publish in, and any other words of wisdom you're willing to pass our way.

As an Associate Publisher for Sams Publishing, I welcome your comments. You can fax, e-mail, or write me directly to let me know what you did or didn't like about this book—as well as what we can do to make our books stronger.

 Note   Please note that I cannot help you with technical problems related to the topic of this book, and that due to the high volume of mail I receive, I might not be able to reply to every message.

When you write, please be sure to include this book's title and author as well as your name and phone or fax number. I will carefully review your comments and share them with the author and editors who worked on the book.

Fax: (317) 581-4770
E-mail: feedback@samspublishing.com
Mail: Linda Engelman, Associate Publisher
          Sams Publishing
          201 West 103rd Street
          Indianapolis, IN 46290 USA

Introduction

Welcome to the next step in the process of learning Visual Basic. This book will bridge the gap between the beginning Visual Basic programmer and the experienced one. While crossing that bridge, you will learn programming design and creative concepts that you can apply to any Windows application you might create in the future. In most beginner books, you learn about the basics of the Visual Basic programming language. These books tend to teach you what the essential pieces are, but not how to put them together to make up a working application.

The promise of this book is that you will be a Visual Basic programmer capable of creating an advanced Windows and/or Web program. This book starts where the *Sams Teach Yourself Visual Basic .NET in 21 Days* ends. Now, don't think that you must read the first book before reading this one—you don't! However, it's assumed that you already have a good understanding of the fundamental Visual Basic concepts.

When More Really Means More

Many books promise more; usually they fall short of that promise. With this book you will learn all the aspects of developing a professional Windows application. You might notice in this book that the term *application* is used instead of *program*. This is to drive home the point that a Windows application is made up of many different components—and, in some cases, several independent programs—that are combined to build the application.

What You Should Know Going In

Before using the book, you should be both familiar and comfortable with the basics of programming in Visual Basic. This book assumes you already know what properties, events, and methods are. You also should know about the different types of events generally used in an application (such as Click and Load). Finally, you should understand the concepts of a Visual Basic project, which include forms and modules. The remainder of this introduction will talk about some of the changes Microsoft has made to Visual Basic, bringing it into the world of Internet/Web programming.

 Note

This book won't step you through the examples used. It assumes that you know how to set properties and add objects to forms.

Welcome to Visual Basic .NET

With the release of Visual Basic .NET, you can use even more functions, features, and tools when creating an application. Even if you've been using Visual Basic 5 or Visual Basic 6, Visual Basic .NET will look a bit different. However, Microsoft has enabled you to customize the interface to make it comfortable for you to use. Microsoft also has enhanced many of the existing controls, added some new Basic language commands, and introduced the capability to design and create Windows or Web applications from within the Visual Basic .NET environment.

By far the largest changes have been made in the area of Web access and the capability to move your application from Windows to the Internet. You can do this by using the new underlying .NET Framework, which you will read a little about in the first week. Everything within Visual Basic has been NET enabled, providing you with many new tools to create Web-enabled applications in addition to the old, standard Windows applications.

With each new release of Visual Basic, I've found new and better ways of performing some basic functions, or adding new functionality to an application. Visual Basic .NET has even more neat stuff that makes it even easier to enhance your applications. There are too many changes in Visual Basic .NET to list in this introduction or even in this entire book. You'll find that almost everything has changed to some degree. But don't be worried—it's still the same Visual Basic you've come to love. In my opinion, all these changes have made developing a Visual Basic application easier.

One change is the way forms are supported. You now can use two separate and unique form packages: one for Windows-based applications and one for Web-based applications. By the time you are finished with this book, you will understand what each are used for and how to use them properly.

Another change to Visual Basic .NET is the menu process. Notice that I didn't mention the Menu Editor. This is because it's no longer part of the Visual Basic environment. Menu creation now is integral to the form design process. You no longer need to use the original and cumbersome Menu Editor from the first release of Visual Basic. Of course, all the changes from Visual Basic 6 are still incorporated into the new release.

Another major change to the Visual Basic language is the capability to create advanced error handling routines using new functionality for error checking. Many other new features have been added to Visual Basic; many will be mentioned in this book. As you are introduced to them, you will see how they will make your job as a programmer easier.

Conventions Used in This Book

All the books in the *Sams Teach Yourself* series enable you to start working and become productive with the product as quickly as possible. Interspersed in each lesson are graphic elements that help you identify special information:

Tips offer advice or suggest easier or alternative methods of doing something.

Notes indicate additional information that might help you avoid problems or that you should consider when using the described features.

Cautions alert you to possible problems or hazards and advise you on how to avoid or fix them.

 This special icon indicates a new term that's defined and explained in a paragraph. The term being defined is formatted in *italic*.

 This icon identifies code that you yourself must type. It usually appears next to a code listing.

You also will find certain typographical conventions used throughout this book:

- Names of all dialog boxes and dialog box options use initial capital letters.
- Messages that appear onscreen, all program code, and Access commands appear in a special monospace font, as in the following example: `Variable undefined`. Text that you are to type appears in **`monospace boldface`**; syntax variables that you need to replace with an appropriate value appear in *`monospace italic`*.
- When a choice is given for code parameters, a pipe symbol (|) is used.

Final Words...

Programming in Visual Basic has been, and continues to be, an enjoyable and profitable experience. I hope this book helps you along the same path that I've taken. Each lesson is meant to take one day to complete and absorb. However, there's no time clock here, so take your time and enjoy the trip.

WEEK 1

At a Glance

In Week 1, you will gain the knowledge and skills needed to design a professional application. An *application* is a program or set of programs that act together to perform a useful task. Generally, the programs that make up an application work with the same body of data, or database. By the end of the first week, you will understand the advanced building blocks that you will use to create Visual Basic .NET applications. More importantly, you will see how to use what you have previously learned about Visual Basic. This week will enhance your knowledge of Visual Basic and cover areas that are often glossed over or ignored altogether. This week will also introduce you to the new .NET Framework, which Microsoft has made the foundation for all of its development languages.

- Day 1, "Writing Professional Visual Basic Applications," will cover the concepts of what makes a professional application, the basics of the project life cycle, and how to prepare for the migration from your Visual Basic 6 applications to the new Visual Basic.NET environment.

- Day 2, "The Face of a Windows Application," will introduce you to the advanced ways of using the Common Dialog forms. You will learn how to use them without having to include the control on a form. You will also see how to use a new object to access information about the files and drives on the computer. Finally, you will see the differences between the different types of application interfaces that you can use to create your application.

1

2

3

4

5

6

7

- Day 3, "Creating Simple Forms," will introduce the concept of templates and explain how to use them. Day 3 will also explain how to create new templates.

- Day 4, "Understanding the .NET Framework," will introduce you to the new .NET Framework and give you an overview of what it will mean to you. Day 4 will also look briefly at how classes are used in the framework. Finally, it will discuss the concept of namespaces.

- Day 5, "Working with Objects, Collections, and Array Processing," will introduce the programming skills that deal with array processing, using the object collections to simplify the program code.

- Day 6, "Understanding Procedures, Functions, and Logic," will explain how functions and subroutines work together to create good applications. It will also take a close look into how subroutines and functions affect the logic of a program.

- Day 7, "Building Complex Forms," will introduce you to complex forms and the techniques and tips to use when creating them.

WEEK 1

DAY 1

Writing Professional Visual Basic Applications

Welcome to the next generation of Visual Basic. In every new release of Visual Basic, Microsoft has added many new features, enhanced some others, and removed or replaced some older capabilities. With the release of Visual Basic. NET, Microsoft has done it again. In fact, Visual Basic .NET (VB .NET) brings together new technologies that will make your applications more efficient, easier to deploy, and Web enabled.

Today you get a quick look at what Visual Basic .NET is and what's new in this version. Along the way you will get an idea of the work involved in upgrading older applications from VB6 to VB .NET. One of the biggest changes Microsoft has made is the inception of the .NET Framework. We will introduce this new environment today and cover it in a little more detail on Day 4, "Understanding the .NET Framework." Additionally, we will explore what it takes to transition from Visual Basic 6 to the new .NET environment.

You also will learn what drives the type of application you're creating. This involves choosing an application that makes sense and creating a life cycle or project plan for the application, taking it from an idea to the final product.

Although you probably already know how to do this, you'll start a new demo project in Visual Basic. This review will help you explore the options available within project properties, focusing on what they can do for you during the development and testing process. Naming conventions also will be covered; however, we won't discuss lists of what they should be. Instead, you'll get an understanding of why you need them and how they should be used.

Finally, at the end of today's lesson, we will cover some of the more advanced controls and features included in Visual Basic. You'll see what they are, how to use them individually and together, and—more important—why you should use them.

A Brief Look at What's New in Visual Basic .NET

Visual Basic .NET is the next version of Visual Basic. Rather than simply add some new features to Visual Basic 6.0, Microsoft reengineered the product to make it easier than ever before to write distributed applications, such as Web and enterprise systems. Visual Basic .NET has two new packages for creating forms (Windows Forms and Web Forms) and a new version of ADO for accessing disconnected data sources. Additionally, it has streamlined the language, removing older, unused keywords among other changes.

These new features will enable you to create both client/server applications and Internet-based applications. With Web Forms and ADO.NET, you now can rapidly develop scalable Web sites. With the addition of inheritance, the language now is an object-oriented programming environment; Windows Forms natively supports accessibility and visual inheritance. Finally, deploying your applications is as simple as copying your executables and components from directory to directory.

Also, Visual Basic .NET is fully integrated with the other Microsoft Visual Studio .NET languages. Not only can you develop application components in different programming languages; your classes also can inherit from classes written in other languages using cross-language inheritance. With the unified debugger, you can debug multiple language applications, whether they are running locally or on remote computers. Finally, whatever language you use, the Microsoft .NET Framework provides a rich set of APIs for use in Windows and the Internet.

Changes to the Visual Basic Language

Whereas earlier versions of Visual Basic were directed toward standard client applications, Visual Basic .NET focuses on creating Web services applications as well as the

1

standard Windows client applications. It does this by generating managed code for the .NET Framework and Common Language Runtime (discussed later in this section). This, of course, required significant changes to the Visual Basic language.

Also, because Visual Basic retained many of its original features, has modified and enhanced others, and added some new ones, some inconsistency and redundancy within the language were inevitable. With the major changes required for the .NET Framework and Runtime, Microsoft thought it was a good opportunity to clean up many of the outdated aspects of the Visual Basic language. Microsoft intended the changes to do the following:

- Simplify the language and make it more consistent
- Add new features that have been requested
- Make the code easier to read and maintain
- Enhance the error processing
- Make applications easier to debug

The New Windows Forms

Windows Forms is part of the new .NET Framework and leverages many new technologies including a common application framework, managed execution environment, integrated security, and object-oriented design principles. Windows Forms also offers full support for quickly and easily connecting to XML Web services and building rich, data-aware applications based on the ADO.NET data model. With the new shared development environment in Visual Studio, developers can create Windows Forms applications with any languages that support the .NET platform.

You can create a Windows Forms application much the same way as you did in previous releases of Visual Basic: Place controls on the form and then position as required. To edit the source code, simply double-click a control to open the Source Editor.

Visual Inheritance

Visual inheritance is one key new feature available in Windows Forms that will enhance developer productivity and facilitate code reuse. For example, you could define a standard main form that contains items such as a standard main menu and perhaps a common toolbar. You can use this form in other applications through inheritance and extend it to meet the requirements of specific applications, promoting a common user interface and reducing the need to re-create the same forms. The creator of this base form or template can specify which elements can be extended and which must be used as is, ensuring that the form is reused appropriately.

Precision Form Design

With the new Windows Forms you have an unprecedented level of control and productivity when designing the look and feel of your applications. Features such as the Menu Designer, anchoring, docking, and many other new controls enable a higher level of power and precision for developers building rich Windows-based user interfaces.

Windows Forms provides you with a rich set of technologies for building Windows-based applications. There are new controls and features for fine-tuning the user interface; Windows Forms also provides flexible deployment and integrated security.

The New Web Forms

Web Forms was created to address the differences between the techniques in use to build a Windows application and those used to create a Web application. With Visual Basic .NET you can rapidly develop applications that will run on the Internet using the exact same techniques you have already learned in Visual Basic. To create a Web application, simply add a Web Form to your project, drag the controls you need onto the page, and then double-click each control to add the code required. Web Forms provides the following advantages:

- Separates the HTML layout from the code behind the page. This separation makes it easier to update either piece independently of the other, simplifying code navigation and enabling code to be versioned more easily.

- Greatly enhances runtime performance because the code behind the HTML page is compiled into an executable—not script, which had to be interpreted every time it was executed.

- Generates HTML pages in HTML 3.2, which means the page can be viewed on any platform, with any browser. Alternatively, you can target the special capabilities of a specific browser or wireless device.

Previous versions of Visual Studio Tools have attempted to simplify Web development. For example, Visual Basic provided support for DHTML clients and WebClasses; Visual InterDev assisted in the development of Active Server Pages (ASP). Web Forms addresses these issues and is the fundamental method of building Web applications with Visual Basic .NET. Web Forms represents an evolution of ASP and WebClasses, providing the best of both models.

Transitioning from Visual Basic 6

Microsoft considered two options when designing Visual Basic .NET: Retrofit the existing code base to run on top of the .NET Framework or build from the ground up, taking full advantage of the platform. To deliver the features most requested by customers (for example, inheritance and threading) and ensure that Visual Basic moves forward into the next generation of Web applications, Microsoft decided to build Visual Basic .NET from the ground up on the new .NET Framework.

Visual Basic .NET enables a fundamental shift from traditional Windows development to building next-generation Web and Windows applications. For this reason your code will need to be upgraded to take advantage of Visual Basic .NET. Thankfully, Microsoft has provided an Upgrade Wizard to help you perform this task. When you open a Visual Basic 6 project in Visual Basic .NET, the Upgrade Wizard will automatically step you through the upgrade process and create a new Visual Basic .NET project, leaving your existing project untouched.

When your project is upgraded, the language is modified for any syntax changes and your Visual Basic 6.0 Forms are converted to Windows Forms. In most cases you will have to make some changes to your code once it's upgraded because certain objects and language features either have no equivalent in Visual Basic .NET, or have an equivalent too different for an automatic upgrade. After the upgrade you also might want to modify your application to take advantage of some newer features in Visual Basic .NET.

When you use the Upgrade Wizard, most required language and object changes will be made for you. The Upgrade Wizard starts when you open a Visual Basic 6 application. It will ask you about the project type and set options for your application (see Figure 1.1). For now, leave the defaults displayed.

FIGURE 1.1

Upgrading your Visual Basic 6 application using the wizard.

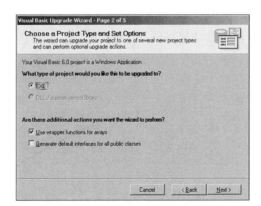

The next step is to specify where you want the new .NET project to be saved. Remember that your original project won't be modified. Once completed, the new project will remain open in the Solutions Explorer. You then can display the Upgrade Report to see what issues you need to resolve as shown in Figure 1.2.

FIGURE **1.2**

Working with the Upgrade Report to resolve Visual Basic language issues.

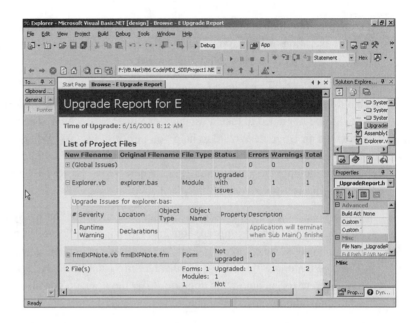

Two very good documents are available from the Microsoft Visual Basic .NET Web site:

- *Preparing Your VB 6 Applications for the Upgrade to VB.NET*
- *The Transition from Visual Basic 6.0 to Visual Basic.NET*

Taking a Brief Look at the .NET Framework

Microsoft .NET will enable the Internet to be the basis of a new operating system. It frees us from the constraints of hardware by making user data available from the Internet. .NET is important to users because it makes information accessible across all devices. It also changes the way developers develop applications by allowing them to hook into Web Services. The framework provides a foundation on which you build and run applications. This foundation allows you to build applications more easily, using a consistent component base.

This framework covers all the layers of software development above the operating system. The .NET Framework actually shields you from the operating system functionality such as file handling and memory allocation. This prepares you to develop an application that ports to a wide variety of hardware and operating system foundations.

The framework actually consists of a group of technologies that form the foundation for the .NET platform. Figure 1.3 shows the major components of the .NET Framework.

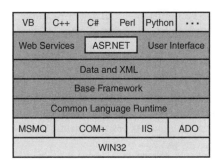

FIGURE 1.3

The .NET Framework consists of several different components, including the Common Language Runtime.

The runtime is responsible for managing your code and providing services to it while it executes, playing a role similar to that of the Visual Basic 6.0 runtime DLL. The .NET programming languages, such as Visual Basic .NET, utilize .NET services and features through a common set of unified classes. The .NET Framework also allows you to deploy your Visual Basic .NET applications without worrying about dependencies in your application as you did in Visual Basic 6. The .NET Framework and the Common Language Runtime will be discussed in greater detail on Day 4, "Understanding the .NET Framework."

Understanding the Common Language Runtime

NEW TERM   The .NET Framework provides a runtime environment called the Common Language Runtime (CLR), which manages the execution of code and provides the services that streamline the development process. Code that you develop with a *language compiler,* which targets the runtime, is called *managed code.* Some of the benefits of the CLR are

- Cross-language integration
- Cross-language exception handling
- Enhanced security
- Versioning
- Deployment support

The CLR automatically handles object layout and manages all the references to those objects, including releasing them when they are no longer being used. CLR provides automatic memory management, which eliminates memory leaks as well as some other common programming errors.

The CLR makes it easy to design components and applications whose objects interact across languages. Objects written in different languages can communicate with each other and their behaviors can be tightly integrated. For example, you can define a class; then, using a different language, derive a class from the original class or call a method on it.

You also can pass an instance of a class to a method on a class written in a different language. This cross-language integration is possible because language compilers and tools that target the runtime use a common type system defined by the runtime. They then follow the runtime's rules for defining new types and create, use, persist, and bind to types.

Visual Basic and the .NET Framework

The runtime file associated with Visual Basic 6 was great at simplifying many of the common programming tasks you required. However, having this simplifying layer meant that you couldn't use new features in an operating system such as DirectX until a Visual Basic–accessible wrapper was created for it.

As a Visual Basic programmer, the most important benefit you get from the .NET Framework is direct and easy access to the underlying .NET platform using a consistent programming model. This means you can build applications with Visual Basic .NET that would not be easy or possible to build with Visual Basic 6. You will appreciate having access to the same features and capabilities as other platform languages. For example, you no longer have to know C++ to create a Windows Service; you can do it all within Visual Basic .NET.

What Makes a Professional Application?

If you read one or more Visual Basic books or have worked with Visual Basic for any length of time, you've probably created many small programs, trying out Visual Basic's different features. By using all the tools, controls, and objects you've learned, you can really impress your friends and family with the things you can get the computer to do. However, after you do this for a while, you've probably asked yourself, "What do I do now?"

NEW TERM To do anything useful on your computer, you need to create larger and more complex programs, or groups of programs called *applications*. Whether the application you're creating is a small inventory program for the house, a personal phone book, or possibly a personnel tracking system for your office, many things go into creating it. If you take a close look at most popular software on the market, such as Microsoft Money, you can see that many different but related routines create the single application.

Whether a seasoned programmer or a newcomer to the industry, everyone dreams of creating an application to sell. Next time you go into a computer store, look at the numerous

1

software applications available; most of them started as one person's idea. If this is where you're heading, you need to know how to plan your application accordingly.

When developing an application, most programmers don't consider what happens when they're done. If you're working for a company, the finished application is handled differently from the way it would be if you were planning to sell the application yourself. Putting everything together into one package takes patience, time, imagination, a little luck, and lots of planning. If all goes well, the finished product will look good and work well.

Application Types

You might not realize it, but you can create three distinct types of applications. If you're just starting out as a developer, this might seem a little strange. An application is an application, right? Wrong! Depending on where you work, the type of application you're creating, and the application's final audience, the package you create will be quite different.

You might create three types of applications:

- A *personal* application is one that you create for yourself and no one else. You probably won't create any help files or a manual for your own application. Also, because it's running on your own PC, you won't create any distribution disks. As you can see, a personal application is like keeping a private journal; no one else will ever know about it unless you tell.

- When working for a company, most applications you develop probably will be *internal* ones used by other employees of that company or by company clients (for example, home banking software). If the application is completely internal, you don't need to consider any issues that deal with marketing the application. However, you do need to create a help system and a manual because you aren't the only one who will be using the application. Users must have some type of documentation to refer to when using the application.

- If the application is for company clients or for *retail* distribution, marketing and advertising must be included in the overall process.

In the current Web-focused environment, these types even extend to the Internet. You can develop applications that run entirely on a Web browser (like many banking applications), or run locally on the PC from the Web without installing the application before using it. Of course, there is the old standard of installing the application directly on the PC.

Picking the Right Application

NEW TERM Before jumping in and creating an application, you must decide what function the application will serve. This decision isn't as easy as it might sound. For every idea you can think up, probably 10 other people have had the same idea. Depending on whether you're creating an application to learn more about programming, to use at home, or to sell, you need to do some *market research* about what the application will do. It's very important to understand the type of person who would use it and how many you might sell, which will help you decide whether to go any further with the idea.

Without doing market research, you might create a great product that nobody wants or a product with so many competitors that your product gets lost in the crowd. If you find that too many other products of the same type are already on the market, you might select a different type of application or place the finished product into the realm of shareware (discussed later in this book). For instance, you don't want to spend time creating a word processing product when products such as Word and WordPerfect are already on the market.

In short, you need to select an idea that's new—or at least different—and run with it. You also have to compare the cost of creating and advertising the product versus your available cash and expected sales. However, once you decide on the application, jump in and start the process. You definitely want to get your product to the public as quickly as you can, with the best quality possible.

Project Life Cycle

NEW TERM When creating an application, you must take several steps to ensure that it's done correctly. These steps generally are grouped together and called the *project life cycle*. Although the number of steps in this cycle can vary depending on the project's complexity, every project must take several universal steps. These steps, called the *standard life cycle* (see Figure 1.4), enable you to plan each section of work and set goals to help verify that you're ready to move on to the next step.

Many newer Windows programmers sidestep this approach, preferring to start coding their application immediately; however, doing so usually causes problems later on. If you don't plan or blueprint your application, you could wind up forgetting something important and redoing large portions of your work just when you thought you were finished.

Design

The most difficult part of creating any application is deciding what it will do. When that's accomplished, the rest becomes relatively easy. The time you spend designing an application is the most important portion of the project. As mentioned earlier, some programmers like to jump right in and start coding. For every hour that you spend designing your application, you could wind up saving as much as a day of debugging time. If you start with a good design, you'll have considered many more of the situations that might cause problems later and resolve them before they occur.

FIGURE 1.4

The standard project life cycle used in the creation of most computer applications.

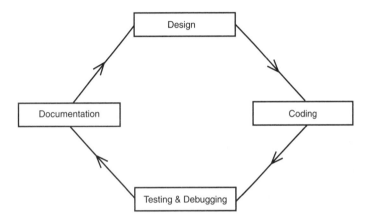

Tip   Fixing design problems on paper is always easier than debugging after they're coded.

In reality, the design step in the life cycle is a cycle itself (see Figure 1.5). Designing an application consists of creating the application's design description, functional definitions, technical definitions, pseudocode, and finally form layouts. From all these steps your actual Visual Basic code will flow. You should expect the design phase of the life cycle to take the largest percentage of time.

FIGURE 1.5

The design phase of the life cycle is a cycle of steps itself.

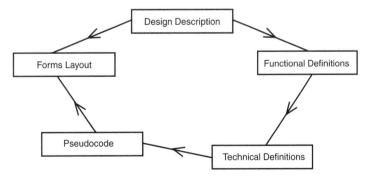

After you write down the functional definitions for your application, you start translating them into a technical definition. As you move from one step to the next, you'll probably find things you missed the first time; if this happens, back up, rewrite that definition, and then continue forward again. In this way, when you start coding, it will be almost a line-for-line translation from your pseudocode to Visual Basic code.

If you think of designing an application the way a house is designed, you would get a good feel for the step-by-step approach you should set up before actually building the application. For example, you wouldn't put the roof of the house up before the walls are put into place, and you wouldn't put the walls up before the foundation is poured. You also wouldn't take a pile of lumber and just start nailing the wood together without a plan. If you did this, your house wouldn't be habitable. It's the same with an application. The plan, or design, is the foundation of the application. If you start with a good foundation, your application will hold up no matter how hard it's used.

To get a good design, you need to understand what the application will consist of. An application must be built according to a carefully laid-out series of steps. In a Visual Basic application you don't want to create any code before you create the forms, or create the forms before you know what types of forms you need or their functions.

If you build the application in the wrong order or leave a part out, it will be that much harder to add the code when the rest of the application is finished. It could take longer to finish—or never work at all. To design an application correctly, you first must understand what you want it to do.

The first step in the design process is to put the overall application definition into words. This usually is done by writing a short paragraph describing exactly what the application is and what it will be able to do; for example:

> **Personal address/phone book**   This application will keep track of names, addresses, and phone numbers by name. It will allow as many different addresses and phone numbers as needed. It also will allow the entry of some personal information (such as birth date, spouse's name, and children's names) to be determined later. It will provide reports in several formats and allow users to search the database for a particular person.

This example presents you with a good idea of what main functions the application will perform, giving you a final goal to aim for as you define the more detailed functions in the application. As an alternative to describing the application in a paragraph, you could list the main functions of the application as follows:

Personal address/phone book

Name/address/phone number entry and display

Personal Information entry

Searching for selected names, state, type, and so forth

Reporting

Data backup and recovery

Multiple database files

This method also provides a road map to follow when defining the functions in more technical detail. A good method for putting the functional definitions on paper is to describe each function in detail. When doing so you should try to describe in sequence all the events, options, and results that might occur when users choose this function in the application.

You also might describe how this function interacts with other functions in the application. Using a conversational style when describing each function makes the purpose of each function easily understandable. A definition of a data entry form in this type of style is as follows:

Data Entry The data entry form will allow entry of the following information: name, address, phone number, spouse, children's names and ages, and other miscellaneous information about the person being added. This function must allow for as many different addresses, phone numbers, family members, and miscellaneous information as necessary; the number can vary from entry to entry. It also will check whether the input is correct (that is, validate that the phone number has the appropriate number of digits). Also, it will verify that the person being added isn't already in the database. Finally, it will support a modification and delete function.

NEW TERM As you can see in this example, the main function is broken into *subfunctions,* which describe each step within the main function, such as what the application will do when the entry form's Update button is clicked.

NEW TERM The next step in the design process is taking these functional definitions and translating them into a technical definition or *pseudocode*. Pseudocode is a style and a technique that allows you to define a function in such great detail that you can almost write the Visual Basic code from the pseudocode. The problem with the technique is that it's not as easy as it sounds because most of us don't think like a computer. However, when you force yourself to create the pseudocode, you'll find that many technical issues you didn't think of are discovered and added to the design or removed from the application. The following simple function demonstrates how pseudocode would look:

```
Duplicate Name Check
Input: Name of person being added to database.
Process:
Get input name
Initialize SQL statement to query the database for the input name
Execute the SQL statement
Check the query resultset
If no records are found - return a 0 to signal that no duplicate records
     were found
If a record was found - return a 1 to signal that the entry is a duplicate
Close the query
Exit function
Error Process:
If an error occurs
Display the error number and message to the user
Return the error number to indicate a problem occurred while checking
     the database
```

As you can see, because this is almost Visual Basic code by itself, translating it into actual Visual Basic code will be far easier than if you didn't do this type of designing.

Finally, you need to define the forms and reports you'll need according to the functions already defined. This is more difficult to do because there's really no set way of doing this type of design. You'll find many tips, concepts, and suggestions about form design (as covered later in this book); however, it really comes down to personal choice. With all that said, remember that the design you finally come up with isn't set in concrete. You can and should go back over the design several times, looking for possible problems before you start creating the actual application. This critical review of your plans is an important part of the design process.

Coding

Well, you've done it. You made it past the design phase of your project. Be proud that you did; more than half of all application projects never make it this far. Now you're ready to start coding—but don't bite off more than you can work on at a time. Also, treat the coding process as if you're peeling an orange. Start by coding the main form of your application with the menu and button bar in place (see Figure 1.6). When you code your application, start with what the user will see when it's started.

At this point if you selected any menu or button options, nothing much would happen because you haven't written any code related to those options. Writing code for the computer isn't as simple as writing a letter. The code placed in a Visual Basic application is organized hierarchically. An application generally consists of one or more modules, including form modules, one for each form in the application; standard modules for shared code; and possibly class modules. Determining which procedures belong in which module depends somewhat on the type of application you're creating.

FIGURE 1.6

Main form of a sample application showing the skeleton of the user interface.

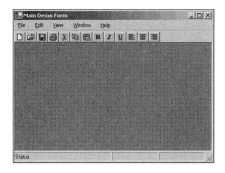

There are certain conventions for formatting and labeling everything in program code. Coding conventions are an attempt to standardize the structure and coding style of any application so that you—and more important, others—can easily read, understand, and maintain the code. Because most applications aren't as simple as the "Hello World" example most books use to teach programming, the organization or structure of your application code becomes very important. Depending on what a section of code does and where it's used, you would place it in different areas of your application. Code is placed in three areas:

- **Event procedures** are subprograms coded to execute in response to specific events in your application.
- **Standard code modules** are subprograms not related to a specific form or control that might be used by objects in different forms.
- **Class modules** contain code and data.

By structuring your code properly and following good coding conventions, your source code will be more precise, readable, and unambiguous and as intuitive as possible.

Note

The object of conventions is to make the application code easy to read and understand without inhibiting your natural creativity with excessive constraints and arbitrary restrictions. For this reason, the conventions suggested here are short and entirely voluntary. This section isn't attempting to tell you how your coding should look or be done; it's only making some suggestions.

Listing 1.1 is a *before* example of a coded function.

LISTING 1.1   Hard-to-Read Code

```
Private Sub save_but_Click()
Me.Cursor = System.Windows.Forms.Cursors.WaitCursor
noupd_ent = False
If new_but.Enabled = False Then
Set logset = logdb.CreateDynaset("cdt_tbl")
logset.FindFirst "[first name] = '" & fname.Text & "' and [last name] =_
        '" & lname.Text & "'"
If Not logset.NoMatch Then
logset.Close
noupd_ent = True
Me.Cursor = System.Windows.Forms.Cursors.Default
MsgBox("Duplicate Candidate Name Entered")
fname.SetFocus
Exit Sub
End If
logset.Close
End If
If data1.Recordset.EOF And data1.Recordset.BOF Then
norecs = True
Else
bk = data1.Recordset.BookMark
norecs = False
End If
If Len(lname.Text) = 0 Then
Me.Cursor = System.Windows.Forms.Cursors.Default
MsgBox("You Must Enter a First and Last Name.", 32, setmsg)
Exit Sub
End If
data1.Recordset.Update
loading = True
cdt_sel = data1.Recordset.Fields("cdt_id").Value
noupd_ent = False
Me.Cursor = System.Windows.Forms.Cursors.Default
End Sub
```

When you enter code, the two easiest things you can do are add comments to the code and consistently indent the code so that different logic blocks become obvious (for example, If...Then...Else...End If). Both conventions improve the overall readability of your code. To continue the trend of commenting your application, you should have a brief comment box at the beginning of each procedure and function to describe what the item does (but not how it does it). Any argument passed to the procedure should be described when its usage isn't obvious or a certain range of values is expected.

You've also probably read about the need for naming conventions. In a Visual Basic application, each object, constant, and variable needs to have a well thought-out name.

Each name should include a prefix that defines the data type. For example,
`strFirstname` tells any programmer that the variable is defined as a string and that it's
used to hold the first name for a data entry. To show you how all this helps, the earlier
sample code has been rewritten with all these conventions (see Listing 1.2).

LISTING 1.2   Properly Formatted Code for Easy Reading

```
Private Sub cmdSaveRecord_Click()
'********
'* This routine will check to see if the person being added to
'* the database is already there. If it is not on the database then
'* it will complete the ADDNEW function by issuing an UPDATE against
'* the database.
'*
'* The variable vntBookMrk is used to pass the pointer to the current
'* record. The variable intNoRecords is used to inform the calling routine
'*                         if the Record was found or not.
'*
'********
  Me.Cursor = System.Windows.Forms.Cursors.WaitCursor
'* If this is a new entry check to see if it already exists
  If cmdNewEntry.Enabled = False Then
      Set recLogRecord = dbLogBook.CreateDynaset("cdt_tbl")
      recLogRecord.FindFirst "[first name] = '" & txtFirstName & _
                        "' and [last name] = '" & txtLastName & "'"
      If Not recLogRecord.NoMatch Then
          recLogRecord.Close
          Me.Cursor = System.Windows.Forms.Cursors.Default
          MsgBox("Duplicate Candidate Name Entered", _
                VBExclamation, Form1.ActiveForm.Text)
          txtFirstName.SetFocus
          Exit Sub
      End If
      recLogRecord.Close
  End If
'* If no records were found set intNoRecords to True
  If datLogEntry.Recordset.EOF And datLogEntry.Recordset.BOF Then
      intNoRecords = True
  Else
      vntBookMrk = datLogEntry.Recordset.BookMark
      intNoRecords = False
  End If
'* If the last name was not entered then display an error message
'* to the user and exit the routine
  If Len(txtLastName) = 0 Then
      Me.Cursor = System.Windows.Forms.Cursors.Default
      MsgBox("You Must Enter a First and Last Name.", _
                VBExclamation, Form1.ActiveForm.Text)
      Exit Sub
```

LISTING 1.2   continued

```
    End If
'* if you got this far update the record.
   datLogEntry.Recordset.Update
   intEntryKey = datLogEntry.Recordset.Fields("cdt_id").Value
   Me.Cursor = System.Windows.Forms.Cursors.Default
End Sub
```

As you can see from this final version of the routine, the code becomes very easy to follow. Related If...End If statements are easy to spot, and the comment box explains the routine's overall purpose.

NEW TERM   In the routine, notice that two variables are *public*—meaning they were not defined by the routine (within the scope of the routine). By being defined earlier in the module, they can be accessed in any routine that might need them. The *scope* of your objects, constants, and variables are important. They should always be defined with the smallest scope possible. Global variables can make the logic of an application extremely difficult to follow. They also make it much more difficult to reuse functions or subprograms in other applications. The concept of scoping is covered later in this book.

Testing and Debugging

NEW TERM   Once you code your application, you must start the process of testing the code to see whether it works and to fix or debug the code that doesn't. Not everyone tests as thoroughly as they should; this is evidenced by all the fixes and upgrades to existing software. Then again, no matter how much you test, there will always be bugs you missed. In addition to bugs that you didn't find in the first place are bugs introduced into an application whenever changes or other fixes are applied to the code. To prevent many of these types of bugs, you should do what's called *regression testing*—retesting everything that has been tested before.

You'll actually be doing two levels of testing:

- **Unit testing**   This is testing individual routines or sections of code. An example of this is to test only the code for the data entry routine and nothing else.
- **Integration testing**   This is testing all the different units as a single system.

When testing your application, avoid using data or input that you know will work. The real art in testing is to pick test data that most likely will cause errors. You also can try the "what if" method: Ask yourself what would happen if the user does something unexpected, such as enter letters in a phone number text box. After you begin testing your code, errors will show themselves.

1

The other half of this term, *debugging*, is the process of identifying the cause of an error and correcting it. (Conversely, testing is the process of detecting the error when it occurs.) On some projects, debugging occupies as much as half of the total development time and, for many programmers, is the hardest part of programming.

The testing and debugging process is a long and arduous task; however, Visual Basic comes with some great tools to help you test and debug your application code. On Day 14, "Testing and Debugging the Application," you'll see how to use all these tools. One thing you must pay close attention to is the usability of the forms you create for your application. Making sure the application you've created is intuitive is part of the total testing process.

Documentation

It doesn't matter how great your forms are; sometimes users will need help. A help system for an application should include online help and a user manual; it also might contain other features such as tool tips, status bars, "what's this?" help, and wizards.

Note

> The software industry is moving away from the old style printed user manuals and have replaced them with either HTML or PDF electronic format.

Online help is important for any application—it's usually the first place users go when they're having problems or have questions. Even a simple application should provide some type of help; not providing help assumes that your users will never have any questions.

Conceptual documentation, whether printed or provided in electronic format such as a Word document, is helpful for all but the simplest applications and can provide information that might be difficult to convey in the shorter help topics. At the very least you should provide documentation in the form of a printable ReadMe text file.

Starting a Demo Project

When you learned the basics of Visual Basic, you were always starting a new project, but the concept of *managing* the project usually was not covered. By definition a Visual Basic project is a collection of files used to build an application. As you work on your application, you'll be working with many different files. Your project will include one or more of the following files:

- Solution file (.SLN)
- Project file (.VBProj)
- Common VB files (.VB, .ResX, .XSD, .SDL)
- Data files (.XSD, .XML)
- Web files (.AS**, .HTM**)

 Note | The files you are used to working with—.FRM, .CLS, .FRX, and .BAS—all are suffixed with .VB in the new version of Visual Basic .NET.

To maintain your project files, you'll use the Solution Explorer window, which always displays a current list of the files in the solution. The Solution Explorer window in Figure 1.7 shows some of the different files that you might have included in your project.

FIGURE 1.7

Every file in your solution or application is listed in the Solution Explorer window.

Whenever you add, remove, or modify any files in your application, you must save your project. Each time you save the project, Visual Basic updates the project file. The project file contains the same list of files shown in the Project Explorer window and contains references to any other objects being used by the project. Figure 1.8 shows an example of a project file's contents.

The Project

When Visual Basic .NET is started, you are presented with the Visual Studio development environment (see Figure 1.9). From here you can start a new project, open an existing project, or select a project you have recently used.

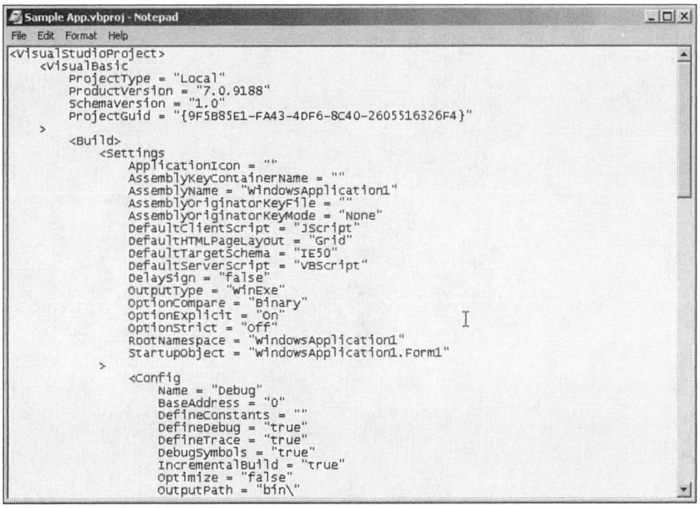

FIGURE 1.8

A project file in Notepad showing the different information saved for the project.

FIGURE 1.9

When Visual Basic .NET is started, you are presented with a Start page.

However, if you don't want this page displayed at startup, you can modify it by selecting My Profile from the list and modify the settings for the development environment as shown in Figure 1.10.

At this point start Visual Basic .NET, and then start a new Windows Application Project. A new solution and project will be created, containing one form. Before you continue, change the name of the solution to TYVB Demo, the project to FileCopy, the form to frmMain, and then save them.

FIGURE 1.10

Modifying the development settings.

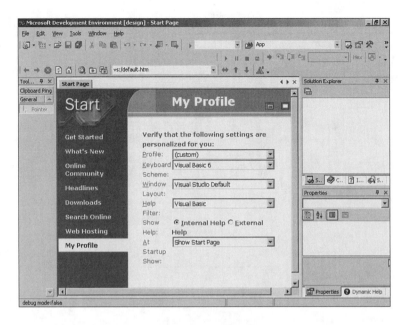

To customize your application project itself, set one or more properties associated with the project. To access the Project Properties dialog box, choose Project _ Properties from the menu (see Figure 1.11). Any changes you make to these properties also are saved to the project file.

FIGURE 1.11

The Project Properties dialog box allows you to customize your applications information and configuration options.

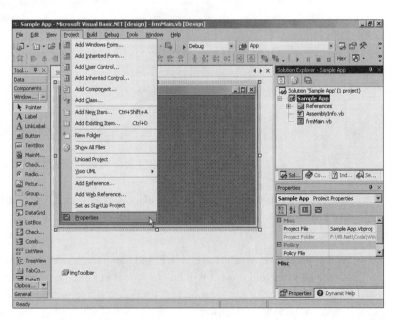

1

The project has two main topics you can modify: Common and Configuration properties. For the moment the two important property sheets are the General and Build sheets. The General properties (see Figure 1.12) allow you to specify the startup object and what type of output you want created when the project is compiled. It also allows you to rename the application namespace and program name.

FIGURE 1.12

The General property sheet provides the standard startup and naming properties for an application.

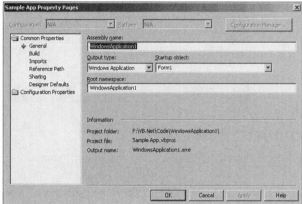

The Build property sheet (see Figure 1.13) lets you set the icon for the application and the three compiler options you want set for the application.

FIGURE 1.13

Setting the compiler options and application icon.

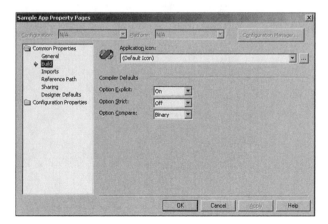

The Configuration topic enables you to set some of the debug options (see Figure 1.14) and optimization properties, which will be covered on Day 19, "Tuning and Tweaking Performance."

FIGURE 1.14

Setting configuration properties for the application.

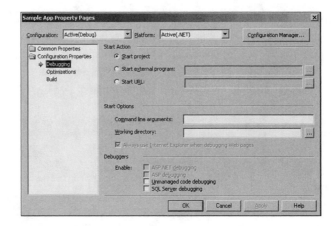

Environment Properties

Finally, you also can modify any settings that control your working environment. To access these options, select Tools, Options from the main menu. This will display the Options dialog with the Environment folder open, as shown in Figure 1.15. As you can see, you can modify almost anything that relates to how the environment interacts with you and your application.

FIGURE 1.15

Modifying the options for the development environment.

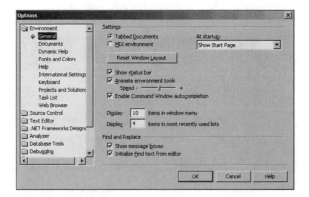

Controls Added to the Toolbox

Okay, time to take a break from all the information that is necessary to creating your application. One neat thing about installing a new version of a development tool such as Visual Basic is seeing the new stuff that has been added. Although most controls in Visual Basic have stayed pretty much the same, some additions should be mentioned before you get into the nitty-gritty of application building. All these controls are available only in the Professional and Enterprise editions of Visual Basic. In the last section of today's lesson you'll see how to combine several of these controls with others in Visual Basic to create more complex interactions with your application's users.

LinkLabel

The LinkLabel control allows you to display text on a form in hyperlink format (see Figure 1.16) and enables you to link to another window in the application or to a Web site. The actual linking action is accomplished with the control's `LinkClicked` event routine.

FIGURE 1.16

Using the new LinkLabel control to display a Web site hyperlink and take the user to that site when clicked.

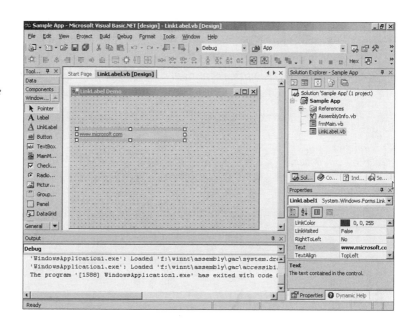

Listing 1.3 shows the code needed to actually perform the link, using a new object or Namespace, `System.Diagnostics`. This namespace provides a method and command, `Process.Start`, which will actually start the default Internet browser passing the URL in the LinkLabel's `Text` property.

LISTING 1.3 Using the LinkLabel Control in Visual Basic .NET

```
Private Sub LinkLabel1_LinkClicked(ByVal sender As System.Object, _
 ByVal e As System.Windows.Forms.LinkLabelLinkClickedEventArgs) _
 Handles LinkLabel1.LinkClicked
    LinkLabel1.LinkVisited = True
    ' Call the Process.Start method to open the default browser
```

LISTING 1.3   continued

```
        ' with a URL:
        System.Diagnostics.Process.Start(LinkLabel1.Text)

    End Sub
```

NotifyIcon

In previous releases of Visual Basic, if you wanted to include a system tray icon in your application, you needed to use some sample code that enabled you to interact with the system tray. However, the actual code was nothing but sample code you needed to modify. In Visual Basic .NET, the use of the system tray is part of the language. The new NotifyIcon control (see Figure 1.17) enables you to display an icon in the Windows System Tray. By using this control in conjunction with the new Context Menu control, you can create sophisticated access to your application from the system tray.

FIGURE 1.17

The NotifyIcon can display a context menu with several options from the application.

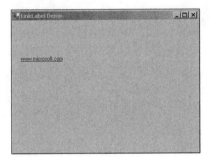

Error Provider

The Error Provider control provides a simple way to tell the user that a control has an error associated with it. When this control is added to the form, all other controls on the form will have a new property added to them. This new property, Error on ErrorProvider, displays an error to the user (see Figure 1.18). Setting the property to a string, which indicates the error, does this. Once this is done, an icon is displayed next to the control in question. The user needs only to move the mouse over the icon to have the error message displayed.

FIGURE 1.18

Using the Error Provider to display a control's associated error message.

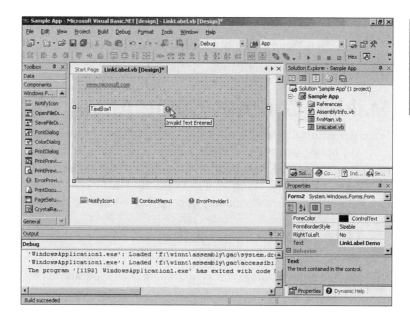

ToolTip

Some controls in Visual Basic have a tool tip property that enables you to display a string to the user when the mouse is moved onto the control. However, many controls don't have a tool tip property. The ToolTip control, when added to a form, will add a tool tip property to all other controls on the form. The only thing you need to do for the tool tip to be displayed is set the new property for the required controls.

Controls that Changed

As in most releases of Visual Basic, many changes have been made to existing controls and features. Although there are too many to mention in this section, two major changes should be mentioned. The first is the change of the single Common Dialog control into individual controls for each common function (discussed on Day 2, "The Face of a Windows Application"). The second is the elimination of the Menu Editor. Rather than have a separate editor to create menus for a form, now you can add the MainMenu control to the form and perform the creation directly on the form as discussed on Day 3, "Creating Simple Forms." There's also a separate ContextMenu control that provides pop-up menu functionality. Here are some other controls that have been modified:

- **Tab**   Replaces the Tab and Tabstrip controls
- **RadioButton**   Replaces the Option Button

- **CheckedListBox**   New in this release
- **DateTimePicker**   Replaces the DTPicker control
- **GroupBox and Panel**   Replaces the Frame control

Making Controls Come Alive

You've probably seen other books that spend most of their time showing you controls and having you try them. At the end of the book you almost feel like saying, "Hey, it's great, but what do I do with it?" Controls are used as the building blocks of all your application forms. Knowing how to use them and when to combine their functionality will help you enhance the way your application interacts with users.

Using Controls Together

Whenever you learn about controls, the one thing left out most often is how to combine them to perform a needed function within your application. This section shows you how to create your own file copy routine and dialog box interface, which will enable users to copy files to other locations and filenames. However, at this point you won't be using the Common Dialog controls to enable users to select the files themselves; that's covered on Day 2.

When most programmers think of copying files within a Visual Basic application, they immediately think of the FileCopy command included in the language. Although FileCopy copies the file properly, there's no way for your application to perform any other tasks while the command is executing. If you want to show your users any type of status information, it would be a before and after status only; not continuous as the command is executed. To create this type of dialog box interface, you'll combine the ProgressBar control and Label control on one form.

In addition to these controls, you also have two command buttons on the form to allow users to start the process and close the form. To create this small application, start a new project and name it FILECOPY. Add the following controls to the form as shown in Figure 1.19:

- Progress Bar
- Label
- Button
- Button

FIGURE 1.19

Creating a custom File Copy dialog box function.

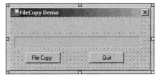

Change the properties for each control as shown in Table 1.1.

TABLE 1.1   Control Properties for the File Copy Function

Property	Value
Form Control	
Name	frmFilecopy
FormBorderStyle	Fixed Dialog
ControlBox	True
MaximizeBox	False
MinimizeBox	False
StartPosition	CenterScreen
ProgressBar Control	
Name	prgStatus
Visible	False
Label Control	
Name	lblDisplay
Text	Leave blank
Button1 Control	
Name	cmdQuit
Text	Quit
Button1 Control	
Name	cmdCopy
Text	File Copy

To get the code to copy the file while your application executes other commands, use the `FileGet` and `FilePut` file statements to read data from the source file and write it to the destination file. Both files will be opened by using the `Binary` option of the `FileOpen` statement. Only two events need code in this application:

- For the cmdQuit_Click event, you need only the command Close to finish the execution of the application.

- For the cmdCopy_Click event, add the code in Listing 1.4 to perform all the necessary tasks.

LISTING 1.4   FRMFILECOPY.TXT: The File Copy Routine to Copy a File Within an Application

```
Private Sub cmdCopy_Click(ByVal sender As System.Object, _
ByVal e As System.EventArgs) Handles cmdCopy.Click

    Dim lngFileSize As Long
    Dim intLoopCtr As Integer
    Dim intBufferCount As Integer
    Dim strInByte As String
    Dim strFrom_filename As String
    Dim strTo_filename As String
    Dim i As Integer, k As Integer
    'Set the length of the strInbyte string
    strInByte = Space(256)
    ' Set the from and to file copy paths
    strFrom_filename = "F:\temp\Testfile.doc"
    strTo_filename = "F:\temp\Copy of Testfile.doc"
    ' If the destination file exists, ask the user if they
    ' want to continue
    If Dir(strTo_filename) <> "" Then
        If MsgBox(strTo_filename & vbCrLf & _
            " already exists. Copy over old file?", _
                MsgBoxStyle.OKCancel) = MsgBoxResult.Cancel Then
                Exit Sub
        End If
    End If

    ' Get the size of the file to copy
    ' and calculate the number of times to loop
    ' the copy routine based on moving 256 bytes at a time
    lngFileSize = FileLen(strFrom_filename)
    intBufferCount = lngFileSize / 256

    ' Set the progressbar min and max properties
    prgStatus.Minimum = 1
    prgStatus.Maximum = 1 + intBufferCount

    ' Open the source and destination files
    FileOpen(1, strFrom_filename, OpenMode.Binary)
    FileOpen(2, strTo_filename, OpenMode.Binary)

    ' Set the label to display the file being copied
    ' and make all of the related controls visible
```

LISTING 1.4   continued

```
        lblDisplay.Text = "Copying.. " & strFrom_filename
        lblDisplay.Visible = True
        prgStatus.Visible = True

        ' This routine loops until the entire file is copied
        For intLoopCtr = 1 To intBufferCount + 1
            FileGet(1, strInByte)
            FilePut(2, strInByte)
            ' change progressbar value to indicate the status of
            ' the copy function
            prgStatus.Value = intLoopCtr

            ' the DoEvents command allows Windows to update
            ' the controls on the form
            Application.DoEvents()

            'Slow the program down to see the progressbar in action
            For i = 1 To 60000
                k = 1
            Next

        Next intLoopCtr

        ' After the copy is complete close both files
        FileClose(1)     ' Close file.
        FileClose(2)     ' Close file.

        ' Stop the animation and make all related controls
        ' invisible
        prgStatus.Visible = False
        lblDisplay.Visible = False

        ' Inform the user that the function is complete
        MsgBox("Copy function complete", MsgBoxStyle.Information)
End Sub
```

Before executing this application, you must change the source file string to a file that exists on your computer and change the destination file string to a valid path and file-name. Execute the application and click the File Copy command button; what you see should closely resemble the Windows File Copy dialog box. This is only one example of what you can do when combining different controls. The only limitation you'll have is your own imagination when thinking of new combinations of controls. Of course, some combinations already exist in Visual Basic, and it's silly to re-create the wheel. Day 2 will enhance this example with the Common Dialog controls.

Summary

Today's lesson covered several different topics that are important to you as a Visual Basic programmer. The first is the need to properly plan out what your application will be and the design of the application. This way you can create an application that will look and perform well. We also discussed the importance of proper programming structure and conventions as you code your application. Testing and documentation proved very important to the final application. By testing the application, you'll hopefully find and fix most problems before users experience them. If users have any questions, the documentation and online help you provide with the application should be detailed enough to answer them.

You've also taken a brief look at what's new in Visual Basic .NET and how to make the transition from Visual Basic 6 to the new release. We briefly discussed the Upgrade Wizard, showing you how Visual Basic .NET helps in the upgrade process. You also were introduced to the new platform that Visual Basic .NET is based on. The .NET Framework provides you with many new features and capabilities to design and deploy more professional applications, both on the desktop computer and the Internet.

You've also reviewed the steps toward starting a new Visual Basic project and how to manage the different components that you can include in the project. Also, the project properties that would affect your application have been discussed so that you can choose to change the ones that make sense for your application. Some of the newer controls available in Visual Basic were covered to give you a flavor for what they can do. You also saw the concept of combining controls to create an integrated, complex dialog box function—the file copy function example.

Q&A

Q What's the difference between a computer program and an application?

A A computer program usually consists of one small executable file; an application is made up of several programs that all contribute to an overall function. For example, Notepad is a Windows program, whereas Microsoft Word is an application with many functions.

Q Can I combine any number of controls on a form?

A Yes, you can combine as many as you need to create a particular function on a form.

Workshop

The Workshop provides quiz questions to help solidify your understanding of the material covered and exercises to give you experience in applying what you've learned. For answers to the quiz questions and exercises, see Appendix A, "Answers to Quizzes and Exercises."

Quiz

1. What's an application?
2. What steps are involved in planning a project life cycle?
3. Describe the difference between testing and debugging.

Exercise

In the FileCopy application that you created today, change the code to move the file rather than copy it.

DAY 2

The Face of a Windows Application

Dialog boxes enable your applications to interact with users using the same forms that Windows currently uses. Today's lesson reviews the different Common Dialog controls available in VB .NET and how to use them. Of course you might be wondering why you need to review this. If you want to create an application that closely resembles the Windows standard, you must understand and use as many of the common features available in Visual Basic as possible. In addition to the review, you'll also gain an understanding of why you should use the Common Dialog controls and—more important—when to use them.

The second half of this chapter will discuss the types of application interfaces that you can create in Visual Basic. When you're designing your application, remember that your user interface probably is the most important feature of the application—if not the most visible. To the users of your application, the interface is the application. No matter how much time and effort you put into designing, writing, and tuning your application code, the success of the application depends on the interface.

Deciding on the type of interface to use can be a little confusing. There are three main types or styles of interfaces that you can choose from: the *Multiple Document Interface* (*MDI*), the *Single Document Interface* (*SDI*) and the *explorer-style* interface. Each style has unique features and gives users certain types of functionality. Therefore, before selecting a particular style for your application, you should be familiar with the different ways each style can be used.

What the Common Dialog Is All About

When the old DOS-based computers changed from black and white to color displays, many new commands had to be created for users to change these new properties. When Windows was introduced, developers knew that users would perform many activities over and over. The outcome of this knowledge was the creation of a set of Windows dialog boxes that interfaced with users. As more programs were written for Windows, many programmers copied the dialog boxes in this set. It was around this time that developers started calling them *common dialogs*.

When Microsoft started producing developer tools such as Visual Basic for the Windows environment, the company created a special tool: the Common Dialog control. With the release of Visual Basic .NET, this control has been separated into an individual control for each of the functions available. The Common Dialog control provides a standard set of dialog boxes for functions such as opening and saving files, setting print options, and changing colors and fonts.

Why Use It?

You might be thinking that the Common Dialog controls are no big deal and that, if you wanted to, you could write your own interfaces for these functions. Through the years, this is exactly what many programmers did, and you could see the differences between different products. No one product looked like another, which made learning how to use various products difficult for users. To get an idea of why these common dialog controls are used by developers, consider what it would take to create just the open dialog. You would need the following controls to create one version of an open dialog form:

- Two simple drop-down controls
- Toolbar with four buttons on it
- Listview control
- TextBox control
- Two command button controls
- Three label controls

You also would have to access several system API functions to get some of the information you want to display.

If all this sounds difficult, it is—and you haven't even considered what the layout of the dialog box will look like yet. Also remember that this is just one dialog box interface. On the other hand, the Common Dialog consist of six different controls that you can use.

Of course, if you use the System File controls included in Visual Basic to create the Open dialog box, the process is easier. However, the resulting interface will look more like the old Windows 3.1 interface than a current Windows display (see Figure 2.1).

FIGURE 2.1

A custom Open Dialog that uses the old System File controls in Visual Basic 6.

> **Note**
>
> Unfortunately, Microsoft no longer supports the System File controls in Visual Basic .NET. These references will be highlighted when you upgrade your application to VB .NET as discussed in the section, "Transitioning from VB 6" on Day 1, "Writing Professional Visual Basic Applications."

As you can see, the best way to put these functions in your application is to use the Common Dialog controls. Although the simple setup is a benefit to you as a programmer, an even bigger bonus is that these dialog boxes are familiar to anyone who has used Windows for more than a day, because they are the exact same dialog boxes that Windows uses.

Interfacing with the Common Dialog Controls

The actual Common Dialog controls are included by default in the Windows Toolbox. As a review, the Common Dialog controls allow you to use the five standard Windows dialog boxes. Visual Basic .NET also includes two new Common Dialogs for use when printing.

- **Open**   Allows users to select files to open.

- **Save As**   Allows users to choose filenames to save.

- **Font**   Lets users choose a base font and set any font attributes they want.

- **Color**   Allows users to choose from a standard color or create a custom color for use in the program.

- **Print**   Lets users select a printer and set some of the printer parameters.

- **PageSetup**   Provides page details for the user to modify.

- **PrintPreview**   Allows the user to select a printer, choose the pages to print, and determine other print related settings.

The Help dialog function that was included in the VB.6 version of the Common Dialogs now is a separate control named HelpProvider.

To access the Common Dialog control, you have to add it to your project from the Components dialog box. You now should see the Common Dialog controls in the Toolbox as shown in Figure 2.2.

FIGURE 2.2

The Common Dialog Controls in the Toolbox.

Start a new Windows Application project and place the five standard Common Dialog controls on the form. They won't actually be shown on the form; you'll see them in the tray at the bottom of the Windows Forms Designer as shown in Figure 2.3. To use any of these different controls, you must set some of the control's properties by using the Properties window.

FIGURE 2.3

Where the Common Dialog Controls are displayed when in Design Mode.

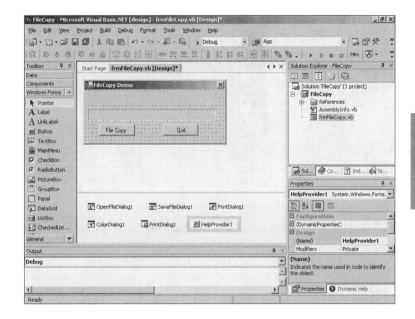

The Many Faces of the Common Dialog Control

One of the most commonly used functions of the Common Dialog control is the capability to select files to open or specify filenames to save. The Open and Save As dialog boxes allow users to specify a drive, directory, filename extension, and filename. With the new dialog controls, the way in which you display one of the dialog boxes is with the same method, ShowDialog.

Open and Save Dialogs

Because the OpenFile and SaveFile dialogs perform very similar functions, this section will cover both of them. As mentioned earlier, the OpenFile dialog box (see Figure 2.4) contains several different component types that work together.

Among these components is the Toolbar control, which allows you to change the way file information is displayed, create new folders, and move up levels in the directory path. You also can use the drop-down box to select a drive or double-click a folder to move down a level in the directory path.

FIGURE 2.4

The Open dialog box contains several simpler controls used to interface with users.

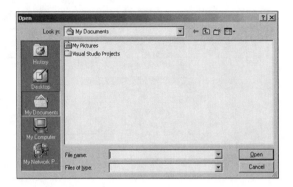

> **Note**
>
> Remember that the Open and Save As dialog boxes don't actually perform any function; they simply get the information from users. It's up to your application code to perform the necessary commands to complete the task.

To see how the Open and Save As dialog boxes can be used, you will create a more robust version of the file copy project than you created on Day 1. This newer version will do the following:

- Allow users to pick a file
- Select whether to copy it or move it
- Specify the destination filename and path
- Check whether the file is being overwritten and warn users if it is

When you work with any of the Common Dialog controls, you will use several properties to set up the interface. In the cases of the Open and Save As dialog boxes, these properties are as follows:

- `Filter` sets the file extension filters displayed in the Type list box.
- `FilterIndex` contains the default filter for the Open and Save As dialog boxes.
- `Filename` contains the path and filename of a selected file.
- `DefaultExt` serves as the extension when a file with no extension is saved.
- `InitialDirectory` sets the initial file directory that's displayed.

The only property that requires more than one or two lines to explain is `Filter`, which provides users with a list of filters to choose from. A pipe (|)separates the description and the filter values from each other. The following is an example of the syntax for setting the `Filter` property:

```
Text (*.txt)|*.txt|Word Documents (*.doc)| *.doc|Any Files|*.*
```

Note

Don't use any spaces before or after the pipe symbol. Any spaces would be displayed with the description and filter values.

This example also allows users to display any file type by selecting the Any Files filter type. You can set several other properties to inform the dialog whether to check if the file or path exists. For the enhanced version of the FileCopy project, you'll add a new form, as shown in Figure 2.5, and modify the original form and the code in the project.

FIGURE 2.5

The new file process form interface for the FileCopy *project.*

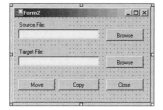

Notice that the new form has several command buttons on it; also it has two text boxes and levels. Of course, it also has the Open and Save file dialogs attached in the tray. In the original form, delete the command button controls from the form and reduce the size to match the form in Figure 2.6. Save this new project by selecting the entire application in the Solutions Explorer and then choosing Save Application As from the File menu, specifying dlgFileOpenCopy as the new project name.

FIGURE 2.6

Changing the old form to enhance the functionality of the project.

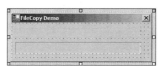

Next, rename the original form to frmStatus and then display its code. Rename the FileCopy_Click routine to FileProcess, and then remove all the other routines in this form. Cut the FileProcess routine from the frmStatus form and paste it into the new frmDialog form. You will make several changes to this code for the enhanced functions. Listing 2.1 shows what the routine should look like. The remaining code controls the action whenever any of the command buttons are clicked. When creating the frmDialog form, the names of the controls should match those in Table 2.1.

TABLE 2.1   Name Properties for the `frmDialog` Controls

Control	Name	Text
OpenFileDialog	dlgFileSelect	
SaveFileDialog	dlgFileSave	
TextBox	txtSourceFile	
TextBox	txtTargetFile	
Button	cmdClose	Close
Button	cmdMove	Move
Button	cmdCopy	Copy
Button	cmdTargetFile	Browse
Button	cmdSourceFile	Browse
Label	lblSourceFile	Source File:
Label	lblTargetFile	Destination File:

Caution   Remember that you are starting with the project that you created in chapter one. The `FileProcess` routine will reference the same controls as before.

LISTING 2.1   FILEPROCESS.BAS: The File Process Routine for Copying and Moving a Selected File

```
Private Sub FileProcess(ByVal FIleAction As Integer)
    Dim frmStat as new frmStatus
    'Set the length of the strInbyte string
    strInByte = Space(256)
    ' Set the file path for the animation file
    ' Set the from and to file copy paths
    strFrom_filename = txtSourceFile.Text
    strTo_filename = txtTargetFile.Text

'   add FileSystemObject code here

    ' Get the size of the file to copy
    ' and calculate the number of times to loop
    ' the copy routine based on moving 256 bytes at a time
    lngFileSize = FileLen(strFrom_filename)
    intBufferCount = lngFileSize / 256
    frmStat.Show()

    ' Set the progressbar min and max properties
    frmStat.prgStatus.Minimum = 1
    frmStat.prgStatus.Maximum = 1 + intBufferCount
```

LISTING 2.1   continued

```
' Open the source and destination files
FileOpen(1, strFrom_filename, OpenMode.Binary)
FileOpen(2, strTo_filename, OpenMode.Binary)

' Set the label to display the file being copied
' and make all of the related controls visible
If FIleAction = ActionCopy Then
    frmStat.lblDisplay.Text = "Copying.. " & strFrom_filename
else
    frmStat.lblDisplay.Text = "Moving.. " & strFrom_filename
End If
frmStat.lblDisplay.Visible = True
frmStat.prgStatus.Visible = True

' This routine loops until the entire file is copied
For intLoopCtr = 1 To intBufferCount + 1
    FileGet(1, strInByte)
    FilePut(2, strInByte)
    ' change progressbar value to indicate the status of
    ' the copy function
    frmStat.prgStatus.Value = intLoopCtr

    ' the DoEvents command allows Windows to update
    ' the controls on the form
    Application.DoEvents()

    'Slow the program down to see the progressbar in action
    For i = 1 To 60000
        k = 1
    Next

Next intLoopCtr

' After the copy is complete close both files
FileClose(1)    ' Close file.
FileClose(2)    ' Close file.

'If the function is a move, erase the source file
If FIleAction = ActionMove Then
    Kill(strFrom_filename)
End If

' Stop the animation and make all related controls
' invisible
frmStat.Hide()

End Sub
```

Listing 2.2 shows the final code. Copy it into the `frmDialog` form's code window; then try running the application and copying or moving a file. The definition statements are located in the General Descriptions area of the form's code. Add the following definitions to the form:

```
Public fileaction As String
Public Const ActionMove = 1
Public Const ActionCopy = 0
Public lngFileSize As Long
Public intLoopCtr As Integer
Public intBufferCount As Integer
Public strInByte As String
Public strFrom_filename As String
Public strTo_filename As String
Public i As Integer, k As Integer
```

LISTING 2.2   FILEOPENCOPY: Command Button Processing Routines

```
Private Sub cmdClose_Click(ByVal sender As System.Object,
        ByVal e As System.EventArgs) Handles cmdClose.Click
    Close()
End Sub

Private Sub cmdCopy_Click(ByVal sender As System.Object,
        ByVal e As System.EventArgs) Handles cmdCopy.Click
    Call FileProcess(ActionCopy)
End Sub

Private Sub cmdMove_Click(ByVal sender As Object,
    ByVal e As System.EventArgs) Handles cmdMove.Click
    Call FileProcess(ActionMove)
End Sub

Private Sub cmdSourceFile_Click(ByVal sender As Object,
    ByVal e As System.EventArgs) Handles cmdSourceFile.Click
    dlgFileSelect.CheckFileExists = True
    dlgFileSelect.ShowDialog()
    txtSourceFile.Text = dlgFileSelect.FileName
End Sub

Private Sub cmdTargetFile_Click(ByVal sender As Object,
    ByVal e As System.EventArgs) Handles cmdTargetFile.Click
    dlgFileSave.OverwritePrompt = True
    dlgFileSave.ShowDialog()
    txtTargetFile.Text = dlgFileSave.FileName
End Sub
```

Notice that two constants are defined to make the code easier to understand. `ActionMove` and `ActionCopy`, instead of the sometimes cryptic 1 or 0, serve to explain what the code segments are doing.

As you can see from this example, the Open and Save dialog boxes can perform some necessary services within your application. The trick is to know how to use them. The application you just created will enable you to copy or move any file to another location on your computer. One of the things you need to do before moving or copying a file is to check whether the target drive has enough room for the file. Since the release of Visual Basic 6, there is a group of objects called the File System Objects, which enable you to get information about the following:

- **Drive or drives attached to your computer**   Enables you to get any information needed about the specified drive or drives
- **Folder or folders**   Enables you to create, delete, or move folders and to access their names, paths, and so on
- **Files**   Enables you to create, delete, or move files and to access their names, paths, and so on
- **FileSystemObject**   Enables you to create, delete, and get information about any of the previous objects

To use these objects, you need to include the Microsoft Scripting Runtime component (Scrrun.dll) in your project by performing these steps:

1. Select Add Reference from the Project Menu.
2. Click the COM tab.
3. Select Microsoft Scripting Runtime from the Component Name list.

For this example, use the File System Objects to get the following information:

- Available space on the target drive
- Total space on the target drive
- Total size of the file being copied

The following code section gets the preceding information and displays it; however, if there isn't enough space for the file, the user will see an error message. You should place the following definitions at the beginning of the `FileProcess` routine that is in the application.

```
Dim Drive_TotalSpace As Long
Dim Drive_AvailableSpace As Long
Dim File_Size As Long
Dim FileInfo As Object
Dim sysInfo As New Scripting.FileSystemObject
```

The next section of code should be placed in the `FileProcess` routine immediately after the `add FileSystemObject code here` comment.

```
Drive_TotalSpace = sysInfo.Drives.Item(Left(strTo_Filename, 3)).TotalSize
Drive_AvailableSpace = sysInfo.Drives.Item(Left(_
                 strTo_Filename, 3)).AvailableSpace
FileInfo = sysInfo.GetFile(strFrom_Filename)
File_Size = FileInfo.Size
If File_Size > Drive_AvailableSpace Then
   MsgBox("There is not enough space to process the file.", _
            vbCritical, Me.Text)
Else
   MsgBox("Total Drive Space: " & CStr(Drive_TotalSpace) & vbCrLf & _
    "Available Drive Space: " & CStr(Drive_AvailableSpace) & vbCrLf & _
    "Source File Size is: " & CStr(File_Size), vbInformation, Me.Text)
End If
```

As you can see from this code, the File System Object makes it easy to access system information you might need for your application. Once you add this code, try running the application to see the sizes of the drive you are using.

Colors

The Color dialog box lets you select the colors that can be used for the foreground or background colors of your forms or controls. When the Color dialog box is displayed to users (see Figure 2.7), it allows them to choose a color.

FIGURE 2.7

The Color dialog box allows users to select a color visually, and returns a numeric value to the program.

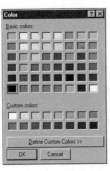

Setting up the Color common dialog control to work with colors requires only that you display the dialog form to use it. The Color dialog box returns only one color at a time, requiring you to call the dialog box for every separate color that you want to be able to change. For example, add the ColorDialog control, naming it `dlgColorSelect`. Also, add one button to the existing `frmDialog` form, and set the button's `Name` property to `cmdColor` and the `Text` to Change Color; then add the following code to the form. The only property used in this routine tells the Color Dialog control to set the initial color.

```
Private Sub cmdColor_Click()
    dlgColorSelect.ShowDialog()
    Me.BackColor = dlgColorSelect.Color
End Sub
```

As you can see, this code changes the color for all the controls on the form. This is a drastic change from the previous releases of Visual Basic. If a control's backcolor property isn't explicitly changed, it will inherit the value from its parent form. In the previous code, you would add the following to preserve the original backcolor:

```
Label1.BackColor = Me.BackColor
    TextBox1.BackColor = Me.BackColor
    Button1.BackColor = Me.BackColor
```

What you've just tried is the basic example of the Color dialog box that every book example uses. Now let's create a separate form that will give users a choice of objects for which they can change the color. Create a new form and name it frmColor. This form will allow users to change the colors of the main form background color and the file-name text box background color. To do this, use several sets of labels and buttons, as shown in Figure 2.8.

FIGURE 2.8

Creating a Color dialog box to interact with users.

The difference with this example is that you're displaying the current color to users before and after it changes. In the Form_Load routine, the labels used to display the current colors will be set. To see this first step in the process, add the following code to your new form:

```
lblAppBack.BackColor = frmDialog.BackColor
lblTxtBack.BackColor = txtSourceFile.BackColor
```

Before running the application, you must change the code in the cmdColor_Click routine to the following:

```
FrmColor.ShowDialog Me
```

This code enables you to display the new form. It also prevents users from doing anything else until they finish with the colors. When you run the application, you'll see the default colors for these properties. Now add the following code to each of the two color labels' double-click routines to change the label name to the respective control:

```
Private Sub lblAppBack_Click(ByVal sender As System.Object,
        ByVal e As System.EventArgs) Handles lblAppBack.Click
    dlgColorSelect.Color = lblAppBack.BackColor
    dlgColorSelect.ShowDialog
    lblAppBack.BackColor = dlgColorSelect.Color
End Sub

Private Sub lblTxtBack_Click(ByVal sender As System.Object,
        ByVal e As System.EventArgs) Handles lblTxtBack.Click
    dlgColorSelect.Color = lblTxtBack.BackColor
    dlgColorSelect.ShowDialog
    lblTxtBack.BackColor = dlgColorSelect.Color
End Sub
```

This code shows the Color dialog box. When the dialog box changes, change the labels'
colors accordingly. Try the application again and change the colors a few times.

Up to this point nothing is really being changed yet. You're giving users two choices
when it comes to actually changing the colors:

- The Apply button changes colors without closing the Color dialog box.
- The Close button changes the colors and then closes the dialog box.

Also, a button on the form will reset the colors to the defaults for the user's computer.
Using the Apply button allows users to see what the selected colors will look like before
leaving the Color dialog box; if they don't like them, they can try different ones. To
finish up the demo, add the following code to the frmColor code:

```
Private Sub cmdApply_Click(ByVal sender As System.Object,
        ByVal e As System.EventArgs) Handles cmdApply.Click
    txtSourceFile.BackColor = lblTxtBack.BackColor
    txtTargetFile.BackColor = lblTxtBack.BackColor
    Me.BackColor = lblAppBack.BackColor
End Sub

Private Sub cmdClose_Click(ByVal sender As System.Object,
        ByVal e As System.EventArgs) Handles cmdClose.Click
    txtSourceFile.BackColor = lblTxtBack.BackColor
    txtTargetFile.BackColor = lblTxtBack.BackColor
    Me.BackColor = lblAppBack.BackColor
    Close()
End Sub

Private Sub cmdReset_Click(ByVal sender As System.Object,
        ByVal e As System.EventArgs) Handles cmdReset.Click
    lblTxtBack.BackColor = vbWindowBackground
    lblAppBack.BackColor = vbButtonFace
End Sub
```

In the cmdReset routine, constant values are used for the related Windows default colors. Run the application one last time and see how this new form works. Don't forget to save this project, as you'll be returning to it later.

> **Note**
>
> When you end the application, any changes you've made to the colors, fonts, or printer options are lost. You can use several different methods to save this information. Later in this book you'll see how to save and retrieve information related to your application properties.

Accessing Fonts

Setting up the Font Dialog control is just as easy as setting it up for the functions already discussed. The first thing you need to do with the Font dialog box is to set the property to specify the font to be selected when the dialog box is displayed. The default font for the Visual Basic IDE is set as the selected font. Using the ShowDialog method, you would display the Font Dialog box as shown in Figure 2.9.

FIGURE 2.9

The Font dialog box allows users to modify all the different font properties available.

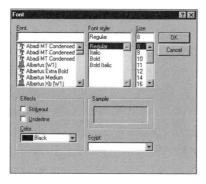

The example I'm using to show you how to use the Font dialog box makes use of a Rich Textbox control and the Open dialog box to get the text file to display. To see how to control fonts, create a new project and format the form as shown in Figure 2.10 by using the Microsoft Rich Textbox control; then add the code in Listing 2.3 to the form.

FIGURE 2.10

*Changing fonts in the
Rich Textbox control
enables you to enhance
text being entered.*

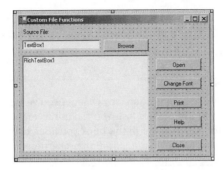

LISTING 2.3   FONTCHANGE.TXT: Using the Font Common Dialog Box to Change Font
Properties

```
Private Sub cmdClose_Click(ByVal sender As System.Object,
        ByVal e As System.EventArgs) Handles cmdClose.Click
    Close()
End Sub

Private Sub cmdFont_Click(ByVal sender As System.Object,
            ByVal e As System.EventArgs) Handles cmdFont.Click
    dlgFontSelect.ShowDialog()
    rtfDisplay.Font = New System.Drawing.Font(_
                FontDialog1.Font.Name, FontDialog1.Font.Size)
    rtfDisplay.Font = New System.Drawing.Font(_
                    rtfDisplay.Font(), dlgFileSelect.Bold)
End Sub

Private Sub cmdOpen_Click(ByVal sender As System.Object,
        ByVal e As System.EventArgs) Handles cmdOpen.Click
    rtfDisplay.LoadFile(txtsourcefile.Text, _
                        RichTextBoxStreamType.PlainText)
End Sub

Private Sub cmdSourceFile_Click(ByVal sender As System.Object,
        ByVal e As System.EventArgs) Handles cmdSourceFile.Click
    dlgFileSelect.ShowDialog()
    txtsourcefile.Text = dlgFileSelect.FileName
End Sub
```

By now you should be able to set the properties for each control based on the code. The
properties for the RTF control set the font information for just the selected text. Run this
application and have some fun with the fonts. You'll see the features of both the Rich
Textbox control and the Font dialog box. As you've seen earlier when working with colors, you can allow users to change any of the application objects fonts by using a separate form to allow selection of each object type.

Setting Print Options

The Print dialog box departs a little from the direct interaction with the visible properties that users can modify by using the Common Dialog controls. This dialog box usually is displayed just before your application sends data to the printer. It allows users to choose which printer to use and set the options for the print process (see Figure 2.11).

FIGURE 2.11

The Print dialog box enables users to set printer options by using a consistent interface.

As in the other dialog boxes, the Print dialog box doesn't actually send anything to your printer; you must code the correct set of Visual Basic statements to perform that task. To the previous sample font project, add a new button control and label it Print; then add the PrintDialog control to the form. The final step is something new in Visual Basic .NET: Add a PrintDocument control to the form. This object connects your document to the Print dialog box. Now add the following code to your form:

```
Private Sub Button1_Click(ByVal sender As System.Object,
        ByVal e As System.EventArgs) Handles Button1.Click
    PrintDialog1.PrinterSettings.PrinterName = "HP LaserJet 6P"
    PrintDialog1.ShowDialog()
End Sub
```

From this sample code you can see that the use of the Print dialog has been simplified. However, you can see that there actually are three different controls you can use:

- Print Dialog
- PrintDocument
- PrintPreview Dialog

The PrintPreview dialog allows you to display your output before printing it, as shown in Figure 2.12.

FIGURE 2.12

Previewing your printed output using the new PrintPreview dialog box.

Although this dialog can have its uses, it does require you to create the code to move the information you want to print, keeping track of several properties, some of which are listed in the following:

- Number of lines already printed
- Height of characters
- Starting position of margins

By using these three controls together, you can create a very professional-looking printer function within your application. Run your application and click the Print button to see how the interaction with the Print dialog box and the related Printer Setup dialog box makes it seem like integrated Windows. On Day 12, "Working with Crystal Reports," you see how to use the Printer dialog box with an advanced printing tool.

Help

You can display a help file to your user by using the HelpProvider control and associating it with the required help file. To use this control properly, you must set the HelpNameSpace property to the name of a formatted Windows help file (.CHM, .HTM., .COL). Once you add the HelpProvider to the form, several properties become available for use by all of the controls on the form (see Table 2.2).

TABLE 2.2 Help Provider Properties

Property	Description
HelpKeyword	The Help Keyword associated with the control
HelpNavigator	The kind of help associated with the control
HelpString	The Help string associated with the control
ShowHelp	Specifies whether Help should be displayed for the control

To see how this works, add the HelpProvider to the form and then set the HelpNameSpace property to an existing help file (.CHM) that is on your computer. Add a Textbox to the form and set its HelpNavigator property to Index and its ShowHelp property to True. Execute the application, select the Textbox, and press F1. When the help file is displayed, users are in the standard Windows help application and can navigate to any area of the help file that they need to go.

The Three Types of Applications

Before you begin the process of designing a professional interface, you need to think about the purpose of your application. If your application is one that will be used constantly, it should be designed differently from one that will be used only occasionally. An application that displays information has a different set of requirements for the interface than an application that gets information. Of course, the type of user who will use the application also influences what the interface will look like. An application for beginners would have a simpler interface than one designed for advanced users.

If you've been using Windows for any length of time, you probably know that not all application interfaces look or act the same. That's because some of them use the SDI (Single Document Interface) style, whereas others use the MDI (Multiple Document Interface) style. The SDI interface is the most straightforward of the three styles you can choose from. An SDI application contains a single data window that users work in and usually doesn't have a Window option on its menu bar (because you can't move between data windows). A good example of an SDI application is the Paint application included with Windows (see Figure 2.13).

FIGURE 2.13

A Single Document Interface application allows users to work with only a single set of data at a time.

The MDI application enables users to work with many different data sets at once. The MDI application also has a Window menu that allows users to switch between windows or documents as required. One of the best examples of an MDI application is Microsoft Word (see Figure 2.14), which allows you to have as many different documents open as you need.

FIGURE 2.14

The MDI application allows you to work with many documents or sets of data.

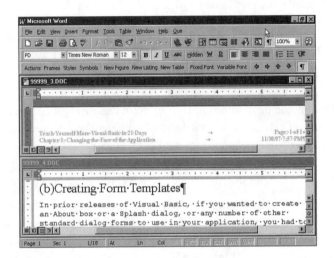

In addition to these most common interface styles, the Explorer-style interface is becoming more popular. This new interface is a single window consisting of two regions: usually a tree-style view on the left and a display or work area on the right. The simplest type of this style application is—no surprise here—the Windows Explorer (see Figure 2.15), which uses a Treeview control on the left and a Listview control on the right.

As you can see, the Explorer style is very useful to work with when the application allows users to select information from a displayed group list. This type of interface lends itself to navigating or browsing large amounts of data. Also, when users select a particular piece of information the working interface can be displayed on the right side of the main application window. An example of this type of usage is Microsoft SQL Server 2000 (see Figure 2.16), which uses the Explorer style to display information on the left of the form; the right is used for whatever type of display or work area is needed.

FIGURE 2.15

The Windows Explorer is the simplest of the Explorer-style applications.

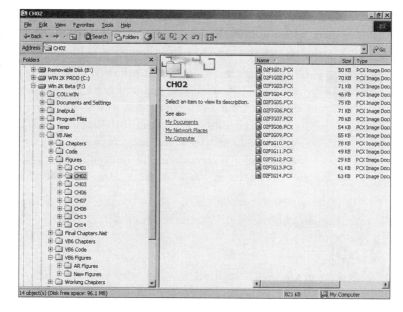

FIGURE 2.16

Microsoft SQL Server 2000 uses the more advanced Explorer-style interface supplied called the Microsoft Management Console.

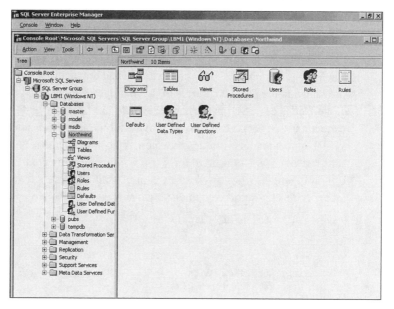

No matter which interface style you choose, be aware of several considerations and techniques:

- Creating a new MDI or SDI application is as simple as setting some of the properties for the forms you add to your application. However, the Explorer-style interface requires you to build a fairly complicated form with several controls on it.

NEW TERM
- Don't think that if you're using the SDI interface, you can't use the Explorer style, or if you have your application start with an Explorer interface, you can't display other forms when needed. Any of the different styles can have multiple forms. The big difference with the MDI application is that it uses a controlling form (or *parent form*) to hold the other forms (*child forms*) that can't appear outside the parent form's boundaries. In SDI applications, you can have as many instances of a form as you need; yet no form is a child of another.

To see how the different application styles operate, you'll build a simple Notepad-style application by using each of the three design styles.

SDI

When you use an SDI application design, what you create will contain a single form with a toolbar, menu, and other functions or features you choose to add. In fact, many of the applications you create will consist of a series of independent forms. Each form is displayed separately from any other forms onscreen and is moved or resized independently. With this type of interface, there's no easy way to organize the forms into a group. Even with this limitation, it's still the interface of choice for many applications you will use.

When using the SDI design to create a Notepad application, you'll work with only one form and add the needed controls to it. Although using the SDI design to create the actual interface is easy, SDI is the hardest type to use because the form with which users interact must be coded carefully to provide all the features users will need. To see how an SDI application is created, start a new project and name it SDINotePad; then name the form frmSDINote. Now add to this form a single Textbox control named txtInput. The form in Figure 2.17 has the Textbox control on it and a simple menu defined. The following code shows you how to display a new copy of the Notepad form:

```
Private Sub mnuFileExit_Click()
    End
End Sub

Private Sub mnuFileNew_Click()
    Dim NewNote As New frmSDINote
    NewNote.Show
End Sub
```

When you execute this application, this small amount of code will cause the text box to expand to cover the entire work area of the form, no matter what size you make the form. Although this application has only one form, you can have as many instances of it as you need (see Figure 2.18). Controlling the application's arrangement on the desktop is entirely up to users.

FIGURE 2.17

Creating the SDI application is as simple as one textbox and a menu.

FIGURE 2.18

Having multiple SDI application instances open at the same time.

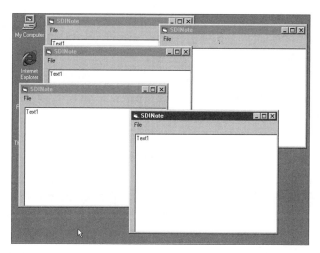

To this simple structure you can add any processing code you need to perform the desired tasks. Some of the tasks you might perform in a Notepad-type application would be opening an existing or new file, saving a file, copying and pasting, and printing.

As you've just seen, the SDI design is really quite easy to put together. However, sometimes you will want to have more than one window open in an application at a time. The next section covers how you can use the MDI interface design to create the same type of application.

MDI

NEW TERM The Single Document Interface allows you to create an application that contains multiple forms within a single container form—the *parent*. When working with an MDI application, you can open multiple windows at the same time and access them from a menu; then, when you minimize the application, all the document windows are mini-mized with only the parent window's icon appearing in the taskbar.

Reviewing the Parent Form

In the previous releases of Visual Basic, the parent form was the container for all the child forms in the application. This form had a number of unique characteristics (listed in the following) that defined how it behaved:

- An application can have only one MDI form.
- Only controls that support the `Align` property can be placed directly on an MDI form.
- You can't use the `Print` method or any graphics methods to display data on an MDI form.

However, in Visual Basic .NET, most of these limitations have been removed. The only unique characteristics of the parent form are

- When you minimize the parent form, it and all its child windows are seen as a sin-gle icon on the taskbar. When the parent form is restored, all the child forms return to their original positions and sizes.
- If the active child form has a menu, you can set the property to determine how the child menu is displayed on the main form.

One new feature to an MDI form is that an application can define more than one MDI parent form. This allows you to create a complex application that contains one or more parent forms, which then contain one or more child forms. The child form also has cer-tain characteristics that affected its behavior:

- Each displayed child window remains within the parent window. It also can't be moved outside the parent window's boundaries.
- When a child form is minimized, its icon is displayed within the parent window—not on the taskbar.
- A maximized child window completely fills the parent form's work area. Its title also is combined with the parent's title and displayed in the parent's title bar.
- When a child form is maximized, any other child forms also are maximized with it.

The .NET release of Visual Basic also has removed the need to define a form as a child. Any form other than a parent form can be used as a child form simply by setting its MDIParent property at run time.

When you're designing the application, you'll work with each form—parent or child—independently of the others. Unfortunately, one of the things that once made MDI forms easy to identify (the icon in the Solution Explorer window) is no longer available. To know which forms are parent and which are child, you must name them accordingly.

Creating the MDI Notepad

Once you create a new project, you must create the MDI parent form. To do this, choose Project, Add a Windows Form, or choose Add Windows Form on the toolbar's Add button. To make this form the MDI parent, set the IsMDIContainer property to True. Once you set this property, the MDI form will look like the one in Figure 2.19.

FIGURE 2.19

MDI forms have a different color background to differentiate it from any other forms in the application.

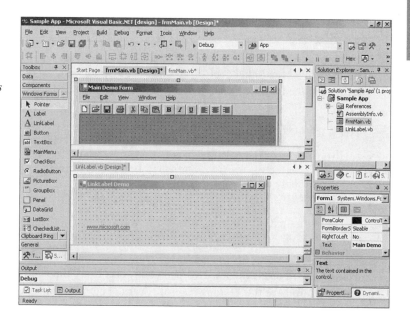

Before going any further, save the project with the name MDINOTEPAD, and name the MDI form frmMDINotepad. You also can set any of the optional properties you might need for your application. Most of these properties are the same ones you would set to control the appearance of any form in your application.

Now add a second form to the project that contains a Textbox control, which will be used as the child form. A child form is just a standard form with its MdiParent property set to the name of the parent form. Thus, everything you know about working with standard forms applies to creating child forms for an MDI application.

In fact, for your application's first child form, you can use the form that's already added to your project and just change its MdiParent property at runtime. Once you have added the new form to the project, add the Textbox control to the form. Now set the properties shown in Table 2.3 for the different objects in your project.

TABLE 2.3   MDINotepad Project Properties

Object	Property	Value
FrmMDINotepad	Text	MDI Notepad Demo
Form1	Name	frmNote
	Text	(blank)
TextBox1	Name	txtInput
	Left	0
	Top	0
	Text	(blank)

By using the MainMenu control, add the menu options shown in Figure 2.19 to the MDI form. Add the following code to the MDI parent form so that this application can display a child form:

```
Dim intFormCtr As Integer

Private Sub mnuFileNew_Click(ByVal sender As System.Object,
        ByVal e As System.EventArgs) Handles mnuFileNew.Click
    Dim NewNote As New frmNote()
    IntFormCtr += 1
    NewNote.MdiParent = Me
    NewNote.Text = "Notepad Version " & IntFormCtr
    NewNote.Show()
End Sub
```

This code will display a new Notepad child form every time you choose File, New from the menu. To have the Textbox control cover the entire child form—no matter what its size—set the following properties at design time:

Property	Value
Multiline	True
Dock	Fill

Because of the way the child forms are displayed, any code you place in the child form is shared by each instance of the form. When you have several copies of the form displayed, each unique form will recognize its own events. Because each form shares the same code, you might wonder how to reference the form that actually has called the code. When you're executing the application, you can display the first child form automatically by putting the following code in the Sub New routine:

```
Dim NewNote As New frmNote()
    IntFormCtr += 1
```

```
rsion " & IntFormCtr
```

;hown when you start the program, don't add this code

e Child Form

ied to make your application more organized, this miss-
cation. The most powerful feature of an MDI applica-
nipulate multiple instances of the child form at the
I applications are made up of only two forms: the MDI
ill the children in the application.

---

t limited to only one type of child form template. For
Basic interface uses many different child form types such
hild form and the Code child form. Also, as you already
as many as you need open at the same time.

---

one child form you must use the MDI form's
returns the child form object with the focus or that's
me light, when you're working with controls on the
ctly which control you're accessing. The
e same way as the `ActiveMdiChild` property by return-
he active child form. The following code shows an
the active child form:

```
eControl.Text = "This is a Demo"
```

---

least one child form loaded when you use the
)erty, an error will occur.

---

i, you need a way to determine whether any of the data
:d and should be saved. By using a Boolean variable,
e Input control's `TextChanged` event routine and reset it
. When unloading the application you can check this
the save routine is needed.

When the MDI form is unloaded, the Closing event is invoked first for the MDI form and then for every open child form. If none of the processing in this event cancels the Close event, each child form is unloaded, and then the MDI form is finally unloaded. Because the Closing event executes before the form actually is unloaded, you can give users a chance to save their data before unloading it. It's in this form that you would check to see if the Boolean variable was set to True.

Running the Application

Now try running the application you have just created to see how the child form is handled at startup time and when you choose New from the File menu (see Figure 2.20).

FIGURE 2.20

Creating several child forms within the MDI application.

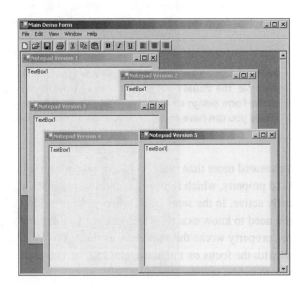

You might have noticed that each time a child form instance is created, it's placed in a different location within the parent. Actually, Windows places these forms onscreen by using a cascading Windows effect, starting at the top left of the screen. To change this default placement and size, you need only to change the WindowState and StartPosition properties to position and size it the way you want it.

Note

The ability to change the WindowState and StartPosition properties for a form used as a child form is new to Visual Basic .NET.

One easier capability to include in an MDI application is to allow users to arrange the child forms in the parent container. The key to this feature is the MDI form's LayoutMdi method, which organizes all the child forms in one of four very familiar patterns. Table 2.4 lists each pattern you can use.

TABLE 2.4   Using the Arrange Method Settings

Constant	Description
Cascade	Arranges all the nonminimized forms behind one another, slightly offset to the right and down from the one behind it.
TileHorizontal	Each form is shown side by side, occupying the full height of the parent.
TileVertical	Each form is displayed on top of each other, occupying the full width of the parent.
ArrangeIcons	This setting arranges the icons of all minimized child forms.

To add this feature to the application, add a new menu option called Window and put four suboptions in it, as shown in Figure 2.21.

FIGURE 2.21

Adding the automatic arrangement processing to your MDI application.

Now add the following to your MDI form code and run your application to see how this works. (Of course you should create several child forms for the best results.)

```
Private Sub mnuWindowCascade_Click(ByVal sender As System.Object,
        ByVal e As System.EventArgs) Handles mnuWindowCascade.Click
    Me.LayoutMdi(System.Windows.Forms.MdiLayout.Cascade)
End Sub

Private Sub mnuWindowVert_Click(ByVal sender As System.Object,
        ByVal e As System.EventArgs) Handles mnuWindowVert.Click
    Me.LayoutMdi(System.Windows.Forms.MdiLayout.TileVertical)
End Sub

Private Sub mnuWindowHoriz_Click(ByVal sender As System.Object,
        ByVal e As System.EventArgs) Handles mnuWindowHoriz.Click
    Me.LayoutMdi(System.Windows.Forms.MdiLayout.TileHorizontal)
End Sub
```

```
Private Sub mnuWindowIcons_Click(ByVal sender As System.Object,
        ByVal e As System.EventArgs) Handles mnuWindowIcons.Click
    Me.LayoutMdi(System.Windows.Forms.MdiLayout.ArrangeIcons)
End Sub
```

One of the best-kept secrets of the MDI form is its capability to keep track of all open child windows and list them in a menu option. To display a list of open child windows, simply set the MDIList property for the Window menu item. This automatically creates a list of the child windows now in the application (see Figure 2.22).

FIGURE 2.22

Automatically displaying all open child windows is easy when using the menu's built-in capability.

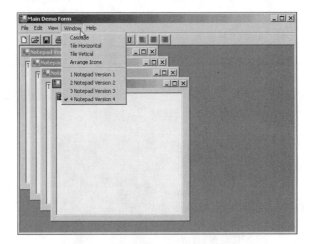

Although you've not really added any substance to this example, the main point to the section was to understand the MDI design process. Now that you've seen what it takes to create and manipulate an MDI application, move to the next section to see how to use the Explorer style for the same application design.

Explorer

Even though the Explorer style is considered an interface, it's really a design that uses several controls on an SDI interface to give users a unique display. The controls that you'll use in creating this interface are

- TreeView
- ListView
- ImageList
- PictureBox

Putting these controls together to get a working Explorer interface requires some special processing to allow users to resize the tree and list areas on the form. You might be wondering how you can use this style to work with document data. A good example of this usage is shown in the Visual Basic Books Online interface (see Figure 2.23).

FIGURE 2.23

The MSDN Books interface uses the Explorer style to display the available books and topics on one side and the topic content on the other.

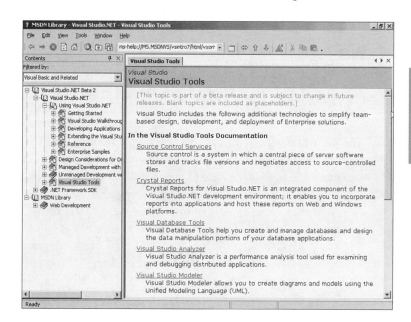

You can see that the two panes used in this application are the TreeView and an HTML-style document browser. For your example, you'll build the same type of interface by using a Textbox control and setting the ListView control's `Visible` property to `False` so that it can't be seen. The TreeView control can display a selection of documents and their related topics; when users double-click a topic it will be displayed in the text box on the right side of the form. To see how this interface works, start a new project and then perform the following:

- Add a TreeView control to the form.
- Change the TreeView Name property to tvTreeView.
- Change the TreeView Dock property to Left.
- Add a Splitter control to the form.
- Add a ListView Control to the form.
- Change the ListView Name property to lvListView.
- Change the ListView Dock property to Fill.
- Change the ListView Visible property to False.
- Add a TextBox control to the Form.

- Change the TextBox Name property to txtInput.
- Change the TextBox Dock property to Fill.

 Note

> If you plan to add a Toolbar to this form, you should do so before adding
> the TreeView, Splitter, and ListView controls. Unless the controls are added in
> this order, the positioning and how the controls interact on the form won't
> be correct. As an example, the Splitter control won't function correctly.

The preceding steps will create the overall interface for you. You still would need to add
the Toolbar, Menus, and any other controls you might need. Of course, you still need to
add the actual application code to this shell. Execute the application and see how the two
displayed areas can be resized by simply dragging the bar between them. To add a couple
of sample documents to the application, add the code in Listing 2.4 to the form and then
add the following line of code to the New routine:

```
Me.Left = GetSetting(Me.Text, "Settings", "MainLeft", 1000)
Me.Top = GetSetting(Me.Text, "Settings", "MainTop", 1000)
Me.Width = GetSetting(Me.Text, "Settings", "MainWidth", 6500)
Me.Height = GetSetting(Me.Text, "Settings", "MainHeight", 6500)
Add_Document()
```

LISTING 2.4   ADD_DOCUMENT.TXT: Adding Nodes to the TreeView Control and Opening
a Text File for Display

```
Public Sub Add_Document()
    tvTreeView.Nodes.Clear()
    'Set the Document Type
    tvTreeView.Nodes.Add("Explorer1")
    'Set the Documents
    tvTreeView.SelectedNode = tvTreeView.Nodes.Item(0)
    tvTreeView.SelectedNode.Nodes.Add("Read Me File")
    tvTreeView.SelectedNode.Nodes.Add("EULA")
    tvTreeView.ExpandAll()
    tvTreeView.ShowLines = True
End Sub

Private Sub tvTreeView_AfterSelect(ByVal sender As System.Object,
            ByVal e As System.Windows.Forms.TreeViewEventArgs)
                                Handles tvTreeView.AfterSelect
    Dim set_File As String
    'Do not execute code if this is the select to build the tree
    If e.Node.Text <> "Explorer1" Then
        set_File = String.Concat("f:\temp\", e.Node.Text, ".txt")
        FileOpen(1, set_File, OpenMode.Input)
```

LISTING 2.4 continued

```
            'ToDo: add code to process the opened file
            txtInput.Text = InputString(1, CInt(LOF(1)))
            FileClose(1)
        End If
End Sub
```

Note The value that is added to the TreeView node should be the name of the text files you are referencing in this application.

This will allow you to select a document, open it, and then display the contents in the text box on the right side of the form.

In the TreeView `AfterSelect` routine, you might not recognize one line of code:

```
txtInput.Text = InputString(1, CInt(LOF(1)))
```

This code line uses three built-in functions to get the total length of the file (`LOF`); convert it to an `Integer` for the `InputString` function. Using this plus the file number that was opened will input the entire file into Textbox control. If you want to allow users to open any text file on the PC, add the `OpenFile` Dialog control to the form and change the Name property to `mnuFileOpen`. Add the code in Listing 2.5 to the `mnuFileOpen_Click` routine. This will display the File Open dialog box and then input the file into the text box.

LISTING 2.5 FILEOPEN.TXT: Enabling Users to Open Any Text File on the Computer

```
Private Sub mnuFileOpen_Click(ByVal sender As System.Object,
        ByVal e As System.EventArgs) Handles mnuFileOpen.Click
    Dim sFile As String
    With OpenFileDialog1
        .Filter = "Text Files (*.txt)|*.txt"
        .ShowDialog()
        If Len(.FileName) = 0 Then
            Exit Sub
        End If
        sFile = .FileName
    End With
    FileOpen(1, sFile, OpenMode.Input)
    txtInput.Text = InputString(1, CInt(LOF(1)))
    FileClose(1)
End Sub
```

Now execute the application. Select each of the two options in the tree list and see how you can work with the data in the Textbox control (see Figure 2.24). At the same time, choose Open from the File menu and select any other text file on your computer to see how it's displayed in the Textbox. Of course, you also can add code for many other menu options and buttons.

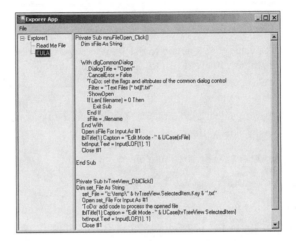

Summary

Today you reviewed how the seven Common Dialog controls are used and learned how to interact with them in a real-world situation. Each different dialog control enables your users to control the look of the application and select the printer and print options they want when printing data from your application. The Open and Save As dialogs enable users to specify which files they want to use when working with the application. If your application allows users to have multiple files to work with, the Open and Save As dialogs definitely are needed. You also saw another method of accessing and displaying these dialog controls to users without adding any controls to your forms.

In the second half of this lesson you learned about the different interface styles you can use. Deciding on the style to use depends entirely on what you want to allow users to do. Although you can use both SDI and MDI for the same type of applications, the Explorer-style interface is most useful when working with a structured application such as a phone book. You've also seen many issues that you need to deal with when using the MDI design.

Q&A

Q **What eight Common Dialog controls are available?**

A The Common Dialog controls provide you with the default Windows dialog boxes:

Open dialog box	Print dialog box
Save dialog box	PrintPreview Dialog box
Font dialog box	Color dialog box
PageSetupDialog	HelpProvider

Q **When using the Open dialog box, is the file selected actually opened by the Common Dialog control?**

A No. The Open dialog control doesn't perform any actual processing.

Q **What makes up an SDI application?**

A An SDI application usually consists of one main form in which most of the application functions take place.

Q **How do SDI and MDI applications vary?**

A An MDI application generally is written to allow users to work with multiple documents or data groups at one time, whereas an SDI application doesn't.

Q **How many MDI parent forms can an application have?**

A An application can have as many MDI parent forms as needed.

Q **Why does the Explorer interface vary from the SDI and MDI interface styles?**

A The Explorer interface isn't actually an interface as much as it is an SDI form design. This interface really is an SDI application with a group of controls designed into a two-pane interface.

Workshop

The Workshop provides quiz questions to solidify your understanding of the material covered and exercises to give you experience in applying what you've learned. For answers to the quiz questions and exercises, see Appendix A, "Answers to Quizzes and Exercises."

Quiz

1. What's the difference between the Help Provider and the Common Dialog controls that you can use?

2. How would you create an MDI application?

3. What controls are used when creating an Explorer interface?

Exercises

1. Use the Common Dialog controls to create an application that asks users for a file to open, and then open that file in Notepad.

2. Enhance the Notepad application that you created today to use the Rich Text Format control instead of the Textbox control.

DAY **3**

Creating Simple Forms

Today's lesson focuses on various aspects of creating forms. Button bars or toolbars are essential for most applications designed for Windows these days. Included with these controls are menus that you can add and manipulate within your application.

NEW TERM After you learn how to use these to features to your benefit, you'll learn how to use forms that you've already created as templates for future forms. With this technique, known as *inheritance,* a new form is created by inheriting the attributes of an existing form.

Working with Toolbars

Unless you've been in a closet for the last several years, you should know that almost every Windows application available has one—if not more—toolbar to enhance the user interface. Toolbars enable users to quickly get at an application's commonly used functions. Depending on the application, one or more toolbars could help with specific tasks, such as the Editor Toolbar in the Visual Basic IDE. Because toolbars are so widely used, most users now expect any desktop application they use to have them.

Adding toolbars to your application has become fairly easy with the Toolbar control supplied with Visual Basic. Creating a simple or complicated toolbar requires that you add the following controls to the form:

- The Toolbar control sets up the buttons of the actual toolbar displayed to users and handles user requests.
- The ImageList control contains the bitmaps used on the toolbar buttons.

To see how these controls interact to form an application toolbar, start a new project and name it Toolbar.

Adding a Toolbar

Here you see how to use the Toolbar control with the ImageList control. Adding a toolbar is as easy as adding the controls to the form and setting some of their properties. Of course, you still need to add the code to make anything actually happen in the application. The next few sections will discuss the process of creating a toolbar on the form.

Selecting the Images for the Buttons

To create a toolbar, place an ImageList control on your form. To begin the process, add the images you want to use on the toolbar by using the Image Collection Editor (see Figure 3.1). You can display this by clicking the Images button in the ImageList properties list.

FIGURE 3.1

Using the Image Collection Editor to add images to the ImageList control.

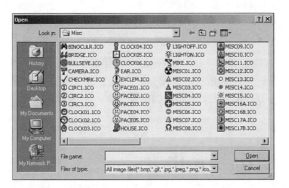

To add an image to the Image collection for the ImageList control, click the Add button. In the Open dialog box that appears, select the image you want to add. When you select the image and click Open, the image is added to the Members list as shown in Figure 3.2.

Find the New and Open bitmaps in /Program Files/ Microsoft Visual Studio.NET/Common7/Graphics/Bitmaps/TLBR_W95 directory and add them to the Image collection. When you're finished, click OK to close the Image Collection Editor.

FIGURE 3.2

Displaying the images already included in the Image collection.

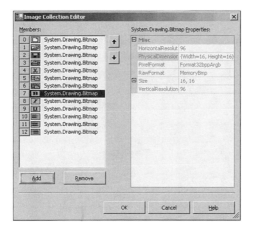

 Tip

Visual Basic installs many different types of graphics files you can use in your applications. You can find any of these files in the /Program Files/Microsoft Visual Studio.NET/Common7/Graphics directory.

To add the toolbar to your project, follow these steps:

1. Place a Toolbar control on the form. It doesn't really matter where you put it; the default Dock property places it at the top of the form.

2. Set the ImageList property to the ImageList control you've just added. This property identifies which ImageList control (if you have more than one on the form) the Toolbar control will use to provide the images for the buttons. (Now you can see why you had to set up the ImageList control first.)

Adding the Buttons

The real action starts when you create the buttons for the toolbar. You'll actually add the buttons by using the ToolBarButton Collection Editor (see Figure 3.3).

To add a button to the toolbar, perform the following steps; then if you want to reposition the button, use the up and down arrows to move it to the correct position on the toolbar.

1. Click the collection button for the Toolbar's Buttons property.

2. In the ToolBarButton Collection Editor, click Add to add a new button to the toolbar.

3. Select the image you want on the button by setting the ImageIndex property, using its associated drop-down list (see Figure 3.4).

FIGURE 3.3

The ToolBarButton Collection Editor allows you to add and modify the buttons and images that you add to the toolbar.

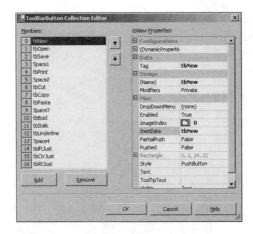

FIGURE 3.4

Selecting the image to use for a toolbar button.

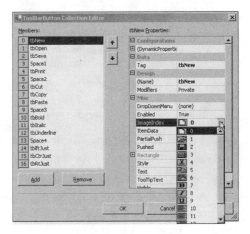

For each button you add, you will need to specify the following properties:

- The ItemData property specifies a string that you can use to identify the button in your code. The value of this property must be unique for each button. You should assign a string that's meaningful to you so you can easily remember it when you're writing your code.

- The ImageIndex property specifies the index of the image you want to appear on the button face. The index corresponds to the index of the picture in the ImageList control. A value of zero for the ImageIndex property will give you a button without an image.

- The Style property determines the type of button you're creating. The button type also determines how the button will behave in the toolbar. Table 3.1 lists the different Style property settings.

TABLE 3.1 Setting Button Behavior with the Style Property

Setting	Description
PushButton (default)	Creates a standard push button
Togglebutton	Indicates that an option is on or off
Separator	Provides a space between other buttons
DropDownButton	Displays a drop-down menu list when the button is clicked

Also, you can set several optional properties for each button:

- Text displays text beneath the image on a button.
- ToolTipText appears when the mouse is placed on the button. (This text appears only if the ShowTips property of the toolbar is set to True.)
- Pushed sets or returns the current state of the button.
- If you set a button style property to DropDownButton, you must set the DropDownMenu property for that button in the ToolBarButton Collection Editor (see Figure 3.5).

FIGURE 3.5

Setting a menu list on the ToolBarButton Collection Editor.

 Note To have a menu to add to the toolbar button, first you must add a ContextMenu control to the form and then set up its menu options. This will be discussed in the next section.

This DropDownMenu feature of the Toolbar offers the functionality included in Visual Basic (see Figure 3.6) and many other Windows-based products.

FIGURE 3.6

Using drop-down menus from a toolbar.

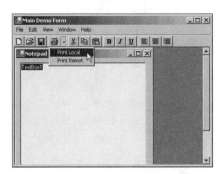

After you add the buttons to your toolbar, click OK to close the Collection Editor and save the changes. Your form should look like the one in Figure 3.7.

FIGURE 3.7

The final project form with the Toolbar and ImageList controls set.

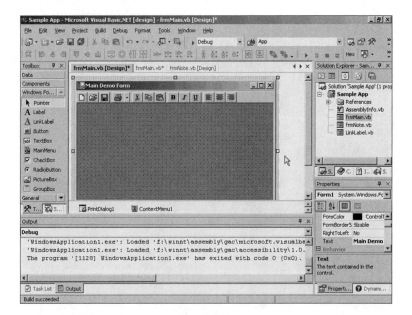

Writing the Button Code

You now have a toolbar on your form. If you execute the application, you can click the buttons and see them respond. However, until you add code to the toolbar's events, the buttons won't perform any functions because they don't have any events of their own.

ButtonClick is the toolbar event in which you'll place your button code. This event passes a set of event arguments in an object to the event procedure called *e,* which allows you to access all the button's properties. In your code, use the value of the ItemData property to determine which button was actually clicked. The following source code is typical for taking actions based on buttons clicked:

```
Private Sub ToolBar1_ButtonClick(ByVal sender As System.Object,
    ByVal e As System.Windows.Forms.ToolBarButtonClickEventArgs)
    Handles ToolBar1.ButtonClick
    Select Case e.Button.ItemData
        Case "New"
            'ToDo: Add 'New' button code.
            MsgBox("Add 'New' button code.")
        Case "Open"
            'ToDo: Add 'Open' button code.
            MsgBox("Add 'Open' button code.")
    End Select
End Sub
```

Tip

In an actual application, these Case statements should call the same code routine as the related menu options. This allows you to program the action once and then call it from both the menu and the toolbar. Doing this makes it easier to maintain your code because then any changes or corrections have to be made only once.

Notice that each Case statement in the Select statement will execute based on the clicked button. Now your toolbar is ready to have the remaining sections of your application code added.

Other Toolbar Features

One of the newest features to be added to Visual Basic is the ToolTip textbox feature. Almost every object and control in Visual Basic can display ToolTips. Using the toolbar, if you set the ShowTips property to True you can specify unique text for each toolbar button. Text placed in the ToolTipText property for a button is displayed during runtime when the mouse pointer remains on a button for a short period of time (see Figure 3.8).

FIGURE 3.8

Use ToolTips to inform users what function each button performs.

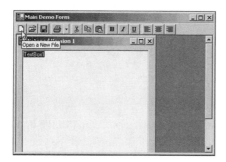

You're now halfway through the process of creating an easy-to-use form for the application. Save this project—you'll be using it to add the menu in the next section.

Adding Menus

Now that you've created a toolbar for your application, you might need to add a menu to enable users to easily select many of the common functions. In most applications, you usually have file functions that allow users to create, edit, and save files. You also have edit functions that allow users to move data around and those for specific tasks in your application. For example, an application I've written has functions for handling pilot information, aircraft data, and log entry functions—in other words, these functions provide lots of things that the users can do.

One of the most important things in any application is allowing users to easily access all its functions. Users are accustomed to accessing most functions with a single mouse click. Also, most users want all the functions located conveniently in one place; to handle this in your application, use toolbars and menus. Visual Basic allows you to quickly and easily create menus with the new MainMenu control, which you create using the actual menu bars located at the top of a form. Pop-up menus that users typically access by right-clicking are created by using the new ContextMenu Control.

Note If you've been using Visual Basic for any length of time, you might be asking, "Where is the Menu Editor?" Well, it's gone! The two new controls, MainMenu and ContextMenu replace the editor, making it easier to work with the menus directly on a form.

Creating an Application Menu

When creating any type of menu system for an application, you must determine what functions you want or need to put on the menu and how you want to organize these functions. By looking at Visual Basic's main menu, you can see that certain functions are organized into groups of similar items (see Figure 3.9).

FIGURE 3.9

Organizing menu items into functional groups.

It is important to group similar menu items according to the application you're creating. In fact, to be consistent with other Windows applications, you should use groups that your users are already familiar with. This way, they have an idea of where to find a particular menu item, even if they've never used this application before. You might find the following standard menu groups in a Windows application:

- **File**—This menu contains any functions related to the opening and closing of files used by your application. Some standard items included in this menu are New, Open, Close, Save, Save As, Print, and Page Setup. The File menu also is the location of the most recently used file list that many applications have. Finally, a File menu generally appears where the Exit command is located.

- **Edit**—The functions on this menu pertain to editing text and documents. Some typical Edit items are Undo, Cut, Copy, Paste, and Clear.

- **View**—This menu can be included if your program supports different views for the same document. For example, a word processor might include a normal view for editing text and a page layout view for positioning document elements.

- **Tools**—This menu is a catchall for any optional programs that might be available from within the application. For example, a spelling checker might be included for a word processor.

- **Window**—If your application supports working with multiple documents at the same time, you should have this menu included in your application. The Window menu is set up to let users arrange the multiple documents or switch rapidly between them.

- **Help**—The Help menu allows users to access your application's help system. It usually includes menu items for a table of contents, an index, a search feature, and an About box.

Use these six menu types as a starting point when creating the menu system for your application. You can include any of them as you need them, but don't think you need to add all six. Also, if you need other menu groups for your application, you can add whatever groups you might need.

Note   When adding other menu groups, be careful not to confuse your users. Whenever possible, place as many of your menu functions in one of the standard menu groups.

Building the Menu Groups

After you decide what functions you want to include in the menu and how to group them, you can start building the menu. When creating a menu for your application, remember that every form in the application can have its own menu defined. To see how to create a menu, start with the project you created previously for the toolbar example. (If you didn't save it, don't panic—just start a new project.)

When creating a menu, you must display the form that you want to add the menu to. Double-click the MainMenu control in the Toolbox to add it to the form. You will see the first menu item on the form ready for you to enter the text (see Figure 3.10).

FIGURE 3.10

Adding menu items to the Main Menu has never been easier. Simply type where it says, "Type Here."

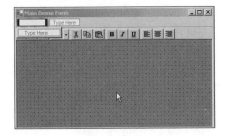

When the MainMenu control is on the form, you can start adding the items that you want in the menu. For each item you want on a menu, you will enter the Text property directly on the menu control at the top of the form. However, the Name property must be changed separately. The Text property is what users see on the menu when using your application; the Name property is what you use in your application code to access the menu item. After you enter a menu item, use the arrow keys to move the cursor and accept the value for the item, moving you to the next menu item (see Figure 3.11).

FIGURE 3.11

The entered menu items on the form.

Note

Remember to change the Name property for each menu item. Otherwise, all menu items will look almost the same in the code, except the number added to the control name.

After you finish entering the menu items for the application, click away from the menu. Your menu will appear on the form exactly as you've entered it.

Adding Menu Levels

If you created a menu as shown in Figure 3.12, it probably will be very clumsy to work with. Every item that you've entered appears on the main menu bar.

FIGURE 3.12

A menu with all the items displayed on the main menu bar.

NEW TERM If your application has only one or two menu options, this might be acceptable; however, if you have many different menu items, the menu bar will run out of space. What you really need to do is set up a menu that uses multiple levels to display multiple menu items. When you click the menu item on the menu bar, the first level of the menu drops down (see Figure 3.13). This level is called a *submenu*.

FIGURE 3.13

Multiple levels of a menu item allow for many options in a small amount of menu space.

Adding subitems to the menu is very easy to do: First select the menu item you want to add the subitem to. This will display a new item entry to the right of the select item (see Figure 3.13). Now click the new subitem displayed and enter the required text. If you want to insert a new item in the menu list, right-click the item below the point where you want to insert the new item and select Insert Item from the pop-up menu.

NEW TERM One other option in a menu is a *separator bar,* which is a line that allows you to group different menu items together with a single menu item's sublevel list (see Figure 3.14). These bars break up a long list of menu items without creating submenus.

Adding a separator bar used to be a bit tricky. However, in Visual Basic .NET, the process has become extremely simple. To add a separator, select the item below the position where you want to add the separator and right-click; then select Insert Separator from the pop-up menu (as in Figure 3.14).

FIGURE 3.14

With separator bars, you can group and organize menu items at the same level.

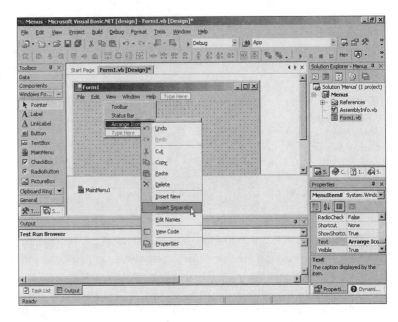

> **Note**
>
> Although separator bars are great to use, don't try to add one to the top level of the menu. You can use them only in submenus.

Enhancing the Menu

If you've been working with Windows applications for any length of time, you've probably noticed that you can access a menu item in several different ways. Usually you can do this using a combination of keystrokes. You can include two different types of access in your menu: hotkeys and shortcuts.

Adding Hotkeys

NEW TERM   *Hotkeys* are something you already know about and use, probably without thinking about it. A hotkey is identified by an underscore beneath the letter in the item's text (for example, the E in Edit). To create a hotkey, place an ampersand (&) in the Text property immediately before the letter you want as the hotkey. For the File menu item, the value of the Text property would be &File. Hotkeys can be used for any item in your menu, including the top-level menu items.

At any given level of a menu, only one unique value can be used as a hotkey. For example, the Visual Basic menu has File and Format at the same top level. If you look closely at them, you'll see that the File menu item has the F as the hotkey, but the Format menu has the o as the hotkey. If you used the F for both menu items, Windows wouldn't know which one you really wanted. However, the same letter can be used in items that appear in different groups, such as the File menu's Print option and the View menu's Page Layout option. For each group or level, you can have at most 36 hotkeys—one for each letter and one for each number.

After you include hotkeys in your menu, you can open a top-level menu simply by holding down the Alt key and pressing the hotkey of choice. When the menu appears, you can press the hotkey for the menu item you want to execute. For example, if you want to start a new project in Visual Basic, you could press Alt+F and then N for the File menu's New Project option.

If there's no conflict with letter selection, you should use the first letter of a menu item as the hotkey. This is what users expect; it also makes it easy to guess what the hotkey is for a particular function.

Adding Shortcuts

NEW TERM   The other way to provide menu access is with shortcuts. *Shortcut keys* provide direct access to any function in a menu, no matter what level it's actually on. You can perform shortcuts with a key combination (such as Ctrl+C for a copy function) or with a single key (such as Delete for the delete function). If you use the default shortcut keys (listed in Table 3.3), users will already know how to perform certain common tasks.

TABLE 3.3   Standard Shortcut Keys Used by Windows Applications

Menu Item	Shortcut Key	Description
Edit Menu		
Cut	Ctrl+X	Removes text or a control and copies it to the Clipboard
Copy	Ctrl+C	Copies the text or control to the Clipboard
Paste	Ctrl+V	Pastes the contents of the Clipboard to the selected area
Undo	Ctrl+Z	Undoes the last change
Find	Ctrl+F	Finds a string

TABLE 3.3 continued

Menu Item	Shortcut Key	Description
		File Menu
Open	Ctrl+O	Opens a file
Save	Ctrl+S	Saves the current file
Print	Ctrl+P	Prints the current data

Assigning shortcut keys is simply a process of selecting the key or keys that you want to use from the Shortcut drop-down list. Shortcut keys are displayed to the right of the menu item both in the selection list (see Figure 3.15) in the Menu Editor and in the actual menu in your application.

FIGURE 3.15

Shortcuts are displayed in the menu item selection list.

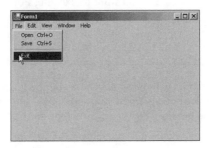

Because of the way shortcut keys work, only one shortcut key can use a given key combination. There also is a new property for each menu item that allows you to choose whether a shortcut key is displayed to the user at any point in the application.

> **Tip**
>
> Just like with hotkeys, the shortcut key should correspond with the first letter of the menu item whenever possible.

Adding the Menu Code

Adding code for the menu is the same as adding code for any other control in your application. There is a Click event for each menu item added to the form. For this reason, giving each menu item a unique name is very important. The Click event is triggered whenever you select the menu item by clicking it, by using the hotkey or the shortcut key. To display the Click event routine for a menu item, simply double-click the menu item you want to work with; its related Click event will appear in the Code Editor window.

Note   If you look at the code that you added to the dlgFileOpenCopy project on Day 2, notice that you had code in the mnuFileOpen_Click routine.

Optional Menu Settings

In addition to the two required properties, each menu item has several other optional properties that you can use to control the menu item:

- Checked determines whether a check mark is displayed next to a menu item when it's selected. This is used to indicate that a particular option has been selected.

- RadioCheck determines whether a dot is displayed instead of a check mark.

- If Enabled is false (not selected), users can see the menu item but can't access it.

- Visible allows you to hide menu items that aren't needed for a particular function or form.

- MergeType determines whether the top-level menu items are displayed while another form is active and contains its own menu.

- MergeOrder determines the actual position of the menu item when the MergeType is MergeItems.

- MDIList is available only when with MDI applications. It displays a list of the current child windows displayed.

When you want to indicate the status of a particular function, use the Checked property to show a check mark in the menu drop-down list for the item selected. Visual Basic uses this property to show which toolboxes are displayed (see Figure 3.16). This property actually toggles back and forth between True and False within the application code itself.

FIGURE 3.16

Using the Checked *property to display a function's status.*

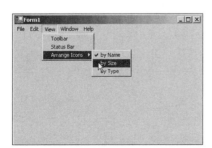

To use the Checked property, add the following code to the Click event of any menu item that with which you want to use it:

```
If <menu item>.Checked then
    <menu item>.Checked = True
Else
    <menu item>.Checked = False
End If
```

 Note

If you try to use the Checked property for a top-level menu item, you'll get an error message. You can't toggle top-level menu items on and off.

The MDIList property specifies that a list of open MDI child forms will be displayed. When this property is set to True, the menu automatically adds items as child forms are opened and removes any closed child forms.

Creating and Using Context Menus

NEW TERM   Menus generally are thought of as being visible and occupying the bar at the top of an application form. Visual Basic allows you to create another type of menu, which appears only when needed and directly next to the area you're working with. These *context menus* often are used to handle functions related to a specific area of the form. For an example of this type of menu, right-click anywhere in Visual Basic's Code Editor window for a code-related menu (see Figure 3.17). Context menus usually appear at the mouse pointer's current location. After you select an option from the menu, it disappears from the screen.

FIGURE 3.17

Context menus offer users many options directly related to the work they're performing.

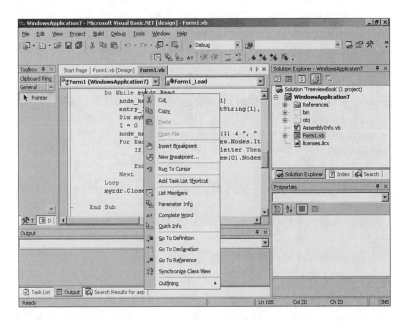

Setting Up a Context Menu

To create a context menu, add the ContextMenu control to the form; then add all the required menu items using the same techniques as the MainMenu control.

The context menu is new to Visual Basic .NET. It has been separated from the Main menu so it's handled independently in the code.

If you want a menu item to appear on the main menu and on the context menu, you must add the same item twice: once on the main menu and once on the context menu.

3

Displaying a Context Menu

To see how the context menu works, add one to your form and insert at least one menu item. The final step is changing the ContextMenu property for the control with which you want to associate the context menu. Once this is done, you can execute the application and right-click the control to display the context menu, as shown in Figure 3.18.

FIGURE 3.18

Using context menus in your application.

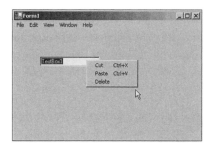

Merging Menus

What does merging menus really do for you? When you're creating an MDI application, you must take care to create your menus properly. If any of the child forms have menus of their own, you must decide which menu bar will be displayed by your application. Whenever a child form has a menu associated with it, its menu will replace the parent form menu when the child form is displayed.

You can deal with menus in an MDI application in one of the following MergeTypes:

• Add   The menu item will be added to the existing menu displayed.

- Replace   The menu item replaces an existing menu item at the same position in a merged menu.

- MergeItems   All submenu items are merged with the existing menu items at the same position in a merged menu.

- Remove   The menu item isn't included in the merged menu.

The MergeOrder property specifies the position a menu item would be placed in when merged with an existing menu on a parent form.

Inheriting Forms

NEW TERM   With Visual Basic .NET, we finally can inherit from one form to another; this capability is called *visual inheritance*. This means we can create a Windows Forms form; then inherit from that form to create other forms with the same layout, controls, and behaviors. We also can use inheritance to create our own versions of Windows Forms controls. For instance, we might want to create an enhanced TextBox control that performs some specialized validation of the input data. This can be accomplished through inheritance by creating a subclass of the original TextBox control class and enhancing it as needed. Finally, the same capability is available when you work with Web forms.

Inheriting Forms in Code

To inherit a form, you first must add the form you want to use to the project. Then, by changing a single line of code, you can inherit the objects from the existing form. To see how this works, start a new project and create a form that resembles the one in Figure 3.19.

FIGURE 3.19

Creating a form to use as a template.

Let's create a new form, Form2, which will resemble the one in Figure 3.20.

FIGURE 3.20

Creating the form that will inherit the objects.

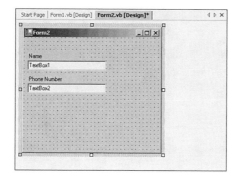

Now that Form2 is created, look at the form's code. You should see the following line at the top of the Public Class Form2:

```
Inherits System.Windows.Forms.Form
```

By changing this line of code to

```
Inherits <ApplicationName>.Form1
```

Form2 also will have the controls from Form1 on it, as shown in Figure 3.21.

FIGURE 3.21

The second form showing the inherited controls and the original controls.

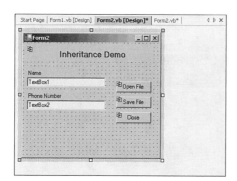

Notice that Form2 now has both sets of controls. This capability isn't just for the controls on a form. If any of these controls had code associated with them, the code also would have been inherited.

The Inheritance Picker

The Inheritance Picker simplifies the process you just completed by presenting you with two dialog boxes, which help you choose the form to inherit and then change the code for you. To use this feature, select Add Inherited Form from the Project menu to display the dialog box shown in Figure 3.22.

FIGURE 3.22

*The Add New Item dia-
log box is shown with
the Inherited Form
option selected.*

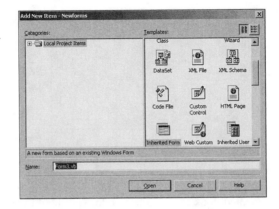

  Caution

For this to work, you must use the Build command to compile the form you
want to use into either an executable file or a DLL before either that form
or DLL can be used by the Inheritance Picker.

On the Inheritance Picker you can specify the name you want to use for the new form.
Once you are satisfied, click the Open button to display the dialog box that lists the
forms that you can use for inheritance (see Figure 3.23).

FIGURE 3.23

*Selecting a form to
inherit.*

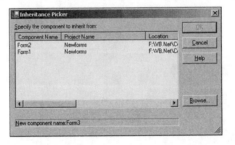

Choose the form that has the controls you want to use and click OK, or click the Browse
button to look for another form in a different application. You can see in Figure 3.24 that
the control inherited from the selected form has a little icon in the upper-left corner that
signifies that the control is inherited.

You should know that inherited controls can't be moved, nor can the inherited code be
changed. These actions can be done only on the original form. It's also important to
know that any changes you make to the base form won't be seen in the inherited forms
until you rebuild the application.

Figure 3.24

The final form with the inherited controls on it.

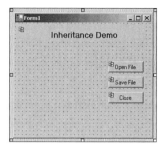

Summary

Today you've seen what it takes to create toolbars and menus that you can use in your application to enable your users to quickly and easily access the application's functions and features. Also you saw how to create context menus that can be used as needed at the precise area in the application that they relate to. Finally, this lesson showed how to inherit existing forms in another project to enable you to reuse forms, code, controls, and menus that have been previously designed and saved. This way you can create multiple applications with a consistent look to them.

Q&A

Q What's the purpose of a toolbar in an application?

A A toolbar enables users to quickly and easily access the most common functions of the application.

Q How does a menu vary from a toolbar?

A Because the menu has more room to work with, it can provide users with access to all functions of the application.

Q How is form inheritance useful when creating an application?

A With inheritance, you can create an application in which many of the forms look like standard Windows forms, or forms that you've already designed for another application, providing a common look to your applications.

Workshop

The Workshop provides quiz questions to help solidify your understanding of the material covered and exercises can apply what you've learned. For answers to the quiz questions and exercises, see Appendix A, "Answers to Quizzes and Exercises."

Quiz

1. What two controls are needed when creating a toolbar?

2. Can a toolbar display text instead of pictures in the buttons?

3. How many top-level menu items can you have?

4. If you use hotkeys, can you have two that start with the same letter?

Exercise

Start a new project and add the necessary controls, toolbar, and menu to allow users to select files to open and close and, when a file is selected, display the text in a control on the form.

Quiz

1. A toolbar requires an ImageList and Toolbar control to be on the form; however, if you want to use drop-down menus in the toolbar you must add a ContextMenu control.

2. Yes, a toolbar can display text, images, or both.

3. You can have as many top-level menu items as you want; however, too many will make your application very hard to use.

4. No. At any given level of a menu item, only one hotkey can use a particular letter.

WEEK 1

DAY 4

Understanding the .NET Framework

Over the past few days, you've seen some of the new features that have been added to Visual Basic .NET. You've also reviewed some of the older features and how they've been changed in the new release. All the while you've been using the new .NET objects, even if you weren't aware of it. Today, you will take a break from the actual programming of Visual Basic and discuss the building blocks on which Visual Basic .NET is built.

Microsoft developed the .NET Framework to provide a common set of components for all Windows and Web programming languages to start with. On Day 1, "Writing Professional Visual Basic Applications," you were briefly introduced to the new .NET Framework and how it relates to Visual Basic .NET. You learned that the .NET Framework provides the basis for the latest releases of the Microsoft development tools. In fact, the Framework allows you to create compiled applications using your choice of programming languages. You also learned that the runtime engines, which have been unique for each language, have been replaced by the Common Language Runtime (CLR), which manages the execution of code and provides the services that make the development process that much easier.

Today, you will take a closer look at what the .NET Framework really is, what makes up the Framework, and how it relates to the Visual Basic .NET environment. You also will look at some of the tools that come with the .NET SDK delivered with any of the Visual Studio .NET products, including Visual Basic .NET.

While reading today's lesson, you might be wondering, "Why do I need to know this stuff?" Well, if you will be designing and creating standalone, fairly simple Visual Basic applications, you probably don't need to understand much about how Visual Basic .NET interacts with the rest of the .NET Framework. However, if you will be creating multitier, multilanguage applications that will be using many of the .NET capabilities, it's a good idea to at least understand the building blocks of the Framework and how they operate. In fact, you will use many of the concepts discussed today in the remainder of this book.

 Note

> If you want more detail about the workings of the .NET Framework, check out *Visual Basic Programmer's Guide to the .NET Framework Class Library* by Lars Powers and Mike Snell (Sams Publishing, ISBN 0-672-32232-3).

What Is the .NET Framework?

In July 2000, Microsoft announced the beginning of what it called the *.NET initiative*. This new platform was to be a new development Framework that contained a new programming interface for all the available Windows services and APIs. It would integrate several different technologies that Microsoft had released over the previous years. The .NET platform includes COM+ services, ASP Web development, and a commitment to the new XML technologies for Web programming. Also, new XML Web services protocols such as SOAP, WSDL, and UDDI are supported by the .NET Framework with the focus of this support on the Internet and Web deployment. The platform consists of four unique product groups:

- Development tools include Visual Basic and C#, the class libraries used to build Web services, and both Web and Windows applications. It also includes the Common Language Runtime.

- Specialized servers are the enterprise servers known separately as SQL Server 2000, Exchange 2000, BizTalk 2000, and so on.

- XML Web services are a selection of commercially programmed components that provide functions to a Web or Windows application.

- Devices in this context are .NET-enabled non-PC devices such as cell phones and handheld computers.

The .NET platform consists of five major pieces (see Figure 4.1). The lowest layer is the operating system, which can be any of the Windows flavors, from Windows Me through Windows 2000 and XP. In fact, it also includes Windows CE, which enables the new technology on handheld and Pocket PCs. The next level is a series of three separate and unique groups of tools that can be used for the development of enterprise applications:

- .NET enterprise server products that simplify the development process for large-scale business systems.

- XML Web services that are reusable across the Web. Microsoft will provide some of these (for a price, of course). Web Services include a calendar, directory, and search services. XML Web services also include the currently available Passport that you can use by any Web site that supports Passport's authentication process. (You will learn how to create your own XML Web services on Day 21, "Working with Web Services.")

- .NET Framework for development and runtime of several different languages.

FIGURE 4.1

The entire Microsoft .NET platform showing the five major components.

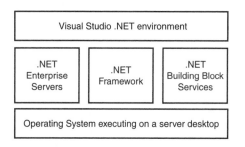

The top level of the platform is the Visual Studio .NET programming environment. The new Visual Studio provides the tools for you to design and create professional, enterprise-wide applications that make full use of the entire .NET platform.

Today's lesson will focus on the center of this level—the .NET Framework. The .NET Framework sits on top of the operating system, which you know can be any of the available Windows environments. The Framework consists of a number of components (see Figure 4.2), some of which you've already seen, and others that you will be introduced to during the remainder of this book.

FIGURE 4.2

The .NET Framework components available for use in Visual Studio .NET.

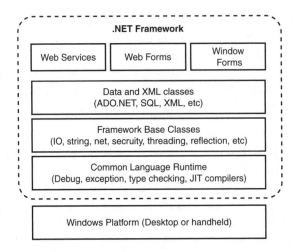

Understanding the Common Language Runtime (CLR)

By far, the most important piece of the .NET Framework is the Common Language Runtime (CLR). The CLR manages the execution of any code written in the .NET languages and is the base of the .NET architecture. This section takes a closer look at the CLR environment.

The CLR was created from scratch, meaning that Microsoft didn't start by using the Visual Basic runtime or the Visual C++ runtime as a starting point. This allowed Microsoft to build an environment in which an application could be written in modules, where each module could be a different language. Any language used to create a .NET application is compiled into files called .NET Portable Executable (PE) files. These PE files can be either .exe or .dll files that you are familiar with from previous releases of Visual Basic. The CLR is the engine that does the following:

- Loads the required classes
- Performs Just-In-Time (JIT) compilation on any required methods
- Enforces security
- Performs other runtime functionality

Note

Just-In-Time compilation means that a PE file will be compiled when it's executed, as opposed to compiling the file once and then deploying it. (JIT will be discussed later today.)

The following are some of the benefits of the CLR:

- Cross-language integration
- Cross-language exception handling
- Enhanced security
- Versioning control
- Deployment support

CLR manages the references to all objects in an application, including releasing the resources used by them when they are no longer being used. The Microsoft .NET executable (PE files) vary from the typical Windows executable in that it carries not only the code and data, but also metadata and Intermediate Language (IL) code (both discussed later in this section) that contains the information the CLR needs to execute the application.

Because the .NET Framework and the CLR are providing cross-language functionality, all .NET languages are now similar in their syntax. If you are a Visual Basic programmer, you might be surprised to see that the syntax of the Visual Basic language has been modified to fit into the new .NET Framework to mirror other object-oriented languages, such as C++ and C#. Listing 4.1 shows a simple Visual Basic .NET program, which should look familiar if you know C#. Whereas C# uses the keyword Using, Visual Basic .NET uses the keyword Import.

LISTING 4.1   FIRSTVBCODE.TXT: A Simple Visual Basic Program

```
Import System
Public Module ModMain
    Sub Main()
        Console.WriteLine ("VB Hello, World")
    End Sub
End Module
```

Another addition to the Visual Basic .NET language is a command-line compiler, VBC.EXE. To compile the Visual Basic .NET code in Listing 4.1, you could execute for the following command:

```
VBC /t:exe /out:Hello.exe Hello.vb
```

The /t option specifies the type of PE file to be created. In this case, because you have specified an .exe, hello.exe will be this command's output.

Explaining the Metadata

NEW TERM   *Metadata* is the machine-readable information about a resource, or "data about data." This information might include details on content, format, size, or other traits of a data source. In .NET, metadata includes type definitions, version information, and other standardized information. For any two components—systems or objects—to be able to work with each other, at least one of them must know something about the other. In COM, this "something" is an interface specification, usually called a *type library*, which allows a development environment or tool to read and create wrapper classes used for the target development language. Although type libraries are extremely rich in COM, many developers complain about their lack of standardization in the coding of these type libraries. The .NET Framework provides a common method for capturing type information, which is called metadata.

The metadata includes descriptions of an assembly and modules, classes, interfaces, methods, properties, fields, events, global methods, and so on. Enough information is provided by the metadata for any runtime, tool, or program to find out almost anything needed to integrate two or more components. Following is a short list of consumers that use the metadata in .NET:

- CLR uses the metadata for verification, security enforcement, memory layout, and execution.
- Class Loader is a component of the CLR that uses metadata to find and load .NET classes.
- Just-In-Time (JIT) compilers use the metadata to compile Microsoft Intermediate Language (IL) code. The .NET JIT compiles the IL into native code before execution.
- Various tools included with the .NET Framework development environment use metadata.

CLR Execution

Now that you've seen the elements of a .NET executable, you can explore what the CLR provides to support the management and execution of the application's executables. This lesson will limit the discussion of the many components contained in the CLR to only the main components. Figure 4.3 shows these components and the order in which they work.

FIGURE 4.3

The major components of the CLR.

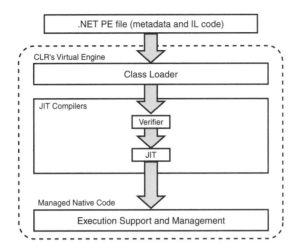

The following are the major components of the CLR:

- Class Loader
- Verifier
- Just-In-Time (JIT) compilers
- Other execution support

The .NET PE files that are created when you compile a Visual Basic .NET program are processed by each component before the program is actually executed. So that you can understand the process, this lesson will briefly discuss each component before continuing.

Class Loader

Whenever a standard Windows application program is executed, the OS loader is executed to actually load the program into memory before it can execute. If the OS loader identifies the program it's loading as a .NET application, it will pass control to the CLR, which finds the entry point (which is usually Main()), and executes it to jump-start the application. Before the application can actually execute, the class loader must find the class that exposes Main() and loads the class. When the Main() routine calls any object of a specific class (any object in Visual Basic, such as a textbox), the class loader is started to perform its tasks the first time a type is referenced. The class loader then loads the .NET classes into memory and prepares them for execution. In performing this task, the class loader locates and loads each target class for the .NET application, and then caches the type information for the class so that it doesn't have to reload the class for the duration of the application. Finally, the class loader uses the appropriate metadata to initialize the static variables for the application.

4

Verifier

Because Microsoft has changed the processing of most languages from an interpreted style of execution to a true compiled execution, the compiled code must be checked to ensure that the types are used correctly and that the code will execute at runtime. The verifier is the component that executes at runtime to verify that the code is safe. It's important to remember that this type verification is done at runtime and that it's a fundamental difference between .NET and other environments.

After the class loader loads a class and before a piece of code can execute, the verifier starts for that code and is responsible for verifying the following:

- The metadata is valid
- The intermediate code is type safe

Both conditions must be met before the JIT compiler can process the code.

JIT Compilers

The JIT compiler plays a major role in the .NET platform because all .NET PE files contain intermediate code and metadata, not native code. This allows the application to run on any platform that supports the .NET Framework, regardless of the language in which it was written. The JIT compiler will convert the intermediate code to native code so that it can execute on the target operating system. For each method verified in the previous step, a JIT compiler in the CLR will compile the method and convert it into managed native code.

The advantage provided by these JIT compilers is that they can dynamically compile code that is optimized for the machine on which it's currently running. If you take the same .NET PE file from a computer with only one CPU to one with two or more, the JIT might be able to compile the code to make use of the extra CPUs.

Other Tools

You should now understand that every component in the CLR uses the metadata and intermediate code in one way or another to successfully allow the .NET application to execute. Several other tasks are done during or after the execution of a .NET application. These tasks are performed by one of the following components:

- The Code Manager controls code execution.
- The CLR detects when objects from your application are no longer being referenced and performs garbage collection to reclaim the unused memory.
- The CLR's exception handling provides a consistent method for error or exception handling within your application.

- The CLR performs various security checks at runtime to ensure that the code is safe to execute and isn't breaking any security requirements.
- The CLR provides enhanced support for debugging.
- The CLR provides interoperation support to allow execution of both managed code (CLR) and unmanaged code (COM) within the same application.

Programming in .NET

Now that you've looked at what .NET really is, it's time to learn how programming in Visual Basic has changed in this environment. The .NET Framework provides a Common Programming Model, which includes the core programming languages and features. If you know other programming languages such as C++, this common Framework gives you the ability to reference your code to other languages. This is possible because the namespaces, classes, methods, and so on have a consistent representation in all the supported languages. This means that by using Visual Basic .NET, you can write a string to the console using the `WriteLine()` method of the `Console` object. Every .NET language will use the same method from the same object. This commonality will require less development training and increase productivity.

NEW TERM   A *namespace* organizes a group of objects, such as the ListBox and TextBox controls, which are both members of the `System.Windows.Forms` namespace. Microsoft created namespaces to prevent ambiguity and simplify references when using large groups of objects such as class libraries.

4

Identifying the Major Namespaces

Most classes and methods that you will use when programming in Visual Basic .NET are members of a namespace. Table 4.1 is a short list of the important namespaces and classes in the .NET Framework. These namespaces are the ones you will find yourself using as you develop a .NET application.

TABLE 4.1   Major System Namespaces

Namespace	Description
System	Includes the basic classes that every program will use, such as `Object`, `Char`, and `String`
System.IO	Provides classes that allow synchronous and asynchronous reading and writing on data streams and files
System.Drawing	Provides access to GDI+ basic graphics functionality
System.Collections	Contains classes that define various collections of objects, such as lists, queues, and arrays

TABLE 4.1   continued

Namespace	Description
System.Threading	Provides classes and interfaces that enable multithreaded programming
System.Reflection	Contains a set of classes and interfaces that provide a managed view of loaded types, methods, and fields
System.Security	Contains a set of classes and namespaces that provide security support to an application, such as Permissions and Policy
System.Net	Provides classes and namespaces for network programming, such as Connection and IP Address
System.Data	Contains the classes and namespaces that constitute the ADO.NET architecture
System.Data.OleDb	Provides the classes for the OLE DB data provider, allowing access to an OLE DB data source
System.Data.SqlClient	Provides the classes for the SQL data provider, allowing access to a SQL Server data source
System.Web.Services	Provides the classes that support the development of XML Web services
System.Web.UI	Provides the classes and namespaces that support development in the new Web Forms environment
System.Windows.Forms	Provides the classes and namespaces that support development in the Windows Forms environment

Remember that you will be using most of these namespaces even if you never realize it. As an example, when you start a new Windows application and start adding controls to a form, you're using the System.Windows.Forms namespace. In fact, if you look at Figure 4.4, you can see that not only does an Inherits statement exist for this namespace, but the references in the project also include several other namespaces in Table 4.1.

Visual Basic and the .NET Framework

Because of these changes in the structure of the Microsoft development environment, Microsoft has taken Visual Basic apart and rebuilt it to support this new .NET Framework, adding support for object-oriented programming. What resulted was Visual Basic .NET, which allows you to do everything that the previous versions of Visual Basic allowed, only more easily.

FIGURE 4.4

Identifying the namespaces used in a project.

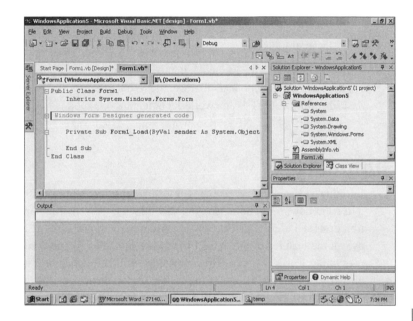

If you are a Visual Basic programmer without knowledge of other object-oriented languages, you will be surprised by the new Visual Basic .NET syntax. However, you will soon realize that the new syntax exists to simplify the process of programming in Visual Basic. In addition to the Visual Basic style Rapid Application Development (RAD) support, Visual Basic .NET has been modernized to give you full access to the .NET Framework. The Visual Basic .NET compiler generates metadata and IL code, making the language an equal to C++ or the new C#. Unlike the older versions of Visual Basic, Visual Basic .NET has no interpreter, so performance drawbacks are no longer an issue for using Visual Basic for large corporate development.

What all this really means to you, the Visual Basic programmer, is that you have a more powerful, easier-to-use programming language that will execute efficiently on any .NET-supported environment.

Working with the .NET Tools

When installing any of the Visual Studio .NET components, such as Visual Basic .NET, the .NET Framework SDK installs the following groups of tools:

- Configuration and deployment tools
- Debugging tools

- Security tools
- General tools

These tools are designed to make it easier for you to create, display, and manage the applications and components that use the .NET Framework. These tools are listed and described in the .NET Framework documentation, which is installed on your computer when you install the .NET Framework.

Summary

In today's lesson, you were exposed to several of the more important concepts of the new .NET Framework. In doing so, you saw how the new environment processes an application designed to use this Framework. Although you probably will never really need to use all the features of the .NET Framework, it's always a good idea to understand how everything works together. This knowledge will help when or if something doesn't work properly in your application. Finally, this lesson introduced the tools that are delivered with the .NET Framework SDK along with what each can be used for.

Starting tomorrow, this book will dive back into the programming of Visual Basic .NET applications and you will see how much of today's lesson will actually start to make sense.

Q&A

Q What are the main components of the .NET Framework?

A The .NET Framework consists of many different components; however, the main ones are CLR, Framework Classes, the components for Web Services, Web Forms, and Windows Forms.

Q What does the .NET Framework mean to me as a Visual Basic programmer?

A At the start, you will need to relearn a few of the concepts that you've been used to with the older versions of Visual Basic. You also will find that developing multitier applications has just become easier.

Q Can I create components that other programmers can use regardless of the language they use?

A Yes. If other programmers are using a .NET language, they will be able to make use of any component, such as a custom control that you might develop.

Workshop

Today's lesson has no quiz questions or exercises.

WEEK 1

DAY 5

Working with Objects, Collections, and Arrays

Now that you've learned a bit more about Visual Basic .NET's capabilities, you should learn some of the theory behind Visual Basic programming. Today's lesson deals with *object* programming using *collections* and arrays. You will see what objects really are, when to use them, and how they relate to the different controls that you use in an application. You also will see how to use collections in your application code, what makes the collection different from arrays, and how to work with both to simplify application programming.

In addition, you will learn how the different loop statements work in relation to the collections you will be using. You will investigate how the loops vary and see when each should be used in the application process. Finally, you will create your own small object, which will enable you to enhance an existing Visual Basic object.

What Are Objects and Collections?

Before you can understand what a collection is, you must know what an object is and what makes it a useful tool for developing Visual Basic applications. Objects are the central concept to Visual Basic programming. Forms, controls, and databases all are considered objects. In fact, everywhere you look in Visual Basic you will see objects.

NEW TERM When you work directly with these objects, you need some way to keep track of them. In Visual Basic, a *collection* is a special object that enables you to keep track of all the other objects in your application. A collection is a way to group a set of related items. In Visual Basic, collections can be used to keep track of many things, such as the forms loaded in your program or the controls on a form.

Objects

Almost everything you use in Visual Basic can be considered an object. In fact, you've already worked with many objects, such as controls, in this book. You've seen that controls all contain properties, methods, and events. Each control also contains code and data items, although you can't see the actual written code. In fact, each control or object, such as the TextBox control, really is a small, self-contained package included with Visual Basic.

NEW TERM When you use the TextBox control, you don't have to write any code to trigger its events or define any of its properties; the TextBox control methods do all the work you will need. This process is termed *encapsulation*. An object is like a space capsule; everything it needs to perform its task is included with the object. All the methods, events, and properties an object uses are defined or coded within the object itself. All objects that share the same features (such as many text boxes on one form) are included in an *object class*.

A single object really is an *instance* of its class definition. Every time you add a new control to a form, you actually are creating a new instance of its class. However, each has its own name, can be separately enabled and disabled, and can be placed anywhere on a form. If you look back at the code you placed in the MDI project on Day 2, "The Face of a Windows Application," you will see the definition of a form object as follows:

```
Dim NewNote As New frmNote
```

This code defines a new object called `NewNote`, which is based on the defined form `frmNote` object and inherits the properties of the original form. You might not realize it, but when you design a form and place controls on it, you are creating your own object. By using existing classes, you automatically inherit the properties, methods, and events from that class. To see this, go no further than the remaining code from the `mnuFileNew_Click` event from the MDI project:

```
intFormCtr = intFormCtr + 1
NewNote.Show
NewNote.Text = "NotePad Version " & intFormCtr
```

Every time you execute the `NewNote.Show` method, another instance of the `frmNote` form is created. Each form has associated with it all the properties and events you coded for the original form. Objects are created as identical copies of their class. Once they exist, their properties can be changed independently from the other objects of the same class on the form.

Collections

Collections are used everywhere in Visual Basic. In the MDI project, when you have more than one `NewNote` form displayed, you can work with them from the point of view of a collection or array of forms. Unlike arrays, collections don't have to be redimensioned every time an object member is added or removed.

When working in Visual Basic, you can use two collections to track the forms and controls that you use in an application. The `FORMS` collection keeps track of every loaded form in an application, whereas the `CONTROL` collection keeps track of every control used within an application. You also can use a third built-in object to define your own collections. By using the generic `Collection` class, you can create as many different instances of the `Collection` objects as needed in your application.

The `Collection` object has three methods that you can use to add, remove, or access the objects in the collection. It also has one property that gives you the number of items in the collection. In the coming sections of today's lesson, you will see how collections offer an easy way to access the objects of your application without writing large amounts of code.

Many objects in Visual Basic have default collections associated with them. One such example is the Treeview control, which has a `Nodes` collection associated with it. Each item in the `Nodes` collection has its own related properties and methods. A better example of an object model is the Data Access Object (DAO) model (see Figure 5.1). DAO's classes are organized into a hierarchy and in turn contain collections. Each collection belongs to the class above it in the hierarchy.

The whole concept of hierarchies simply means that objects can contain other objects, which in turn contain other objects. As you might have figured out, the terms *object* and *class* are related, where a class is actually the defined structure for a given object.

5

When an object is declared in the code, Visual Basic uses the related class to "know" how to define the object you want to create.

FIGURE 5.1

The classes, objects, and collections of the Data Access Object.

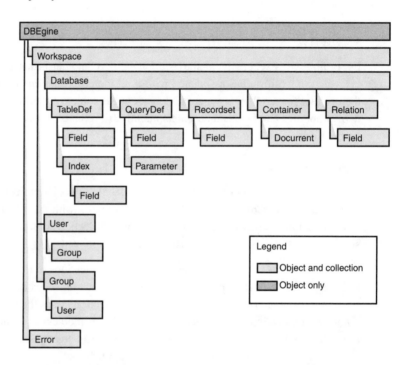

Using System Objects

NEW TERM Besides the objects that you can declare, such as forms, several other objects are included with Visual Basic to make your life as a programmer easier. These *system objects* can be used anywhere in an application. Although you can't define new instances of these objects or pass them as variables to other routines, they still are very useful.

> **Note**
>
> Although Visual Basic .NET has replaced many of these system objects with methods in a namespace, most of the functionality that you might have previously used is still available in a different way.

The original system objects are discussed in the following section along with the new namespace that has replaced them. The new way to access some of the older functionality also is discussed.

App **Object**

Most of the App object information was version related and has been replaced by Assembly attributes. Version information was set in the Project Properties dialog box; now this information is set by editing the project's AssemblyInfo file. Figure 5.2 shows this file open in the editor.

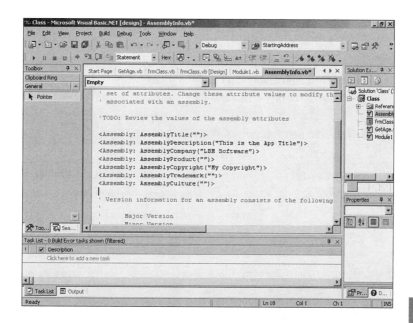

One of the App object's more useful features was the ability to define a title string anywhere in the application. Although this property no longer exists, you can use the AssemblyDescription as a title variable. To use this value in your application, you must define a Public variable for your application and assign it to this value as follows:

```
Public AppTitle As String = _
System.Diagnostics.FileVersionInfo.GetVersionInfo(
System.Reflection.Assembly.GetExecutingAssembly.Location)
.Comments
```

You now can use this public variable to display the application title whenever you need it. For example, when using the MSGBOX statement to display a message to the user, you would want the caption to reflect the application's title. To do so, you could enter the application title as a string every time you use a MSGBOX, or you can use the AssemblyInfo file with its associated variables. The MSGBOX statement would resemble the following:

```
MSGBOX("Incorrect Date entered. Try Again!", MsgBoxStyle.Critical, AppTitle)
```

You can do many different things with these variables.

As you can see, the AssemblyInfo file provides runtime information about the current application.

Screen **Object**

In older versions of Visual Basic, the Screen object provides global information about your application, and in some cases, allows you to set these global properties. In Visual Basic .NET, there's no equivalent object; however, most of the functionality can be duplicated by using features in the .NET Framework. Table 5.1 lists some of the more useful Screen object properties and their Visual Basic .NET equivalents.

TABLE 5.1 Screen Properties in Visual Basic .NET

Property	.NET Equivalent
ActiveControl	System.Windows.Forms.Application.ActiveForm.ActiveControl
ActiveForm	System.Windows.Forms.Application.ActiveForm
Fonts	System.Drawing.FontFamilies
Mousepointer	System.Drawing.Cursor.Current
Height	System.Windows.Forms.Screen.PrimaryScreen.Bounds.Height
Width	System.Windows.Forms.Screen.PrimaryScreen.Bounds.Width

Clipboard **Object**

The Clipboard enables you to offer your application users the standard Windows copy and paste functionality. If you decide to include the Edit menu's Copy and Paste options, Clipboard functionality would be used to provide that actual function. To see how this works, open the dlgFileOpenCopy project you created on Day 2. To this project, add a menu with only two main options, Copy and Paste; then add the code in Listing 5.1 to the form.

Note
> The Clipboard object has been replaced by the System.Windows.Forms.Clipboard namespace.

LISTING 5.1 CLIPBOARD.TXT: Adding Copy and Paste to Your Application

```
Private Sub mnuCopy_Click()
    Dim datobj As New System.Windows.Forms.DataObject
```

LISTING 5.1   continued

```
        datobj.SetData System.Windows.Forms.DataFormats.Text, _
            txtSourceFile.Text
        System.Windows.Forms.Clipboard.SetDataObject datobj
    End Sub

    Private Sub mnuPaste_Click()
        txtTargetFile.Text = _
            System.Windows.Forms.Clipboard.GetDataObject.GetData( _
            System.Windows.Forms.DataFormats.Text)
    End Sub
```

When you run this application you can copy text from the Source text box and then paste it into the Target text box. Of course, in this example the object being copied and pasted is hard coded into the routine. To make this a truly generic routine, you can use a property of the Form namespace; the ActiveControl property gives you access to whatever control is active on the form at that moment.

When creating a copy and paste routine, you must identify the type of data you are copying, because the Windows Clipboard handles text and graphics differently. Also, when users paste the data from the Windows Clipboard, you must make sure they are pasting the data to a field with the same data type as the data that was copied.

As a rule, you also should empty the Clipboard before copying any data into it. This entire process uses several different methods and properties of the Clipboard, Form, and Control objects. The code in Listing 5.2 shows the generic copy and paste routines you can add to your application code.

5

LISTING 5.2   COPYPASTE.TXT: Checking the Data Type Before Copying and Pasting Data with the Clipboard

```
    Private Sub MenuItem1_Click(ByVal sender As System.Object, _
        ByVal e As System.EventArgs) Handles MenuItem1.Click
            Dim datobj As New DataObject()
            If TypeOf Me.ActiveControl Is TextBox Then
                datobj.SetData(DataFormats.Text, Me.ActiveControl.Text)
                Clipboard.SetDataObject(datobj)
            elseIf TypeOf Me.ActiveControl Is PictureBox Then
                datobj.SetData(DataFormats.Text, Me.ActiveControl.Text)
                Clipboard.SetDataObject(datobj)
            End If
        End Sub

    Private Sub MenuItem2_Click(ByVal sender As System.Object, _
        ByVal e As System.EventArgs) Handles MenuItem2.Click
```

LISTING 5.2   continued

```
        If TypeOf Me.ActiveControl Is TextBox Then
            If Clipboard.GetDataObject.GetDataPresent(DataFormats.Text) Then
                Me.ActiveControl.Text = Clipboard.GetDataObject.GetData( _
                DataFormats.Text)
            Else
                MsgBox("Invalid data in clipboard", _
                    MsgBoxStyle.Information, Me.Text)
            End If
        ElseIf TypeOf Me.ActiveControl Is PictureBox Then
            If Clipboard.GetDataObject.GetDataPresent(DataFormats.Bitmap) _
              Then
                Me.ActiveControl.Text = Clipboard.GetDataObject.GetData( _
                DataFormats.Bitmap)
            Else
                MsgBox("Invalid data in clipboard", _
                    MsgBoxStyle.Information, Me.Text)
            End If
        End If
    End Sub
```

Accessing Objects

Accessing or working with Visual Basic objects really is quite simple when you use the available statements, properties, and methods. In the previous section, you saw how to create a copy and paste routine using several new Visual Basic statements and functions. By using the Clipboard's GetFormat method and the TypeOf...Is expression, you can test for any data type or control type in the application.

Finding the Object's Class

Use the TypeOf keyword to determine the type of object you are working with. It can be used only as part of an If...Then statement and returns True or False depending on the object you are checking. In the following code, a True condition would be returned if the active control is a check box:

```
If TypeOf Me.ActiveControl Is Checkbox Then
```

In addition to the TypeOf keyword, if you must retrieve the type of a particular object, you can use the TypeName function. The TypeName function is much more flexible than the TypeOf keyword because you can use it anywhere in your code and it returns the object's class name as a string. This enables you to change a section of code from this:

```
If TypeOf Me.ActiveControl Is Textbox Then
    MSGBOX("This control is a Textbox.")
EndIf
```

to this:

```
MSGBOX("This control is a " & TypeName(Me.ActiveControl))
```

By simplifying your code, you make it easier to perform maintenance or add new features at a later time. This also allows you to modify the copy and paste routine again. Now the object type of the object you are copying can be compared to the object type of the object into which you are trying to paste the data:

```
If TypeName(Me.ActiveControl) = TypeName(CopyObj) Then
```

This statement will compare the type of the active control with the type of CopyObj. CopyObj is an object variable that you define and create in the application and set in the Copy routine using the following line of code:

```
CopyObj = Me.ActiveControl
```

Both the TypeOf keyword and the TypeName function are very useful when you must know the type of the object because some objects don't support a particular property or method that you must reference.

Creating Objects

You can create an object in your application in several different ways; the easiest is to place a control on a form. Every time you add a form or control to the application project, you create another object or instance of a class. Another way to create an object requires you to add some code to your application. First you must define the object in the declarations section of the application as follows:

```
Public myForm as NEW frmNote
```

This declaration actually creates an object at the time of the declaration. If you look at the following code for the mnuFileNew_Click routine in the MDI project you created on Day 2, you would see that every time you selected File, New from the menu, a new instance of the form object was created.

```
Private Sub mnuFileNew_Click()
    Dim NewNote As New frmNote
    intFormCtr = intFormCtr + 1
    NewNote.Show
    NewNote.Caption = "NotePad Version " & intFormCtr
End Sub
```

The third way to create an object also is done in code by assigning an object variable to the form by using the NEW keyword as shown:

```
MyObj = New frmNote
```

5

This would enable you to create objects without having to define unique variables for each type of object you might create. Thus the `mnuFileNew_Click` routine could be changed to the following:

```
Private Sub mnuFileNew_Click()
    intFormCtr = intFormCtr + 1
    NewNoteObj = New frmNote
    NewNote.Show
    NewNote.Caption = "NotePad Version " & intFormCtr
End Sub
```

The `NewNoteObj` variable is defined at the beginning of the Form code as follows:

```
Public NewNoteObj as Object
```

Because the object variable, `NewNoteObj`, is defined as an object, it can be set to whatever object you must create for the application.

Acting on Objects and Collections

As you add more controls to a form, working with these controls becomes a little cumbersome. Because the same types of objects are members of the same class (that is, every text box on a form is a member of the text box class), you can program these objects with more flexibility than you would have thought. Look at a section of code that you normally would see in almost every application. This code sets several properties for a single object: a text box. In this code you can see that the control name is duplicated on every line:

```
txtFirstName.Text = "Demo"
txtFirstName.BackColor = BackColor.Red
txtFirstName.Font = New System.Drawing.Font("Ariel", 12)
txtFirstName.Font = New System.Drawing.Font(txtFirstName().Font, _
    FontStyle.Bold )
```

By using the `With...End With` command set, you can easily set several properties for the same object. The preceding code could be rewritten as

```
With txtFirstName
    .Text = "Demo2"
    .BackColor = BackColor.Bisque
    .Font = New System.Drawing.Font("Ariel", 12)
    .Font = New System.Drawing.Font(.Font, FontStyle.Bold)
End With
```

Later today you'll see how to use this command with collections to reduce the amount of code in your application and increase the performance at the same time.

Most collections you will use in your applications will be created, destroyed, and managed by Visual Basic itself. They will take one of the following forms:

- Forms
- Controls
- Grid columns and rows
- List items
- Treeview nodes
- Data recordset fields
- Others

Arrays

Except for a few differences, working with collections is much the same as working with *arrays*. An array is a list of variables accessed by using the same variable name and an index value. With arrays, you can store many occurrences of data. The application code can treat each array element as a standard variable. The difference is the index value that specifies which array element to access.

One restriction of an array is that all elements must contain data of the same data type. Another restriction is that you must define the array with an exact number of elements before you can access it. You do this by using the following line of code:

```
Public Array_Demo(9) As String
```

This will define an array, `Array_Demo`, with 10 string elements in it. However, if you don't know the maximum number of elements you might need, you could use the `ReDim` definition statement to change the number of elements in the array:

```
ReDim Preserve Array_Demo(25)
```

You can see that you aren't redefining the array itself; just the amount of memory it needs in the application. The Preserve keyword tells Visual Basic not to clear any existing data from the array during the process.

5

Note

All arrays in Visual Basic .NET have a starting element value of zero. Thus, an array defined as

```
Public Array_Demo(25) As String
```

really has bounds from 0 thru 24.

Collections

Collections play an important role in the programming of a Visual Basic application. They are always present and are updated automatically as things change in the application. For example, if you want to know how many controls are on a form, the Forms collection's Count property is updated by Visual Basic. Besides any predefined collections that Visual Basic provides, you also can define your own.

The advantages of using a collection over an array is that collections add new elements without requiring that you code anything special as with arrays. A collection also can contain almost any combination of objects, although if you are using a collection, it probably will be for a specific reason; thus, the objects in it will be of the same type.

When you create your own collection, you must manage it yourself. Any collection that you create will be a member of the Collection class as defined by Visual Basic. To define a collection, add the following code at the module level of your application:

```
Public colMyTextInput As New Collection
```

As with any other variable definition, it could be defined as Public or Private depending on your needs. A collection is like an empty file cabinet. You can add objects, remove objects, count the number of objects in it, or reference an object. The Collection class has three methods and one property that you can use:

- The Add method adds items to the collection.
- The Remove method deletes items from the collection by using an index or key.
- The Item method accesses a collection element by index or key.
- The Count property returns the current number of items in the collection.

The key to adding objects to the collection is the Add method. The syntax for this method is

```
Sub Add (item as Object [, key As String = Nothing] [, _
    before As Object = Nothing] [, after As Object = Nothing])
```

For example, to add a new name object to a collection of names using the person's Social Security number as the key, you would code the following:

```
ColEmployees.Add NewName, SSNum
```

This assumes that the SSNum is a string. If the value you are using for the key is a number, you must use CStr to convert it to a string. The key value accepts only strings as input. Also, if you are adding objects to the collection in a particular order, you can use the before and after parameters to specify the exact position to add the object.

 Caution Because collection objects maintain their numeric index numbers automatically as you add and delete items, the index of a given item will change over time. Don't save an index and expect it to retrieve the same item later in your program. Use keys for this purpose.

Because collections also can contain objects instead of values, you can access any object's properties without having to first place it in an object variable. You can reference the properties directly from the collection as in the following:

```
ColTextInputLines.Item(1). Text = "Please enter your First name."
```

The reason this works is the way Visual Basic processes the statement. It evaluates the expression from left to right. When it comes to the collection's Item method, it gets the reference to the indexed item and uses it to evaluate the remaining parts of the line. Although this is a faster way of writing code to access a collection object's properties, if you're going to use more than one property or method of an object in the collection, copy the object reference to a defined object variable first. Using an object reference while it's in the collection is slower than using it after placing it in an object variable. The following is an example of this concept:

```
Dim txtInputCurrent As TextBox
TxtInputCurrent.Text = ColTextInputLines.Item(1)
```

For some design requirements you can use a collection object; you will never use an array. Rather than using an array that must be declared to a certain size and can contain only one data type, you can add items to and remove items from the collection without worrying about the storage it needs. If you need the user to input an unknown number of names, phone numbers, or any other type of data, you could use an array as follows:

```
Dim Input_List() as String
Dim Current_Value as String
Dim Counter as Long
    Counter = 0
Get_Next_Number:
        Current_Value = InputBox("Enter the Phone Number", , "NA")
        If Current_Value <> "NA" Then
            ReDim Preserve Input_List(Counter)
            Input_List(Counter) = Current_Value
            Counter = Counter + 1
        End If
        If Current_Value = "END" Then Exit Sub
        Goto Get_Next_Number
```

As you can see, when using arrays you must keep track of the index value and resize it every time you need to add a new element to it. With a collection, the same routine would resemble the following:

```
Dim Input_List as New Collection
Dim Current_Value as String
Get_Next_Number:
    Current_Value = Inputbox("Enter the Phone Number",,"NA")
    If Current_Value <> "NA" then
        Input_List.Add(Current_Value)
    End If
```

5

```
If Current_Value = "END" Then Exit Sub
Goto Get_Next_Number
```

With a collection, the process becomes simpler and easier to manage.

Creating Your Own Class

If you've been programming for any length of time, you know that most programmers collect a library of functions and routines that they can use in any application requiring them. In Visual Basic you can define your own data types to meet certain application design requirements; you can use classes in much the same way. Although classes don't replace functions in your application code, they do provide a convenient way to organize those routines and the data they use. If you look closely at any object classes included in Visual Basic, such as a text box, you'll see that the class combines data and procedure code into one succinct unit.

Although you don't want to create a class for every routine you write, you can create a class from it if the routine will be useful in many different applications. This will enable you to add the class to an application if you need it. To add a class to your application, you first must create one. For the purposes of this lesson, you will create a small class that will calculate a person's age based on birth date. If the age is greater than an age limit passed to the class, an event will be triggered to enable the application to act on that information. Although classes can become very complicated, the creation process is the same no matter what type of class procedure you create.

To create your class, you will add a Class object to your project. The first step is to start a new project. Don't do anything with the form that's automatically added to the project; you will use it later. Add the new class to your project by choosing Add New Item from the Project menu. The new class you will build, called GetAge, will have the properties, methods, and events listed in Table 5.2.

TABLE 5.2 New Class Definitions

Name	Data Type	Description
	Properties	
Birthdate	String	Input date to calculate a person's age
AgeLimit	Integer	Sets the age limit for the event calculation
Age	Integer	Read-only value containing the calculated age
	Method	
CalcAge		Class procedure that calculates the age

TABLE 5.2   continued

Name	Data Type	Description
	Events	
Underage		Triggered if the calculated age is under the AgeLimit value
OverAge		Triggered if the calculated age is over the AgeLimit value

When you have the class object in your project, all you need to do is add the different routines to define the methods, events, and properties for the class. The final step is to add the required code to access the class in the form.

Adding Class Methods

The methods of a class are nothing more than public routines or functions you've declared for the class. There is only one method for the example class we are creating. You should place the following code in the class module immediately following the declaration section. It takes the entered date as input and calculates the difference between that date and the current date. It then compares that numeric difference with the age to check against and raises the appropriate event depending on whether the difference is less than or greater than the specified age to check against.

```
Public Sub CalcAge()
    mvarAge = DateDiff(Microsoft.VisualBasic.DateInterval.Year, _
        mvarBirthdate, Now)
    If mvarAge <= mvarAgeLimit Then
        RaiseEvent UnderAge()
    Else
        RaiseEvent OverAge()
    End If
End Sub
```

As you can see from this code, the age is being calculated with the built-in function DATEDIFF; it is compared to the AgeLimit property value. If it's less than the age limit, the UnderAge event is triggered; otherwise, the OverAge event is triggered.

Adding Class Properties

NEW TERM   Properties store information in an object. They also control how values are set or returned by using *property procedures*. A property procedure is a series of Visual Basic statements that manipulate a custom property within a class.

A property itself is defined by a block of code enclosed within the Property and End Property statements. Inside this block each property procedure is enclosed within a declaration statement (Get or Set) and an End statement. In a Get procedure, the return value

5

is supplied to the calling expression as the value of the property. In a Set procedure, the new property value is passed through the argument of the Set statement.

A property procedure is invoked implicitly by code that references to the property. The code uses the property's name the same way it would use a variable's name, except that it must provide values for all arguments that aren't optional and enclose the argument list in parentheses.

For this example you must define three properties: Birthdate and AgeLimit as read/write properties and Age as a read-only property. The following code shows how to declare the first two properties for read/write using the Get and Set statements. You should place this code in the class module following the CalcAge method code:

```
Public Property Birthdate() As String
    Get
        'used when retrieving value of a property, on the
        ' right side of an assignment.
        Birthdate = mvarBirthdate
    End Get
    Set(ByVal Value As String)
        'used when assigning a value to the property, on the
        ' left side of an assignment.
        mvarBirthdate = Value
    End Set
End Property

Public Property AgeLimit() As Short
    Get
        'used when retrieving value of a property, on the
        ' right side of an assignment.
        AgeLimit = mvarAgeLimit
    End Get
    Set(ByVal Value As Short)
        'used when assigning a value to the property, on the
        ' left side of an assignment.
        mvarAgeLimit = Value
    End Set
End Property
```

The third property is read-only and has just a Get code block:

```
Public ReadOnly Property Age() As Integer
    Get
        'used when retrieving value of a property, on the
        ' right side of an assignment.
        Age = mvarAge
    End Get
End Property
```

Adding Class Events

Events are added to a class by declaring them with the Events statement at the beginning of the module. For this class, you must add only two events:

```
Public Event UnderAge()
Public Event OverAge()
```

You also must declare several variables to use within this class for processing. These are local variables to hold the age, birth date, and age limit values that were passed to the class object. Add the following to the beginning of the class module before the event declarations:

```
'local variable(s) to hold property value(s)
Public mvarAgeLimit As Short 'local copy
'local variable(s) to hold property value(s)
Public mvarBirthdate As Date 'local copy
Public mvarAge As Short 'local copy
```

Creating the Form

To use the class, you have to add a few lines of code to define the class in the application, create a new instance of the class, and finally add the code for the event routine of the class. Add a NumericUpDown control, Masked Edit box, two labels, and a button to the form in the project as shown in Figure 5.3. This will allow you to enter a birth date and then call the GetAge method.

 Note You can use the Masked Edit control in an application by adding it to the Toolbox (right-click the toolbox and choose Customize Toolbox from the pop-up menu). Then select the Masked Edit control in the COM tab to add it to the toolbox.

5

FIGURE 5.3

Creating a form to accept a birth date to pass to the class routine.

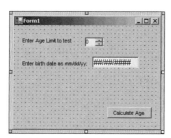

You can see NumericUpDown control allows users to change the age limit value by clicking the up or down arrows. I also added some standard property settings for the form and the button. These will center the form onscreen and set the button to the default so that users can press Enter to calculate the age.

Now add the code in Listing 5.3 to the form's code and run the application. This code will verify that the data entered in the text boxes has the correct data type; if the information is okay the CalcAge method of GetAge will be invoked.

LISTING 5.3   NEWCLASS.TXT: Application Code for the CLASS Project, Showing How to Create and Use a Class

```
Private WithEvents NewAge As GetAge

Private Sub cmdcalcage_Click(ByVal eventSender As System.Object, _
    ByVal eventArgs As System.EventArgs) Handles cmdCalcAge.Click
        NewAge = New GetAge()
        If Not IsNumeric(txtAgeLimit.Text) Then
            MsgBox("Please enter a valid age limit", _
                MsgBoxStyle.Critical, Me.Text)
            Exit Sub
        ElseIf Not IsDate(mskDate.FormattedText) Then
            MsgBox("An invalid date was entered.", _
                MsgBoxStyle.Critical, Me.Text)
            Exit Sub
        End If
        NewAge.AgeLimit = CShort(txtAgeLimit.Text)
        NewAge.Birthdate = mskDate.FormattedText
        NewAge.CalcAge()
    End Sub

Private Sub newage_underage() Handles NewAge.underage
    MsgBox("This person is under the age limit of: " & _
        NewAge.AgeLimit & " with an age of: " & NewAge.Age)
End Sub

Private Sub newage_overage() Handles NewAge.overage
    MsgBox("This person is over the age limit of: " & _
        NewAge.AgeLimit & " with an age of: " & NewAge.Age)
End Sub
```

Start the application, enter an age limit for the application to use, then enter a date and click the Calculate Age button. If the date is less than the age limit you entered, you will get the message shown in Figure 5.4.

Of course, in more sophisticated class modules, these methods and events would perform much more complicated processes than what's shown in this example. The neat thing about this topic is that after the class is created and saved, you can add it to any other application project.

FIGURE 5.4

For each event of the GetAge *class, a different message box appears.*

Browsing Your Objects

When working with classes you've created, or with any class that comes with Visual Basic, you can view all their associated properties, methods, and events by using the Object Browser. The Object Browser comes with Visual Basic and gives you a single location in which to look for objects and object information that is included in your project. When you first open the Object Browser by choosing Other Windows and then Object Browser from the View menu, the default browser appears in a pane(see Figure 5.5).

FIGURE 5.5

The Object Browser displays all your application's object information.

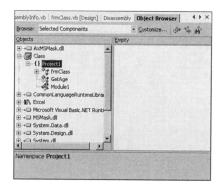

NEW TERM By default, the Object Browser displays information contained in objects and *type libraries* included in your project. A type library contains the detailed information about classes and their properties, events, methods, defined constants, and more. For every class you create, for objects included in your application, or even for information about other applications (such as Microsoft Excel), Visual Basic creates type library information to display. To add other libraries or objects to the browser for you to display, click the Customize button to display the Selected Components dialog box (see Figure 5.6).

To add more components, click the add button to display the Component Selector dialog box shown in Figure 5.7; then locate and select the components you want to browse.

5

FIGURE 5.6

Adding new objects to display in the Object Browser.

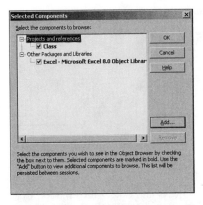

FIGURE 5.7

Selecting components to browse.

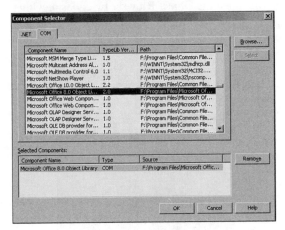

After you select the components you want, click OK twice to close the Component Selector and Selected Components dialog boxes. You will see the new components displayed in the browser (see Figure 5.8).

FIGURE 5.8

Displaying the Excel components in the Object Browser.

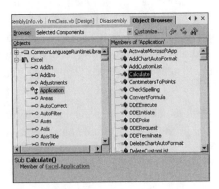

The Object Browser will even show the component for the project you created with Visual Basic. To see what's associated with the class you just created, expand your project's name in the Objects list box to display all the objects included in your project; then select the new class that you created. You will see all the properties, methods, and events that you added to the class (see Figure 5.9). This tool is very useful if you can't remember a property name or, if you must use a Visual Basic constant, you can look it up in the Object Browser.

FIGURE 5.9

Listing all the associated information for a class.

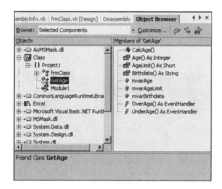

Processing Loops

NEW TERM   One of the most useful control statements in Visual Basic is the *loop*. Loops perform most of the repetitive tasks in any application. You can use two types of loops when creating a Visual Basic application: *conditional* loops, which perform a task until a specified condition occurs and *counter* loops, which execute for a set number of times. If you search the Visual Basic Help system for the word *loops*, several topics are listed. All these topics fall into one of these two loop types.

Counter Loops

In programming languages, a counter loop usually is a For or For...Next loop. Regarding today's lesson, there actually is a third version of this loop, For Each...Next, which is used specifically for collections and arrays. Each loop is defined at the beginning with a For statement and ends with a Next statement. The syntax of a standard For...Next loop is

```
For counter = start To end [Step step]
[statements]
[Exit For]
[statements]
Next [counter]
```

In the `For` statement, you specify the counter variable and the starting and ending values. At the end of the loop, the `Next` statement instructs the computer to add 1 to the counter variable and then go back to the `For` statement, where the counter is compared to the ending value. If the counter is larger, the loop is ended. To see exactly what happens, a `For` loop can be coded without using the `For...Next` statements:

```
Counter = Start_Value
Top_Of_Loop:
    If Counter <=End_Value then
        [Code Statements]
        Counter = Counter + 1
        Goto Top_Of_Loop
    End If
```

As you can see, `For...Next` statements do a lot of work for you. By using the `Step` keyword, you also can specify the value that's added or subtracted from the counter variable. Finally, if you must exit the loop early, you can use the `Exit For` statement. When the loop process is completed, program processing continues at the first line of code after the `Next` statement.

> **Tip**
>
> For debugging purposes, always include the counter variable name in the `Next` statement so you can identify the `For...Next` relationship when several loops are nested within each other.

The other type of counter loop is `For Each...Next`. This statement enables you to use a counter loop without knowing how many elements are in the array or collection. The syntax of this statement (shown in the following code) is very similar to the first `For...Next` statement; however, there are a few differences, as shown here:

```
For Each element In group
[statements]
[Exit For]
[statements]
Next [element]
```

In this case you must specify an object-defined variable as the element; the group is either the array or the collection with which you want to work. The remaining sections of the statement are identical to the first `For...Next` statement.

> **Tip**
>
> If you plan to access all elements in a collection, the `For Each...Next` statement performs better than if you use the index values with a standard `For...Next` loop.

You can use this loop statement with other object-related functions mentioned earlier today to access every control on a form to set their properties. For example, if you had an application in which you wanted to set the font of all labels, command buttons, and text boxes to a specific size, you could do it in your application code with the following code snippet:

```
Dim myobj As Object
For Each myobj In Me.Controls
    If TypeOf myobj Is TextBox Or _
       TypeOf myobj Is Button Or _
       TypeOf myobj Is Label Then
       myobj.Font = New System.Drawing.Font("Ariel", 12)
    End If
Next
```

This type of programming logic enables you to create single routines that will process any object on a form.

Conditional Loops

Just like with counter loops, you can use several different types of conditional loops: Do and While. Each shares one key feature: the *condition*. The condition is any valid Visual Basic expression that can be evaluated to True or False. The Do statement actually has two main types that you can use: Do While and Do Until. The following is the syntax for both statements:

```
Do [{While | Until} condition]
[statements]
[Exit Do]
[statements]
Loop
```

As you can see, the Do statement syntax closely resembles the For...Next syntax. In fact, the same principles apply.

The Do While statement tells the application to process the statements in the loop while a specified condition is true. When the condition becomes false, the loop is exited. Do Until works the same way as Do While, except that the loop is processed until a condition becomes true. This can be seen in the following two segments of code:

```
Do While Not EOF(1)
' Process Statements
Loop

Do Until EOF(1)
' Process Statements
Loop
```

5

Both versions of the Do statement check the condition before entering the loop and then at the beginning of each iteration. As an example, in the Do Until statement, if the file was already at the end, the code contained in the loop won't be processed. To confuse matters a little, both Do statements can be coded differently:

```
Do
[statements]
[Exit Do]
[statements]
Loop [{While | Until} condition]
```

At first glance, they might not look any different, but notice that the While or Until condition occurs at the bottom of the loop instead of at the top. This allows the code contained in the loop process to be executed at least once no matter what the state of the condition is.

Depending on the type of loop processing you must do, you must select the appropriate type of loop statement. For example, most file access routines that require you to read all the records returned that would use loop processing usually will use the Do Until method checking for the end of file condition to be True. Many times the type of loop you use is more for documentation purposes than for performance.

Summary

Today you learned how to work with objects and collections in your application. Accessing collections is no harder than working with arrays, although collection objects provide better performance and easier coding compared with array processing.

You also learned several different ways to work with multiple controls, with the focus on how to simplify the code you are writing. You've also seen how to create your own classes to package a process with its related data elements so that you can use them in any application. Finally, you had a short overview of the different loop processing statements that you can use when working with collections and objects.

Q&A

Q What's the difference between a control array and the control collection?

A A control array is a standard array in which the elements are controls of the same type. The control collection is a system-created array that contains all controls on the form, no matter what type they are.

Q What do objects of the same class share?

A Objects of the same class share all properties, methods, and events.

Q What's the benefit of creating your own collection?

A Because a collection can contain any type of element, you can include any of the different objects that you are working with, including forms, controls, and variables.

Q Why should I create my own class?

A A custom class module enables you to bundle a function as a separate unit and use it as an object in any application by adding the saved class to the new project.

Workshop

The Workshop provides quiz questions to solidify your understanding of the material covered and exercises so you can apply what you've learned. For answers to the quiz questions and exercises, see Appendix A, "Answers to Quizzes and Exercises."

Quiz

1. Name two different ways to programmatically check an object's class.

2. Why is using the `With...End With` statements not recommended with the following code?

```
With txtInputFile
    .Text = "TextFile.TXT"
    .Maxlength = 10
End With
```

3. Name the four objects that all collections share.

4. How do you create a new instance of an object or class?

Exercise

Write an application that will put a new text box control on the form every time you click the button.

DAY 6

Understanding Procedures, Functions, and Logic

You've seen many different tools and features that you can use when creating a Visual Basic application. Following this book's examples, you've worked with built-in functions, statements, and event procedures, and have even created your own class module. What you didn't know (or many programmers didn't care about) was how the information was being passed to and from the application's different routines. You've seen routines that start like this

```
Private Sub Main()
```

but didn't understand why the parentheses were needed or what `Private` really meant. The only thing that you knew was that they were needed for the application to run properly. Today's lesson discusses how variables are declared in an application and the different ways in which Visual Basic handles them. Also, you will learn the differences between subprocedures and functions, and how each are used. Finally, you will review the concept of writing a logical application and see how to use some of your old programming friends in a different way.

Scoping Out the Variables

By now you've probably noticed that a Visual Basic application has different types of source files containing the program instructions that make up your application. These files, such as forms, code, and class modules, often contain multiple procedures. A form module might have event procedures for each control on the form. The form modules also might contain general routines used by several event procedures. The standard code modules also can contain multiple procedures. These procedures can be in the form of functions or subroutines.

NEW TERM   When a module contains multiple routines, those routines often must share data between them. Creating a variable in one routine with a `Dim` statement doesn't automatically make that variable available to any of the other routines. To understand how to use variables properly, you must understand how to define variables in your application. *Declaring* variables simply means that the application knows that the variable exists and what values or type of data is valid for that variable. Also, how a variable is defined affects how its data can be shared within the application.

Defining the Variables

If the only routines a form module contains are the event procedures, you don't have to worry about sharing data. As you've seen in many of the sample projects you've created, all modules, including form modules, have a Declarations section that contains the definitions for many of the variables your application is using. You can view this section by selecting General from the Object drop-down list and Declarations from the Procedure drop-down list in the Code Editor (see Figure 6.1).

With only event procedures, you would have no need to declare any variables. Any variables you declare generally are used to store data temporarily when performing calculations within the application. For example, you might want to calculate several values, compare them, and then perform some operations on them, depending on the comparison's result. You must keep the values if you want to compare them, but you don't need to store them in an object property.

NEW TERM   Besides variables, you also can declare some data for your application as *constants*. As the name implies, these values remain constant throughout the life of the application. Using constants, you can make your code more readable by providing meaningful names instead of numbers or hard-coded strings. In fact, you've been using constants all along, even if you haven't realized it. When you code a statement like the following, you are using a built-in constant:

```
frmNote.Visible = True
```

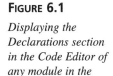

FIGURE 6.1

Displaying the Declarations section in the Code Editor of any module in the application.

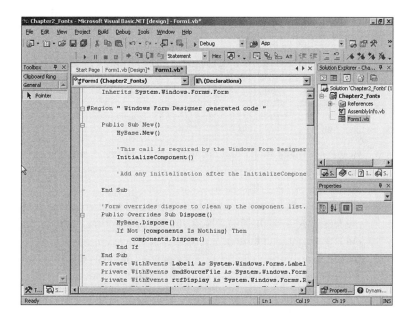

The variable name `True` actually is a constant with a value of -1. You could have written this line of code as follows:

```
frmNote.Visible = -1
```

Of course, the first version of the statement is much more readable, even if you know the -1 means `True`.

As you begin to add code to the event procedures in your application, you might find that you want several procedures to work with data in the same variable. For example, you could store the value of a text box in a variable when a command button is clicked. However, suppose you declare the variable inside the procedure as follows:

```
Private Sub cmdSalesComplete()
Dim Sale_Amt As Single
    Sale_Amt = Csng(txtAmt_Total.Text)
'   Any remaining code would go here
End Sub
```

Unfortunately, no other procedure could access this variable. `Sale_Amt` is considered local to only that procedure because you declared it inside the procedure itself. If you want to enable other procedures to access the variable, you must move its declaration into the module's Declarations section.

As you might have discovered accidentally, there are several ways to declare variables in your application. If you simply type variable names into your code as shown in the

6

following code, you don't need to declare the variable before using it unless the `Option Explicit` statement is used:

```
Private Sub cmdCalcAmt_Click(ByVal sender As System.Object, _
      ByVal e As System.EventArgs)
   TempAmt = Csng(txtAmt_Total.Text)
   TempAmt = TempAmt * 1.06
   MsgBox "This is the final total: " & TempAmt
End Sub
```

However, Visual Basic will automatically create a variable that you can use, just as if you declared it yourself. Although this is convenient, it can lead to errors in your code if you misspell a variable. To see how easily this could happen, try this on your computer: Start a new project and add a command button and text box to the default form; then add the preceding code to the form. Now run the application, enter a number in the text box, and click the command button. You should see a message box with a valid number being displayed. Now, to see what would happen if you misspelled the variable somewhere in the code, change the second line to the following:

```
TempAmt = TemAmt * 1.06
```

Now run the application again. This time you shouldn't see any number when the message box is displayed. Because the `TempAmt` variable was misspelled on the next-to-last line of the code, this function will always display a zero on the message box. Whenever Visual Basic encounters a new variable name, it doesn't know whether you mean to declare a new variable or that you've just misspelled an existing one, so it creates a new variable for you. To avoid this problem, you can tell Visual Basic to warn you whenever it encounters a name that wasn't explicitly declared as a variable. Placing the `Option Explicit` statement in the Declarations section of any module in your application prevents you from having this problem.

Note

> Visual Basic 6 required you to insert this statement in any modules where you wanted to prevent dynamic declarations. In VB .NET, you no longer need to enter them in your code. By selecting the `Option Explicit` option in the Project Properties, Common properties, Build Dialog, all variables will be verified for declarations before the application is compiled.

Where Do Variables Live?

NEW TERM   A variable's *scope* specifies which sections of your application code can access that variable. When you declare a variable within a procedure, only the code in that procedure can access or modify the data stored in that variable. This variable is said to have a scope that's *local* to that procedure. However, you might need to use a variable with a wider scope, such as one whose data is available to all procedures within one module or to all procedures in the entire application. Visual Basic enables you to specify the scope of any variable when you declare it. Depending on how a variable is declared, it's scoped as either a local or global variable:

- **Private**   The variable is accessible only to the code within the procedure in which it was declared (that is, any variable defined as private in a class is accessible to all the functions/subroutines within that class).

- **Public**   The variable can be used by any procedure in the module in which it was declared (that is, any variable defined as public would be exposed and accessible outside of the class).

As you add more modules to your project, you might find that the private variables defined within the procedures are no longer enough for your applications needs. You might need to access a variable from one module in another module. To do this, you will need to declare the variable as public.

Note   Public variables can be declared only in a module's Declarations section. They can never be declared inside a procedure.

Besides the `Public` statement, you also can declare variables using the `Private` and `Dim` statements. The `Private` statement will declare a variable that can be accessed only in the module or procedure in which it was declared. Both the `Dim` and `Private` statements declare variables essentially the same way, however, by using `Private`, you are implicitly setting the variable's scope to the class or routine it is declared in.

Tip   When writing code for your application, you should use the `Private` statement instead of `Dim` to ensure that the variable's scope is what you intended.

6

Note   Even the procedures with which you work have a scope. Generally, they are private to the module in which they are located and only other procedures in that module can access each other. However, if you declare a procedure as `Public`, it will be available anywhere in the application.

In this new release of Visual Basic, a new level of scope has been added. Previously, any variables declared within a block of code were still accessible outside that block of code in the same procedure. In Visual Basic .NET there is now block scope, and any variables declared inside a block of code are no longer accessible outside it. The following examples show the change in the scope.

In VB6:

```
For I = 1 to 10
    Dim N as Long    ' N is accessible anywhere within the current procedure
    N = N + Incr(I)
Next
W = Base * N          ' N is still accessible outside the block
                      ' it is declared in.
```

In VB .NET:

```
Dim N as Long    ' N is now declared outside the block and is
                 ' accessible anywhere in the current procedure
For I = 1 to 10
    N = N + Incr(I)
Next
W = Base * N           ' N is still accessible, but I is not.
```

If using public variables can cause problems in the application, why should you use them? In most cases you should use public variables in the following situations:

- When you must access information anywhere in your application (such as custom color and font information)
- When you are creating constants to be used in your application (constants can't be declared as private)
- To allow access to a database workspace without opening multiple instances of the database
- When you must access Windows API calls in the application

 Tip

> If you must use any public variables, you should declare them in a standard module rather than in one of the form modules in the application. This gives you a centralized location for all these variables so you won't accidentally declare another public variable with the same name.

Watching Out for Problems

The more public a variable becomes, the more cluttered your programs become and the easier it is for bugs to enter the picture. Although public variables sound useful, you don't want to use them unless it is absolutely necessary. Typically, only a few procedures must share the same data values; most procedures don't need to share data at all.

One of the most common mistakes a programmer can make is to use the same variable name in multiple places for different reasons. If that variable is explicitly declared as private in the different routines, no harm is done except for the issue of duplicate names from a documentation perspective. However, if that variable is declared as module level or as public, you would wind up changing the value in the variable that might still be used in another routine in the application. This causes one of the hardest types of bugs to find and fix.

You've seen that variables can be either local (private) or global (public) and that routines often must share data among themselves. However, you now know that when you declare public variables, you expose yourself to problems that could occur by reusing variable names. An overwhelming problem is that you must share data between procedures but you've been told that you shouldn't include module-level and public variables in your applications. To get around this dilemma, pass the data that a procedure needs directly to that procedure.

You also should be careful not to use the same name when you declare two separate public variables. If one variable is local in a procedure and the other is public, the local variable will hide the scope of the public one. When the local variable is no longer accessible, the application will use the public one. The problem with this is you probably won't realize there are two variables with the same name, and you'll use them both as if they were one variable. Of course, the results will be anything but expected.

Passing Information

Okay, now you know that working with local variables is safer than working with global or public variables. Given this fact, and that local variables can be used only by the procedure in which they were declared, what happens when you have multiple procedures that must work with the same data? Just because the procedures are separate doesn't mean they must work with separate data.

If one procedure calculates an array that's printed by another procedure later in the application but the array is local to the first routine, the second one wouldn't be able to access it. No routine can use another routine's local data until you set up some type of sharing mechanism between them. When passing data between two routines, one routine (the calling procedure) passes data to the second routine (the receiving procedure). If the receiving routine modifies or calculates a value that the calling routine needs, the receiving routine can return that value to the calling routine.

6

NEW TERM When passing a local variable from one routine to another, you are really passing an argument from the calling routine to the receiving one. Of course, you can pass more than one argument or variable at a time from the calling routine. The receiving routine is said to *receive* a parameter or variable from the calling routine. Whether you call these passed variables arguments or parameters, the important thing is that you are sending local variables from one routine to another.

Note

You might not realize it, but you already know how to pass arguments to a routine. Every time you use the MSGBOX function you are passing data. All information inside the parentheses is passed as arguments. The MSGBOX function will receive these values and display them.

The parentheses hold the names of the variables you are passing or the variables being received. To pass a local variable from one routine to another, you would place the local variable in parentheses inboth the calling and receiving routines as follows:

```
Call Calc_Total_Sales(Units, Unit_Price)
```

```
Public Sub Calc_Total_Sales (ByRef cUnits as Integer, ByRef cUnit_Price As Single)
```

If the parentheses are empty, nothing is being passed to the procedure. That's why many event routines have the parentheses in the declarations statement.

Caution

Never pass a public variable. This would confuse Visual Basic to no end. Besides, there's no reason to pass a variable that's already accessible in the receiving routine.

Subroutines and Functions

Now that you know how to pass a variable, the next step is to understand to what type of procedure you are passing the data. Since the advent of programming you could use two types of procedures: the subroutine and the function. The only difference between them is the way the data is returned to the calling routine and how the routine is accessed. You probably will code most of your application by using routines. As you design your applications, you will execute many sections of code from different areas of the application (such as input edit routines). By segregating this code in routines, you are making it easier to read the source code and it will make modifying the code easier.

Subroutines

One of the most common elements of a Visual Basic application is the *subroutine,* a procedure that performs a certain task and returns control to the routine that called it. *Calling* a subroutine refers to the transferring of execution control from the current code section to the subroutine. Suppose you have a subroutine that displays a message box saying that you got to the subroutine. Now you want to print a text string to the form, call the subroutine, and then print another text string to the form when you click a command button. Your application will resemble the code in Listing 6.1.

LISTING 6.1   CALLSUB.TXT: Calling a Subroutine from the Main Code

```
Private Sub cmdDemo_Click(ByVal sender As System.Object, _
        ByVal e As System.EventArgs)
    Label1.Text = "Starting the application"
    Call ShowMSGBOX
    Label1.Text = "Ending the application"
End Sub

Private Sub ShowMSGBOX()
    Msgbox "I am currently in the sub-routine"
End Sub
```

If you look closely at this code, notice two separate subroutines. The first is the command button Click event routine, which is executed when you click the command button. When you run this application, you will see the first line being displayed in a Label control and then a message box being displayed (see Figure 6.2). Until you click OK on the message box, the second assignment statement in the Click routine won't be executed.

FIGURE 6.2

Displaying a message box in the called subroutine halts execution until the message box is closed.

6

Looking at this very simple example, you might wonder whether you can just put the line of code directly in the calling routine. In this instance, not only could you, but you should because a one-line subroutine is a very inefficient way to write code. However, if you are creating a task that requires many lines of code, using a subroutine will make your code a lot easier to understand.

When creating subroutines, you should keep the following things in mind:

- Try to group related tasks into one subroutine.
- If you have a task that's repetitive or will be called from many different places in the application, it should be created as a subroutine.

By keeping these in mind, you won't create many small subroutines that take action on the same group of information, such as a name and its related address, or retype the same section of code repeatedly in different sections of the application. Another added benefit of using subroutines for complicated tasks is that if you must change the way it works, you would need to change it only in the subroutine. If you didn't use a subroutine, you would need to search the entire application looking for the code to change.

Like any other procedure, a subroutine starts at the top of its executable code and finishes at the bottom. If the subroutine must finish before it gets to the `End Sub` statement, you would add an `Exit Sub` statement to the code. This statement works just like the `Exit Do` and `Exit For` statements used to end a loop early. The following code shows how you use the `Exit Sub` statement to exit a routine before reaching the end of the routine:

```
Public Sub Get_Input()
    Dim Data As Integer
    Data = InputBox("Enter a Number", Me.Text, "0")
    If Data = 0 Then
        MsgBox("Zero Entered, Process Cancelled")
        Exit Sub
    End If
    MsgBox("The number entered was: " & Data.ToString())
End Sub
```

Functions

NEW TERM   When working with subroutines, you can see that even though they can accept parameters, they return no values other than any modifications they might make to the passed variables. To create a subroutine that can return a value that's not a modification of a parameter that was passed, you would use a special form of the subroutine called a *function*. The only difference between a function and a subroutine is that a function can return a value to the calling routine. Both functions and subroutines can have variables passed to them, and they both accept the same types of arguments. The syntax of a function is only slightly different from a subroutine and is shown here:

```
[Public | Private | Friend] [Overloads] [Overrides] [Protected]
                         Function name [(arglist)] [As type]
    [statements]
    [name = expression]
End Function
```

To return a value from a function, you only need to assign the value to the function name as in the following:

```
Public Function CalcTotal() as Single
    [Function Code]
    CalcTotal = Sale_Amount
End Function
```

This code would return the final sale amount to the calling procedure. You would call this routine as follows:

```
Invoice_Line_Amt = CalcTotal
```

If you are passing arguments to the function, the calling statement would look like this:

```
Invoice_Line_Amt = CalcTotal(Qty, Price)
```

Again, if you must exit the function before the entire routine is executed, you would use an Exit function. A function's return value can be used in various ways. It can be assigned to a variable as just shown, or the function call can be used in a statement as follows:

```
If CalcTotal <= 0 Then
    Msgbox("Invalid Sale Amount Entered")
End If
```

When you create subroutines and functions, which type of routine you will create depends on whether you need a value returned. In Visual Basic you can use several built-in functions either as subroutines or as functions. Visual Basic figures out which way to process the routine based on its position in the code. As an example, here are two lines of code using a MsgBox. One is a subroutine and the other is a function:

```
If MsgBox("Do you want to continue?", MsgBoxStyle.Question + _
        MsgBoxStyle.YesNo, Me.Text) = MsgBoxResult.Yes Then
    MsgBox("We will continue processing the data")
End If
```

6

If a routine is used as a value as in the previous If statement, it's assumed to be a function. However, if no return value is expected, it's assumed to be a subroutine. You can't create a routine that's both a subroutine and a function.

Reference or Value

NEW TERM You must understand only one other important issue about passing variables: how the passed data is referenced. There are two ways to reference data: by value and by reference. By default, all Visual Basic routines pass data by *reference,* which means that the arguments can be changed by their receiving routines. If you want to keep the data from being changed in the receiving routine, you must pass the arguments by *value* instead of by reference. To pass an argument by value, you would add the ByVal keyword in front of a parameter in the receiving routine's declaration statement:

```
Public Sub CalcTotal (ByVal Qty, ByVal Price)
```

When you are passing a variable by reference, the subroutine actually is working with the data variable from the calling routine. In contrast, passing variables by value will pass the actual data to the receiving routine, and it will be placed into a local variable in that routine. To see the difference between these, start a new project, add two command buttons to the form, and then copy the code in Listing 6.2 to the project's code section.

LISTING 6.2   VALREF.TXT: Passing Variables by Reference and by Value for Very Different Results

```
Private Var1 As String
    Private Var2 As String
    Private Var3 As Integer

Private Sub demo_Reference(ByRef pVar1 as String, ByRef pVar2 as String, _
        ByRef pVar3 as Integer)
    pVar1 = "Var One has been changed"
    pVar2 = "So has Var Two"
    pVar3 = 33
End Sub

Private Sub demo_Value(ByVal pVar1 as String, ByVal pVar2 as String, _
        ByVal pVar3 as Integer)
    pVar1 = "Var One has been changed"
    pVar2 = "So has Var Two"
    pVar3 = 33
End Sub

Private Sub Button1_Click(ByVal sender As System.Object, _
        ByVal e As System.EventArgs) Handles Button1.Click
    Var1 = "This is the ByRef Demo"
    Var2 = "Call the demo_Reference Routine"
    Var3 = 10
    Call demo_Reference(Var1, Var2, Var3)
    MsgBox("Var1=" & Var1 & vbCrLf & "Var2=" & Var2 & vbCrLf & _
        "Var3=" & Var3)
    End Sub
```

LISTING 6.2   continued

```
Private Sub Button2_Click(ByVal sender As System.Object, _
        ByVal e As System.EventArgs) Handles Button2.Click
    Var1 = "This is the ByVal Demo"
    Var2 = "Call the demo_Value Routine"
    Var3 = 10
    Call demo_Value(Var1, Var2, Var3)
    MsgBox("Var1=" & Var1 & vbCrLf & "Var2=" & Var2 & vbCrLf & _
        "Var3=" & Var3)
End Sub
```

Now run the application. Click the first command button; then click the second one. As you can see, the routine passing the variables by reference actually is changing the original variable data (see Figure 6.3), whereas the routine using by value doesn't change the original data (see Figure 6.4).

FIGURE 6.3

Passing variables can cause the original data to be changed unintentionally.

FIGURE 6.4

Unless the data must be changed in the routine, using ByVal *is the accepted method of passing arguments.*

6

To summarize, when you create routines—either subroutines or functions—you must decide how the data will be processed. Remember that declaring all your variables as public will make it easier for you to write the initial code, but when you must test and fix problems, public variables will give you very bad headaches.

> **Note** You also can define arguments for a subroutine or function as `Optional`, which allows you to pass data in that parameter only when needed.

The Vulcan Way or Adding Logic to the Program

Using functions and subroutines is but one way to affect how your application code will be processed. When designing complex database applications, many sections of code will perform the same process—just on different data. For example, your application could accept dates as one of its inputs. Besides editing the data to see whether it's a valid date, you might have to check to see whether the date is allowed. However, you might be performing this edit check on several different data input fields at different times in the application. Calling a function and passing the date variable—and possibly the range against which to check it—would enable you to check the return value for any errors.

If the function could return more than just a `True` or `False` condition, you would need to write code that would check for each of the possible return values that might be returned. The process of checking the return value of a function or comparing any two variables or values in your application is what makes the application perform. Without the capability to change the flow of execution, your application wouldn't be very flexible—and wouldn't work very well. The creation of your application really is the process of logically handling the data that the user will input.

NEW TERM Unfortunately, in programming there's no one way to do something. This still holds true even in Visual Basic. Your application will process the data that it's given by testing and comparing the data, and then execute different sections of code based on the results. This process is commonly referred to as *condition execution* of the code.

> **Note** When designing your application and creating the code, you should try to keep the code's execution as logical as possible.

Changing the Flow

NEW TERM To conditionally execute any code in your application, you first must be able to test it. This test is called a *condition*. If the condition is `True`, the related code will be executed; if the condition is `False`, the related code will be skipped. The way most programming languages, including Visual Basic, perform this testing is with one of two types of statement groups. The first and oldest of the two is the `If...Then...End If` statement block. The second—and sexier—of the two is the `Select Case` statement group. Both statement groups use expressions that you can create with operators, variables, and functions.

If...Then, What Next?

You might think that you know the `If...Then` statement like the back of your hand, but you probably aren't aware of a few ways to use it. Several variations of the `If...Then` statement also help when developing the application for multiple operating systems. A typical `If...Then` statement in an application tests a particular input data value and, if it isn't in the database, processes it accordingly. The following code uses several of the concepts that you've already seen during this first week:

```
If (keyascii < 48 Or keyascii > 58) And keyascii <> 8 Then
    Beep
    keyascii = 0
End If
```

This simple, boring way to use the `If...Then` statement only enables you to conditionally execute a single section of code. However, if you want to execute one section if the condition is true and another if it's false, you would use the `Else` clause of the `If...Then` statement. The code would resemble the following:

```
If IsDate(entdate.Text) Then
        entdate.Text = DateAdd("d", 1, entdate.Text)
    Else
        Beep
End If
```

NEW TERM   As you can see, the `Else` statement works as if you are talking to someone (that is, *if* the condition is true, *then* add the date, *else* if not, beep). With the `Else` statement you are testing for two conditions at the same time. But can you use the `If...Then` statement to test for multiple conditions? By using the `ElseIf` statement along with the rest of the `If...Then...Else` statements, you can test as many conditions as you need. This creates a section of code that's called a *nested* `If` statement. The following is the syntax of this extended version:

```
If condition Then
    [statements]
[ElseIf condition-n Then
    [elseifstatements] ...
[Else
    [elsestatements]]
End If
```

6

Notice from the preceding code snippet that the `If...Then` statements to be executed are indented. The reason for this becomes very clear as you use this extended version of the statement. If all of the code were aligned to the left of the page, finding the matching `If...ElseIf...Else...End If` statements would be very difficult. If you lose track of the matching statements when you are coding the application, you could wind up having some sections of code execute incorrectly.

Many programmers use the `If` statement to test a variable that has been modified just before the `If` statement itself:

```
RetCode = MsgBox("Okay to Delete Record", MsgBoxStyle.Question +
            MsgBoxStyle.OKCancel, Me.Text)
    If (RetCode = vbOK) Then
        'Perform delete code
    End If
```

You've just seen earlier in this lesson that you can use the `MsgBox` to return a value directly into an expression, so this code can be rewritten as

```
If (MsgBox("Okay to Delete Record", MsgBoxStyle.Question +
            MsgBoxStyle.OKCancel, Me.Text) = MsgBoxResult.Yes) Then
            'Perform delete code
End If
```

There's no limit to the number of nested `If` statements that you can string together. However, there is a mental limit. You don't want to create a section of code that is so complex you can't figure out what it does. There are other ways to create a conditional test block for many different cases.

Before leaving the `If...Then` statement, look at some of the other ways it can be used. You probably know that you can code an `If...Then` statement on one line if only one code statement must be executed. For example:

```
'If the sale was over $500 give a 10% discount
If Sales_Amt > 500 Then Sales_Amt = Sales_Amt * .90
```

Whenever you must execute more than one line of code, you should use the `If...Then...End If` block. Now, did you know that you can execute several lines of code on a single line? This actually is a holdover from the old DOS Basic days. For example, the following code:

```
If (keyascii < 48 Or keyascii > 58) And keyascii <> 8 Then
    Beep
    keyascii = 0
End If
```

could have been written as follows:

```
If (keyascii < 48 Or keyascii > 58) And keyascii <> 8 Then _
    Beep : keyascii = 0
```

By separating each statement with a colon (:), you can execute several lines of code without using the End If block. Most programmers have never used the If statement differently from the way it has been shown here. However, the statements that you can execute when a condition is true aren't limited to standard lines of code. If you must test a condition and then loop through an array to process the information, you could call a subroutine that loops through the array, or you could code the following:

```
If Update_Records Then
    Do Until (EOF(1))
        'processing code
    Loop
Else
    MsgBox("No records have been updated.")
End If
```

Thus, when needed you can mix any type of Visual Basic statement with the If...Then statement block.

The last version of the If...Then statement enables you to set sections of code to be used only when certain conditions occur. The #If...Then...#Else directive instructs the Visual Basic compiler to conditionally compile different sections of code. The following code produces different executable files depending on the operating system on which it was compiled:

```
' If Win16 evaluates as true, do the statements following the #If.
#If Win16 Then
'. Place exclusively Win16 statements here.
    '...
' Otherwise, if it is a 32-bit Windows program, do this:
#ElseIf Win32 Then
'. Place exclusively 32-bit Windows statements here.
    '...
' Otherwise, if it is neither, do this:
#Else
'. Place other platform statements here.
    '...
#End If
```

Try this code in your application. If your computer is running Windows 95 or Windows NT/2000, you will have only the conditional code in the #ElseIf Win32 section of the statement block executed. This special version of the statement typically is used to compile the same application for different operating systems.

The Select Case Statement

The Select Case statement is another way to test for multiple conditions and then execute the related program code. However, it provides a much easier section of code to maintain. Here is the syntax:

6

```
Select Case testexpression
[Case expressionlist-n
    [statements-n]] ...
[Case Else
    [elsestatements]]
End Select
```

Just like with the If...Then statement, the statements that can be executed in the Case
block can be a mixture of any standard Visual Basic statements, including other Select
statements. In the Select statement, an expression is evaluated in the opening Select
Case statement; then the Case statements within the Select...End Select block test the
resulting value against one or more values or expressions. For example, if you want to
perform one section of code if an expression is zero, another if it's odd, and a third section of code if it's even, with a maximum value of 10, you could code an If statement
with an elaborate expression to figure out whether the number is odd or even, or you
could use the Select Case statement as shown here:

```
Select Case Input_Number
    Case 0
        MsgBox("The Value is Zero")
    Case 1,3,5,7,9
        MsgBox("The Value is Odd")
    Case 2,4,6,8,10
        MsgBox("The Value is Even")
    Case Else
        MsgBox("The number is invalid")
End Select
```

Again, depending on what you need for your application, the `Select Case` statement would be very useful for testing values being input into the application.

Other Functions

Two other functions are worth mentioning in this section:

- `Choose` selects and returns a value from a list of arguments based on an index value.

- `IIf` returns one of two values depending on the expression.

Each function provides a unique method of choosing a particular value or expression. The `Choose` function enables you to use an index value to select from a list of strings or numbers. This works particularly if the index represents the value in an option group. The following is the syntax of the `Choose` function:

```
Choose(index, choice-1[, choice-2, ... [, choice-n]])
```

This function will enable you to choose from as many different values as you need to include in the parameter list. Using the `Choose` function is quite easy. The following is an example of how to use it:

```
Shipper = Choose(index, "FedEx", "Airborne", "DHL")
```

If the index value is between 1 and 3, the appropriate string will be placed in the variable `Shipper`. If the index value is less than 1 or greater than the number of choices from which it must choose, it will return a `Null` value. The other function, `IIf`, will return one of two expressions, depending on the value of a conditional expression. Here is the syntax of this function:

```
IIf(expr, truepart, falsepart)
```

This function also is fairly easy to use and represents the old two-door method of choosing. If *expr* is true, the first value or expression is returned; if *expr* is false, the second one is returned. This function could be used to calculate a discount based on a single condition as shown here:

```
Sales_Total = IIf( Sales_Amt>500, Sales_Amt * .90, Sales_Amt)
```

However, remember one thing if you decide to use this function: The `IIf` function always evaluates both the true and false expressions, even though it will return only one of them. If evaluating the false expression results in an error, an error will occur even if *expr* is true.

6

Summary

Today you learned what it takes to use variables properly within your application. Many things can go wrong when you are creating an application; however, if you plan and declare your variables correctly, you will have one less thing to worry about. Complex applications usually require many types of functions and subroutines to perform specific tasks that might be repeated at different locations in the application.

You also learned the different ways to affect application program flow. This will enable you to see how different sections of code execute depending on the current data being processed. This allows you to create a much more flexible application than if you had to anticipate everything that the user might do and code for each of them separately.

Q&A

Q What two types of procedures can you use to perform tasks in Visual Basic?

A You can use both subroutines and functions to perform tasks in an application.

Q What kind of variable has the broadest scope?

A A variable that's declared as `Public` has the broadest scope in an application.

Q What are the different ways to change the flow of execution in an application?

A There are many different ways to change program flow; however, when writing the code for an application, the best ways are by using the `If...Then` and `Select Case` statements.

Q Can a subroutine call another subroutine?

A Yes, any subroutine or function can call any other routine in the application to which it has access, according to the routine's scope.

Q What's the difference between the `If...Then` and `Select Case` statements?

A An `If...Then` statement enables you to test for different expressions on each occurrence of the `If` statement. The `Select Case` statement works with only one expression.

Workshop

The Workshop provides quiz questions to solidify your understanding of the material covered, and exercises so you can use what you've learned. Try to understand the quiz and exercise answers before continuing on to the next day's lesson. Answers are provided in Appendix A, "Answers to Quizzes and Exercises."

Quiz

1. How many values can a function routine return?
2. What's the difference between a subroutine and a function?
3. Why is using public variables not recommended?
4. How can you leave a subroutine before you come to the `End Sub` statement?
5. What type of scope has been added to Visual Basic?

Exercise

Write a program that contains public variables, public constants, and module- and procedure-level variables. Have one command button call the procedure and print all the variables in the application. Now try having a second command button print all the variables to see what would happen.

6

DAY 7

Building Complex Forms

If you are fairly new to Visual Basic programming, the forms you've created probably have a simple design. However, most applications require a few complex forms along with the simple ones. Today's lesson will discuss form design—the visual aspect of forms and the function of each form. You also will look at some built-in functions and coding techniques that you can use to enhance a form, giving users an easier interface. Finally, you will see how to bring everything you've learned this week into well thought-out, usable forms and their related code.

Designing the Form

You know that a Windows application really is a collection of related forms that enable users to interact easily with data. As you might have seen in other Windows applications, some forms can be very useful but very boring to look at—or more important, to use—whereas others are very confusing to figure out. By using your Visual Basic knowledge and some design standards (which you'll learn about here), you can create an application that looks good and is easy to use. However, your application's forms to some degree will reflect your personality.

Because the form is the most important part of any application, few people will use it if the interface isn't easy to follow or if it's confusing. When designing the forms, you should take into account user experience level. The GUI (Graphical User Interface) offers a wide variety of ways to make users feel comfortable with the application.

The Good, the Bad, and the Ugly

Perhaps the most important concept to learn is simplicity. If the form design in your application looks difficult, it probably is difficult. Spending some time designing the forms can help you create an interface that works well and is easy to use. Also, from a visual point of view, a clean, simple design is always preferable. A common mistake that most programmers make is to design the forms after their real-world paper versions. This creates some problems for users. The size and shape of paper forms are very different from that of a screen display; if you were to duplicate the paper form exactly, you would be limited to text boxes and check boxes. What's more, there's no added user benefit. In Figure 7.1 you can see an entry form that uses several of the Visual Basic controls, which allows the form to remain on one screen.

FIGURE 7.1

Advanced controls allow more information to be displayed on a single screen form with no scrolling required.

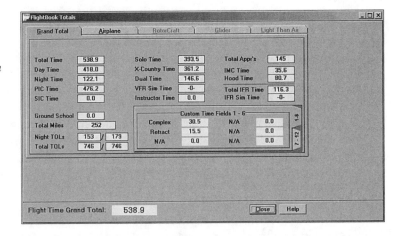

If this information were placed on the form all at the same time, not only would users have to search for some of the fields; they also would have to scroll to see every section of the form. When designing an application that replaces a paper-based system, you could provide users with a version of the input form that mirrors the original paper form and could be printed. This would become a reporting issue—not a form design problem.

One thing a paper form can't provide is a list of valid choices for some of the input areas. By using controls such as the list box, preloaded with choices, you can reduce the amount of typing users must do. You also can simplify the application by moving rarely used functions to their own forms and displaying them only when needed. That said, you can prevent many form problems or design issues by using the following design principles:

- Make the forms as consistent as possible within an application.
- Apply the same standards throughout the application.
- Place the command buttons on all forms in the same position and order, whenever possible.
- Use color to highlight important information.
- Don't clutter the forms with too much information.
- Group related information together on the form.
- Keep the data entry forms simple.

These design principles aren't very difficult to understand when you've either seen examples of them or have used an application that doesn't conform to them.

When designing a user interface, begin by looking at some of the applications already available. You will find that they have many design concepts and objects in common. Objects such as toolbars, status bars, ToolTips, menus, and tabbed dialogs are used to enhance the interface. Therefore, it should come as no surprise that Visual Basic enables you to add any or all of these objects to your application.

Making Use of Space

NEW TERM   What is space? It's not the final frontier, at least not when it comes to application design. By using space effectively in your forms, you can emphasize different controls and improve the usability of your application. This concept generally is called *whitespace*. Whitespace doesn't have to be white; it really refers to the empty areas around and between a form's controls. If you place too many controls on a form (see Figure 7.2), the form will look cluttered and intimidating, making it difficult for users to find any single field or control. By using some of the framing type controls, such as the Tab control, you can display only sections of the form in the same space, making the display less cluttered.

Adding Color and Pictures to Your Application

You can use color in your application to make it very visually appealing; however, it's easy to go overboard. Color preferences vary radically; a user's taste in color might not be the same as yours. Some colors can evoke very strong emotions, and if your application will be used overseas, some colors can have a cultural significance of which you are completely unaware. To play it safe, it's best to stay with the softer, more neutral, colors. In fact, when Windows itself was developed, color was considered very important—so much that it created many different color scheme options (see Figure 7.3) in the screen settings property page.

7

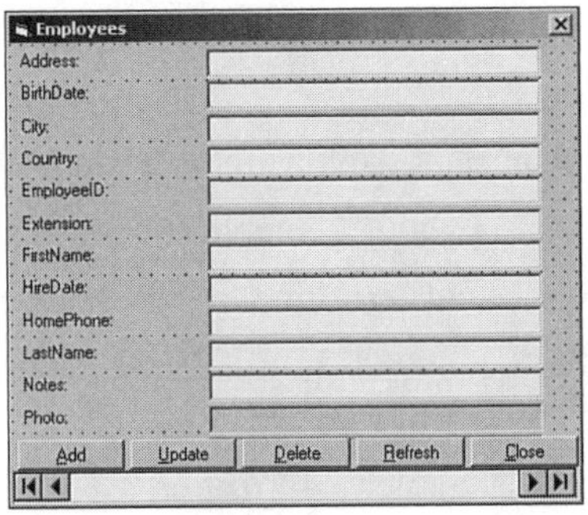

FIGURE 7.2

Too many controls overpower the visual image of the form and make it difficult to use.

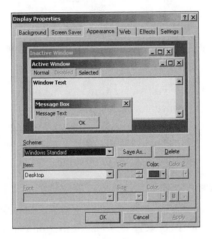

FIGURE 7.3

Windows users can choose many different color schemes for their computers.

You also can change any of the individual colors in the scheme to fit your personality. Of course, the colors that you choose for your application probably will be influenced by the type of audience or the mood you are trying to convey in your application. Although using colors such as bright reds, yellows, and greens would work well for a children's application, you wouldn't want to use them if you were creating a financial application. Using bright colors in small doses can effectively draw users' attention to an important area or, in the case of the form in Figure 7.4, notify users when something requires the user to perform some action.

Other features that you can use to enhance the overall look and effectiveness of your forms are icons and pictures. As everyone knows, one picture is worth a thousand words; you can use pictures to convey information without needing text. However, you must be careful about which images you choose because images can be perceived differently by different people. Having icons in toolbar buttons to represent different functions is very useful—unless users can't identify the function represented by the icon. As you learned on Day 3, "Creating Simple Forms," Visual Basic helps you in this respect by supplying the standard icons used in a Windows application toolbar. If you decide to create your own icons or pictures, try to keep them simple. Complex, colorful images don't translate well into a 16×16-pixel icon.

FIGURE 7.4

Color can be used to signify exceptions in the displayed data.

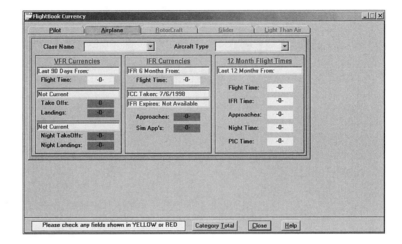

Consistency and Standards

Some objects in most forms that you will design will be more important than others. When actually laying out the form, you want to make sure users easily recognize the more important objects. Because of the way you learned to read (left to right and top to bottom), your eyes would be drawn to the upper-left portion of the screen first, so you should place the most important objects there. Objects such as command buttons (OK or Continue) should be placed in the lower-right portion of the screen, because users won't use those buttons until they have finished working with the form.

The way you group the different controls on the forms also is important. Grouping controls in a logical order according to their function or relationship with other controls on the form enables users to work with their data in the same way. When entering name and address information, having all the fields placed in the same area of a form is far better than scattering them all over the form.

In many cases, other controls such as the GroupBox control can be used to contain groups of controls, reinforcing the relationship of these controls. Figure 7.5 shows a form that wasn't designed using relationships and groupings. You can see that the input fields were placed on the form as the designer thought of them.

7

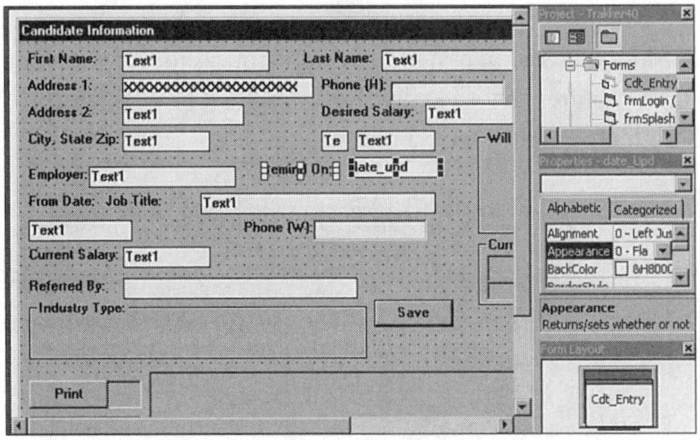

FIGURE 7.5

Haphazard placement of controls on a form creates confusion for users.

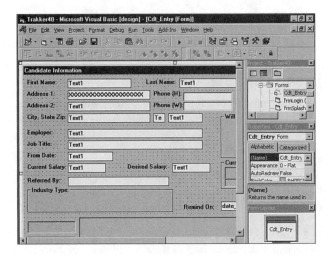

In Figure 7.6, the same form has been redesigned by placing the different input controls into logical groupings. Immediately, you can see how much easier it is to use this version of the form.

FIGURE 7.6

Grouping the input controls creates an efficient-looking form.

Also, because this form is used to enter date-related information, the data input field is placed in the form's upper-left position. If you decide on a style to use when designing your forms, stick with it. If all your forms have a consistent look to them, users will find them easier to use.

Consistency enables you to create harmony in your application. When users look at your application, everything on the forms should fit together. Keep in mind that inconsistency can be confusing and make your application appear disorganized. The best way to provide consistency in your application is to establish a strategy and style for your forms before you begin designing them. You must consider the following elements:

- Size of the controls (buttons, text boxes, and so on)
- Font style, size, and properties
- Types of controls to use

Because Visual Basic comes with many different controls, using all of them in an application can be very tempting for a developer. You should try to avoid this by choosing the subset of controls that best fits your application design and image that you want to present. As an example, the following controls are used to present lists of data to users; however, each one has specific reasons for you to select them:

- List view
- Combo box
- DataGrid
- Treeview

In most applications, the standard way to display a list from which to choose is by using a combo box. However, if you are displaying data from a database, the DataGrid control usually is the control of choice. Also, try not to use controls for a purpose for which they weren't designed. Although text box controls can be set to read-only and used to display data, a label control is more often used for this purpose. Not only is a label designed to display read-only information, it takes up less system resources than a text box control.

Unless you are planning to distribute fonts with your application, you should use only the standard Windows fonts, such as Arial, Times New Roman, or System. If you deviate from these and users' PCs don't have the font you use, the font will be substituted for the next font listed alphabetically in the font list. This usually can be fixed by installing the font, but it can be very frustrating to users until the problem is resolved. Figure 7.7 shows how a form looks using the font Wide Latin if the font wasn't available on the computer. This happens because of the way Windows searched for a replacement font. The font that would be used is completely dependent on the fonts installed on the reader's computer. The next font in the list is Wing Dings, which as you can see isn't exactly English.

Keep the same style as you move from form to form. Don't change fonts, colors, or control sizes on different forms; this only annoys users. Finally, design your forms with some thought, and then step back and look at them. If you don't think they look good, users probably won't, either.

7

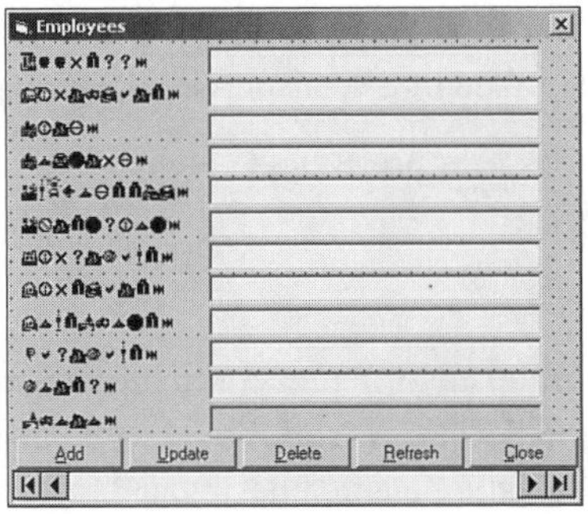

FIGURE 7.7

Choosing standard fonts will prevent very strange substitutions by the Windows operating system.

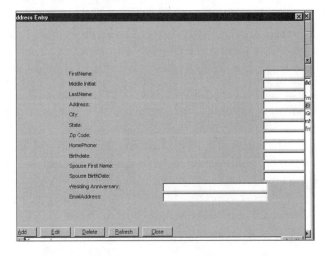

What Size Is It?

When designing and creating forms for your application, you might want to consider what resolution users might have on their PCs. Screen resolution and color depth can be changed on every PC on which your application might run. Even though Visual Basic handles many Windows issues for you, this is one that it doesn't handle. In Figure 7.8, you can see what happens when a form designed at 1024×768 resolution is displayed on a PC with the resolution set at 640×480.

FIGURE 7.8

Displaying a larger form in a smaller resolution cuts off some of the form.

If you want to create forms and controls that have the same proportions no matter what screen resolution you use, you must either design your forms at the lowest resolution or add code to your program that changes the forms. The easiest way to prevent this type of problem is to design your forms in 640×480 resolution. However, if you prefer to work at a higher resolution, you still must be aware of how your form will look at a lower resolution.

Tip

One way to stay alert to how your form will look in a lower resolution is to create a 640×480–pixel solid color bitmap and set the form's Picture property to the bitmap. This will show you where the lower-resolution form will end. However, don't forget to remove the bitmap when you are finished designing the form.

Note

Although my comments in this section are directed toward a 640×480 screen size, most users leave their screen in 800×600 size.

One other way of dealing with resolution changes is to create different versions of each form and have the application use the correct set of forms for the resolution being used. If you use this method, realize that you would be multiplying your effort by the number of screen sizes you want to support.

When designing your application, you also must consider the color display capabilities of the computers on which it might run. Some computers can display 256 or more colors; others are limited to 16. If you design a form that uses the 256-color palette and it's displayed on a computer limited to 16 colors, it will dither or mix the colors of your form to simulate the ones that aren't available. This probably will cause some of the controls on the form to disappear or look very strange when displayed.

To prevent this from happening, stick with the 16 standard Windows colors when you create the forms for your application. These colors are represented by the Visual Basic color constants (`Black`, `Blue`, `Cyan`, and so on). Even if it's necessary to use more than 16 colors in your application, stick with the standard colors for text, buttons, and other interface elements.

Tip

If you must use the 256-color palette, use the standard colors for any text, buttons, or other important interface objects. This way, users will be guaranteed to see them no matter what colors the computer can display.

Using the Form Editor Features

When designing your forms, several features are available from the Visual Basic form editor. These functions are listed in the Format menu and in the Layout toolbar, as shown in Figure 7.9. They enable you to simultaneously position, size, and align the controls

7

you place on the form. If you didn't have them to use, you would have to perform these tasks manually on each control. Figure 7.10 shows a form with many text boxes that must be sized the same.

FIGURE 7.9

The form editor tools are available from the toolbar and the menu.

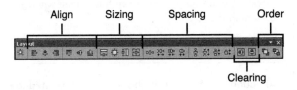

FIGURE 7.10

Formatting the controls on the form using the editor tools.

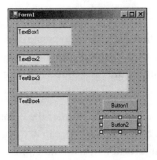

To manually size these controls, select each one individually, and set the height and width to the required settings, or use your eyes to visually change the sizes. However, if you use the editor tools, you can select all the controls at once as shown in Figure 7.11 and then click the appropriate form editor button.

FIGURE 7.11

Selecting all the controls to format at once.

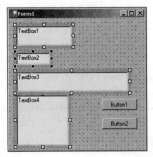

The only thing you must remember when using these group formatting functions is that the last control selected is the one that will be used as the template for the sizing or placement of all selected controls.

Tip

The control used as the template can be identified by the black sizing boxes; all the other selected controls will have white sizing boxes, as seen in Figure 7.11.

Another function is present in the property list for most controls. The Locked property actually locks and unlocks controls on the form. This prevents you from accidentally moving or resizing the controls after you position them all properly. You can lock or unlock all controls selected at the same time.

NEW TERM One final feature deserves to be mentioned here: the capability to display and modify the tab order of a form's controls. The *tab order* specifies what control gets the focus when you press the Tab key. By selecting Tab Order from the View menu, the default order numbers are displayed on each control (see Figure 7.12). You can change this order by simply clicking a control to change the number.

FIGURE 7.12

Displaying and modifying a control's tab order.

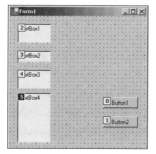

Putting It All Together

Think of each form in an application as having a distinct job to do. Most applications you design will contain many types of forms. No matter which application interface style you decide to use, there will always be one main form that will act as the focal point for every function in the application. When deciding how many forms you need for your application, you should start by drawing a flowchart that lists each different form and how users would get to it. Figure 7.13 shows a diagram for an Address Book application using the MDI style interface.

From what you've seen, designing the application form is more than just throwing controls on the form and some buttons for navigation. You want to take everything you've learned and combine it into your application. Whatever style application interface you eventually decide to use, they all have certain elements included on them.

7

FIGURE 7.13

When designing the form interaction, flow-charts usually help in the design process.

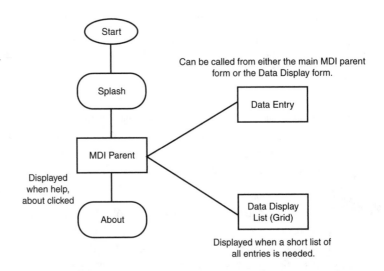

One feature of Visual Basic is the capability to *prototype* your application. This means to create an application structure with all the forms and navigation in it, but none of the unique application code included. You can start this application and navigate from form to form, testing each button or menu option without spending time on the detailed code until you are satisfied with the form's design.

NEW TERM

During this first week you've seen how to create each of the different building blocks available for your application. Now it's time to put them together and learn what happens when you do that. When you are working with only one feature during the learning process, no user issues might appear. However, when your application is finished and users are in the middle of entering new information, for example, what happens if they click the Add Entry button again? This sounds simple, but think about it: Your application is in the middle of a database add function when users request another add function. You have the following choices for what the application could do:

- Cancel the previous Add, losing any data entered.
- Prompt users to save the previous entry and then continue.
- Prevent the second add request while the entry form is in use.

Each choice carries its own set of program design issues. To see how everything comes together, you are going to build the prototype application defined in Figure 7.13. Start a new project and name it ADDRBOOK. Then change the initial form to an MDI parent, naming it mdiMainForm. Add two more forms to the project, one for the data-entry function and one for the search function. Change their names to frmEntry and frmSrch, respectively and remember to change their MDIParent properties to the MDI parent form in the application. The only controls that you will add to these forms will be a Button control. Add one button to each form that will close that form when clicked. Don't worry about the other forms shown in the diagram; you will add them later.

Menus

You are going to add a menu to this main form, but first you must decide which options you want to provide on the menu. An address book application usually needs the following options:

- Open/save address book database
- Edit entry
- Add/delete entry
- Application preferences
- Search
- Print reports
- Help
- Back up database

These options would be grouped into only a few main menu options that should remain consistent with the Windows standard interface.

From this diagram you can add the menu to the MDI form. You must make one other design decision before actually creating the menu: whether to use unique names for each menu option or to create a menu collection array. Each of these has good points and bad points. Using unique names for each option will enable you to separate each menu option routine. This makes the maintenance of the menu code a little easier to follow because you can find a particular menu routine by clicking on the menu option directly while in design mode. However, it does create more subroutines for the application to keep track of.

Once you design the menu and add it the form, you should place a MSGBOX statement for each option's Click event so that when testing the prototype, you will know whether the selection process really works, as shown in the following code:

```
MSGBOX("Place Menu Option " & <Option> & " Code Here.")
```

This MSGBOX also serves as a reminder to you if you forget the code for any particular menu option as you are coding the application. Once you complete the menus, you should run the application and click each menu option to ensure that you didn't miss one.

Besides the main form, you might want to add menu options to the child forms. However, as discussed earlier in the book, you don't really want to add menu options to the child forms if they share several of the same options as the main menu. What you

7

should do is add the extra menu selections to the main menu and make them visible only when needed.

This brings you to the topic of which menu options are available when. If you choose the Add New Entry menu option, you can disable it so that users can't select it again until the entry process is completed. You do this in the menu click routine with the following code:

```
MnuFileNew.Enabled = False
```

NEW TERM This statement will *gray out* the menu option instead of hiding it. This is a visual cue used to tell users that this option isn't currently available. When the Entry form is closed, the statement setting this property to True is placed in the form's `Closing` event. This type of process enables you to turn on and off any menu options that you don't need to keep available at all times.

However, when working with menu options that are specific for a child window, these should be hidden except when the related child window is displayed. Figure 7.14 shows the main menu with no child forms displayed, and Figure 7.15 shows the same menu with the Add child form displayed.

FIGURE 7.14

The starting main menu with no child form menu options visible.

FIGURE 7.15

When a child form is displayed, some main options will be grayed out and others will be made visible.

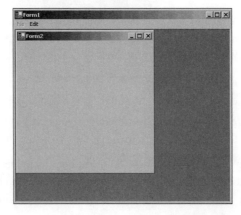

Go through the menu events and set each of them as needed, remembering to set the Add Entry event to display the Add child form and the Search event to display the Search form. Also, in each of the child forms, add at least the Close button to enable you to close the form and return to the main form. Also add the code that will set the Enabled property for the menu option back to True. Run the application and see how the menu options work.

Toolbars

When adding the toolbar to the main menu, the first question is which options are going to be available on the toolbar. If you place every menu option on the toolbar, it probably will take up a good percentage of the work area in the application. Therefore, most applications place only the most used options on the toolbar, enabling users to add other menu options to the toolbar as they want. This customization is supported by the Toolbar control, so it's easy for you to give it to the users. Your only requirement is to add the initial buttons and the related code to the toolbar click event.

When you click the toolbar, only one event is triggered no matter which button you click. The toolbar click event uses a SELECT CASE statement to determine which button was clicked. You should call the related menu routine from the toolbar click event routine as shown in Listing 7.1.

LISTING 7.1   TOOLOPTIONS.TXT: Directly Accessing the Related Unique Menu Option Routine

```
Private Sub ToolBar1_ButtonClick(ByVal sender As System.Object,
    ByVal e As System.Windows.Forms.ToolBarButtonClickEventArgs)
    Handles ToolBar1.ButtonClick
        Select Case e.Button.ItemData
            Case "New"
                Call mnuFileNew_Click()
            Case "Open"
                Call mnuFileOpen_Click()
            Case "Save"
                Call mnuFileSave_Click()
        End Select
    End Sub
```

Your MDI parent form should now look like the one shown in Figure 7.16.

If you are adding a toolbar to the child forms, you should remember that the toolbar would be merged with the one from the MDI parent.

If you decide to add a toolbar to a child form, your application could look like the one shown in Figure 7.17.

7

FIGURE 7.16

The MDI parent form with both the menu and toolbar in place.

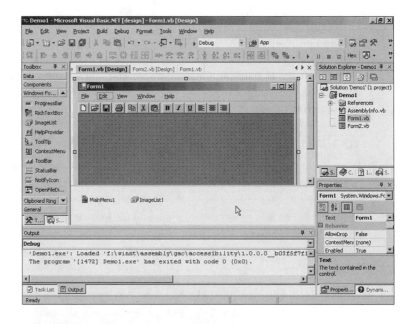

FIGURE 7.17

Multiple toolbars don't look very good in an application.

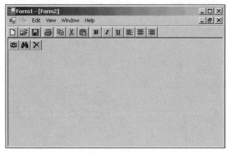

Another option you can add to a toolbar is a drop-down button that will display a menu style list to users (see Figure 7.18).

FIGURE 7.18

Using the toolbar to present multiple options.

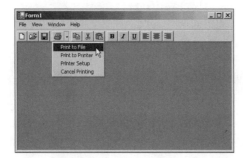

By setting the Style property of the Toolbar button to DropDownButton, you can add menu items to the button using the ToolBarButton Collections Editor. This enables you to create toolbars that look and work exactly like the ones in Visual Basic and other Microsoft products.

Note
Remember to include a ContextMenu control on the form if you want to make use of the DropDown Button feature.

This new feature enables you to keep the toolbar small, yet still present users with many options to select from.

Standard Forms

Every application can have other related forms that can give users information about the application or its status. By utilizing these form styles, you can add some flavor to your application while displaying information to users. The splash form in Figure 7.19 was originally created as a way to inform users of the following while the application is starting:

- Version number
- User name
- Serial number
- Application name
- Copyright warning

FIGURE 7.19

Using a splash form as the main startup form for an application tells users that something is happening.

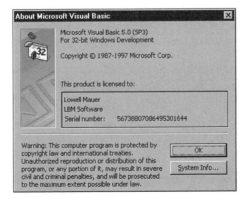

If you want to use this style of form, you must create it at least once. As soon as it's created, you can use this form in any application in which you want a splash form displayed. This form usually is displayed while the application is performing its initialization process and is closed when the application is ready for use.

To use this form, you must add the code to display the form in the Sub NEW routine and then close the form when the main form has finished loading.

Another form you can add to your application is the About form. This is the same standard form that you see whenever you choose About from the Help menu in most Windows applications (see Figure 7.20). This dialog box usually is shown only from the Help menu.

FIGURE 7.20

Displaying information about the application from the About help dialog box.

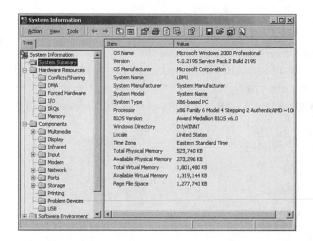

Also, the About form usually has a button on it that executes the Microsoft System Information application that displays many different types of system-related information (see Figure 7.21).

The information displayed on both of these forms can be retrieved directly from the application. The location of most of the information is the Assembly.VB file that's included automatically in the project. When you create your application project, you would enter the information shown in Figure 7.22. This information can be accessed using the following reference. Depending on the information you want, you would select the associated object from the drop-down list.

```
System.Diagnostics.FileVersionInfo.GetVersionInfo(
System.Reflection.Assembly.GetExecutingAssembly.Location
).<Object>
```

FIGURE 7.21

The Microsoft System Information application displays important information about the programs that the computer is processing.

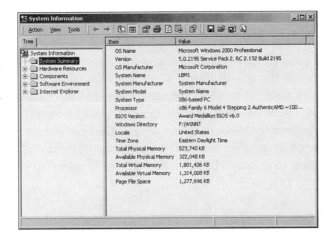

FIGURE 7.22

Setting the Application information in the Assembly.VB file.

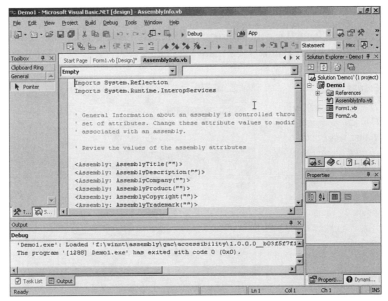

Although you can display a lot of good information using this technique and system reference, it does require some typing to get it done. The best way to use this information anywhere in the program is to set several string variables at the start of the application that will hold the application information. This will reduce the amount of typing you will need when using the information later in the program.

7

Status Bars

This next feature isn't a form that you can add to the application; it's a control that's included in the Windows common control that comes with Visual Basic. The status bar provides a window, usually located at the bottom of a main form, which can display various types of status information. The StatusBar control can be divided into as many separate `Panel` objects which are contained in a `Panels` collection. This allows you to display different information in the status bar separated in these panels. This control enables you to use one of seven values for the `Style` property to automatically display common data such as the system date and time or the status of the following keyboard keys:

- Scroll
- Insert
- Num Lock
- Caps Lock

The StatusBar control properties are set during design time in the StatusBarPanel Collection Editor (see Figure 7.23).

FIGURE 7.23

The StatusBarPanel Collection Editor allows you to add panels and modify its properties.

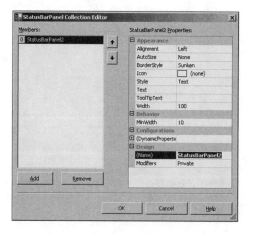

This control displays pertinent information about whatever form or function is being performed at the moment. Add this control to the `mdiMainForm`; then add three panels: one for status text, date, and time. The date and time values will be updated by the control itself when your application is executing. To use the status bar to inform users where they are, you can simply add two lines of code for each form in the application. The first line of code will display text in the first panel describing what function the form performs. The following line of code should be inserted into the child form's `LOAD` routine:

```
StatusBar1.Panels.Item(1).Text = "Address book detail display"
```

In the form's `Closing` routine, this property should be set back to blanks to remove the displayed information. At this point your `mdiMainForm` should resemble the one shown in Figure 7.24.

FIGURE 7.24

The final MDI parent form for the sample application showing the menu, toolbar, and status bar.

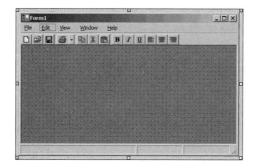

Although you should now have a working Windows application, you should add only one more thing to the application prototype: the common dialog functions.

Common Dialog Controls

You've already seen what you can do with the Common Dialog controls. However, now you want to add these features to the application. For the File Open and Save functions, just add the code to display the common dialogs when the option is clicked.

For the Color and Font functions, you really want to display a form that lists the different objects and features of these objects that can be modified using these common dialog boxes. For example, you might want to allow users to change the background color of all the forms or change the font style for just the buttons, labels, or input text areas. Besides letting users change these options, you must have a way to save the settings for the next time the application is executed. Before Windows 95, most applications used an initialization file or .ini to save application-related information. With the advent of Windows 95 and Visual Basic 5, programmers also can use the system registry to save application-related information instead of an .ini file.

When you must save application-execution information in between the times you run it, you can use the `SaveSetting` command to save the information in the user's system registry file. Conversely, you can retrieve these settings from the registry by using the `GetSetting` command. The syntax basically is the same for both, as you can see here:

```
SaveSetting appname, section, key, setting
GetSetting(appname, section, key[, default])
```

7

The following are the parameters for each command:

- *appname* is a string containing the name of the application or project whose key setting is requested.
- *section* is a string containing the section name where the key setting is found.
- *key* is a string containing the name of the key setting to return.
- *setting* is an expression containing the value to which the key is being set.
- *default* is the value to return if no value is set in the key setting.

When users change any colors or fonts, you should save them in the registry. When the application is started, these settings should be retrieved during the New routine to set the objects. To understand how this actually works, go back and open the dlgFileOpenCopy project from Day 2, "The Face of a Windows Application." When you execute the application and then change the colors on the form, the changes aren't saved anywhere. Thus, when you close the application and restart it, the colors are reset to the defaults. You can use the SaveSetting and GetSetting functions to save the color change and then retrieve it when the application is started. In the cmdColor_Click routine, place the following line of code after the call to the common dialog function:

```
SaveSetting "FileCopy", "Colors", "frmBackColor", frmDialog.BackColor
```

In the form's New routine, add the following line of code:

```
frmDialog.BackColor = GetSetting("FileCopy", "Colors", "frmBackColor",_
    vb3DFace)
```

This code line will get the color value and set the application's background color using it. Now when you run the application and change the color, it will be saved for future use. These two lines of code must be used for every color value or font-related value that you let users change. You also might want to set the original colors as constants in the application. By doing this, you can enable users to reset the colors or fonts to the default settings.

The Tab Control

The Tab control enables you to add a group of tabs to a form, with each one acting as a container for other controls. Only one tab will be active in the control at a time, displaying the controls it contains to users while hiding the controls on the other tabs. This allows you to display large numbers of controls to users without cluttering up the form.

A Tab control acts like the dividers in a notebook. By using the Tab control, you can define multiple pages for the same area of a window or dialog box in your application. The properties of this control allow you to

- Set the number of tabs that are displayed.
- Organize the tabs into one or more rows.
- Assign the text caption for each tab.
- Display a graphic on each tab.
- Set the style of the tabs.
- Size the tabs.

When using this control, you must add it to the form before you start placing the controls you want into the tab area. Each tab can contain its own unique set of controls for users to interact with.

Using the Date Controls

Almost every windows application requires users to enter dates in one format or another. Originally, most programmers used text boxes and then coded all the edit and input routines required to enable users to enter dates properly. The Masked Edit control was introduced allowing the programmer to specify an input length and format for the data. Along the way, many "calendar" custom controls were created to display a visual calendar to users.

Visual Basic .NET now provides two controls that give you the most robust date interaction yet possible:

- The MonthCalendar control makes it easy for users to view and set date information using a calendar interface.
- DateTimePicker displays date and time information and allows users to modify the date and time information.

Each control addresses a particular date display function, as discussed in the following sections.

The MonthCalendar Control

The MonthCalendar control should be used whenever you want to display date information to users in an easy-to-follow, calendar-style format. Allowing users to choose a date using the mouse instead of typing a date value makes it easier to work with dates within an application. In addition to the standard one-month view, the control has the capability to display as many as 12 months at one time on a form. This feature can be used when you want to enable users to view date information around a specified date. Let's look at the MonthCalendar control's display (see Figure 7.25).

7

FIGURE 7.25

The MonthCalendar
control displayed at
runtime can be
accessed with the
mouse or the keyboard.

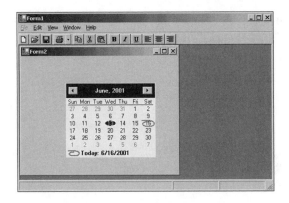

Buttons displayed in the top portion of the MonthCalendar control are used to scroll the months in and out of view. Users can navigate using either the keyboard or the mouse. You also can see that the specified date is highlighted while the current date is circled. To see how this control works, start a new project in Visual Basic and add the MonthCalendar control to the toolbox. Add the MonthCalendar control and two buttons to the form as shown in Figure 7.26.

FIGURE 7.26

Adding the MonthView
control to a form.

Set the Name properties for the controls as shown in Table 7.1.

TABLE 7.1   Setting the Properties for the MonthView Demo

Control	Property	Value
Monthcalendar	Name	mvDate
Button1	Name	cmdShowDate
	Text	Show Date
Button2	Name	cmdQuit
	Text	Quit

In the mvDate_DateSelected routine, add the following line of code:

```
MsgBox ("You have selected the date: " & e.Start, MsgBoxStyle.Information)
```

When you run this application, this code line will display a message dialog telling you the date that you clicked on the MonthCalendar control. The control has several properties that assist you in obtaining the selected date or dates. To access the date from anywhere in the application, you would use one of the following:

- SelectionStart
- SelectionEnd

These both also have a series of properties associated with them, which return specific date information:

- Month returns a value (1–12) of the month containing the currently selected date.
- Day returns the day number (1–31) currently selected.
- DayOfWeek indicates the day of the week on which the selected date falls.
- DayOfYear indicates the day of the year the selected date falls on.
- Year returns the year of the selected date.
- Date returns the full date selected.
- UtcNow returns the current date and time corrected for Greenwich Mean Time.

In addition to the preceding properties, there are many useful methods, such as the capability to add days to the selected date. You also can find out how many days in the month or whether the year is a leap year.

Selecting a Date Range

If your application requires users to enter a date range, you can use the MonthCalendar control to display or select a date range. To allow the selection of more than one date, the MaxSelectionCount property must be set to a number greater than 1; in fact, the default when you add the control to a form is 7. This property also acts as the control for the maximum number of days that can be selected. The Start and End properties will contain the starting and ending dates in a range. However, if only one date is selected, both properties will contain the same date. When a range of dates are selected, they all will be highlighted as shown in Figure 7.27.

Displaying Multiple Months

To display more than one month on the control, you would use the CalendarDimensions property. This is used to specify how many months will be displayed. To display 6 months, set the Height property to 2 and the Width property to 3. The resulting display would resemble the one in Figure 7.28.

7

FIGURE 7.27

Selecting a date range will highlight all the selected dates on the control.

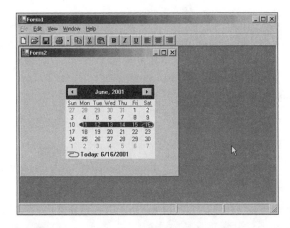

FIGURE 7.28

Certain types of applications require multiple months displayed at the same time.

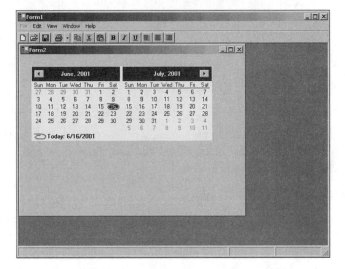

Clicking the arrow buttons at the top of the control would scroll the next 6 months or the previous 6 months into view. However, you can see that this takes up large amounts of space on the form.

Formatting the Calendar

Besides the standard type of formatting properties to modify the background and foreground colors of the control, you also can specify which day of the week will appear as the first day by changing the value of the FirstDayOfWeek property. Also, the ShowWeekNumbers property specifies whether week numbers will be displayed in a separate column on the control. Finally, the current date can be displayed at the bottom of the control by setting the ShowToday property to True. Any day number on the control can have its font set to bold by using the AddBoldedDate method. This enables you to draw the users' attention to specific dates (such as holidays, vacations, and so forth).

Although this control is very useful, it does take up a lot of space on a form. When you have space requirements or don't need to display a calendar all the time, consider using the other new date control, called DateTimePicker.

The DateTimePicker Control

If you are short of space on a form, but need a date control on the form, use the DateTimePicker control. This control presents itself as a drop-down box (see Figure 7.29).

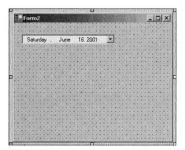

When the DateTimePicker is dropped down, a MonthCalendar calendar is displayed. Depending on whether you are working with dates or times, the control allows you to display either the MonthCalendar or use scroll buttons to change the time in the input area. The control can be used to display the date in several preset formats and you can specify custom formats using the standard format strings.

Because the DateTimePicker acts like a masked edit control, each part of the date or time is treated as a separate field within the edit portion of the control. Try using this control by adding it to the demo form and then executing the application. Then, when you click the arrow button of the control, the MonthCalendar will be displayed as shown in Figure 7.30.

The best feature of these controls is that you can bind them to a date field in the database recordset. This provides a codeless method of inputting and displaying date information from a database.

7

FIGURE 7.30

*Selecting a date from
the displayed
MonthView calendar.*

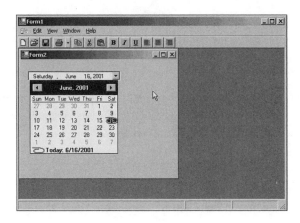

Summary

Today you've seen that designing forms takes a little more effort than just putting controls on the form. You must understand what the function of each form will be and how you want to present the information to users. You've also seen how to combine all the different elements available in Visual Basic to create a form design that gives users good information about the functions they are performing and a method for navigating to and from the different forms. The menus and toolbars also give users quick access to the application's functions and features without having to remember what keystroke they must make to perform the action. You also learned how to use other features to enhance the interface, including the MonthCalendar and DateTimePicker controls.

Q&A

Q How can I use the Windows registry to save information from the application?

A You can access the system registry for the application by using the Visual Basic functions `GetSetting` and `SaveSetting`.

Q What's the difference between the MonthView and DateTimePicker controls?

A The biggest difference between these two controls is that the MonthCalendar control displays a calendar style display at all times, whereas the DateTimePicker will display the calendar only when the dropdown button is clicked.

Workshop

The Workshop provides quiz questions to solidify your understanding of the material covered and exercises to provide you with experience in using what you've learned.

Try to understand the quiz and exercise answers before continuing on to tomorrow's lesson. Answers are provided in Appendix A, "Answers to Quizzes and Exercises."

Quiz

1. What are the six main design concepts for good forms design?
2. Can any object be placed on an MDI parent form?
3. What's the difference between an Explorer and SDI style interface?

Exercise

Create an application that uses the MDI interface and contains a menu, toolbar, status bar, and one child window. Enable only the File | New menu option and the New button on the toolbar. When either of these is clicked, display another child form in the application. Also have the current date and time displayed on the status bar.

WEEK 1

In Review

The first week provided you with the knowledge and skills that you need to design a professional application. This was done by introducing you to the advanced building blocks that you can use to create a Windows application. You also saw how to use what you had previously learned about the basic concepts of Visual Basic to enhance your applications by making both the user interface and the code easier to use and maintain. Finally, you were introduced to the new .NET Framework and how it affects you as a Visual Basic programmer. Along the way, you saw some of the new features in VB .NET and how some of the old standards had changed.

Professional Applications and the Windows Interface

On Day 1, the concepts of deciding what type of application to create and the process you should use to design it were discussed in the idea of a project life cycle. This included designing, coding, testing, debugging, and documenting. By following these concepts and guidelines, you can design and create a good application that will also work well. You also took your first look at the .NET Framework and what it means to a Visual Basic programmer. The transition from Visual Basic 6 to the new .NET environment was also discussed. On Day 1, "Writing Professional Visual Basic Applications," you also looked at some of the options to set for the entire solution and project within Visual Basic that will help you while you are coding and testing your application. You then saw some of the newer controls that have been added to Visual Basic. Finally, you created a small application that used some of the standard programming concepts of Visual Basic and the new controls to enhance a plain file copy utility.

On Day 2, "The Face of a Windows Application," you visited with an old friend, the Windows Common Dialog control. You saw that it has been changed and enhanced into individual controls to facilitate easier use. You first reviewed how these controls worked and then used them to enhance the file copy utility that you created on Day 1. In the second half of Day 2, you reviewed the three existing applications types: SDI, MDI, and the Explorer style application interface. Along the way, you saw some of the changes that were made to existing controls and functions.

Day 3, "Creating Simple Forms," started investigating the concepts of what Windows applications use to provide the user with multiple ways of accessing the application's features. The Toolbar control was covered in depth along with the new features that were added in VB .NET. The second topic in Day 3's lesson was how to make use of the new MainMenu and ContextMenu controls to add menu functionality to your application, including the creation and use of pop-up menus within the application. These two new controls have replaced the old Menu Editor that you used in previous releases of Visual Basic. The final topic for Day 3 was the use of existing forms as starting points for new forms in an application.

In Day 4, "Understanding the .NET Framework," you had an in-depth look at the .NET Framework, including what it is and how it relates to you as a Visual Basic programmer. Among the new concepts were namespaces and classes. You saw how the .NET Framework provides you with a more stable environment in which to create applications.

Using Collections and Other VB Concepts

In addition to all the Windows-oriented features of Visual Basic are many standard programming features that are still available to you to help create an application that performs well. Days 5, "Working with Objects, Collections, and Array Processing," and 6, "Understanding Procedures, Functions, and Logic," covered many topics that you might have quickly covered in previous books, but in greater detail so you not only know how to use the features, but why you should use them in certain situations. Among all these features is the added ability to create your own application classes that can be used like any other object within your Visual Basic application.

Designing Complex Forms

Day 7, "Building Complex Forms," actually looked at some topics that usually are not discussed in a "normal" Visual Basic programming book—what goes into designing good forms that are easy for the user to read and use. Day 7 also showed you how to take all of the different features and controls that you learned in that week and use them in a professional style application. Finally, Day 7 discussed a couple of performance and usage tips that allow you to add easier ways for the user to access the features and data fields that appear in your application.

WEEK 2

At a Glance

Week 2 will start by defining what databases really are, the types that are available for you to use, and how to choose the best one for your application. Week 2 will also present a quick refresher on what SQL language is and how to use it. After that is done, the actual application design process will begin. You will see how to combine everything that you have learned so far into an application definition and a working prototype for that application. You will also see how to create Custom controls that can be used to enhance and simplify the application that you are building. Next, Week 2 will discuss using Crystal Reports to get the data from the database onto printed reports. The last two days of this week will cover topics that the average programmer normally forgets about. Error handling, performance, testing, and debugging are all covered during this week.

- Day 8, "Designing the Database Application," will show you how to design the application along with the database. This includes the application flow, the related tasks that it will perform, and what forms are needed and how to create them.

- Day 9, "Processing Data," will review the concepts of database design and creation. It will also give a quick course in using SQL to access the database.

- Day 10, "Accessing the Database," will cover the newest ways to access data from the database. You will see how to use the new ADO.NET features of the Visual Basic .NET development environment. You will also review the other data access capabilities of Visual Basic .NET.

8

9

10

11

12

13

14

- Day 11, "Enhancing the Application with Custom Objects," will cover the much-talked about topic of Custom control creation. Instead of having you create a simple control that is not really useful in an actual application, this chapter will show you how to create custom controls from the data access forms you created earlier. This will enable you to add these forms as another control to the Explorer interface.

- Day 12, "Working with Crystal Reports," will introduce you to the Crystal Reports reporting tool that is packaged with Visual Basic. Besides understanding what it will do for you, you will see how to add reporting capabilities to your application using Crystal Reports.

- Day 13, "Coping with Error Handling," covers the forgotten child of programming. The importance of error handling will be discussed as well as different issues that will pop up as you develop an application. The Error handling functionality available in Visual Basic .NET will be discussed. Some helpful tips and techniques that you can use in your application will also be covered.

- Day 14, "Testing and Debugging the Application," will cover an area that many programmers don't fully understand. You will gain an understanding of what testing really means, why it should be done, and how to use the debugging facilities that come with Visual Basic. The concept of regression testing and scripting will also be discussed. In the process, you will see how to work with the new Debug facilities of Visual Basic .NET.

DAY **8**

Designing a Database Application

In previous lessons you've seen what comprises a good application, and some of the Visual Basic tools and features you can use to create an application. We also reinforced some good programming concepts. Today's lesson will bring all these building blocks together, add a few new ones, and show you the progression from the initial idea to the working prototype of an application.

You'll see that creating an application takes more effort (read: thinking) than you realize—you can't simply design and build the database, throw controls on the forms, and then expect the application to work properly. In fact, with the Internet becoming the central spoke in the ever-increasing application environment, you also must understand how to access databases from a Web-based application. As we discuss database design, you will understand some of the pitfalls and how Visual Basic provides help in the design process.

What Is a Database?

NEW TERM   Before you design a database, it's important to understand exactly what a database is and what types of databases you have to choose from. The application type will affect the database type that you choose. A database actually is a system that contains many different objects used together to allow your application fast and efficient access to the data. You can use many examples of databases with your application; here are the most common:

- Microsoft Access
- SQL Server Personal Edition
- Oracle Personal 7
- Sybase SQL Anywhere

All these databases can run on a standalone computer and enable you to create very complex databases for your applications. Choosing the right database for your application is very important; the wrong one will affect performance and complicate your job as a developer. When deciding what type of database to use, you also should consider where the application likely will execute. If it's a Web application or a multiuser application, you probably will want to use a larger, more robust, server-based database such as Oracle, SQL Server, DB2, or Sybase.

Before starting the design process, you must select a database. When working with Visual Basic, the database options fall into two distinct groups: *Local databases* can be accessed directly from Visual Basic through Visual Basic's database Jet engine; *remote databases* can't be accessed by using Visual Basic's standard database access capabilities. Understanding the differences will help you select the correct database for your application.

However, in Visual Basic .NET, you can access both local and remote databases using the same database access controls and objects known as the *ActiveX Data Objects* *(ADO)*. An addition to this access is the new *ADO.NET*, which provides total access to a database from either a client application or a Web application.

Local Databases

Local databases generally are much smaller in physical size and the amount of data they store, whereas remote databases are much larger and in the data they store. The following databases and data sources fall into this category:

- Microsoft Access
- Microsoft SQL Server Personal Edition

- Lotus Worksheets
- Microsoft Excel Worksheets
- dBASE
- Paradox
- ASCII
- Oracle Personal

As you can see, these PC-resident database types have been around for a while and are available from almost any computer software store. Accessing these databases doesn't require that you install any other software on the PC, nor does it require special knowledge of how to work with them. However, the size of local databases is restricted. For example, Microsoft Access 2002 databases can't exceed 2GB (gigabyte).

Local databases generally are used for single-user applications such as checkbooks, address books, and personal information managers. Some enterprising teenagers have created database applications that keep track of their baseball cards or videotapes. Deciding what your application will address and how it will be used helps you in the database selection process.

Remote Databases

NEW TERM   By definition, remote databases don't reside on user PCs, but this isn't always true. In fact, a remote database is any type of database that requires an *ODBC* (*Open Database Connectivity*) or an OLE DB driver for an application to access it. ODBC databases fall into two main categories: those that run on a single PC and the larger corporate ones that require large, very powerful computers (called *servers*) with large amounts of available disk space. Database servers are used to separate the workload between the client PC (where the application executes) and the database system (where the database queries are performed). This provides the application with fast data access without slowing down PCs.

Most large server-type databases provide versions that will run on standalone PCs. Most large corporations use one of the following database systems (although this isn't to say that others aren't out there):

- Oracle
- Sybase
- Microsoft SQL Server

If you're designing an application that will use one of these larger databases, the best way to design and test the application is to use the single-PC version during the design, development, and testing process. When the application is complete, switch the database connection to the larger, server-based version.

Building the Initial Design

Back on Day 1, "Writing Professional Visual Basic Applications," you learned that creating an application is a lot like building a house. For a well-built house, you need a blueprint to follow; to create a good blueprint, you need to know who's going to live in the house and what his or her living style will be. This will help you decide the number and sizes of the rooms, what colors to use, and so on. With an application, the blueprint is the *technical specs;* the *functional specs* are what you need to know to create the technical specs. Many books teach the overall application design process by using very simplistic example applications; that's not what will happen here.

Let's revisit the application discussed on Day 1. The starting description of that application is as follows:

> **Personal Address/Phone Book**—This application will keep track of names, addresses, and phone numbers by name. It will allow as many different addresses and phone numbers as needed. Also it will allow the entry of some personal information (such as birth date, spouse's name, and children's names) to be determined later. It also will provide reports in several formats and allow users to search the database for a particular person.

Although this application is fairly simple when compared with applications such as Microsoft Money or Microsoft Outlook, it still requires all the same components to perform properly. From this simple paragraph a mighty application will grow; however, it takes patience and time. Once you decide on the type of application you want to create, the next step is to decide the main tasks it will perform.

Choosing the Tasks

Defining the tasks for the application sometimes will define its complexity. For example, this application is an address/phone book; to enable users to select a phone number and have the computer dial it for them would require additional code to interact with a phone modem connected to the computer. To add this functionality to the application, you need to know how to test for the existence of a modem, connect to that modem, and then actually dial the number. If you don't know how to add this functionality, you might consider waiting to add it until after the initial version of the application is created and tested. This is what releasing new versions is all about.

Keep the initial version of this application at a simpler level. The best way to design an application is to ask yourself, "What would I want the application to do if I were the user?" Basically, you're the first and most important user of the application. This approach might not work for the larger, corporate-type application but it does work for the smaller, more personal types.

Even before you list the different tasks that the application will perform, you need to decide what type of application interface to use for this application. For this sample application, use the Explorer-style interface. To review this style, the initial form that users see and remain in for most of the application will resemble the one shown in Figure 8.1.

FIGURE 8.1

This interface includes many of the controls you learned about earlier in this book including menus, toolbars, and a status bar.

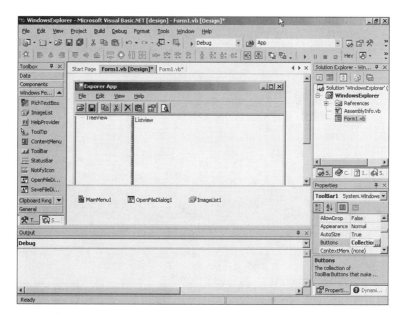

Okay, you've picked the application that you'll create—now you need to list the main functions that it will perform. Think of the purpose of the application; then list what you want it to do. From this reasoning, you should get the following list:

- Keep names and addresses.

- Search for a particular name.

- Print different types of reports.

- Allow for different users.

- Enable easy maintenance of the application.

If this list seems simplistic, that's because it is. You then would expand each item in this list until you're satisfied with the result. Let's expand each of the preceding tasks and add a bit more detail to the definition.

Keeping Names and Addresses

What do you really mean when you say, "Keep names and addresses?" Usually it means you want to keep track of the standard information found in any paper phonebook you would look at. The first step in defining all the mini-tasks required for this topic is to list the data elements you want to put in the database. Table 8.1 lists the data elements you can use for this type of application.

TABLE 8.1   Data Elements You Can Include in the Application Database

Name	Type
First Name	String
Last Name	String
Spouse Name	String
Child Name	String
Address	String
City	String
State	String
Zip	Integer
Email Address	String
Phone	Long
Birth Date	Date
Notes	String

This list is pretty straightforward—but look more closely at it. It has elements such as phone number and birth date. Can't a person have more than one phone number? Also, if you're allowing users to enter the names of the person's spouse and children, you could have more than one birth date to enter. When you create the tables for this database you'll need to design for the capability to handle multiple copies of these types of elements. How do you want users to see the information? This section of the application will require a Book Entry form and a Detailed Entry display.

Although only two forms are involved with the data entry and display, each form performs quite a bit of processing. The first form gives users an easy way of entering information. Depending on how fancy you want to get, you could create a form that uses many of the more advanced Visual Basic controls. Figure 8.2 shows an example of this entry form. Notice this form enables users to select from a list of phone number types to use to enter a number. A similar approach is used for entering child and spouse information.

FIGURE 8.2

One concept of the Data Entry form, using many of the advanced Visual Basic controls.

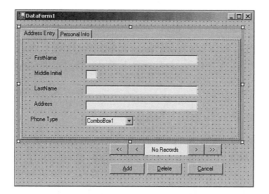

Additionally, you can see that the form is split in two with the TabControl control to make unique areas for business and personal information for that entry. What tasks must this form perform when a new entry is added? This list is fairly standard for most database applications; some of these tasks are code related; others are database related:

- Validate the dates entered.
- Edit the phone numbers for the correct amount of digits.
- Verify this person isn't already in the database.
- Allow users to cancel the process, if needed.
- Provide easy ways to select static information (such as state names).
- Give positive feedback to users when the data is finally added.

The second form enables users to display all the information in an entry without having to change sections of the display. For this to look good, you have to decide how to display the information. Some applications use the same form as the entry form but set it up so that the data can't be modified. Today's lesson uses the same form with some modifications. This version of the form would have the following extra Buttons visible on the form:

- Update
- Next (entry)
- Previous (entry)
- Delete
- Print

Figure 8.2 shows these extra Buttons as *disabled* (grayed out), although in the actual application you probably would hide these controls unless you need them. Then again, some applications combine the Add form and the display/modify form into one single form by including one more button on the form to request the add process.

Note

> Be aware that the forms, data elements, and database design in this lesson are only one way to design and create this particular application.

Searching for a Particular Name

The next task that this application will provide is the capability to search the database for a particular entry. When you use the Explorer-style interface, it doesn't make much sense to allow users to search by a person's last name. However, you might need to find someone in the database in many other ways, including the following:

- First Name
- Zip Code
- Spouse Name
- Child Name
- City
- State

A search form basically is the same in most applications, so you can use the design concepts of any application you use. Figure 8.3 shows the form in the sample application. Notice that a ComboBox control allows users to enter the actual data to search for or to select from previously entered values. This form uses the search text and the database functionality to perform the actual search.

FIGURE 8.3

Search forms are very similar in design for many Windows applications.

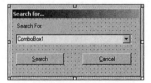

Printing Different Report Types

This task starts out simple but can quickly become the most complex task in the application. What types of reports do you want to get from this application? Is "report"

8

even the correct term for this process? Reports usually are associated with bigger applications such as checkbooks, accounts payable, and so on.

This application will provide users with a list of the entries in the database. But what format should the list be in? Some people will want to print a list of names and numbers to
carry in their briefcase or wallet. Others will want a detailed printed copy of the entire
database information in book format. The actual creation of these lists is covered on Day
12, "Working with Crystal Reports." However, you need to enable users to select the output type that they want. Different applications perform this in different ways:

- Some display a dialog box listing each available report. Users select the one they
  want and click a button to continue (see Figure 8.4).

FIGURE 8.4

*One method of report
selection is fairly stat-
ic, giving users a list
of available reports but
no options.*

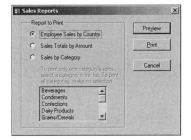

- Other applications enable users to choose from a list of options that would modify
  the application's standard reports. This way you can design and create a few standard reports that users could modify to print many different versions.
- Another way is to add search capability to the report selection. Each type of report
  selection depends completely on the reporting tool being used to create and display
  the reports.

Allowing for Different Users

Many database applications can work with multiple copies of the database or display
records that are associated with a single user in one database. This allows more than one
person in the household to use the application, yet each have his or her own private
address/phone book database. You can go even further by requiring a password to allow
access to the database when it's first opened. This type of process usually is available
from the main application menu or toolbar, as shown in Figure 8.5.

Of course, this capability comes with its own problems and requirements. The most
important one you need to supply with the application is an empty copy of the database
that will be used to create each different working copy that users want.

FIGURE 8.5

*Enabling users to
select different data-
bases to use in the
application.*

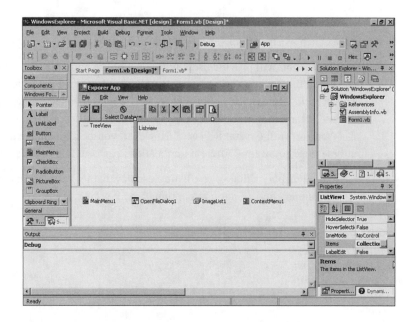

Easily Maintaining the Application

What does maintenance really mean to users? The only thing they're interested in is
whether the application will work every time they use it. Well, a good design and good
testing should take care of this concern—but what if something goes wrong and they lose
the database files or accidentally delete the files? Your application must allow users to
create backup copies of the database files so if the unthinkable happens, they can simply
restore their data from the backup copy. Referring back to multiple databases, this backup system will have to recognize which database is being backed up.

Setting the Limits

Setting the limits of an application covers two distinct areas of the design process. When
designing an application, you'll probably develop a list of functions and features you
want to see in the application; however, you might not have the knowledge or the time to
add them to the application. The issue of having enough time really depends on whether
you're planning to sell the application and when it needs to be ready for market.

One of the biggest traps developers fall into is the "one-more-feature" syndrome. Have
you ever finished a project at home, sat back, and said, "That looks great, but just let me
change one thing … ?" If you have, you already know about this deadly trap. If you keep
changing "just one more thing," the application will never be complete. This is known as
Scope Creep and will usually slow the development of an application almost to a stop.

To prevent this from happening to you, develop the list of tasks (functions and features) for your application and stick with it. If you find something you think would be nice to have in the application, put it on the "next release" list. This way you don't lose the idea, yet it won't affect the initial version of the application. However, if you find a task that must be in the application but isn't, you have to add it no matter what effect it might have on the completion date of the application.

A second limit to set for the application is the amount of data to add. Although you want to create a fairly flexible application, enabling users to add new data fields usually backfires in the form of errors and lost data. Imagine what would happen if you allowed users to create new phone number elements when needed. This could lead to a single entry having hundreds of phone numbers associated with it, which in turn would cause a problem with printing the entry—and how would users easily display this information?

Usually the limits put on data in a database depend on the database engine and how much data it can safely support. In the case of Microsoft Access 2000, the database file can't exceed 1GB (gigabyte). For an application such as an address book, this is an awful lot of names.

Creating the Database

Once you know what types of forms you need and how they will look, you must create the database that will contain the information required for this application. You've already learned that if you have information with several duplicate data elements related to it, you should create multiple tables. In this application, each entry can contain one or more of the following pieces of information:

- Addresses (home, PO box, business, shipping)
- Phone numbers (home, business, fax, cell, pager)
- Children's names

NEW TERM The process of listing these possibilities helps you decide how many tables you'll need in the database. In addition to these main tables in the database, you'll probably need other tables, called *reference* or *support tables* to provide all the capabilities to users.

Building the Tables

Depending on which database system you will be using, the actual method and tools you would use to create a table will differ. This application will need the following tables:

- Address entry
- Phones
- Offspring
- Comments
- Reports

Note

For the purposes of the next few chapters that deal with database access, I will be using SQL Server Personal Edition as my database selection.

You also could add several optional reference tables to the application to make it easier for users to enter the information:

- A zip code/city cross reference would allow users to enter a zip code and have the city automatically entered.
- Valid area codes would help in the validation process of phone numbers.

Of course, adding these types of reference tables requires you to type all the information, or have access to a data file containing this information so you can load it into the database. For each required table, you must define the columns they contain. Table 8.2 lists each database table and its related column definition.

TABLE 8.2   Adding Column Definitions to the New Tables

Column Name	Description/Commentary
Address Entry Table[1]	
Entry key	Uniquely identifies each record
Date updated	Tells you when the record was last updated
First name	
Middle initial	
Last name	
Address	
City	
State	
Zip code	Allows for the zip+4 format
Home phone	Holds the area code and the phone number
Birth date	

8

TABLE 8.2   continued

Column Name	Description/Commentary
Address Entry Table[1]	
Spouse's first name	
Spouse's birth date	
Wedding anniversary	
E-mail address	
Phones Table[2]	
Phone key	Uniquely identifies each record
Entry Fkey	The foreign key used to join to the Address Entry table
Phone type	Identifies the type of phone number in the record
Phone number	The actual phone number
Phone ext	The extension to dial if the phone type is Business
Offspring Table[3]	
Offspring key	Uniquely identifies each record
Entry Fkey	The foreign key used to join to the Address Entry table
Child first name	
Child birth date	
Child sex	Notes whether the child is a boy or a girl
Comments Table[4]	
Note key	Uniquely identifies each record
Entry Fkey	The foreign key used to join to the Address Entry table
Note	Contains the actual text of the note
Reports Table[5]	
Report key	Uniquely identifies each record
Report desc	Contains the description of the report
Report filename	
Report sort order	Defines the sort position of the report in the display list and allows you to reorder the report list when needed

[1]*This is the main table that will hold the basic address information.*
[2]*Each record in this table will hold one phone number that's related to a specific Address Entry.*
[3]*Each record in this table will hold the information for one child who's related to a specific entry.*
[4]*This table will contain any notes for the Address Entry.*
[5]*This table maintains the list of reports available in the application. It allows future expansion of the report list.*

By looking at the information in Table 8.2, notice that only the information that can occur in multiples has its own table. Any other information related to the address book entry is contained in the primary or master table. Also, the reports table is used only by the reporting dialog form to display the available reports to users. Finally, you also should notice that each table has two types of key fields in them: one used for system control of the records and one used to define the relationships between tables.

Defining the Indexes

The indexes you define for the database tables are directly related to the types of searches you'll allow users to perform in the application. If you don't define indexes, application performance slows as the database grows; if you add too many indexes, the application's performance will slow down. This happens because if the field being searched isn't indexed, during table searches the database engine will have to read the entire table to find matching records. Imagine looking for a name in a phone book that isn't in alphabetical order. You would have to read every name in the book looking for the one you wanted. With the top-of-page indexing that the phone books usually have, finding a name is easy and quick. Database indexes work the same way.

When working with indexes, sometimes you'll need to use more than one column to create a unique index value. What happens if two people have the same last name, such as Smith? You would need to look at the first name to see which one you want. Thus for the application, you need to create at least six indexes—one for each table.

For the three supporting tables, the index should be on the Entry Fkey field, which relates the record to a given address entry. Therefore, all records with the same key value should be grouped together. For the primary table, you should start by creating a primary index using the first and last name fields individually; one using a unique id number; then creating two more indexes using the first and last name fields together.

When combining fields into one index, it's important to remember that the order in which they're listed in the index affects the way the index will work. When an index is created with the two fields in the wrong order, the returned query result will have incorrect information. For this application, add the indexes listed in Table 8.3 for much better performance when accessing the tables.

TABLE 8.3   Adding the Necessary Indexes to the Database

Table Name	Index Name	Field Name
Address Entry	idxFirst	First Name
	idxLast	Last Name
	idxPrimary	Last Name; First Name

TABLE 8.3 continued

Table Name	Index Name	Field Name
Phones	idxPhones	Entry Fkey
Offspring	idxChild	Entry Fkey
Comments	idxComment	Entry Fkey
Reports	idxReports	Report Key

8

If you're wondering why built-in SQL queries haven't been mentioned yet, keep in mind that these types of queries are used primarily to speed up the SQL process and to answer specific data needs in an application. Unfortunately, most query requirements aren't known until you get to that section in the application creation process.

Note

If, while creating this application, you decide you want to include other data items in the address entry information, feel free to add them. However, remember that the forms also will have to be modified to accommodate the new fields.

Building the Application Prototype

Now that you've defined the database and have decided on each form you need, the next step is to actually create the application prototype. Start a new project in Visual Basic called AddressBook. Now add the controls to the initial form to create an Explorer-style interface. Add a MainMenu control to the form and add the items shown in Figure 8.6; then add the toolbar as shown in Figure 8.7.

To complete the process, save the project. If you look at the Solution Explorer window in the upper right of the VB .NET IDE, notice all the form and module files added to the project (see Figure 8.8).

You now have an application skeleton. Unfortunately, nothing will work when you execute the project because you must add the code as discussed on Day 7, "Building Complex Forms." Once you do this, try a few of the menu options and toolbar buttons. You can see that you have a working prototype, although it's only half completed—you still need to add the search, data entry, and report selection forms to the application.

FIGURE 8.6

*The Main Menu items
for the Address Book
Application.*

FIGURE 8.6

*The Main Menu items
for the Address Book
Application.*

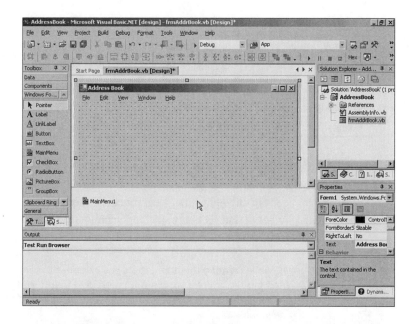

FIGURE 8.7

*Adding the toolbar to
the initial form.*

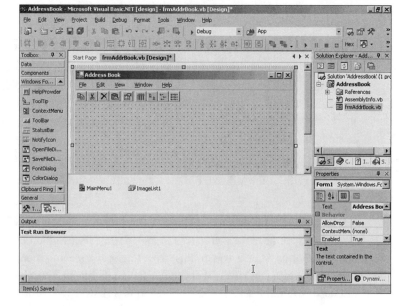

FIGURE 8.8

The Solution Explorer displays all the forms and related files needed for the application.

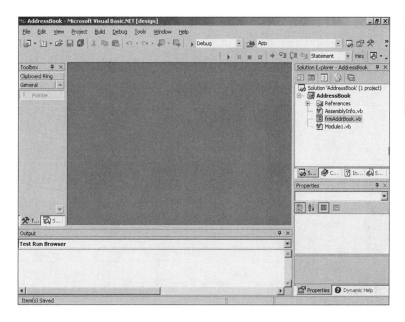

Using the Data Form Wizard

Adding the data access forms to the application can be very interesting; however, Visual Basic includes a tool that helps you with the creation process. The Data Form Wizard takes you through several dialog boxes in which you'll specify the dataset you are creating, what database you're using, and the types of forms you want to create. The final data access forms you'll use in the application won't resemble the forms this wizard creates. You'll use the wizard to generate the initial forms, which will have all the necessary data access code to use as a starting point. You must add only two forms to the application for data access: the data entry form and a grid-style display form. Let's start with the grid-style form.

To invoke the Data Form Wizard, choose Add Windows Form from the Project menu, select Data Form Wizard, change the name of the form at the bottom of the dialog, and then click Open to start the wizard. When the introduction dialog box appears, click Next to continue. The next dialog box asks you which dataset you want to use or to create a new one. A dataset defines the tables and columns you will be using in the application.

After entering a new name or selecting a dataset that already exists in the application, click Next to specify what database you're using. If you haven't already created a connection to a database, you can do that now by clicking the New Connection button on this form, which will display the Data Link properties dialog as shown in Figure 8.9. This dialog allows you to select the connection type and the database you want to use.

FIGURE 8.9

Creating a new connection for the application.

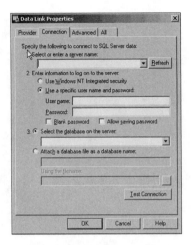

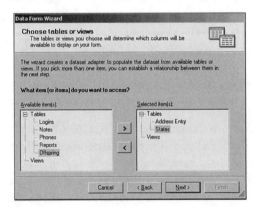

> **Note**
>
> Once you define a connection to a database it's displayed in the Server Explorer window whenever you start Visual Basic.

After you select the database, click Next to continue. You now can select the tables, views, and stored procedures you want to include in the new dataset being created (see Figure 8.10).

FIGURE 8.10

Choosing the tables, views, and stored procedures to use in the dataset.

Once you select the tables, click Next to define the type of relationship you want for the tables and which columns to include (see Figures 8.11 and 8.12).

FIGURE 8.11

Choosing the table relationships.

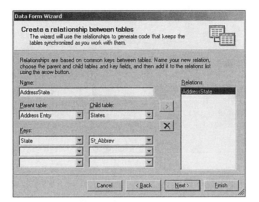

FIGURE 8.12

Choosing the columns.

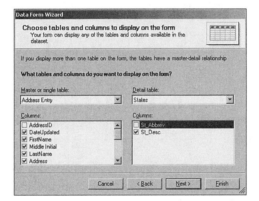

For this example, select the following columns from the table:

- First Name
- Last Name
- Address
- City
- State
- Home Phone

After selecting these columns, click Next to select how you want the data displayed, either in a grid showing all rows at the same time or a single record at a time. Again, for this example select the grid display and click Finish to have the form created as shown in Figure 8.13.

FIGURE 8.13

*The finished data grid
display form with only
the Close button and
DataControl displayed.*

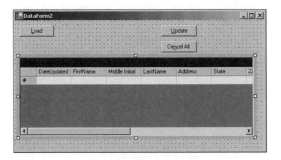

After you create this form you must add a menu option and a Toolbar button to give
users a way to display this form. Of course, in the true sense of this application interface,
you'll actually incorporate the data grid display into the Explorer window without using
another form.

> **Note**
>
> On Day 11, "Enhancing the Application with Custom Objects," you'll see
> how to create custom controls. Use these data forms as a guide so that you
> can add these dialog boxes into the Explorer interface without it looking as
> if separate forms were in the application.

Next you want to reuse the Data Form Wizard for the data entry form, creating a single-
record display for this form. Also choose every field from the Address Entry table except
Entry Key and the DateUpdated. These fields are used by the application; users don't need
to see them. Finally, click the Finish button to create the form as shown in Figure 8.14.

Remember to add the menu option and Toolbar buttons to allow users to display the data
entry form. Once you complete this step, you're almost finished. The final step is to add
the unrelated forms to the application.

Adding Forms

The only forms left to add—if you haven't been keeping track—are Search and Report
Selection. The Search form is pretty easy; however, the code behind it is a bit tougher.
For now create the form as shown in Figure 8.3. The only code line you need to add to
the form is in the Close button's click event to close the form.

The Report Selection form is by far the most difficult form to create—not in what you
need to place on the form, but in how you want the form to look. I'm partial to a treeview selection list of reports (see Figure 8.15), although some developers prefer command buttons or option controls (see Figure 8.16). It's your choice; choose one and create the form, again by adding only the code to unload it.

Figure 8.14

The data entry form has every field from the Address Entry table.

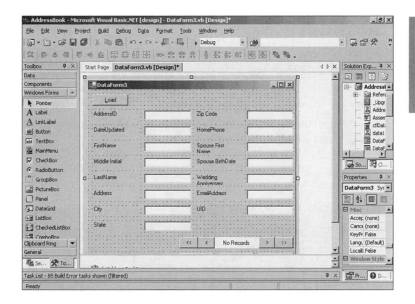

Figure 8.15

Giving users an Explorer-style treeview to select reports from.

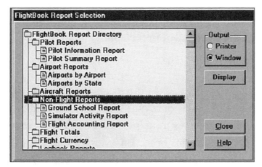

Figure 8.16

With a small number of reports, option controls or command buttons work just as well.

Now that everything is created, run the application and exercise the different options and buttons in the application to see how it all works. In the following lessons you'll see how to add the code needed to activate the functions and features for which you've created these forms.

Summary

Today's lesson begins the process of creating a real application you can use to keep track of phone numbers and addresses on your computer. It discusses the need to identify the different tasks the application will perform, identify the required tables and fields, and choose the indexes to create. Finally, you learned how to create the application prototype. You've created every form you need; now the hard part starts—adding the code that will make this a unique, working application.

Q&A

Q How does the Data Form Wizard help create a database application?

A The Data Form Wizard prompts you for the necessary information and then builds a form with enough data access code already included. This gives you a head start on the modifications when customizing the form later.

Q What are the two main form types usually included in an application?

A An application generally has a main application interface form, such as an MDI parent or the Explorer interface form. If the application uses a database, data-bound forms also are included in the application.

Workshop

The Workshop normally provides quiz questions to help solidify your understanding of the material covered and exercises to help you use what you've learned. Today's lesson really is about how to create forms based on a design that's already in place. There's nothing else I could ask you to do that you haven't already done in the lesson; for this reason, there are no quiz questions and no exercise for this lesson. However, you should look at the things you do at home or at work and try to envision the types of data and table structures you would create to hold this type of information.

DAY 9

Processing Data

Database processing has become an integral part of almost any type of complex application on the market. Databases are used to store data, whether it's your address book, your checkbook, or your company's accounts payable. Even though databases can be used by any size application, the design concepts are the same, no matter what application will use it.

With Visual Basic you can create very powerful database-oriented applications with a little bit of planning and some effort. However, planning a good database requires that you understand exactly what a database is and what makes a good one. A poorly designed database causes even the best application to perform badly. On the other hand, a well-designed database makes the application process that much easier.

Designing a database requires you to use the same process as designing your application. The difference in designing the database and designing the application is determined by the type of application you're creating. Some applications, such as a word processor, don't use database systems at all; others have a simple database and a complex user interface. Still other applications, such as an accounts payable system, make extensive use of database systems.

This lesson will show you how to define the data you'll need in your database, the structure of the database itself, and what it takes to actually create the working database. Finally, you'll get a short lesson in what *SQL (Structured Query Language)* is and how to use it.

Designing a Database

The same steps for designing an application can be applied to database design. Before designing the first form, you must have a completed data design to work with. When you design your application, you not only need to design your program code for performance; you also must pay attention to the logical and physical design of the database. A good database design does the following for your application:

- Allows data to be stored efficiently so that the database doesn't get larger than absolutely necessary
- Provides for easy data updates
- Provides a flexible design to allow for the addition of new functions, tables, or data
- Makes it easy to perform quick searches

 Note

> Although the database design is completed, changes probably will be made to it as you design the application. Don't worry about these changes; if the original design is good, the changes should be easy to apply.

NEW TERM All of these are provided in a *relational database.* Relational databases got their name because they contain tables that are related to one another by certain key data in the table. For example, if you keep employee records for a company, you might have two separate tables: one to keep private employee information and one to keep job-related information for each employee. The employee table would have a row for each person and columns for each unique piece of data. The job table might have multiple rows for each employee (depending on how many different jobs that person has held in the company) and, of course, columns to hold the specific data.

If you were looking for a particular person's job description, you would go to the employee table and find the name of that person. By using his or her employee number, you would go to the job table, find the employee number, and look at the job description. This method of connecting data from different tables is what makes a relational database what it is.

As soon as you understand the basic idea of relational databases, you'll begin to see tables, rows, and columns everywhere. You've always seen tables; however, you probably didn't think of them as such. Everyday information that you read in the paper actually is tables of information containing rows and columns of data. Things such as the stock market report or football standings all can be placed into a database table.

Laying Out the Database Structure

You should meet several objectives when designing the tables in your database. Although the ideal is to meet all of these objectives, sometimes it's just not possible, as you'll see:

- Prevent storage of repetitive data
- Provide capability to find unique records quickly
- Make it easy to maintain the database
- Make it easy to perform changes to the database structure

By striving for these objectives you'll create a database that can grow with your application. The beginning steps in designing your database actually take place in the application design itself. Initially you must define what tasks your application will perform. As you're defining the tasks to be performed in the functional specification, you're actually performing the first step in the database design process. These functional specifications enable you to lay out the tables and necessary related data. The remaining steps are as follows:

1. Define the data needed for the application.
2. Organize the data into tables.
3. Set the relationships between the tables.
4. Create any necessary table indexes.
5. Define any data validation requirements.
6. Define any additional queries the application might need.

Once you determine the data your application needs, organize the data into groups that make it easy to retrieve the information. Within the database, the data will be stored in one or more tables.

Setting Up Tables and Columns

NEW TERM A *table* actually is a collection of related data for a particular idea. By deciding what the main idea is for a table, you can determine whether a given piece of information belongs in that table. For example, a library wants to keep track of books and videos it has available to loan. The designer might be tempted to put all the data into one table; however, when the data required for each type of record is listed, you can see that certain pieces of information aren't common for both items.

In creating one table, many entries would be blank for the books; there also would be some blank ones for the videos. You also would have to add a column to distinguish between a video and a book. Creating the database this way would result in a lot of wasted space and could result in poorer application performance. Figure 9.1 shows a database table with the two types of information combined; Figure 9.2 shows the same information separated into two tables. In Figure 9.1, you can see that both employees and customers are kept in the same table, whereas in Figure 9.2 they are separated into two different tables. In the Employee table, you can see the Employee Number column, which is used to uniquely identify each row in the table; the Customer table does not have a column that identifies each row.

Employee : Table

Record Type	Name	State	Employee Nun	Hours Worked
C	Barb Smith	NY		
E	Chris Stone	NY	12319	15
C	Joe Minor	NJ		
C	Josh Tanner	NJ		
E	Mike Rogers	NY	9648	25
			0	0

Record: 6 of 6

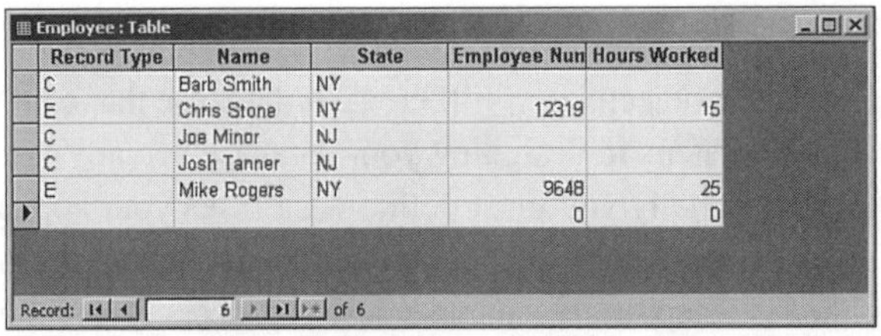

FIGURE 9.1

Combining information into one table can waste space.

Employee : Table

Name	State	Employee Nun	Hours Worked
Chris Stone	NY	12319	15
Mike Rogers	NY	9648	25
		0	0

Record: 3 of 3

Customer : Table

Name	State
Barb Smith	NY
Joe Minor	NJ
Josh Tanner	NJ

Record: 4 of 4

FIGURE 9.2

Dividing information into separate tables provides each table with only the relevant data.

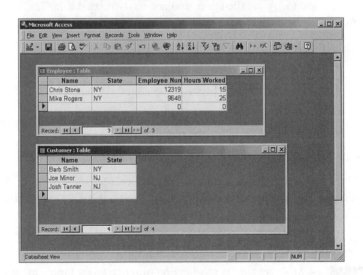

As you can see, when the data is separated into two tables, the wasted space is reduced to almost nothing. When deciding what data should be in which tables, remember that if the information would result in wasted space for many rows in the table, the data doesn't belong there.

Understanding What's Normal

NEW TERM   *Normalizing a database* is the process used to minimize the storage space and create a more effective database structure. The process of normalization involves five steps, each one reducing the amount of redundant data in the tables; however, most database developers today do not implement the fourth and fifth normal forms. In fact, in most cases, the developers "denormalize" the data to improve performance. Look at a table designed to keep employee information. Figure 9.3 shows the original table before the normalization process.

FIGURE 9.3

The unnormalized Employee table.

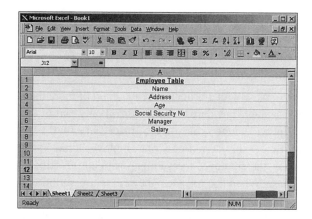

First Normal Form

NEW TERM   Move the data into separate tables where the data in each table is of a similar type, and give each table a main or *primary key* (unique label or identifier). This will eliminate any repeating groups of data. The employee information now is separated into two tables, as shown in Figure 9.4.

Name	Address	Age	Skills
John Smith	2 1st Ave	23	ASP, VB, COM
Jane Doe	3 2nd Ave	22	HTML, ASP, CSS

When separating the data, you can see that some information is directly related to the employee and the other information is related to their skills. The Name column in the employee table is the key; the skill table would require both the name and the skill to define a unique row in the table. By using a name, you could get all the skills related to that employee. If you look closely at the skill table you'll see that some information is related only to the skill; not the employee. Separating the skills from the employee information leads to the next step in the process.

FIGURE 9.4

The Employee information in the first normal form of design.

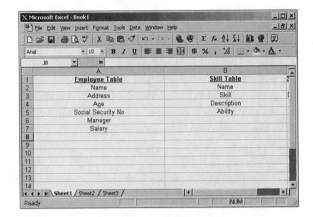

Second Normal Form

After you have a table with a primary key made up of more than one column, you need
to take out of that table any data that depends on only part of the key. In this example,
the skill description and the skill would be placed in a third table where the key would be
only the skill. Before this step, if only one employee knew Visual Basic and that person
left the company, the employee record along with all the skills related would be deleted
from the database. When this happens, the skill and description for Visual Basic would
vanish. After applying the second normal form to the database, a skill can exist even if
no one has it. Further, your application could allow new skills to be added in advance of
anyone having them. Figure 9.5 now shows the tables in second normal form.

FIGURE 9.5

Second normal form allows data to be kept even if it's not related to any current information.

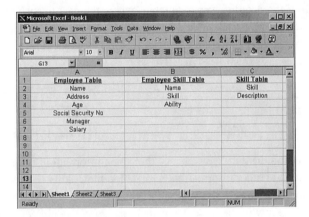

Third Normal Form

The third normal form is the final step in the process toward a well-designed database. This step gets rid of any data in the tables that doesn't solely depend on the primary key. If the employee changes jobs, you would update his or her record with the new job information. However, the job description and location doesn't depend on the employee. This data would be placed into its own table. In this form your database can handle any changes to the information without requiring changes to the structure. Figure 9.6 shows the final result of the normalization process.

9

FIGURE 9.6

Third normal form is the final step in reducing redundant data in a database.

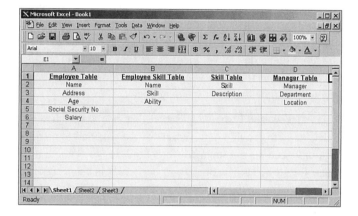

NEW TERM Many other tables can be added to the database. Some of these are like the skill description table in the preceding example. This type of table is called a *lookup table*. Lookup tables are used to store common information such as skill descriptions or static information such as state codes and their names.

 Note

Although putting your database into third normal form will completely eliminate redundant data, sometimes it's more practical to deviate from this method to improve performance. If your application tracks salespeople and you need to display a total sales amount that requires a calculation of thousands of rows of data, you might want to include this total column in the salespeople table and update it every time a sale is made. This will affect performance a little because of the extra processing required for the update process; however, overall you'll notice better performance because the large calculations are unnecessary. You always can make tradeoffs between application performance and database design. For every application, you must find a middle ground that you're comfortable with and that gives you the optimal performance you want.

Indexing the Information

NEW TERM When you put data into database tables, the individual records usually are stored in the order in which they were entered. This is called the *physical order* of the data. Unfortunately, usually you want to work with the data in an order different from the order in the database itself. For you to work with the data in the order you want, you need to define a *logical order* in which the data will be stored. Also, usually you need to find specific records in a table quickly. Indexing the data in the tables enables you to order the data.

NEW TERM An *index* actually is another database table that contains the key data for each record in the indexed table. The index itself is stored in a specific logic order maintained by the database. It also contains pointers that the database uses to find the actual record in the data table. Indexes are very similar to the index in the back of this book. To find a specific topic you would look for it in the alphabetical listing; then go directly to that topic using the page number.

Because indexes usually are small tables that can be searched very quickly, they're used in all databases to provide quick access to the data and to retrieve the data in a particular order. A table can have as many different indexes as needed; however, the more indexes a table has, the slower the database will perform when adding or deleting records from the table. This is because the database must update each index table for every change made to the actual table it references.

Establishing Relationships

Once you normalize the tables and define the required indexes, you must define how the tables relate to one another. This operation usually is performed on paper and added to the database diagram, as shown in Figure 9.7.

In Figure 9.7, you also should notice that the column in the Titles table, PubID is used to relate the Titles table to the Publishers table using the primary key in the Publishers table, PubID. The column in the Titles table is known as a *foreign key,* meaning a column that is used to relate to another table in the database. These columns can be defined in some database applications, such as Microsoft SQL Server and Oracle. When accessing data from a database, you would have to define the relationship of the tables for every SQL statement you would create. The relationships actually are defined in the From clause of the SQL statement. The following SQL statement accesses the tables from the PUBS database that comes with SQL Server 2000:

```
SELECT Titles.Title_Id, Titles.Title, Authors.city
FROM Titles
     Inner Join
        titleauthor
        On Titles.Title_ID = titleauthor.Title_id
```

```
Inner Join
    Authors
    On Authors.Au_ID = titleauthor.Au_ID
```

FIGURE 9.7

*Database table rela-
tionships usually are
defined in the database
design diagram.*

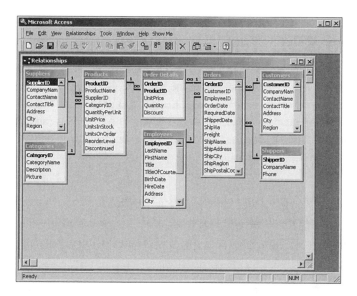

9

As you can see, the relationship actually is defined by using the keys in the different
tables that have matching information. When the database executes this SQL statement, it
looks for records in the first table where the data in the key field matches the data in the
second table's key field. It returns only records where there's a match between these
keys.

Defining Queries

The problem with using databases in an application is that every time you need to access
more than one table, you must redefine the relationships and fields you want in a SQL
statement. If you're designing an application with very little database interaction, you
probably could get away with doing this; a more complex application would very quickly
become difficult to maintain. If you need to change the data that is being retrieved, you
must modify the SQL statement. *Queries* are a feature you can use in most databases.

NEW TERM   A query or *view* is nothing more than a SQL statement defined directly in the
                 database. When using these defined queries, the database processes the data
request faster. If you need to access data from three tables as shown in the previous SQL
statement you can define a query in the database so that your SQL statement is
simplified as

```
Select * from ThreeTableQuery
```

Most relational database management systems provide tools that enable you to define queries in the database, which allows you to concentrate on the design of your application.

Using SQL: The Short Course

Once you understand what goes into a database design, you need to understand the language used to access the data in the database. SQL is the language most computer programs use to access the database. Learning to use SQL is like learning any other programming language; once you learn how to use SQL you can access any database that supports SQL access. Just as Visual Basic conforms to standards and each command or statement has a specific syntax, so does SQL. SQL actually is divided into two types of statements:

- *Data definition language* (*DDL*) is used to define the database itself.
- *Data manipulation language* (*DML*) is used to access the database.

This section covers a short discussion of the DML SQL language.

NEW TERM *SQL statements* allow you to perform processing in one line or a few lines of SQL code that would take many lines of BASIC code to do. SQL statements create queries that define the fields, tables, and range of records needed in a particular process. When a query is processed, the data usually is returned in a *dynaset*. A dynaset is an updatable list that contains a collection of pointers to the data. SQL statements consist of the following three sections:

- **Parameter declarations** are optional parameters passed by the program code to the SQL statement.
- **Manipulative statements** tell the database engine what kind of process it will perform.
- **Options declarations** define and filter conditions, groupings, or sorts that need to be applied to the data being processed.

The syntax for a SQL statement is as follows:

```
[Parameters] Manipulative statement [Options]
```

The following section discusses some manipulative statements and related options you can use. The manipulative statement tells the database engine what action to perform; the options declarations tell it what fields to process. SQL statements can perform a wide variety of tasks that mirror the actions users would need to perform on their data. These actions fall into one of five distinct manipulative statements:

- SELECT is used to retrieve a group of records from the database and places them into a dynaset.
- INSERT INTO adds a group of records to a table.
- UPDATE updates the values in a table.
- DELETE FROM removes the specified records from the database.
- TRANSFORM creates a new summary table by using the contents of one field as the names of the columns.

9

Note

> You can't use SQL statements directly in a Visual Basic application. They're used with data controls or ActiveX Data Objects.

Using the SELECT Statement

In most basic applications, the SQL statement type you'll use most often is SELECT. The SELECT statement is used to retrieve records from the database and places them into a dynaset for access by the application code. The syntax of the SELECT statement is as follows:

```
SELECT [predicate] fieldlist FROM tablelist [table relations]
    [range options] [sort options] [group options]
```

Although you can create very complex SQL statements, as you can see from the syntax, the simplest form of the SELECT statement will retrieve all fields from a table. The following statement retrieves all fields and rows from the Contact table:

```
SELECT * FROM Contact
```

The asterisk (*) serves as a wildcard to specify all the columns of a table in the SELECT statement. The fieldlist defines the fields included in the output recordset. The fieldlist can include all fields in a table, only selected fields, or calculated values based on fields in the table. Also, by using the AS clause, you can rename a field to use in the recordset.

Caution

> Renaming fields doesn't affect the actual database field name—only the name used by the application to access that field in that particular recordset.

Because SQL allows you to retrieve data from multiple tables, you can even specify which table a field should be retrieved from. The syntax of the fieldlist section is as follows:

```
[tablename.]field1 [AS alt1][,[tablename.]field2 [AS alt2]]
```

By using this syntax, you can retrieve only the first and last name of a contact, as follows:

```
SELECT [First Name], [Last Name] from Contact
```

 Note

> Although it is recommended that you avoid using blanks in a field name, you can (if needed) by enclosing the name in brackets.

Accessing Multiple Tables

Because of the normalization process, data can be placed in many different tables to reduce the amount of duplicate data. When you need to retrieve this information from the related tables, you must create a SQL statement that will combine this information. To select data from multiple tables, you need to specify three things:

- The table from which to retrieve the field
- The fields that need to be retrieved
- The relationship between the tables

When specifying the fields to be retrieved in the fieldlist, you must place the table name and a period in front of the field name (for example, Contact.[First Name]). If you need to retrieve some fields from one table and all fields from another, you can still use the wildcard character (for example, Contact.[First Name], Sales.*). The next step is to specify the tables you're using in the FROM clause of the SELECT statement. Finally, the relationship between the tables is specified by using a WHERE clause of a JOIN condition. The WHERE clause is used more often than the JOIN condition when creating SQL statements. The final SQL statement would look like the following:

```
SELECT Contact.[First Name], Contact.[Last Name], Sales.*
       FROM Contact
       INNER JOIN Sales
           ON Contact.ID = Sales.ID
```

This statement retrieves the first and last name from the Contact table, and all the related sales information from the Sales table.

Note

> You can omit table names from the fieldlist as long as the field name is unique in the tables listed.

Creating Calculated Values

In the preceding SQL example, the sales-related information for each contact is retrieved. Suppose you also need to work with the average sale made for that contact. You can calculate this value by dividing the two values in your program code or use a calculated field in the SELECT statement. A calculated field can be the result of an arithmetic operation or the result of a string operation. In addition to the standard arithmetic and string operations, each database supports many operations and functions unique to that database. For example, Microsoft Access allows you to use the same set of functions as Visual Basic, such as MID$ or UCASE$. The following SQL statement shows how to get the average sale made for the contact as part of the query:

```
SELECT Contact.[First Name], Contact.[Last Name], Sales.*,
       Sales.[Sale Total] / Sales.[Sale Units] as [Avg Sale]
       FROM Contact, Sales WHERE Contact.ID = Sales.ID
```

Although this SQL statement will create a recordset that you can update, any calculated field in the recordset is read-only.

Changing the Tables Names

Of the names of the tables you're using, the SQL statement could get very long when supplying the table names in the fieldlist. To prevent this from happening and simplify the SQL code, you can assign a short name to any table in the statement, much the same as you can rename a field in the fieldlist. By using aliases in the FROM clause, you can assign a name that makes sense to you to each table. For example, the preceding SQL statement could be rewritten as follows:

```
SELECT CT.[First Name], CT.[Last Name], SA.*,
       SA.[Sale Total] / SA.[Sale Units] as [Avg Sale]
       FROM Contact as CT, Sales as SA WHERE CT.ID = SA.ID
```

As you can see, this approach makes the SQL statement a little easier to read.

Filtering the Data

One of the more powerful features of SQL is its capability to control the range of records to be processed by specifying a filter condition. You can use many types of filters, such as [Last name] = "Jones", Units > 1, or [Order Date] between #5/1/94# and #5/31/94#.

Note   Although the SELECT statement is being reviewed, the basics of filtering can be used in other SQL statements, such as DELETE and UPDATE.

Filter conditions in a SQL command are specified in the WHERE clause. The syntax of the WHERE clause is as follows:

WHERE *logical-expression*

Four types of logical statements define the condition you can use with the WHERE clause:

- A comparison is used to compare a field to another field or a given value (for example, [Sales Quantity] > 10).
- LIKE compares a field to a specified pattern (for example, SM*).
- IN compares a field to a list of acceptable values (for example, State IN ("NY", "NJ", "CT")).
- BETWEEN compares a field to a value range (for example, [Order Date] BETWEEN #01/01/96# and #02/28/96#).

Each predicate has many different options and wildcard values you can use. Because some of them vary depending on the database, you should review these options for the database you're working with.

The WHERE clause enables you to specify multiple conditions to filter on more than one field at a time. Each individual condition follows the syntax discussed earlier but are combined using the logical operators AND and OR. By using multiple-condition statements, you can find all the contacts in New York and New Jersey, or anyone whose first or last name begins with Rich:

```
SELECT * FROM Contact WHERE State IN ('NY', 'NJ') or
    ([Last Name] LIKE 'RICH*' OR [First Name] LIKE 'RICH*')
```

In addition to specifying the records to be retrieved, you also can use the SELECT statement to specify the order in which you want the records to appear in the dynaset. To sort the records, you would use the ORDER BY clause of the SELECT statement. You can specify the sort order with a single field or with multiple fields. If you use multiple fields, the individual fields must be separated by commas. When specifying a sort, the default direction is ascending; to change the sort order for a given field, use the DESC keyword after the field name. To sort contact information alphabetically by state and then by last name in a descending order, use the following SQL statement:

```
SELECT * FROM Contact WHERE State IN ('NY', 'NJ') ORDER BY State,
    [Last Name] DESC
```

Working with SQL can be very frustrating at times; however, it makes your life as a programmer easier because of the functions it performs for you. Without SQL and relational databases, every data access function would need to be coded within your application. This review was only for the SELECT statement and a few of the many possible actions you can perform with SQL. In the following lessons, you'll see how to use SQL while designing the data forms and data access processes in your application.

> **Note** During the following discussions of views, stored procedures, and triggers, we will use the Northwind database that is included with SQL Server 2000. You also will learn how to use the Visual Database Tools that are included with Visual Basic .NET to create and modify views, stored procedures, and triggers in a SQL Server or Oracle database.

Using Table Views

A *view* is nothing more than a virtual table whose columns are defined using a SELECT statement. As with an actual table, a view consists of a set of named columns and rows of data. However, a view doesn't actually exist as a physical table in the database. The rows and columns of data come from the tables referenced in the SELECT statement that defines the view, and are produced dynamically whenever the view is referenced.

Views enable you to look at data in the database without duplicating that data. A view provides you with a method to filter the data referenced in the SELECT statement that is used to define the view. This SELECT statement can reference one or more tables or other views in the current database or other databases.

You might be wondering, "What can I really use views for?" The answer is everything. You can use views to limit the data that can be accessed by an application's process or as a way of simplifying access to the data.

> **Note** Because a view is defined in the database, a user or application program can access a view as if it were a regular table. Thus views are used to restrict, index, or even filter the data with a WHERE clause.

The types of views you can create range from the very simple to the very complex. A view is nothing more than a SELECT statement that retrieves data from one or more tables. When creating a view, you use a specific syntax, as shown here:

```
Create View [<database name>.] [<owner>.] view_name
[(Column [ ,...n])]
[With <view_attribute> [ ,...n]]
As
Select_statement
```

Table 9.1 lists each argument in the preceding syntax, along with a brief explanation.

TABLE 9.1 The Arguments for Creating a View

Argument	Description
`View_name`	The name of the view you are creating. You can optionally specify the owner and database names as well (for example, `Northwind.dbo.newView`).
`Column`	One or more columns that will be included in the view when executed.
`Select_statement`	The `SELECT` statement that actually defines the view.

To understand views, start with a standard `SELECT` statement as shown:

```
SELECT * FROM Employees
```

As you can see, the `SELECT` statement would return all the columns requested in the `Employees` table. Let's trim this down a little: Suppose the process you are working on needs only the name of the employee and his region. The new `SELECT` statement would look like this:

```
SELECT EmployeeID, LastName, FirstName,
       Region
FROM Employees
```

Okay, so far so good—but what if you know your application will need this selection of data over and over again? Well, one way to resolve this is to keep rewriting this `SELECT` statement whenever you need it. Alternatively, you can create a view that will return only this data. The following listing will create such a view when executed as a SQL statement.

```
CREATE VIEW Employees_VIEW
AS SELECT EmployeeID as Emp_ID, LastName as Lname,
          FirstName as Fname, Region as State
FROM Employees
```

The preceding `CREATE` statement consists of the `CREATE VIEW` command and the associated `SELECT` statement. You might notice that a new statement is included in this listing. The `GO` statement tells the server to execute all the commands that precede it before continuing. This is required because a `CREATE VIEW` statement must be the first statement in a batch.

The preceding `SELECT` statement also provides alias names for the columns. When you use this view, you can reference those alias names as if they were the actual column names or use the star (*) notation to select all the columns in the view.

```
Select * from Employees_View
```

As you can see, the star (*) notation returns only the columns that were referenced in the creation of the view; not all the columns in the table.

Note

Once you create a view, it will continue to exist in the database until you explicitly delete it.

The Server Explorer in Visual Basic .NET allows you to see what views exist in the selected database (see Figure 9.8).

FIGURE 9.8

Listing all views contained in a database.

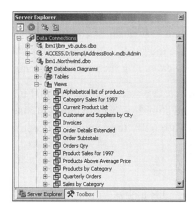

Any syntax you can use for accessing a table with a SELECT statement can be used to access a view. When you create a view you can create it with many of the options that are available in a normal SELECT statement. However, you should know about a few restrictions:

- You may not use an ORDER BY or a COMPUTE clause when creating a view; however, you can use them when accessing a view.

- If you create aliases for the column names in a view, the aliases must be valid column names according to the naming rules.

Tip

As you can probably figure out, if you want to prevent a SQL query from accessing some of the columns in the database, simply create a view that doesn't reference those columns.

Working with Stored Procedures

NEW TERM A *stored procedure* is nothing more than one or more SQL statements stored in the database that can then be executed by name. They provide a number of benefits, including enhanced control of data, straightforward access to complex data operations, and improved performance. In some applications, a Database Administrator or DBA might decide that procedures should be the only interface to the data.

> Not all databases support stored procedures. However, the most widely used databases, such as Microsoft SQL Server and Oracle, do support stored procedures.

A stored procedure should contain a logical set of commands that are executed more than once for that database. They enable the programmer to simply call the stored procedure as a function instead of repeatedly executing the same statements inside a SQL script.

In the following section we will create a stored procedure that inserts a new order into the Orders table and then a second stored procedure that will insert detail rows into the Order Detail table. Finally, we will modify these stored procedures so that they except parameters instead of static data.

Using the INSERT Statement

Let's start with the procedure that adds a new order to the Orders table. The procedure will need to check to see whether the order number being inserted has already been used. If the order number is already in use and the order is still open, we will use that orderID. If not, we will create a new order. For now, let's keep it simple. We'll add a new open order for the customer, QuickStop (CustomerID 'QUICK') and use the open orderID in the Order Details insert procedure. The following SQL code shows the insert statement to add the new order.

```
INSERT INTO [Northwind].[dbo].[Orders] (
    [CustomerID],
    [EmployeeID],
    [OrderClosed]
) VALUES(
    'QUICK',
    2,
    'N')
```

This procedure adds a row to the Orders table for the customer 'Quick' and employee #2. The 'N' is the OrderClosed field; it tells us that this is an open order. We'll allow the details of the order (dates, shipping method, addresses) to be null until we close the order.

At the core of the procedure is a simple INSERT statement:

```
INSERT INTO [Order Details] (
    [OrderID],
    [ProductID],
    [UnitPrice],
    [Quantity],
    [Discount]
) VALUES (
    11078,
    3,
    10.00,
    6,
    0
)
```

If you execute only the statement (not as a procedure), you'll add a row to the Order Details table.

Let's write the INSERT statement as a procedure using the create procedure statement. Procedures are objects, so the procedure will require a name. The name must be unique among all objects in the database (so a procedure can't have the same name as a table or view that it accesses).

We'll use prAddItemToCart for the name of the procedure. Listing 9.1 provides the statements that create the new procedure.

LISTING 9.1   A Simple Stored Procedure

```
 1: create proc prAddItemToCart
 2: as
 3: INSERT INTO [Northwind].[dbo].[Order Details] (
 4:     [OrderID],
 5:     [ProductID],
 6:     [UnitPrice],
 7:     [Quantity],
 8:     [Discount]
 9: ) VALUES (
10:     11078,
11:     3,
12:     10.00,
13:     6,
14:     0
15: )
16: return
```

When you successfully create a procedure, it doesn't insert or return data, and it doesn't return any messages; it does create a new object in your database. Let's look at the procedure itself:

ANALYSIS Lines 1 and 2 declare the type and name of the object. You can use the words proc and procedure interchangeably. After the name you indicate that the actual batch of statements follows with the keyword as. Lines 3–15 are the query itself. Line 16 contains a return statement. return statements are optional at the end of procedures; however, they are recommended. In the section "Returning Procedure Status" later today, you will see how you can use the return statement to let a calling program know whether the procedure worked properly.

The syntax for the Create Procedure statement is

```
create proc[edure] <procedure-name>
as
<SQL statements>
return
```

What about the output? SQL Server responds in the same way to all CREATE statements: total silence. No "procedure created" or "attaboys" here. In SQL Server no news is good news. To actually execute this stored procedure, you must use the keyword Execute as part of the SQL statement you are executing as shown here:

```
Execute prAddItemToCart
```

Working with Parameters

There is only one problem with our procedure as we have created it. It works great if we have only one customer who buys only one item, but what if that customer wants to buy something else? What if we have another customer? Should we write a separate procedure to handle each customer? One for each product? Of course not. Instead we'll change the procedure to enable you to pass the customer ID, the order ID, and the product ID as *parameters*.

NEW TERM A parameter is a mechanism enabling a calling program to pass a value to a procedure so the procedure can operate in response to that value. Here is the syntax for creating or altering procedures that accept parameters:

```
create | alter proc[edure] <procedure-name>
[ ( @parameter-name datatype [ = defaultvalue ] [, ...] ) ]
as
<SQL statements>
return
```

To use a parameter in a stored procedure, it needs to be declared in the create proc statement or added later using the Alter Procedure statement. You then can use the parameter the same way you would use any value or variable in the procedure. Listing 9.2 shows you how to modify the procedure to access parameters for each of the insert values. Notice you use alter proc to change an existing procedure.

LISTING 9.2   Using Parameters to Pass Item Information to the Stored Procedures

```
 1: alter proc prAddItemToCart (
 2:     @OrderID int,
 3:     @ProductID int,
 4:     @UnitPrice money,
 5:     @Quantity smallint,
 6:     @Discount real
 7: ) as
 8: INSERT INTO [Order Details] (
 9:     [OrderID],
10:     [ProductID],
11:     [UnitPrice],
12:     [Quantity],
13:     [Discount]
14: ) VALUES (
15:     @OrderID,
16:     @ProductID,
17:     @UnitPrice,
18:     @Quantity,
19:     @Discount
20: )
21: return
```

ANALYSIS   In Listing 9.2 you can see that lines 2–6 define the list of parameters used in the stored procedure. The declaration of a parameter requires a system or user-defined data type. The data type should match the column data type if it will be used in a where clause or in a values list, as in lines 15–19 in the example.

Query performance is considerably better if the data type of the parameter is an exact match for the column data type. You should take the time to look up the data type in the Query Analyzer when you are writing a stored procedure.

Passing Parameters to Procedures

How do you pass a parameter to a procedure? (You have already been doing it with the system procedures.) Parameters are passed in the same statement after the parameter name. In the following statement, all the values that follow the stored procedure name are treated as parameters.

```
Execute prAddItemToCart
    11078,
    4,
    10.00,
    6,
    0
```

The procedure now enables the user to add any item to any cart based on his parameters.

Using Triggers

NEW TERM A *trigger* is a special class of stored procedure that is designed to execute automatically when an UPDATE, INSERT, or DELETE statement is issued against a table
or view in the database. A trigger also can query other tables and can include complex
SQL statements. For example, you could control whether to allow an order to be added
to the database based on the customer's current account status.

Some of the advantages of using triggers are

- Because triggers are automatic, they are activated immediately after any modification to the table's data, such as a manual entry or an application action.
- They can cascade any changes through related tables in the database.
- They can be used to enforce restrictions that are more complex than those defined
in the table definitions.

Writing Your First Trigger

The best way to see how a trigger works is to create one. Let's create a simple trigger for
the Employees table on the Northwind database. A CREATE TRIGGER statement looks a lot
like the CREATE PROCEDURE statement, with two exceptions:

- A trigger is associated with a table or view, and with one or more actions that will
be performed on that table or view.
- A trigger takes no parameters for input or output.

The following is a sample trigger on the Employees table in the Northwind database,
which we will use to see how triggers work:

```
Create Trigger trg_employees
On Employees
For insert, update
As
Raiserror ('%d rows modified (This is the trigger message) ', 0,1,@@rowcount)
```

This trigger will execute whenever you insert or update rows in the Employees table.
When the trigger executes, it will display the number of rows modified by the statement
calling the trigger (@@rowcount); that is, when it is called by an INSERT or UPDATE
statement.

Note Remember that a trigger isn't executed directly; it is executed by the server
when the FOR clause is met.

Triggers are very much like stored procedures in that you must define them to store them in the database. Additionally, like a stored procedure, triggers aren't executed when you create them. However, the difference between stored procedures and triggers comes in when they are executed. You control when a stored procedure is executed, whereas the SQL Server controls when a trigger is executed.

Understanding When Triggers Fire

A trigger is executed based on how you have defined that particular trigger. You can specify one of the following options:

- AFTER specifies the action that, when performed, will fire the trigger. The trigger will execute after the action is performed on the database. This is the default option.

- FOR specifies the action that, when performed, will fire the trigger. The trigger will execute after the action is performed on the database. Specifying FOR is the same as specifying AFTER.

- INSTEAD OF specifies that this trigger should execute instead of the trigging action.

Even if the triggering statement modified no rows, the trigger will still execute. This is important to remember because when you start writing triggers, you will need to take into account all the following possibilities:

- One row was modified
- Two or more rows were modified
- No rows were modified

You will find that the trigger code you write will be more complex than most of the other code because of these possibilities.

Working with the Visual Database Tools

Once you design the database you can actually create it. You can design your database by using the tools supplied by the database application system. Alternatively, you can use the database capabilities within Visual Basic to execute the SQL DDL to create the database and tables. Also, if you are working with Microsoft SQL Server or Oracle you can make use of the Visual Database Tools that are included with Visual Basic .NET.

You can use Visual Basic's Data Access in your application to access the data in an existing database or in a program written to create a database for use by your application. Writing programs that create databases can be an entire development effort all by itself. Unless you need to build the database when the application is executed the first time, it's usually better to create the empty database structure and include it with your application files.

Note

> Most databases won't allow you to create new tables or columns using the Visual Basic access methods; instead you must use the utilities that are included with that database or code the SQL DDL scripts that will add the necessary objects.

The Visual Database Tools provide you with an interactive set of tools that allow you to create and modify databases on your computer. It also enable you to create and maintain the following:

- Views
- Queries
- Stored procedures
- Triggers
- New table (SQL Server and Oracle only)
- New table columns (SQL Server and Oracle only)
- New database (SQL Server only)

You can use this tool to create the database structure you've designed for your application.

Exploring Data in the Server Explorer

The Visual Basic .NET Server Explorer (see Figure 9.9) enables you to view and define database connections that can be used in a Visual Basic application, and to access any SQL Server and Oracle database server available on your network.

FIGURE 9.9

Displaying database connections in Server Explorer.

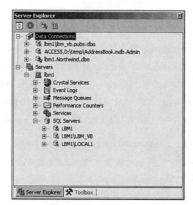

To see what databases are available, start Visual Basic .NET and display the Server Explorer. Expand the server that contains the databases you want to work with. If you are working with either SQL Server or Oracle you will see a folder for the database server. You then can expand the database server folder to see the different databases on that server as shown in Figure 9.9. Through the Server Explorer interface, you can access the Visual Database Tools and use them to work with your database.

Note

Defining new database connections for use in your applications will be covered on Day 10, "Accessing the Database". The remainder of this chapter will cover the use of the Visual Database Tools.

Creating the Database

Creating a new database in either SQL Server is as simple as right-clicking the database server where you want the new database to reside and selecting New Database from the pop-up menu. This will display the Create Database dialog (see Figure 9.10), which will enable you to enter the name of the new database and the security you want to use to access it.

FIGURE 9.10

Defining the new Database to the server.

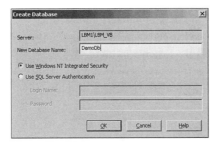

Caution

When creating a database this way, remember that the properties of the database should match the defined defaults for that database server. You can't modify them directly in the Visual Database Tools; you will need to either execute SQL DDL to ALTER these properties or, in the case of SQL Server, use the Enterprise Manager for that database.

Adding Tables and Columns

After you create the database file, the next step is to create the tables you need in the database. To create a new table, right-click the Tables node of the target database and choose New Table from the pop-up menu. The Table Designer will appear (see Figure 9.11).

FIGURE 9.11

Adding columns to a Table with the Table Designer.

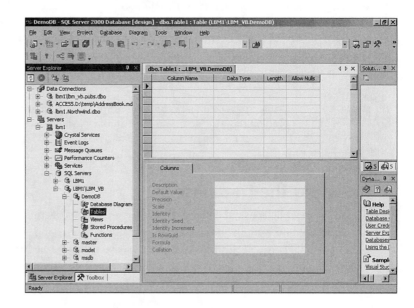

When the table is displayed, the default name is Table1 if this is the first table. To change the name of the table, click the Property Pages icon in the Properties window to display the properties for the table itself as shown in Figure 9.12.

FIGURE 9.12

Modifying the properties for the Table.

The top half of the Table Designer allows you to add columns and specify the datatype, length, and whether the column can contain null values. You also can specify any optional settings, such as a default value, for each column. After you enter all the necessary information, click OK to add the field to the table. Repeat this process until you've added all the fields you need in the table. Once a table is defined in the database, you can always modify it by right-clicking it and selecting Design Table from the pop-up menu.

Caution

Make sure you enter the information for each field correctly. Even though you can modify some of the properties for the fields, many can't be changed. You would need to delete and re-add the field to change these settings.

Adding an Index to a Table

The Indexes/Keys tab on the Table Designer Property Pages also allows you to add, modify, or delete indexes for a table. Any indexes now in the table are displayed in the Index List in the center of the form. To add a new index, click the New button (see Figure 9.13).

FIGURE 9.13

Adding a new Index to the Table.

To actually add the index, modify an index name (if you don't want to use the default name); then select the fields you want included in the index by selecting them in the Columns list. After defining the fields for the index, you can specify whether you want this index to be unique or to be the primary index for the table. After you properly define the index, click Close to save it.

Adding Views

To add a view to the database, right-click the Views node and choose New View from the
pop-up menu. This will display the Query and View designer with the Add Table dialog
to allow you to select the tables you want in the view (see Figure 9.14). The Add Table
dialog allows you to select any Tables, Views, or Functions that are available in the
database.

FIGURE 9.14

*Selecting the Tables for
the View.*

Note For this section the Northwind database will be used to create a new view.

Select the tables you want by either double-clicking each table or selecting all of them
and clicking Add. Once you select all required tables, click Close to continue. Once the
tables have been selected, you will be using the Query Designer to finish the creation
process. The Query Designer consists of four unique sections or panes:

- **Diagram pane** displays the tables you are querying. Each box represents a table,
  and shows the available data columns and icons that indicate how each column is
  used in the query. Joins are indicated by lines between the boxes.
- **Grid pane** contains a spreadsheet-like grid in which you specify options, such as
  which data columns to display, what rows to select, how to group rows, and so on.
- **SQL pane** displays the SQL statement for the query or view. You can edit the SQL
  statement created by the Designer or you can enter your own SQL statement. It is
  particularly useful for entering SQL statements that can't be created using the
  Diagram and Grid panes.

- **Results pane** shows a grid with data retrieved by the query or view. In the Query Designer, the pane shows the results of the most recently executed Select query. You can modify the database by editing values in the cells of the grid, and add or delete rows.

To add columns to the view, you can either select a column using the drop-down list as shown in Figure 9.15, or drag a column from a table in the diagram pane and drop it in a column row in the Grid pane.

FIGURE 9.15

Selecting a column using the drop-down list.

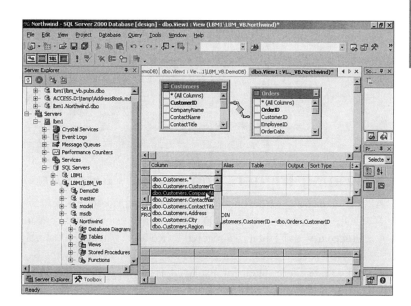

As you add columns to the view, notice that the SQL pane changes to reflect the actual Select statement required to retrieve the data. The Grid pane also allows you to specify the following properties for each column in the view. You can test this view by clicking the Run Query button in the toolbar to execute the query and display the results in the Run pane as shown in Figure 9.16.

- Sort Order
- Sort Type
- Grouping
- Selection Criteria

FIGURE 9.16

Displaying the data in the Run Pane.

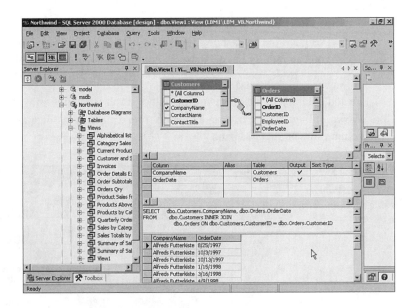

Adding Triggers and Stored Procedures

As you learned earlier in the day, triggers and stored procedures are created using SQL DDL statements. The Visual Database Tools enable you to create and modify both Stored Procedures and Triggers. A Stored Procedure is created by simply right-clicking the Stored Procedures node for the database; this will display the SQL Editor with an empty stored procedure statement displayed as shown in Figure 9.17.

FIGURE 9.17

Adding a new Stored Procedure to a database.

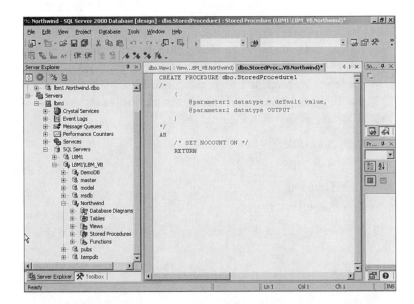

You also can modify a Stored Procedure by right-clicking an existing procedure and selecting Edit Stored Procedure from the pop-up menu. This will display the SQL code for the procedure along with the correct ALTER statement syntax as shown in Figure 9.18.

FIGURE 9.18

Modifying an existing Stored Procedure.

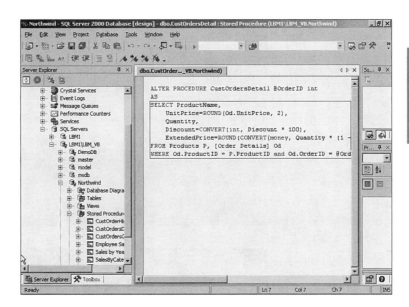

Triggers are created and modified much the same as a Stored Procedure with only one exception: Because Triggers are associated with a particular table, you would right-click the table to which you want to add a trigger or modify an existing trigger. This would display the SQL Editor with the correct syntax as shown in Figure 9.19.

Displaying Data from a Table

Another feature of the Visual Database Tools is the capability to display data from any table in a database. This is done by double-clicking the selected table to display the data in a grid as shown in Figure 9.20.

Using the Database Designer

The Database Designer enables you to design and visualize a database to which you are connected. When designing a database, you can use the Database Designer to create, edit, or delete tables, columns, keys, indexes, relationships, and constraints. To visualize a database, you can create one or more diagrams illustrating some or all of the tables, columns, keys, and relationships in it. To create a new database design, you can right-click the Database Diagram node and select New Diagram. This will display an Add Tables dialog, which enables you to select the tables you want in the diagram.

FIGURE 9.19

Working with triggers.

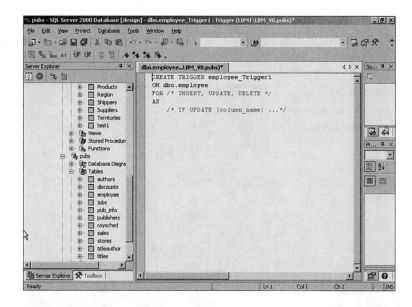

FIGURE 9.20

*Displaying data using
the Visual Database
Tools.*

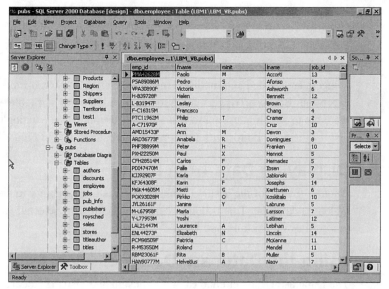

Once you have selected the tables, click the Close button to display the diagram. Figure 9.21 shows a diagram with the Orders and Order Details tables. You should notice that if relationships are defined in the database, these also are displayed.

FIGURE 9.21

Tables in the Database Diagram along with defined relationships.

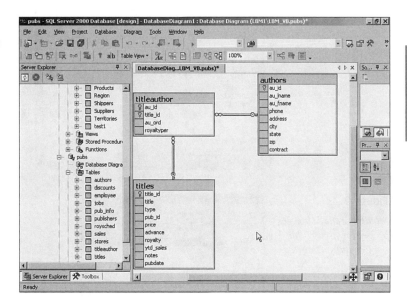

For any database, you can create as many database diagrams as you like; each database table can appear on any number of diagrams. Thus, you can create different diagrams to visualize different portions of the database or accentuate different aspects of the design. For example, you can create a large diagram showing all tables and columns, and create a smaller diagram showing all tables without showing the columns.

You also can use the Database Diagram as the central location in which to maintain the database you are working with. From within the diagram, you can perform all the tasks previously discussed in relation to the Visual Database Tools. You can add new tables or modify an existing table. Right-clicking a displayed table provides you with many options as shown in Figure 9.22. You also can display the Property Pages for the table, and modify any of the existing properties or names in the table as shown in Figure 9.23.

FIGURE 9.22

Using the Database Diagram to access the different options for a table.

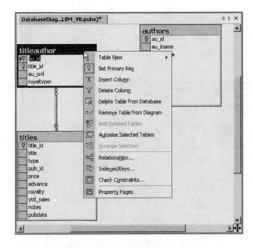

FIGURE 9.23

Modifying the Table properties from within the Database Diagram.

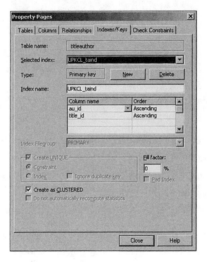

Summary

Today you explored the requirements and rules to follow when designing a database. We discussed the database normalization process, which includes reducing the duplicate data usually found in some databases. Also, you received a short overview of what SQL is and how to code the SELECT statement. Finally, you saw how to use the Visual Database Tools to create and maintain the database you need for your application. In the next lesson you'll see how to design a specific database application and the database it uses.

Q&A

Q What's the difference between a local and a remote database?

A A local database is accessible directly from Visual Basic through the Jet database engine. A remote database is any other database type that uses the ODBC connections for the application to access them.

Q How many tables can I have in a database?

A Depending on the amount of storage on the computer, a database can contain as many tables as are needed for the application. For example, Access allows up to 32,768 total objects in a database.

Q Why should I use indexes in a database?

A Indexes speed up the data access process by creating sorted tables that the database engine uses to find the required data.

Q Does Visual Basic come with a tool I can use to create and maintain a database?

A Visual Basic comes with the Visual Database Tools, which allow you to create and maintain many different types of databases.

Workshop

The Workshop provides quiz questions to solidify your understanding of the material covered and exercises to help you use what you've learned. The answers to the quiz questions and exercises are provided in Appendix A, "Answers to Quizzes and Exercises."

Quiz

1. What are the four main objectives when designing a database?

2. How many different main SQL commands are there?

3. What does *normalization* mean?

4. What is SQL?

Exercise

List the tables and columns you would want to include in a database designed for an address book application.

DAY **10**

Accessing the Database

In the last few days you've seen what a database is, how to create one, and how to use the SQL language to access the data contained in it. We also discussed the process of creating a database application, and you used the Data Form Wizard to create two different data forms with different types of display characteristics.

You also learned how to use the Visual Database Tools to interact with the database and to design and create queries. With the advent of ADO.NET as the latest access method, the way you were used to accessing the database has changed somewhat. Today you will look at these different methods and how you can combine them to perform complex application functions. In the process, you will learn how to use the different methods for the different types of database access you might need for your application.

Visual Basic and Data Access

Visual Basic was designed to enable you to create database applications for the Windows environment quickly and easily. If you want to access an existing database, Visual Basic makes it easy for you to write a complete data management application with almost no programming; you just need to drop a few controls on a form and set the properties. In fact, Visual Basic makes it so easy that it even creates the data forms for you. The components that make all these capabilities possible are the new ADO.NET dataset objects, which then are bound to the different controls on a form to display the data. With these controls you can create a wide variety of complex applications.

In addition to the new ADO.NET capabilities, you still can use the ADO Data Control and the ADODB objects in your application. However, there have been some changes in the way you would use them to display data on a form, which will be covered later today.

Of course, as your applications become more complex you'll need to add code to them. However, before building complex applications you should have a good understanding of the tools available for you to use.

Data Access Objects

When database access was originally added to the Visual Basic product, it came in the form of the Data Control and Access Objects. This allowed the programmer to access any type of database needed by the application. However, it worked best with Access/Jet engine databases that existed on the local PC. As PC use grew in the workplace, larger, more company-inclusive applications were required to use databases such as Microsoft SQL Server and Oracle.

Accessing these larger, enterprise-wide databases requires a more robust control. Successive releases of Visual Basic not only include the original Data Access Objects (DAO); they include a new Remote Data Control and Objects, which are specially designed to access remote databases using an ODBC connection. Visual Basic 6 also includes a third data access method to the product, which combines the best parts of both of its predecessors. ActiveX Data Objects (ADO) and its related control provided database access to both local and remote databases without the need to choose the appropriate data access control or object. Again, Microsoft has made changes to the data access available in Visual Basic.

Although the ActiveX Data Objects and control are still available for compatibility reasons, the recommended access method is now ADO.NET, which provides a more robust data access for both Windows and Web applications.

ADO versus ADO.NET

In traditional client/server applications, connecting to a database and keeping it open while the application was running was important to provide many simultaneous users with immediate access to the data. Unfortunately, sometimes this approach can be impractical for the following reasons:

- Open database connections take up valuable system resources. Also, most databases can maintain only a small number of concurrent connections.

- An application that requires an open database connection cannot be modified easily to allow hundreds of users concurrently.

- In an Internet or Web application, most components are completely disconnected from each other. Under these conditions, maintaining an open database isn't viable. It's impossible to know whether any given request will need additional access to the database.

For these reasons and many more, ADO.NET has been created to answer these issues and allow for greater flexibility in designing Web-based applications. To allow for the smoothest transition to ADO.NET, Microsoft has made the ADO.NET programming model very similar to the ADO model. You must understand only a few key concepts to use ADO.NET. The biggest difference you will notice is that ADO.NET is simpler than previous access methods. It contains a unified data access method for all typical data access requirements: local, network, and Internet.

10

Before diving into the new ADO.NET concepts, let's take a brief look at how the ADO Data Control has changed in Visual Basic .NET and how you can still use it. We also will explore the ADO data objects and how they can be used.

Working with the ActiveX Data Control

The ActiveX Data Control is still supported in Visual Basic .NET by the included compatibility layer. As you will see, because of the changes made to the control, it's no longer the recommended method for accessing data in your application. In Visual Basic 6, the ActiveX Data Control provides quick access to your data. By setting only a few parameters for the control, you can attach to the database and access data from a SQL query without writing any code at all.

The ActiveX Data Control accesses any database type required—either directly, for Jet-supported databases, or remotely, using an OLE DB–supported access method. In addition to this flexibility, program code is used to change the properties of the Data Control and enhance its capabilities. In fact, setting up and using the Data Control requires only three easy steps:

1. Place the Data Control on the form.
2. Build the database connection string for the database you want to access.

3. Set the `RecordSource` property to the SQL query you want to access in the database.

The Data Control provides the navigation functions automatically using the arrow keys included with the control. Figure 10.1 shows the original Data Control including the navigation keys. By using these keys, there is no need to add any code that provides the navigation capabilities.

FIGURE 10.1

The ActiveX Data control provides its own navigation.

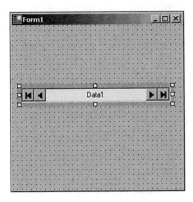

In Visual Basic .NET, this control is still available; however, you must add it to the toolbox to access it. Adding it to the toolbox also adds the references to the compatibility layer required for its use. Figure 10.2 shows the references added for the Data Control and the Data Control itself in the toolbox.

FIGURE 10.2

Adding the ActiveX Data Control to the solution.

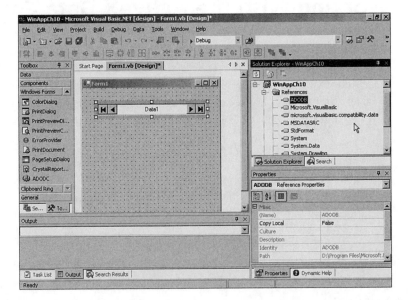

Using the ActiveX Data Control

Because this probably is the first time you've heard about the changes to the ActiveX Data control, let's take a quick look at how to use it to access a database and display the requested data:

Note If you have a previous version of Visual Basic, you can use the Access database NWIND.MDB for this example. Otherwise, make any changes to the example to use whichever database you have access to. For the example, I will be using the Northwind database available in SQL Server.

1. Start a new project.
2. Add the ADODC to the Toolbox by right-clicking the toolbox and selecting Customize Toolbox from the pop-up menu.
3. In the Customize Toolbox dialog (see Figure 10.3), select ADODC from the .NET Framework Components list and click OK to add the control.
4. Add the controls in Table 10.1 to the form as shown in Figure 10.4.

FIGURE 10.3

Adding the ActiveX Data Control to the Toolbox.

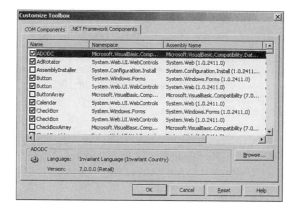

TABLE 10.1 ActiveX Data Control Demo Form Setup

Object	Property	Value
ADODC	Name	adcProducts
Textbox	Name	txtProduct
Label	Text	Product Name
Button	Name	cmdQuit
	Text	Quit

10

TABLE 10.1   continued

Object	Property	Value
Button	Name	cmdNext
	Text	Next
Button	Name	cmdPrev
	Text	Previous

FIGURE 10.4

The ActiveX Data Control Demo showing the controls to add to the Form.

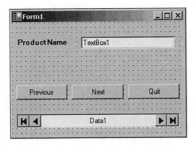

The next step is to define the connection string for the Data Control. Unfortunately, here is the first change to the Data Control. In the previous release you can use the Data Connection Wizard to define the connection for the control directly. Now you can either enter the connectionstring property information yourself in the code or the property page. The following code segment shows the connection information you need to enter:

```
Provider=SQLOLEDB.1;Persist Security Info=False;User ID=sa;
Initial Catalog=Northwind;Data Source=lbm1;Use Procedure for Prepare=1;
Auto Translate=True;Packet Size=4096;Workstation ID=LBM1;
Use Encryption for Data=False;
Tag with column collation when possible=False
```

Not all parameters are needed; however, you can see that this is a little complicated. The way I add the connection information is to use an OLEDB connection object to define the connection string by adding it to the form as shown in Figure 10.5. This will enable you to define the connection you want to use.

After the connection object is added, click the ConnectionString property and select New Connection from the drop-down list. This will display the Data Link Properties dialog. To define a database connection, select the provider for the database you are using (see Figure 10.6); then specify the connection information (see Figure 10.7).

Before clicking OK to save this connection information, test the connection by clicking the Test Connection button at the bottom of the form. A message box should appear, informing you that the test connection succeeded. If the test passed, click Finish to complete the process.

FIGURE 10.5

Adding an OLEDB *connection object to the form.*

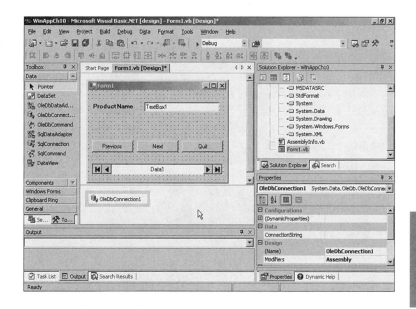

FIGURE 10.6

Selecting the OLE DB provider for the database used in the application.

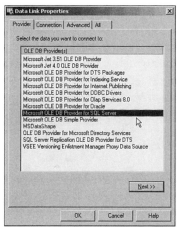

After you define the connection string, you can either copy the information from the OLEDB connection string property or paste it into the ADODC connectionstring property. If you copy the information, you can delete the OLEDB connection object from the project. The other method is to simply add a statement to the form that sets the ADODC property to the OLEDB property as shown:

```
adcProducts.ConnectionString = OleDbConnection1.ConnectionString
```

10

FIGURE **10.7**

*Specifying the location
of the required
database.*

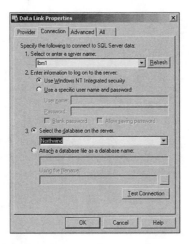

The next step is to specify the SQL statement that the connection will use as the record
source. Again, you have a choice: You can code the SQL statement yourself and place it
into the RecordSource property for the ADODC or use the OLEDB command object. If
you use the OLEDB object, you first must leave the OLEDB connection object on the form;
then add an OLEDB command object to the form and click the CommandText property. This
will display the Query Builder dialog, which you learned about on Day 9, "Processing
Data." You will use the query builder to define the SQL statement you want to use for
this connection, as shown in Figure 10.8.

FIGURE **10.8**

*Defining the SQL
statement for the data-
base connection.*

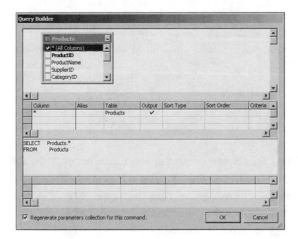

Once you define the SQL statement, you can paste it into the ADODC RecordSource property or use the following statement in the code to set the property at runtime. If you paste the information, remember to remove both OLEDB objects from the project:

```
adcProducts.RecordSource = OleDbCommand1.CommandText
```

 Note If your database requires a login, remember to set the User ID and Password information in the Data Control.

The final step in using the actual Data Control is to open the connection. Unlike previous releases, the connection isn't automatically opened with the recordset positioned at the beginning. You must use the Refresh method to activate the connection.

Displaying the Data on the Form

One of the biggest changes in using the ADO Data control is that the other data display-ing objects can't bind to it, which means to display or modify data using these objects (such as Textbox), you must add program code to accomplish it. To display data from the current record, you can add code to the Data Control's MoveComplete event procedure:

```
txtProduct.Text = adcProducts.Recordset.Fields("ProductName").Value
```

This code assigns the Product name to the Textbox's Text property on the form. The last step is to add the following code to the Command buttons allowing you to navigate the SQL statement:

```
Private Sub CmdNext_Click(ByVal sender As System.Object,
        ByVal e As System.EventArgs) Handles CmdNext.Click
        adcProducts.Recordset.MoveNext()
End Sub

Private Sub CmdPrev_Click(ByVal sender As System.Object,
        ByVal e As System.EventArgs) Handles CmdPrev.Click
    adcProducts.Recordset.MovePrevious()
End Sub

Private Sub CmdQuit_Click(ByVal sender As System.Object,
        ByVal e As System.EventArgs) Handles CmdQuit.Click
        Me.Close()
End Sub
```

Now run the application and try moving around the rows. You can see that the operation of the ADODC is almost identical to the original Data control.

10

The ADODC also provides the record navigation functions that users and the application need to access the data. With these buttons (refer to Figure 10.4), users can move to the first or last record in the recordset, or to the next or previous record in the recordset. The button design is similar to the buttons you would find on a VCR or CD player, making the buttons very easy to understand.

The Data control also has a `Caption` property you can use to display any important information, such as the last name of the address record you're browsing. You can't set the `Caption` property automatically; you do it by adding the following line of code to the ADODC's `MoveComplete` routine:

```
adcProducts.Caption = adcProducts.Recordset.Fields("ProductName").Value
```

This actually is using the capabilities of the ActiveX Data Objects, which enable you to access the database from within your application code. As you can see, the Data control has many capabilities.

When you invoke the Data control's `Delete` method, the current record is deleted from the database but is still held in the Data control's buffer until a `Move` method is executed. If you don't explicitly move to another record, an error will occur.

Although Data controls are covered in every book written about Visual Basic, they're always shown as a single control on a form. To use the capabilities to quickly add database access, many complex applications that need access to different tables and queries will use multiple Data controls on the same form. Also, often the Data control itself isn't visible on the form when the application is executing. This means even the four functions that it supplies must be added to the form using additional code.

Knowing the Current Record

A recordset has a pointer that keeps track of the current record. There's only one current record for a Data control at any time. A recordset also has special positions known as *beginning of file* (`BOF`), before the first record, and *end of file* (`EOF`), after the last record. Because there's no current record when the record pointer is positioned at either of these, problems can occur.

By default, the Data control prevents these problems by setting the record pointer to the first record when the `BOF` is reached or by setting the pointer to the last record when the `EOF` is reached. This way, there's always a current record for viewing or editing. However, sometimes you need to know when you've actually reached the `BOF` or `EOF` position while using the Data control. You can control what the Data control does by setting the control's `BOFAction` and `EOFAction` properties.

The `BOFAction` property tells the Data control what action to take when the beginning of the file is reached. This property has two settings:

- 0 - adDoMoveFirst, the default setting, executes the MoveFirst method to set the record pointer at the first record and the BOF flag to False.
- 1 - adStayBOF sets the BOF flag to True.

The EOFAction property tells the Data control what action to take when the end of the file is reached. This property has three possible values:

- 0 - adDoMoveLast, the default setting, executes the MoveLast method to set the record pointer to the last record and the EOF flag to False.
- 1 - adStayEOF sets the EOF flag to True.
- 2 - adAddNew executes the AddNew method to prepare for the addition of a new record.

Note

> The BOF and EOF actions are triggered only when users reach the beginning or end of the file by using the Data control's navigation buttons. They have no effect if you're using data access methods (such as MoveNext) in your code.

10

Programmed Access with the Data Control

To manipulate the Data control, you would add code to the events for the Data control and possibly for the controls displaying the data. Here are some ways you can use code with the Data control:

- Change the properties of the Data control or the bound controls during program execution.
- Provide capabilities that the Data control doesn't have by using the recordset methods.

Like with any other control, you can change the Data control's properties at runtime. You can change the control's Connection or RecordSource properties to set specific conditions on the data users want to see. This can take the form of filters or sort orders, or your application might have the filters set as part of an access control scheme.

If you need to set the properties at runtime, simply set the properties with code:

```
DtaMyDatabase.RecordSource = "Select * from Titles"
DtaMyDatabase.ReQuery
```

After setting the properties, use the Data control's Requery method to apply the changes, as shown in the last line of the code. The changes to the Data control take effect only after the Requery method is invoked.

You can use several key events to manipulate the way the Data control performs:

- `WillChangeRecord`, `WillChangeRecordset`, and `WillChangeField` process any data before the record is updated.
- `Error` is triggered for any data access error.
- `MoveComplete` performs calculations based on data in the current record or to change the form in response to data in the current record.

Although most of the Data control's actions are handled automatically, these events can help you add enhanced capabilities to your application.

Validating the Data

When you need to add validation processing to your application, you use the `WillChangeField` event, which is triggered just before a value of one or more Field objects in the Recordset is changed. However, if a method such as `Update`, `Delete`, or `AddNew` is executed, you use the `WillChangeRecord` event to perform the validation for the entire record. This event occurs when users process a navigation button on the Data control or when the form containing the Data control is unloaded.

The `WillChangeField` event is triggered whenever a field in the current record is changed and an `Update` or `Move` method is executed. The parameters used by the `WillChangeField` event are

- `cFields`, which contains the number of field objects currently in the `Fields` collection
- `Fields`, the collection that contains the `Field` objects with the pending changes
- `adStatus`, which contains the status of the change event
- `pRecordset`, which contains the reference to the current recordset

The values for the `adStatus` parameter enable you to specify whether to allow or prevent the change of the field's data. When you are using a method that affects the entire record, the `WillChangeRecord` event is triggered. Besides the `adStatus` parameter, this event contains the parameter `adReason`, which tells you which method invoked this event. By checking the `adReason` parameter, you can perform different processes depending on the type of action taken against the Data control. Table 10.2 lists the values of the `adReason` parameter.

TABLE 10.2 The `adReason` Parameter Values for the `WillChangeRecord` Event

Constant	Value	Description
adRsnAddNew	1	AddNew
adRsnDelete	2	Delete

TABLE 10.2 continued

Constant	Value	Description
adRsnUpdate	3	Update
adRsnUndoUpdate	4	Undo the Update
adRsnUndoAddNew	5	Undo the AddNew
adRsnUndoDelete	6	Undo the Delete
adRsnRequery	7	Requery the database
adRsnReSync	8	Resync the query with the database
adRsnClose	9	The Close method of the Data control was used
adRsnMove	10	Move
adRsnFirstChange	11	FirstChange
adRsnMoveFirst	12	MoveFirst
adRsnMoveNext	13	MoveNext
adRsnMovePrevious	14	MovePrevious
adRsnMoveLast	15	MoveLast

The code you place in these events can be as complex as you need. An example
WillChangeField routine is as follows:

```
Private Sub Adodc1_WillChangeField(ByVal cFields As Integer, _
        ByRef fields As Object, ByRef adStatus As ADODB.EventStatusEnum, _
        ByVal pRecordset As ADODB.Recordset) Handles Adodc1.WillChangeField
    If Not IsDate(txtDate.Text) Then
        MsgBox("The Flight date you entered is Invalid" & _
                vbCRLF & "Please Re-enter!", vbCritical, Me.Text)
        adStatus = adStatusCancel
        txtDate.DataChanged = False
        txtDate.Text = "??/??/??"
    End If
End Sub
```

If any field changes are incorrect, set the adStatus parameter to adStatusCancel to
cancel the entire operation.

The MoveComplete Event

This event is triggered after the current record pointer is moved to another record. You
can use this event to control the movement of related Data controls on a form. For example, if you're creating an order entry display and select a new customer, you might want
to change the recordset of the orders Data control by changing the RecordSource property and then invoking the Requery method for the second Data control.

ActiveX Data Objects

Now that you've seen how to access database information with the ActiveX Data Control, we will make further use of the ActiveX Data Objects to program complex database functions into your application. You can use Visual Basic's ADO to create complete database applications. ADO acts as an application's internal representation of the physical data stored in some type of database or data management system. You can think of the data objects as special types of program variables. These variables represent data stored outside the application, rather than data stored in the computer's memory while the application is running.

ADO and programming code also provide the structure for many actions used by the Data control and the bound controls to access the database. To see the similarities and differences between ADO and the ADODC, you'll create the same data form as the one you created by using the Data control.

The main reason for using ADO is the flexibility it gives you over and above what's available with the Data control. You can perform more complex input validation than is possible with just the data engine because the commands don't directly access the database. You also can cancel changes to your edited data without using transactions. Using ADO commands also provides an efficient way to handle data input and searches that doesn't require user interaction. An example is looking up the price of an item in a table for the ordering process. ADO commands also enable you to do transaction processing when needed.

Opening a Database

The first step in writing most database applications is to connect or open the database you'll be working with. Opening a database is a lot like opening a file, except you're using the ADODB commands instead of the simple Basic Open statement. When you open a database, you're actually creating a Database object that will be used by the other Data Access Objects. To access the ADODB command set, you must include in your project a reference for Microsoft *ActiveX Data Object Library* (*ADODB*), which contains all the ADODB command objects.

The database is represented in the application by the ADODB Connection object. A working database session is defined by creating RecordSet objects within the Connection object. You then can open a query with the RecordSet object's Open method. To use the Open method, create a RecordSet object and call the method, as follows:

```
Dim cnn1 As ADODB.Connection
Dim cmd1 As ADODB.Command
Dim rstProducts As ADODB.Recordset
```

```
Dim strCnn As String
Dim varDate As Date
' Open connection.
  cnn1 = New ADODB.Connection()
  cnn1.ConnectionString = "driver={SQL Server};server=lbm1;" & _
                          "uid=sa;pwd=sa;database=northwind"
  cnn1.CursorLocation = ADODB.CursorLocationEnum.adUseClient
  cnn1.Open()
  cmd1 = New ADODB.Command()
```

After you open the connection, only a link from your application to the database is created; you still can't access the data in the database. To access the data, you need to create and open a `Recordset` object that links to the data stored in the database. When creating a `Recordset` object in your application, you can access an entire table, specific fields and records from a table, or a specific combination of records and fields from several tables.

NEW TERM   A *query* is a grouping of data from one or more tables in a database. This data is selected with a SQL statement, which usually contains field name filters. Queries address the records present in the base tables at the time the query was created, and enable users to make changes in the data and store it back into the database. However, queries don't automatically reflect additions or deletions of records made by other code, users, or applications after the query was created.

Using queries enable you to do the following:

- Join data from multiple tables.
- Limit the number of fields or records retrieved from the database.
- Use filters and sort order properties to change the data view.

Queries also have a limitation that you should be aware of:

- The query won't automatically reflect any changes made to the data in the base tables; you have to requery it.

Opening a recordset requires nothing more than a reference to a SQL statement and the active connection. The `Recordset`'s `Open` method executes the specified SQL statement and connects to the data. The following code is the simplest form of creating a query, in which all the records and fields are selected from a table with no other condition specified. This type of query is created by a Data control as a default.

```
RstProducts = New ADODB.Recordset()
RstProducts.Open("select * from products", cnn1)
```

When you create a query, you can use any valid SQL statement you need to select the correct data from the database.

10

Accessing the Data

Now that you have an understanding of what it takes to create and open recordsets, you can see how to use them in an application. As you've already seen, to display data with the Data control and bound controls, you simply draw the controls on the form and then set the appropriate data field properties for the controls. The display process itself is automatic.

You can access data through a recordset's Fields collection in several ways. For example, to retrieve the contents of a field named "Title" in a recordset called MyDyn and place it into a text box named Text1, you could do the following:

- Use the field's ordinal position in the Fields collection as Text1.Text = MyDyn.Fields(0).Value.

- Use the field's name to retrieve it from the Fields collection as Text1.Text = MyDyn.Fields("Title").Value.

- Use the recordset collection's default to access the field as Text1.Text = MyDyn("Title").Value.

As an example, redo the demo you created with the Data control. Start a new project and add two text boxes to the default form to hold the data from the query, as shown in Figure 10.9.

FIGURE 10.9

Using ActiveX Data Objects to access the database.

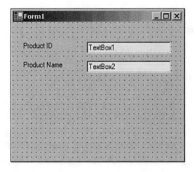

To set up the query for use, you must open a database connection and then open a recordset by using the Open method. In the form's Declarations section, add the Dim statements for the objects required as shown:

```
Dim cnn1 As ADODB.Connection
Dim cmd1 As ADODB.Command
Dim rstProducts As ADODB.Recordset
```

You then open the connection and query in the Form_Load event routine, as shown in Listing 10.1.

LISTING 10.1   ADOEX1.TXT: Opening the Database and Recordset in the Form_Load Event

```
cnn1 = New ADODB.Connection()
cnn1.ConnectionString = "driver={SQL Server};server=lbm1;" & _
                        "uid=sa;pwd=sa;database=northwind"
cnn1.CursorLocation = ADODB.CursorLocationEnum.adUseClient
cnn1.Open()
cmd1 = New ADODB.Command()
rstProducts = New ADODB.Recordset()
rstProducts.Open("select * from products", cnn1)
rstProducts.MoveFirst()
Call DisplayFields()
```

Now the query is open and you're positioned at the first record in the recordset. To display the data, assign the value of the desired data fields to the display properties of the controls containing the data. For this type of processing, it's recommended that you create a subroutine (as shown in Listing 10.2) to perform the assignment of the controls from the current record in the recordset. This same routine can be called from a number of button events rather than repeat the code in each event. This way, the code is more efficient and easier to maintain.

LISTING 10.2   ADOEX2.TXT: Adding Data Fields to the Controls' Display Properties

```
Private Sub DisplayFields()
    TextBox1.Text = rstProducts.Fields("productid").Value
    TextBox2.Text = rstProducts.Fields ("productname").Value
End Sub
```

When you execute the application you will see only one record's information displayed (see Figure 10.10).

FIGURE 10.10

Display the information for a single record.

However, when accessing data this way, you can't move from one record to another in the application. You also should have noticed in the Form_Load event that after the query was created, a MoveFirst method was executed to ensure that the current record pointer points to the first record. Because you're now controlling access to the data, you must add each navigation button that you want available to users. Generally, you would use the Move methods to provide this functionality. To see how this is done, add four command buttons to the form, as shown in Figure 10.11.

FIGURE 10.11

Adding the manual navigation buttons to the form.

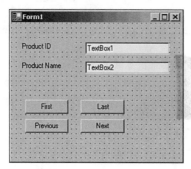

Now add the code in Listing 10.3 to allow each button to perform the specified action.

LISTING 10.3   ADOEX3.TXT: Adding Navigation Command Buttons to the Form

```
Private Sub cmdFirst_Click(ByVal sender As System.Object,
        ByVal e As System.EventArgs) Handles cmdFirst.Click
    rstProducts.MoveFirst()
    Call DisplayFields()
End Sub

Private Sub cmdlast_Click(ByVal sender As System.Object,
        ByVal e As System.EventArgs) Handles cmdlast.Click
    rstProducts.MoveLast()
    Call DisplayFields()
End Sub

Private Sub cmdnext_Click(ByVal sender As System.Object,
        ByVal e As System.EventArgs) Handles cmdnext.Click
    rstProducts.MoveNext()
    Call DisplayFields()
End Sub

Private Sub cmdprevious_Click(ByVal sender As System.Object,
        ByVal e As System.EventArgs) Handles cmdprevious.Click
    rstProducts.MovePrevious()
    Call DisplayFields()
End Sub
```

Now execute the application and try using the buttons that you just added. You should be able to move around the records in the query. However, you'll still have to deal with one problem when you try to move past the beginning or end of the recordset. You should get an error message as shown in Figure 10.12.

FIGURE 10.12

Trying to move past the beginning or end of a record will result in an error.

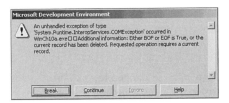

To prevent this from happening, you need to check the EOF and BOF properties of the recordset when moving forward or backward in the recordset. Listing 10.4 shows the additional code you need for this function.

10

LISTING 10.4   ADOEX4.TXT: Checking for the EOF or BOF Conditions

```
Private Sub cmdnext_Click(ByVal sender As System.Object,
        ByVal e As System.EventArgs) Handles cmdnext.Click
    rstProducts.MoveNext()
    If rstProducts.EOF Then
        MsgBox("Last record displayed", vbInformation, Me.Text)
        rstProducts.MoveLast()
    End If
    Call DisplayFields()
End Sub

Private Sub cmdprevious_Click(ByVal sender As System.Object,
        ByVal e As System.EventArgs) Handles cmdprevious.Click
    rstProducts.MovePrevious()
    If rstProducts.EOF Then
        MsgBox("Last record displayed", vbInformation, Me.Text)
        rstProducts.MoveFirst()
    End If
    Call DisplayFields()
End Sub
```

Besides displaying the data on a form, you can use ADO to modify, add, or delete data in the database. The AddNew method used to add a new record to a recordset doesn't actually add the record; instead, it clears the copy buffer to allow data for the new record to be input. To add the record physically after you put data into the record's fields, you use the Update method. Listing 10.5 shows how to use the AddNew method to add a new record to the recordset.

LISTING 10.5   ADOEX5.TXT: Adding a Record to the Recordset

```
Private Sub cmdAdd_Click(ByVal sender As System.Object,
        ByVal e As System.EventArgs) Handles cmdAdd.Click
        rstProducts.AddNew()
        Call DisplayFields()
        rstProducts.Update()
End Sub
```

 Caution

Because the new data isn't added to the database until an Update method is executed, reusing the AddNew method or moving the record pointer with any Move or Find method will clear the copy buffer, and any data that has been entered will be lost.

Just as a routine is used to move the data from the recordset to the controls, a routine should be used to move the data from the controls to the recordset. To make changes to a record, a copy of the current record is placed into the copy buffer so that data can be changed. After a user changes the data, you would need to execute the Update method. As with the AddNew method, the changes take effect only when the Update method is executed (see Listing 10.6).

LISTING 10.6   ADOEX6.TXT: Adding the Edit Routine to the Application

```
Private Sub CmdUpdate_Click(ByVal sender As System.Object,
        ByVal e As System.EventArgs) Handles cmdUpdate.Click
        rstProducts.Fields("ProductName").Value = "This is my Book"
        rstProducts.Update()
        Call DisplayFields()
End Sub
```

The Update method used with the AddNew and Edit methods writes the data from the copy buffer to the recordset. In the case of AddNew, Update also creates a blank record in the recordset to which the data is written.

Note

When you edit a record and are updating it, never try to update the primary key fields in the data. This usually causes an error to occur.

Finally, if you need to delete a record, use the Delete method (see Listing 10.7). This method removes the record from the recordset and sets the record pointer to a null value.

LISTING 10.7 ADOEX7.TXT: Adding the Delete Process to the Form

```
Private Sub CmdDelete_Click(ByVal sender As System.Object,
      ByVal e As System.EventArgs) Handles CmdDelete.Click
   rstProducts.Delete
   MsgBox("Record has been deleted", vbInformation, Me.Text)
   Call cmdNext_Click
End Sub
```

As you can see, after the Delete method is executed, the cmdNext click routine is called to move the current record pointer to the next valid record in the recordset. If this isn't done, an error will occur. To see how all this works, add three more command buttons to the form, as shown in Figure 10.13; then add the code for each action. Run the application again and try each action to see how it works.

FIGURE 10.13

Adding the data modification processing to the example.

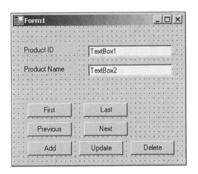

Introducing ADO.NET

Now that you've reviewed the ActiveX Data Objects methods and the changes that have been made, we'll discuss the new ADO.NET access methods. The first thing you might be asking yourself is, "Why ADO.NET?" And, "What can it do for me?" Well, ADO.NET is the redesigned ADO access method to allow for distributed Internet applications. It uses the same access methods for local, client/server, or Internet applications that access a database. Although ADO.NET resembles the older ADO methods, there are some significant differences.

ADO.NET provides access to data sources such as Microsoft SQL Server and any data source accessible through either OLE DB (such as Oracle and Sybase) or XML. The biggest change is that ADO.NET separates database processing into data access and data manipulation using the DataSet and the .NET data providers. By providing data access is this manner, the application—either on the client or on the Web—is completely disconnected from the database. This allows larger numbers of users to access the data without managing the resources that would be necessary if everyone was directly connected the entire time.

The DataSet is one of two components of the disconnected architecture of ADO.NET. The DataSet is designed to provide independent data access of any data source. As a result, multiple and differing data sources can be used at the same time. The DataSet contains a collection of one or more `DataTable` objects made up of rows and columns of data, and primary key, foreign key, constraint, and relation information about the data in the `DataTable` objects.

The second component is the .NET data providers, which are designed to provide fast, efficient data manipulation. You can use the following four data providers in your application:

- **Connection** provides connectivity to a data source.
- **Command** enables access to database commands, which return data, modify data, run stored procedures, and send or retrieve parameter information.
- **DataReader** provides a high-performance stream of data from the data source.
- **DataAdapter** provides the connection between the `DataSet` object and the data source.

The DataAdapter uses `Command` objects to execute SQL commands at the data source to both load the DataSet with data and reconcile changes made to the data in the DataSet back to the data source. Two .NET data providers are included with Visual Basic .NET:

- **SQL Server** provides access to Microsoft SQL Server 7 or later.
- **OLE DB** provides access to any database that supports OLE DB access.

We will spend the remainder of this lesson discussing the DataSet and .NET data providers, and how you can use them in your applications. Finally, you will create two simple data access applications: one to provide read-only support and one to allow you to update data in the database.

Working with DataSets

ADO.NET doesn't support a `Recordset` class to access data from a database. For most data access requirements, the more flexible DataSet has replaced the Recordset concept. Also, the `DataReader` object provides fast, read-only access to the data. As you've seen earlier in this lesson, the Recordset object is still available for compatibility and for a few application requirements in which a traditional ADO access is still superior (direct connection to database).

A DataSet is a collection of small tables or recordsets (don't get confused with the Recordset object) and the relationships between them. A DataSet can be considered a mini–relational database that you've defined, which is kept in memory for use by your application. Also, the DataSet is completely disconnected from the original data source, containing a copy of the data specified in the SQL command and used for local processing. Any operations done to this data are performed on the local copy. When all processing is complete, this local DataSet is sent back to the database to be resolved with the original data; any changes, additions, or deletions found will be posted to the original database.

Creating a DataSet

Each DataSet contains one or more DataTable objects, which are defined during the creation process. For the DataTable to contain data, the Rows collection must have some rows with columns defined. You can generate a DataSet for your project in two ways; the one you use depends on how you will be accessing the data. If you will use the data provider objects directly in your code, you can create a DataSet by adding one directly to the project. Do so by selecting Add New Item from the Project menu. This will display an empty DataSet editor (see Figure 10.14), which will allow you to drag the data you want from the Server Explorer directly into the editor.

FIGURE 10.14

Creating a new DataSet manually.

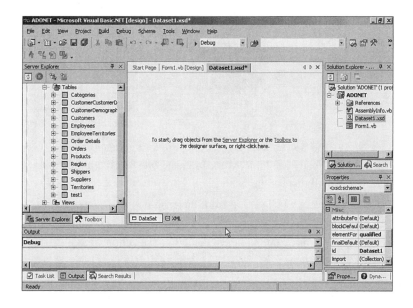

After you drag the data columns required, the DataSet editor will reflect these changes as shown in Figure 10.15. The DataSet generated from this action then can be used within the code by referencing it in a data adapter object.

FIGURE 10.15

Creating a DataSet with a data connection and adapter.

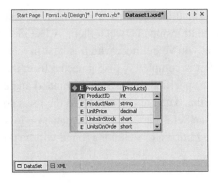

The easier method of creating a DataSet is by adding a data adapter to your form. This will start the Data Adapter Configuration Wizard (see Figure 10.16), which steps you through the process of defining and creating a DataSet.

FIGURE 10.16

Adding a data adapter to the form to generate a DataSet.

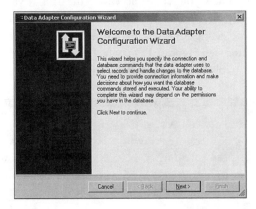

- The first step in the process is to select a data connection to use. If one isn't already available, you can create one by clicking the New Connection button. This will display the Data Link Properties dialog that was discussed earlier today.

- Select a connection from the drop-down list and click Next to continue the process.

- The next step asks if you will be using a SQL statement or a stored procedure. For this example leave the default selection of SQL Statement and click Next to continue.

- To define what data you want to select, you will use the Query Builder discussed in Day 9, "Processing Data," to build the query. Click the Query Builder button to display the tool as shown in Figure 10.17. Use the Query Builder Tool to define the SQL Statement used to create the DataSet.

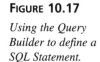

FIGURE 10.17

Using the Query Builder to define a SQL Statement.

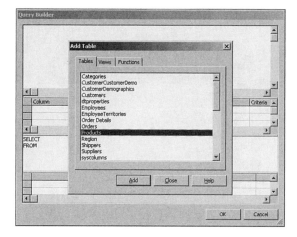

This example uses the Orders, Order Details, and Products tables from the Northwind database. When these tables are selected you can see that the defined relationships are displayed in the diagram pane (see Figure 10.18).

FIGURE 10.18

Building a SQL Statement.

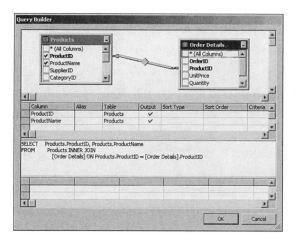

Select the columns you want to work with by clicking them in the diagram pane; then click OK to return to the Data Adapter Wizard. You should see the SQL Statement you've just defined in the Data Adapter dialog window (see Figure 10.19).

FIGURE 10.19

The final SQL Statement displayed in the Data Adapter.

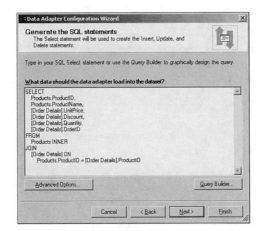

Click Next to see if the wizard has detected any issues with the generation process. Figure 10.20 shows the results for this example. Notice that several messages inform you that the Insert, Update, and Delete commands can't be created properly because only a few columns from different tables have been selected.

FIGURE 10.20

Checking the build process in the wizard.

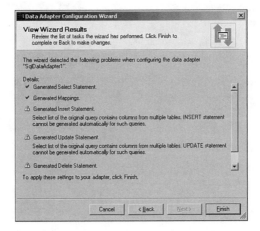

If you are satisfied with the results, click Finish to complete the process. You should see both the Data Adapter and Data Connection objects displayed in the form's work area. The final step is to actually create the DataSet definition. To do this, right-click the Data Adapter object and select Generate DataSet from the pop-up menu to display the Generate DataSet dialog (see Figure 10.21). This dialog allows you to name the DataSet file and to select the tables you want to include in it.

FIGURE 10.21

Generating the DataSet.

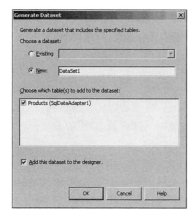

After you make the required selections, click OK to complete this process. You should see a `DataSet` object in the form's work area and the DataSet file in the Solution Explorer.

Retrieving and Viewing Data

Retrieving data can be done in one of two ways. The first is to use a Data Reader to retrieve and display the data. However, if you use a Data Reader you can't modify the data and then update the database. To modify data you must use the different methods of theDataAdapter. In this section you will learn how to use the different methods of the DataAdapter to retrieve, display, and modify the data specified. This can be done either in a data grid or in individual Textbox control. Later today you will learn how to use the DataReader to populate a TreeView control.

Note

> Although all the examples in this section use SQL Server and the
> SQLdataAdapter, the syntax, methods, and commands are identical when
> using the OLEDBdataAdapter.

Populating a DataGrid

Populating a DataGrid requires only a few simple changes to the DataGrid properties and one line of code in the form. First add a DataGrid control to the form as shown in Figure 10.22; then, in the `DataSource` property, select `DataSet11` as the data source. In the `DataMember` property, select `Employees`.

FIGURE 10.22

Adding a DataGrid to the form.

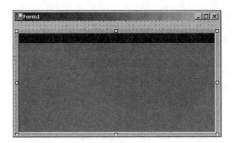

 Note

Although you can select `DataSet11.Employees` as the `DataSource`, it will prevent you from changing the `DataMember` property in the application code if needed.

As the last step, add the following line of code to the form's `Sub New` routine immediately after the call to `InitializeComponent()`:

```
SqlDataAdapter1.Fill(DataSet11)
```

This statement will execute the SQL Statement defined in the SQLDataAdapter and populate the DataSet. Figure 10.23 shows the data grid populated with data from the database.

FIGURE 10.23

Displaying data in the DataGrid.

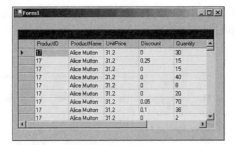

Displaying a Single Row of Data

In this section you will see how to bind different controls to the SQLDataSet and display the requested data. For this example, the demo in the ADO DB section will be used. Delete the DataGrid from the form; then add the controls listed in Table 10.3 to the form as shown in Figure 10.24.

TABLE 10.3   Adding ADO.NET Objects to the Form

Control	Property	Value
Textbox	Name	txtFname
	Text	Leave blank
	DataBindings.Text	Employees.FirstName
Textbox	Name	txtLname
	Text	Leave blank
	DataBindings.Text	Employees.LastName
Textbox	Name	txtTitle
	Text	Leave blank
	DataBindings.Text	Employees.Title
Label	Text	Employee Id
Label	Name	lblEmpId
	DataBindings.Text	Employees.EmployeeID
Textbox	Name	txtRecordCnt
	ReadOnly	True
	BackColor	White
Label	Text	First Name
Label	Text	Last Name
Label	Text	Title
Button	Name	cmdNext
	Text	&Next
Button	Name	cmdPrev
	Text	&Previous

10

FIGURE 10.24

Displaying data using individual controls on a form.

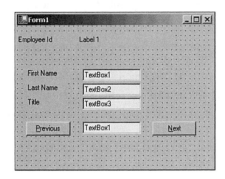

You can see in Table 10.3 that the Textbox controls and one label also have their `DataSource` and `DataMember` properties set. Listing 10.8 shows the code you need to add to the buttons to move records to display and a routine that gets the number of records in the query.

LISTING 10.8   ADONET1.TXT: Adding Move Routines to the Button

```
Private Sub cmdPrev_Click(ByVal sender_
➥As System.Object, ByVal e As System.EventArgs) Handles cmdPrev.Click
        Me.BindingContext(DataSet11, "employees").Position -= 1
        ShowPosition()

End Sub

Private Sub cmdNext_Click(ByVal sender As System.Object, ByVal e
➥As System.EventArgs) Handles cmdNext.Click
        Me.BindingContext(DataSet11, "employees").Position += 1
        ShowPosition()

End Sub

Private Sub ShowPosition()
        Dim iCnt As Integer
        Dim iPos As Integer
        iCnt = Me.BindingContext(DataSet11, "employees").Count
        If iCnt = 0 Then
            txtRecordcnt.Text = "(No records)"
        Else
            iPos = Me.BindingContext(DataSet11, "employees").Position + 1
            txtRecordcnt.Text = iPos.ToString & " of " & iCnt.ToString
        End If
End Sub
```

Finally, place a call to ShowPosition in the Sub New routine right after the line that fills the dataset.

Updating the Data

Updating data in a dataset requires that you use the Update method of the SQLdataAdapter. To change the data in any field, simply modify the data and then instruct the data adapter to send the changes back to the database. The following code would perform this action:

```
Me.BindingContext(DataSet11, "employees").EndCurrentEdit()
SqlDataAdapter1.Update(DataSet11)
```

The first line ends the edit function, which saves the changes into the dataset in memory; the second statement sends the update back to the database.

Using the Data Reader

The data reader provides you with fast, read-only data access to your dataset. It allows you to loop through the data, displaying it as needed. In this example we will create a phonebook-style form that displays the names and phone information of the employees on a form using a Treeview and Listview control. The data reader will be used to initialize both controls as needed. Start a new project and add a Treeview control to the form.

> **Note**
>
> The data reader doesn't use the data adapter to connect to the database; you must define a SQL command for this to work. The reason for this is the data adapter provides disconnected access to the database, which allows updates to the data. Because the data reader provides read-only functionality, the data adapter isn't needed.

10

Rather than add a data adapter to the form, add a SQL command. When you do this, the query builder is displayed for you to design the query needed for the application. In this example, the employees table will again be used.

Populating the TreeView Control

The TreeView control is the center of all activity in an address book application. Initially, it will display a standard alphabetic selection list, as shown in Figure 10.25. This will enable users to go directly to a given letter in the alphabet to find a particular entry.

FIGURE 10.25

The initial TreeView listing with the letters of the alphabet.

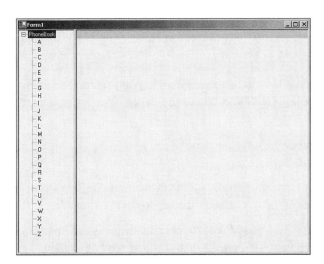

Initializing the TreeView control really has nothing to do with data access; however, it's required before adding any entry names. The code in Listing 10.9 sets the TreeView control. For each added node, the associated letter is used as the key, allowing you to access that node directly later in the process.

LISTING **10.9**   ADONETEX1.TXT: Initializing the TreeView Control at the Start of the Application

```
Dim I as integer
Dim node_letter As String
        tvTreeView.Nodes.Clear()

        'Set the Document Type
        tvTreeView.Nodes.Add("PhoneBook")

        'Set the Documents
        tvTreeView.SelectedNode = tvTreeView.Nodes.Item(0)

        tvTreeView.ExpandAll()
        tvTreeView.ShowLines = True
        tvTreeView.ShowPlusMinus = True
        For I = 1 To 26
            node_letter = Chr(64+I)
            tvTreeView.SelectedNode.Nodes.Add(node_letter)
        Next I
```

Note   Don't forget that the TreeView needs an Image control if you want the different nodes to have pictures associated with them.

Now that you have the TreeView control ready to accept data, you can create the code needed to perform this action. To add the entry names as shown in Figure 10.26, do the following:

1. Define a SQL connection.
2. Open a SQL command.
3. Loop through records, adding the name to the TreeView control by using the first letter of the last name as the key to the current node.

For this application, add the last name followed by the first name to the list. Also, the Tag to each item will be the EmployeeID, to provide a unique key for each node. It also will allow you to access the EmployeeID later in the application to display an entry.

FIGURE 10.26

Displaying the entry names in the TreeView.

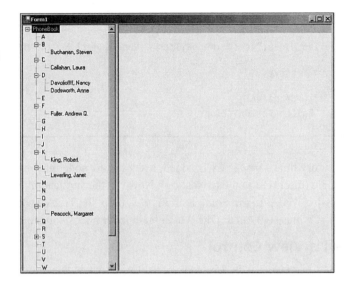

The code in Listing 10.10 can be placed in the Form_Load routine for the application so that the TreeView control is initialized when the application is started. However, if you're allowing users to select an address book database to use, and there might be several different ones, you should place this initialization code into a separate subroutine that can be called when needed.

LISTING 10.10   ADONETEX2.TXT: Adding the TreeView Control Data Initialization Code as a Routine Called from the Form_Load Event

```
Private Sub Form1_Load(ByVal sender As System.Object,
      ByVal e As System.EventArgs) Handles MyBase.Load
       Dim myrdr As SqlClient.SqlDataReader
       Dim node_key As String
       Dim entry_letter As String
       Dim node_name As String

       Set_NewTree()

       SqlCommand1.Connection.Open()
       myrdr = SqlCommand1.ExecuteReader(CommandBehavior.CloseConnection)
       Do While myrdr.Read
           node_key = myrdr.GetString(1)
           entry_letter = Mid(myrdr.GetString(1), 1, 1)
           Dim myNode As TreeNode
           I = 0
           node_name = myrdr.GetString(1) & ", " & myrdr.GetString(2)
           For Each myNode In tvTreeView.Nodes.Item(0).Nodes
               If myNode.Text = entry_letter Then
```

LISTING 10.10   continued

```
tvTreeView.Nodes.Item(0).Nodes.Item(myNode.Index).Nodes.Add(node_name)
                End If
            Next
        Loop
        myrdr.Close()
        SqlConnection1.Close()
End Sub
```

Also, every time a new entry is added, a single new node must be added using the same key logic (discussed in a later section). Now run the application to see how TreeView processing works. In the example in Figure 10.26, the TreeView control automatically provides a plus sign (+) to note which main letter nodes contain data entries.

The ListView Control

The data displayed in the ListView control will change whenever users select a different letter in the TreeView control, much the same way as Windows Explorer displays the contents of a directory that was selected. To do this, you need to know when a new letter was selected in the TreeView and then clear the ListView to reinitialize it.

The first step in the process is to recognize when a node is selected; the second is to know if the selected node is a letter or a name. The AfterSelect event routine is triggered whenever a node is selected in the TreeView control. The code in Listing 10.11 checks to see whether the node was a letter or a name and then calls the appropriate routines, passing the selected letter as an argument.

LISTING 10.11   ADONETEX3.TXT: Checking for a Letter Node to Call the ListView Initialization Routine

```
Private Sub set_Listview(ByVal KeyCode As String)
        SqlCommand2.CommandText = sqlstr & " Where LastName Like '" & KeyCode &
➥"%'"
        SqlCommand2.Connection.Open()
        myrdr = SqlCommand2.ExecuteReader(CommandBehavior.CloseConnection)
        ListView1.Items.Clear()
        Dim lstAdd As ListViewItem
        I = 0
        ListView1.Columns.Clear()
        ListView1.Columns.Add("Name", 140, HorizontalAlignment.Left)
        ListView1.Columns.Add("Address", 70, HorizontalAlignment.Left)
        ListView1.Columns.Add("Phone", 70, HorizontalAlignment.Left)
        Do While myrdr.Read
```

LISTING 10.11 continued

```
            node_key = myrdr.GetString(1) & ", " & myrdr.GetString(2)
            ListView1.Items.Add(node_key)
            ListView1.Items(I).SubItems.Add(myrdr.GetString(3))
            ListView1.Items(I).SubItems.Add(myrdr.GetString(5))
            I += 1
        Loop
        myrdr.Close()
End Sub
```

For this application, the only display option that makes any sense for the ListView control is Report. The data that should be displayed for each entry is up to you. However, the minimum should be that shown in Figure 10.27.

FIGURE 10.27

The final ListView display showing data from the address entry table.

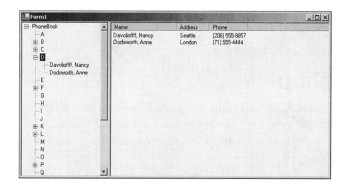

10

Summary

Well, you've had a busy day. You've learned how to use the ActiveX Data Control to automatically access, display, modify, and delete information. Also, you saw how to perform the same actions by using ActiveX Data Objects.

After you saw how the older data access worked, we discussed the new ADO.Net features when accessing data from a database. You saw how to use these methods to add some initialization code to the address book application. All this allows you to create a feature-rich database application that your users can work with.

During Week 3, on Day 17, "Adding Data Access to the Web," you will see how to use the new ADO.NET capabilities for an Internet project.

Q&A

Q Can any or all of the access methods be used in the same routine?

A Yes, you can use any of the different access methods in the same routine or application. It all depends on what you need to accomplish.

Q What methods can you use to position the database to a particular record?

A You would use the `Find` and `Move` methods to position the database: `Find`, `MoveLast`, `MoveFirst`, `MoveNext`, and `MoveLast`.

Q What do the `EOF` and `BOF` values determine?

A `EOF` determines the end of the file; `BOF` determines the beginning of the file.

Q Why would a Data Reader be used?

A The Data Reader provides fast, read-only access to data within a database. You should use it whenever you need to access data, without any requirement to modify it.

Workshop

The Workshop provides quiz questions to solidify your understanding of the material covered and exercises to help you use what you've learned. The answers to the quiz questions and exercises are provided in Appendix A, "Answers to Quizzes and Exercises."

Quiz

1. What's the difference between ActiveX Data Control access and ActiveX Data Objects?

2. What does the `MoveComplete` routine do?

3. How do you delete a record from the database?

Exercise

Add a search form to the address book application that will allow users to search for a first or last name and display the results in a list box control. Users should be able to select a name and have it displayed in the `frmAddressEntry` form.

DAY 11

Enhancing the Application with Custom Controls

Over the last few days you've learned about designing databases, creating data forms, and accessing data through code. Today you'll switch gears and see what a custom control is, how to create a fairly simple one, and then—finally—how to convert an existing form into a custom control. You'll also see the reasons for converting a form into a custom control.

Custom controls are one of the most exciting features of the Visual Basic product. They allow you to combine existing controls with code and create new controls that meet your application's specific design needs. Of course, you also can create custom controls as applications so that other developers can use them in their applications.

You'll see how to create a custom control; however, the process is by no means simple. You also will take a brief look at how to create a custom control that will be used by a Web application. The best today's lesson can do is whet your appetite for more information about controls.

Using Custom Controls

Before creating a custom control you must understand what they are and the different types of custom controls you can create. If you can create a Visual Basic form, you can create a custom control. The steps and skills necessary to create controls are practically identical to those used to create a form. What's more, control creation possibilities are virtually unlimited.

Why Use Custom Controls?

Creating custom controls is like teaching an old dog a new trick. Although Visual Basic provides many different controls and many other companies produce custom controls to provide particular functionality, at some point you'll need to perform some task that the existing controls don't perform.

For example, if you want users to be able to enter a new value in a combo box, you need to have some code in the combo box's Leave routine. That's easy; however, if the new entry requires more information to actually add the new value, you need to display another form to get that information. Here's the problem: When the second form is closed, the new record normally is committed to the database. Unfortunately, any changes made to data on the form all are committed at once. This might cause errors when users try to finish the entry and update the database.

By creating a custom control that does the initial add and update of the reference information, you aren't unloading a form and you actually can code the update process differently; you also can use this control in other applications. Custom controls allow you to create any type of control you need to solve a unique problem in your application. The only limiting factor is your own imagination.

Knowing the Models

A large part of creating a quality custom control lies in the details—that is, verifying the design and runtime settings of every property, method, event, and user input. Defining these ahead of time will go a long way toward helping you succeed. Before creating the control, you should know that you can follow three different models; each model addresses a specific area of the design concept:

- Enhancing existing controls
- Building complex controls from existing controls
- Creating user-drawn controls

Enhancing Existing Controls

In this model your control contains a single existing control. Most of this control's properties, methods, and events are mapped to your control's public properties, methods, and events. Your control can add new properties or events or otherwise modify the behavior of the standard control. For example, you could implement a text box that will convert all the text entered to uppercase characters.

The biggest advantage of enhancing an existing control is that it's extremely easy to do: You use the existing properties, methods, and events of the existing controls. Although this is the easiest method, you might want to use another approach for the following reasons:

- Each existing control defines its own behavior and drawing characteristics. There are limits to what you can do to modify the control.

- Existing controls are always in run mode when your control is active, making it impossible to set the control's design time properties even though the new control is in design mode. For example, if you want to create an enhanced list box that supports single and multiple selection modes, you need to place two separate list box controls into your control: one for single selection and one for multiple selection.

- As soon as you go beyond the built-in controls or redistributable controls provided by Microsoft, you run into licensing issues. For your control to work in the design environment, each existing control must be properly licensed.

Building Complex Controls from Existing Controls

This model really is a superset of the preceding model, except that rather than map your public properties and events to a single control, you map them to any or all existing controls in the new control. It's also possible to map the same property to more than one control.

Creating User-drawn Controls

The two preceding approaches have the advantage of being incredible easy to use. User-drawn controls represent one of the most exciting approaches you can use for control creation, although the difficulty jumps astronomically. With this type of control you work primarily with properties and events of the UserControl object. User-drawn controls are used whenever your new control had nothing in common with any existing controls. You would actually define all the control's properties, methods, and events while drawing the control so that it looks exactly the way you want it to.

11

With any of these three methods, the custom control you create will look and act like any other controls. You can insert them into the toolbox windows, double-click the control to add it to the form, and select its properties from the Properties window.

Creating a Small Custom Control

To gain an understanding of what it takes to create a custom control, you'll create a small, fairly simple custom control with the properties, methods, events, and controls listed in Table 11.1.

TABLE 11.1 Simple Custom Control Elements

Name	Description
Properties	
TableName	Contains the table name or a SQL statement
DisplayField	Contains the number of columns displayed
Method	
Refresh	Refreshes the database query when executed
Event	
Click	Triggered when users click the control's return button
Controls	
ComboBox	Displays the data from the specified field in the table
Button	Returns control to the calling form

By combining these items with the data-access programming you learned yesterday, you can design a control that will solve the problem described earlier. In this section you'll create the basic control interface and set the properties, methods, and events for the control. In the next section you'll add code to this control to include the enhanced functionality you want.

To begin building the new control, open a new project, selecting Windows Control Library as the project type as shown in Figure 11.1. After you open a new Windows control project, notice some differences in the display (see Figure 11.2).

The biggest difference is that the displayed work area has no title bar or borders like standard form work areas. This serves as a reminder that you're not creating a form. When creating a new control, Visual Basic generates a default control class called UserControl1. Visual Basic then assigns default properties, events, and methods to the control. To go beyond these defaults, modify these values and routines to make the control perform the way you want it to.

FIGURE 11.1

Starting a Windows Control Library project to contain the new custom control.

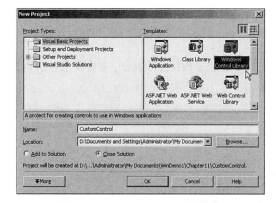

FIGURE 11.2

The custom control design window doesn't have a title bar or a border.

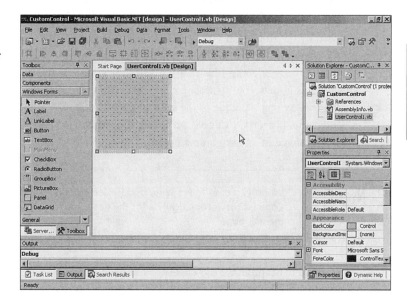

Okay, now add some existing controls to the control as shown in Figure 11.3. This will give you the tools to create the unique process you need to perform.

FIGURE 11.3

The initial controls added to the new custom control being created.

Don't forget to change the name of the project from UserControl1 to something a little more meaningful. For this example, name the control AdvDBAdd, referring to this control's function (Advanced Database Add). Also change the control's bitmap image. This image will appear in the toolbox whenever you add the control to an application. Now activate some properties, methods, and events for the new control.

Adding Properties, Methods, and Events

Deciding which properties, methods, and events to add to your new control usually is the most difficult step in the creation process. You must decide which events in the custom control you want to users to have access to; you also must decide which properties and methods are available. Adding properties and methods is easier than adding events—a method is any public procedure you declare in your control class; a property can be declared by using a Property statement in Visual Basic.

Implementing Properties

The controls that make up a user control normally are declared private and thus can't be accessed by developers. If you want to make properties of these controls available to users of the new control, you must expose them to users. A property of a base control is exposed in the user control by creating a new property via the Get and Set statements. This process allows you to either expose an existing property of a base control or create a new property that's unique to the custom control you're creating. The Get procedure is called when a property's value is retrieved; the Set procedure is called when a property's value is changed in an assignment operation.

 Note   When you enter a Property declaration statement in the Code Editor, the Code Editor automatically adds the Get...End Get and Set...End Set statement groups.

For the simple example we are creating, you need to add only two properties to the custom control. Listing 11.1 shows the code required to define these properties.

LISTING 11.1   PROPERTYADD.TXT: Adding Properties to the Custom Control

```
' Defining local variables to store the property values.
Private m_DisplayField As Integer
Private m_TableName As String

    Public Property DisplayField() As Integer
        Get
```

LISTING **11.1**   continued

```
            DisplayField = m_DisplayField
        End Get
        Set(ByVal Value As Integer)
            m_DisplayField = Value
        End Set
    End Property

    Public Property TableName() As String
        Get
            TableName = m_TableName
        End Get
        Set(ByVal Value As String)
            m_TableName = Value
        End Set
    End Property
```

You also must define local variables within the custom control to store and work with the properties you've added. Within these property procedures, you can add as much complex code as you might need to perform the required tasks for your custom control.

You've just defined two custom properties for the new control. However, you also might need to access properties from the base controls, such as the Text property from the ComboBox control. You would do this by defining a custom property that also sets the Text property of the ComboBox. Listing 11.2 shows you how to do this.

11

LISTING **11.2**   BASEPROPERTY.TXT: Adding Access to a Base Control's Property

```
Private m_cboAuthorsText As String

    Public Property cboAuthorsText() As String
        Get
            cboAuthorsText = m_cboAuthorsText
            cboAuthorsText = cboAuthors.Text()
        End Get
        Set(ByVal Value As String)
            m_cboAuthorsText = Value
            cboAuthors.Text = Value
        End Set
    End Property
```

Remember that you must define a private variable for each property to expose in your custom control.

Adding Events to the control

NEW TERM Events are ways for your control to communicate with the rest of the program. You *raise* an event in code after predetermined conditions are met. For example, when a user clicks a button in the custom control, you can raise a click event that the calling form can access. When an event is raised, it can be *handled* by the hosting form or control, or it can be ignored altogether. To raise an event, you would use the RaiseEvent statement:

```
RaiseEvent cmdReturnClick()
```

This will cause the named event to be triggered in the hosting form. In addition to using RaiseEvent, you also must define the new event as shown:

```
Public Event cmdReturnClick()
```

This statement defines the event and makes it accessible to the hosting form. Listing 11.3 shows the code required to activate the Return button's click routine.

LISTING 11.3   RETURNCLICK.TXT: Accessing the Return Button's Click Routine

```
Public Event cmdReturnClick()

Private Sub cmdReturn_Click(ByVal sender As Object, _
    ByVal e As System.EventArgs) Handles cmdReturn.Click
        m_cboAuthorsText = cboAuthors.Text
        RaiseEvent cmdReturnClick()
End Sub
```

Including Methods in the Custom Control

A method is implemented in a control in the same manner a method would be implemented in any other component. If a method is required to return a value, it's implemented as a Public Function. If no value is returned, it's implemented as a Public Sub.

For this example, you need to define only one method to perform a refresh of the database query used to populate the combobox drop-down list.

Note

> You will be using many of the techniques that you learned yesterday to access the database table to display the list of authors in the combobox.

Listing 11.4 displays the code required to open a database connection and populate the combobox drop-down list. This subroutine will be called during the initialization process of the hosting form by refreshing the Refresh method that will be added next.

LISTING **11.4**   DBREFRESH.TXT: Getting Data from the Database for the Drop-Down List

```
Private Sub Init_Combo()
        Dim conn1 As New OleDb.OleDbConnection()
        Dim cmd1 As New OleDb.OleDbCommand()
        Dim MyReader As OleDb.OleDbDataReader
        conn1.ConnectionString = "Provider=SQLOLEDB;data source=lbm1\lbm_vb;" & _
                            "integrated security=SSPI;initial
catalog=pubs;"
        cmd1.CommandText = m_TableName
        cmd1.Connection = conn1
        cmd1.Connection.Open()
        cboAuthors.Items.Clear()
        MyReader = cmd1.ExecuteReader(CommandBehavior.CloseConnection)
        'Loop until there are no more reports to add
        While MyReader.Read
            cboAuthors.Items.Add(MyReader(m_Displayfield))
        End While
        MyReader.Close()
        conn1.Close()
End Sub
```

To add the Refresh method, include only the following code in your custom control:

```
Public Sub adbRefresh()
    Call Init_Combo()
End Sub
```

This will provide access to the routine in the hosting form as shown in Figure 11.4.

FIGURE **11.4**

Accessing the new method from the hosting form.

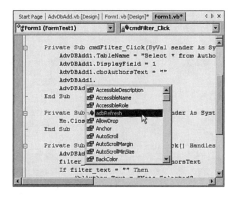

Testing the Control

Before testing the control you've just created, you must build the custom control. Now add a new project to the solution you're working with. The next step is to add a reference for this control to the new project by right-clicking the references folder and selecting Add Reference. Then click the Projects tab to select and add the custom control reference (see Figure 11.5).

FIGURE 11.5

Adding a reference to the new control.

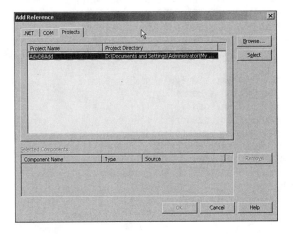

This will add the control to the toolbox for the project. The new custom control should appear in the Windows Forms toolbox list, as shown in Figure 11.6.

FIGURE 11.6

Accessing the new custom control from the Toolbox.

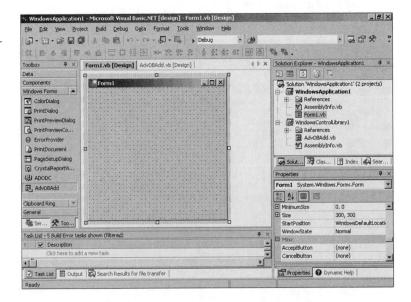

Now add the custom control and the remaining controls listed in Table 11.2 to the form as shown in Figure 11.7.

TABLE 11.2 Creating the Hosting Form to Test the Custom Control

Control	Property	Value
New Custom Control	Name	AdvDBAdd1
	DisplayField	1
	TableName	Select * From Authors
	Visible	False
	CboAuthorsText	Leave blank
Button	Name	cmdQuit
	Text	&Quit
Button	Name	cmdFilter
	Text	&Filter
Label	Text	Author Selected
Label	Name	lblAuthor
	Text	Leave blank

11

FIGURE 11.7

Creating the final Filter form.

 Note   The custom control will only be seen if users click the Filter button to select a different author.

The final step is to add the code to the required events for the form to perform properly. The first step is to add a reference as shown to the custom controls refresh method in the New subroutine to initialize the drop-down list:

```
AdvDbAdd1.adbRefresh()
```

Next add the code in Listing 11.5 to the custom control's click routine to check if an author's name has been selected. It also will set the properties for the custom control and show it to users.

LISTING 11.5   CHKAUTHOR.TXT: Checking to See Whether an Author Has Been Selected

```
Dim filter_text As String

Private Sub cmdFilter_Click(ByVal sender As System.Object,
        ByVal e As System.EventArgs) Handles cmdFilter.Click
    AdvDBAdd1.TableName = "Select * from Authors"
    AdvDBAdd1.DisplayField = 1
    AdvDBAdd1.cboAuthorsText = ""
    AdvDBAdd1.adbRefresh()
    AdvDBAdd1.Visible = True
End Sub

Private Sub cmdQuit_Click(ByVal sender As System.Object,
        ByVal e As System.EventArgs) Handles cmdQuit.Click
    Me.Close()
End Sub

Private Sub AdvDBAdd1_cmdReturnClick() Handles AdvDBAdd1.cmdReturnClick
    AdvDBAdd1.Visible = False
    filter_text = AdvDBAdd1.cboAuthorsText
    If filter_text = "" Then
        lblAuthor.Text = "None Selected"
    Else
        lblAuthor.Text = filter_text
    End If
End Sub
```

At this point you can test the control much like any other code in the solution. To see how to use the testing capabilities of Visual Basic, refer to Day 14, "Testing and Debugging the Application."

Summary

What you've seen today can be overwhelming at first, but you'll find that custom controls are just another tool now available for you to use in Visual Basic. By creating and using custom controls, you can create a single form application that can do anything you need done. Additionally, any time you need a unique function for your application design, you know how to create it yourself.

Q&A

Q **Why should I create my own custom controls?**

A When you need a unique process for an application, consider creating a custom control. Also, if the process you're creating might be used in other applications, a custom control makes it easier to copy the process.

Q **Should I worry about any limitations when creating a custom control?**

A You are limited only by your imagination. However, before spending days or weeks creating a custom control, investigate to see if it has already been created so you can buy it rather than waste the time and effort to create it.

Workshop

The Workshop provides quiz questions to help you solidify your understanding of the material covered and exercises to provide you with experience in using what you've learned. The answers to the quiz questions and exercises are provided in Appendix B, "Answers to Quizzes and Exercises."

Quiz

1. What makes up a solution?

Exercise

By using the process discussed in today's lesson, convert the address data entry form to a custom control that can be used in the Address Book application.

11

DAY **12**

Working with Crystal Reports

One of the most important features that you can add to an application is the capability to print the data in the application's database. In this day and age, users have come to expect professional-looking, easy-to-use reports from the applications they use. Since Visual Basic 3, Microsoft has included a version of Crystal Reports with the development product. However, it was never fully integrated with the Visual Studio IDE. You were always running a separate design tool independent of Visual Basic. In Visual Basic .NET, that final step has been taken, and Crystal Reports is now a fully integrated component of the development environment. Crystal Reports provides a complete reporting design, creation, and viewing tool for you to use within your Visual Basic Windows and Web applications.

In today's lesson, you will learn how to use Crystal Reports to design and create reports that you can add to your application. We also will take a close look at how to incorporate these reports into your application by creating a report selection form. Finally, the CommonDialog Print dialog box will be added to the form, enabling users to modify the Printer Setup options. At the end of the process, users will be able to select a report, choose some filter options, and then run the report.

What Is Crystal Reports?

Crystal Reports is a powerful reporting application that allows you to create custom reports, lists, and labels from the data in your application database. When Crystal Reports connects to the database, it reads in the values from the fields you selected and places them into a report, either as is or as part of a formula that generates more complex values.

You can use a wide range of built-in tools to manipulate data to fit the report's requirements. These tools enable you to

- Create calculations.
- Calculate subtotals and grand totals.
- Calculate averages.
- Count the total number of records in a query.
- Test for the presence of specific values.
- Filter database records.

The data from your database can be placed and formatted exactly where you need it when designing the report. By using Crystal Reports, your reports can be as simple or as complex as your needs require. After you design a report for your application, you can use it within the application or as a template to create other similar reports.

Although most database programs include their own report generators, they are usually too difficult for non-technical people to use, and they generally require a good understanding of how that database program works. Crystal Reports is both an end-user reporting tool and a report development tool.

In keeping with the Visual Basic design concept, Crystal Reports can connect to almost any database available. You do so by using one of the following methods:

- OLE DB (ADO)
- ADO.NET
- ODBC (RDO or RDS)
- Database file (Local files; that is, dBASE)

Note	Although ODBC and OLE DB are generally used to connect to the more complex server databases, such as SQL Server 2000 and Oracle, they can also be used to access Paradoxand, if needed, Microsoft Access.

Taking a Look Around

When working with the Crystal Report Designer, you are presented with two main windows and their associated toolbars (see Figure 12.1). This designer automatically launches when you add a new Crystal Reports object to your project, or when you double-click an existing Crystal Reports object in your project.

FIGURE 12.1

The Crystal Report Designer you use to access all the features when designing a report.

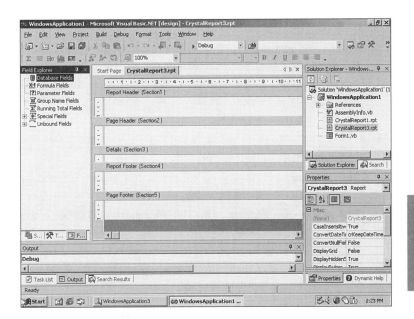

The Main Report Window

The Main Report window is divided into report sections, such as section headers, footers, and details. You drag objects from the Field Explorer on the right side of the window into a report section. The data that appears in the finished report is based on your design choices. In particular, the report data will vary depending on the sections that you choose to insert the fields or functions. For example, if you insert a chart object into the report header section, the chart will appear only once at the top of the report and will contain only summarized data for the entire report. You access the functions and features available in Crystal Reports via the Field Explorer by dragging the object onto the designer and then using the property window to format the object. Some report objects that you can add to your report and format according to your needs include

- Database fields
- Formula fields
- Parameter fields
- Group Name fields
- Running Total fields
- Summary fields
- Charts
- Subreports

When creating a new report, you first select the database to use, and then the Main Report window is displayed to enable you to insert and format the data you need in your report. When you start a new report, the five sections listed in Table 12.1 are created automatically in the designer.

TABLE 12.1 Sections Automatically Created by the Report Designer

Section Name	Description
Report Header	Displays the report title, data, and any other information that needs to appear at the top of the report. Information displayed here is shown only once.
Page Header	Similar to the Title section; this information is displayed at the top of every page.
Details	Displays the detail information from the query.
Page Footer	Usually displays the page number and any other information that you want at the bottom of each page.
Report Footer	Displays information only on the last page of your report.

You build reports by inserting data fields, formulas, and other objects into one of the preceding sections in the Design window. You use the Field Explorer to select or build the fields you want to insert on the report. You add subtotals and other group values by selecting a field and then building the conditions to generate the new subtotal or group value (that is, change of state). These group sections are created as needed, and the values are placed in the appropriate section. If you want the value to be some other place on the report, you simply select it and drag it where you want it.

Using the Crystal Report Experts

Crystal Reports contains several experts or wizards that you can use when creating reports. When you start a new report by inserting a new Crystal Report object into your project, the Crystal Report Gallery dialog box appears (see Figure 12.2).

FIGURE 12.2

The Crystal Report Gallery dialog box shows each Report Expert from which you can choose.

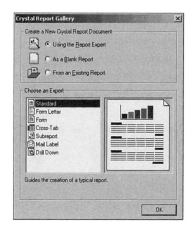

The Crystal Report Gallery provides you with the following options:

- Use a Report Expert to guide you through the report creation process.
- Open a blank report.
- Create a new report from an existing report.

If you choose to use the Report Experts, you must then select the report type you want to create from the bottom section of the dialog box.

> **Note**
>
> The Crystal Report Designer in Visual Basic .NET is much like the Crystal Reports designer available in Visual Basic 6.

Each expert takes you through the steps required to build that style report.

Adding Calculated Values

Crystal Reports uses formulas and functions to do the kind of number crunching and data manipulation needed for an advanced database report. You use the Formula Editor window (see Figure 12.3) to create the calculated fields in the report.

12

FIGURE 12.3

You can build simple and complex calculations in the Formula Editor.

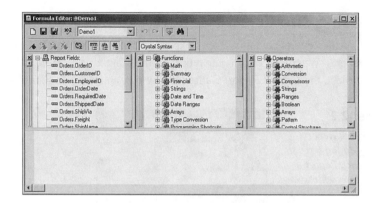

NEW TERM The Formula Editor enables you to work with both formulas and functions. A formula is a set of instructions that calculate the information you can't directly receive from the database. If a database record has two fields, Unit Price and Quantity Sold, but you need the total sales price, you would have to multiply the two fields to calculate the total sales price. This process is accomplished by using a formula that you place in the report.

This type of formula is simple, because it uses the standard arithmetic operators. However, not all the calculations you need are simple formulas. Sometimes you will require complex calculations or manipulations of the database fields. If you want to display the average monthly sales for the previous year, rounded to the nearest unit, you need a mathematical formula. The functions required to perform these activities involve a fair amount of data manipulation. Whereas some of this can be done using only Crystal Reports operators, many of them can't be done without the use of functions.

Functions are built-in procedures or subroutines used to evaluate, calculate, or transform data from the database. The Formula Editor is divided into four subwindows used to create the calculation (refer to Figure 12.3):

- The Fields window lists all available database fields based on the tables previously selected.
- The Functions window lists all the functions you can use to create a calculated field.
- The Operators window lists all the operators you can use.
- The largest window is the Formula Text window, where you build the actual calculation.

You can choose to use the different windows to select items or, if you know the correct syntax, type directly into the Formula Text area.

You can combine fields, functions, operators, and other calculations to create complex calculated fields. This enables you to create complex calculations in steps (small calculated fields) and then combine them to form the finished calculation.

Filtering Your Data

When you select a field for the report, every row or query in the table will be printed. However, in many cases, you may need only specific rows of data from the database rather than all the rows. For example, you may want only New York customer data, or only invoices that fall within a particular date range. Crystal Reports includes a Select Expert (see Figure 12.4) that allows you to specify the filtering criteria for your report either against detail rows of data or against groups of data based on the grouping information you've defined for the report.

FIGURE 12.4

Setting the filter information for your report.

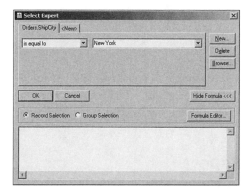

Designing the Report

Of course, like anything else in the application process, designing reports requires some thought before you can actually create them. For each report that you are creating, you should answer the following questions:

- What is the report's purpose?
- What data will the report include?
- Does it need filter capabilities?
- How should the report be laid out?

If you have the answers to these questions, your reports will perform well. Before starting the creation process, you should sketch out what the report will look like and also list the fields needed for the report. The report that we will design in this section will use the Northwind database, which is available either in SQL Server 2000 or Microsoft Access.

12

The data will be used to simulate an address book style report. An address book application usually needs several types of reports, including mailing label, phone lists, and a complete address book report.

Although you will learn enough about Crystal Reports to create most reports you need, today's lesson is really meant to show you how to integrate Crystal Reports into an application while providing users with several advanced features. We will create an address/phone list report, which will contain the following information:

- Name
- Address
- City
- State
- ZIP Code
- Home Phone
- Office Phone, if any

Although this report is fairly simple, it will allow you to learn the necessary skills to create any type of report. After you list the fields, you next need to sketch the report's layout. After you are satisfied with the layout, you then add a new Crystal Report item for the project.

Creating the Report

To start the process, follow these steps:

1. Start a new project.
2. Choose Add New Item from the Project menu (or right-click in the Solution Explorer and select Add, Add New Item).
3. Select Crystal Report from the Add New Item dialog box (see Figure 12.5). Remember to change the default name of the report to something meaningful for your application. For this example, name the report AddressBook1.rpt. Click the Open button to invoke the Crystal Report Designer for this new report.

Use the Standard expert for the example report; however, Crystal Reports can assist in creating many different styles of reports from this dialog box:

- *Standard* creates a standard report with rows and columns. It often has summary information at the bottom of the columns.
- *Form Letter* creates a simple form letter for you to merge address information from the database.

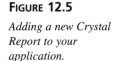

FIGURE 12.5

Adding a new Crystal Report to your application.

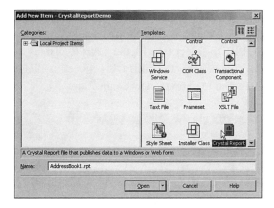

- *Cross-Tab* inverts the order of a standard columnar report. It's often used to obtain a quick summary view of a more complex set of data.

- *Mail Label* creates items such as mailing labels or name tags from the information in your database.

- *Form* creates a report that can use a preset form to display the data (that is, Invoice).

- *Sub-Report* allows you to use multiple queries to display master-detail style reports that can also contain charts.

- *Drill Down* shows the supporting information, or detail information, for each record.

After you select the Standard report expert from the Crystal Report Designer main dialog box and click OK, the related report expert is automatically started. For the style selected, eight steps (shown as tabs in Figure 12.6) are involved in creating the initial report.

12

FIGURE 12.6

The Report Expert guides you through the report creation process.

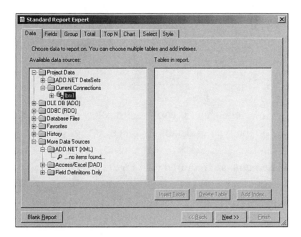

The logical starting point of any report is to select the database required for the report. The first tab will display the data access choices available to use in the report. For this example, open the OLE DB folder (see Figure 12.7) to display any available connections. If there are no active connections, the OLE DB connection dialog box appears (see Figure 12.8), allowing you to define a new connection.

FIGURE 12.7

Selecting the database connection to use for the new report.

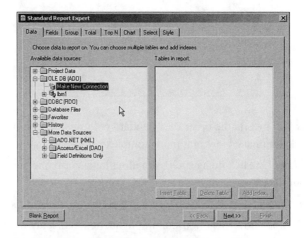

FIGURE 12.8

Selecting the OLE DB connection to use.

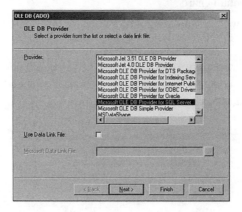

When defining a new connection, you need to select only the OLE DB connector and then, depending on the type of database you are using, specify the connection information. For this example, SQL Server 2000 is used, so the server name, sign-on information, and database name are required (see Figure 12.9).

FIGURE 12.9

Specifying the connection information needed for the selected database type.

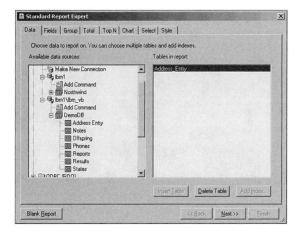

If you've created the Address Book database, you can select it from this dialog box. However, if you haven't created this database, with some minor changes to the report, you can use any other database you have available that contains contact information. The example will use the Northwind database from SQL Server 2000. After you select the database, all tables and queries contained in it are available for you to use, and displayed in the data sources frame in the report expert (see Figure 12.10).

FIGURE 12.10

Choosing the tables and/or views to use in the report.

12

From this dialog box, select the table(s) you want to use and then click Next to continue the creation process. If you choose more than one table, a ninth tab is added as the next option. This Link tab allows you to define or modify the join information already defined in the database. Because the join information has already been defined, you will see the joins displayed as shown in Figure 12.11.

FIGURE 12.11

Defining or modifying the join information for a report.

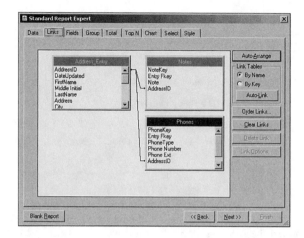

If the joins are correct, you can click Next to continue to the third tab. This tab (see Figure 12.12) enables you to select the fields from each of the tables that you need in the report.

FIGURE 12.12

Selecting the data fields from the included tables and views.

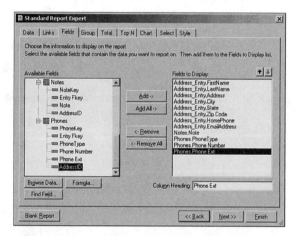

You add the fields to the report data list by double-clicking each field in the Database Fields list or by highlighting the fields that you want and clicking the Add button. You also can set the order of the fields in the report. For each field selected, you can also enter a custom column heading in the text box below the list. Select the fields listed in Table 12.2 and add them to the fields list.

TABLE 12.2   Required Fields for the Address/Phone List Report

Table	Field
Address Entry	First Name
	Last Name
	Address
	City
	State
	Zip
	Home Phone
	EmailAddress
Notes	Note
Phones	Phone Type
	Phone Number
	Phone Ext

You will need to set the Join Type for the Notes and Phones table to Left Outer Join using the Options dialog box on the Links tab, as shown in Figure 12.13.

FIGURE 12.13

Setting Left Outer Join for the report query.

12

During the report design, you will sometimes require some manipulation of the fields you've selected, by performing either a mathematical process or a string process. Although you will need to manipulate some of the fields, you will see how to do that a little later in this section.

After you select all the fields for the report, you could either preview the report or continue refining it by adding other options. Clicking Next displays the Group tab (see Figure 12.14).

FIGURE 12.14

Choosing the fields and grouping process using the Group tab in the report expert.

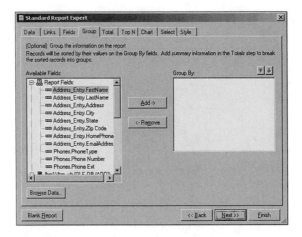

The Group tab enables you to select the fields you want to sort and group, specifying what order or direction to sort them. In this report, the only sort needed would be on the Last Name field. After you set the group options, click Next five times to bypass the next several tabs, which aren't used for this example. As their names imply, the Totals tab lets you define summary fields for the report, whereas the Select tab lets you set filter conditions for the report.

Note After you see how a report is viewed in your application, you will modify the groupings to use a neat feature of the new report viewer.

The final tab displayed is Style (see Figure 12.15), on which you choose from a list of default styles for your report. You can also enter a Title for your report on this tab.

FIGURE 12.15

Setting the report's style by selecting it from a list.

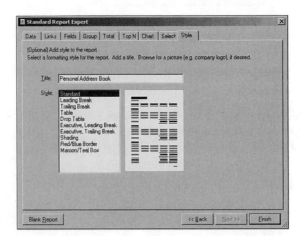

Choose the Standard style and enter **Personal Address Book** as the report's title. To complete the creation process, click Finish. You should now be in the main report window with the report layout displayed, as shown in Figure 12.16.

FIGURE 12.16

The initial report shown in the main report window with the default layout.

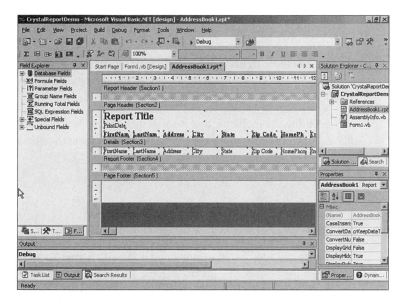

Enhancing the Output

Now that you've created the basic report, you are ready to add a few extra fields to it and enhance its format. Figure 12.17 shows the finished report as it's displayed in a Visual Basic application.

12

FIGURE 12.17

The initial version of the address book report.

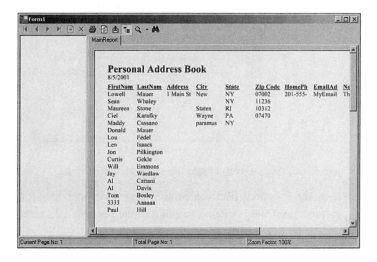

As you can see, the report still needs a little work to make it look professional. Some fields need to be formatted and the following items need to be added to the report:

- A Page Header
- A System Date
- Page Numbering

You can add these fields to the report by using the Special Fields objects in the Field Explorer. To add one of these fields, select and then drag it to the location on the report where you want the field to be placed.

The most important change that we will make to the report is to create a calculated field that will take the city, state, and zip fields and put them together while removing all extra blanks. This will convert a line like

```
New York              NY  11236
```

to a more compact, space-saving version:

```
New York, NY 11236
```

Also notice the addition of a comma after the city name. To add a new calculated field, right-click the Formula Fields node in the Fields Explorer and select New from the pop-up menu. You will need to enter **CityStZip** as the formula name and click OK. This displays the Formula Editor with the name of the formula in the window's title bar (see Figure 12.18).

FIGURE 12.18

Creating a new formula with the Formula Editor.

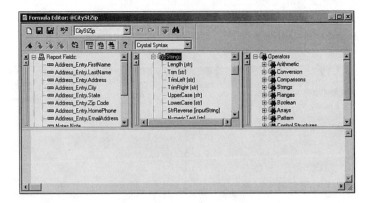

Now follow these steps to create the new calculated field:

1. In the Functions list, locate the Strings folder and open it to find the TrimRight(x) function. Double-click it to add it to the Formula edit area.

2. Find the City field in the Report Fields list. In the Formula edit area, notice that the cursor is between the open and close parentheses. This enables you to double-click the City field to have it placed in the function.

3. After you add the City field, move the cursor to the end of the line and enter **&** or **+**, which can be found in the Operators list in the Strings folder, or you can just type it in. Either character will perform a string concatenation using the trimmed City field and the next field that you will add.

4. Add a string constant that contains a comma and a blank (**, **). You need to type this in yourself. Then add another concatenation character after the string.

5. Find the State field in the Fields list and double-click it to add it to the formula. This is assuming that the State field is two characters; if you aren't sure, you should also trim the field.

6. Add another string constant that contains two blanks ( ), which will position the Zip field properly. You will need to type this in yourself. Remember to add a + before and after the string.

7. Add the Zip field to the formula, and click the Check button to verify that no errors are in the formula. The formula should be the same as this:

```
TrimRight ({Entry.City}) + ", " + { Entry.State} + "  " + { Entry.Zip}
```

If there are no errors, click the Accept button to place the new field in your report.

> **Note**
>
> Every formula is created the same way. The only difference is the complexity of the formula.

12

Depending on what type of field you are formatting, you can either right-click the field to see the pop-up menu, or if the field is a string, you need to create a calculated field that adds the required information. If the phone number fields were strings, you would need to create a formula that resembles this one:

```
"(" & {Publishers.Telephone}[1 to 3] & ") " & {Publishers.Telephone}[4 to 6]_
 & "-" & {Publishers.Telephone}[7 to 10]
```

If the phone number were defined as a numeric field, you would first have to convert it to a string and then create the preceding formula. However, if you use a string, you could force users to enter the formatted string by using the TextBox control formatting and include the literal characters with the text.

After you make all the changes discussed, the report should resemble the one shown in Figure 12.19.

FIGURE **12.19**

The Address/Phone list report with the calculated fields added.

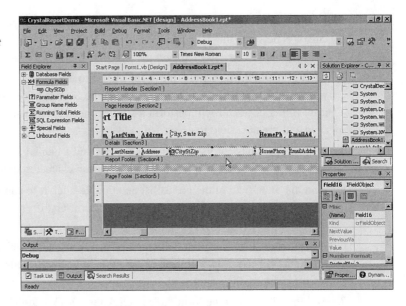

Adding Grouping to the Report

When you add a grouping to your report, the report viewer (discussed in the next section) will allow you to display the groupings in a separate window. This provides users with the ability to select a particular group value and have its report data displayed. To use this feature, you need to set a grouping in the report. For the address book report, the grouping should be based on the first letter of the last name. To do this, create a new calculation using the following:

```
Left ({Orders.LastName}, 1)
```

This will create a field that contains only the first letter of the last name. Of course, you need to add this field to the report. When you add this field, you don't really need it shown in the actual report, so you should right-click the field and select Format to display the Format Editor for this field (see Figure 12.20). Then select Suppress If Duplicated to prevent this field from being displayed in the report. To save the change, click OK.

The next step is to set a grouping based on this field. To do this, right-click in the Field Explorer and select Insert Group from the pop-up menu. This will display the Insert Group dialog box (see Figure 12.21). This dialog box allows you to select the field to group on, the order to sort the group, and other options, such as keeping the group together.

FIGURE 12.20

Setting formatting information for a report field.

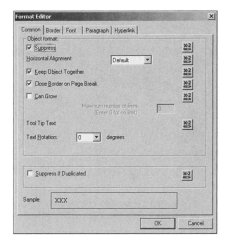

FIGURE 12.21

Setting the Grouping options for the Address Book report.

12

For this report, group by the new FirstLetter field and set the Keep Group Together option (this prevents a page break in the middle of a grouping, if possible). You will see how this works with the Report Viewer in the next section.

Adding the Crystal Reports Control to Your Application

The first step in displaying a Crystal Report in your application is to add the Crystal Report Viewer to a new form in the project (see Figure 12.22). Through this viewer, users can choose the report from the main form. It should also include a button that will allow users to close the form when finished with the report.

FIGURE 12.22

The Crystal Report Viewer in the Toolbox and on a form.

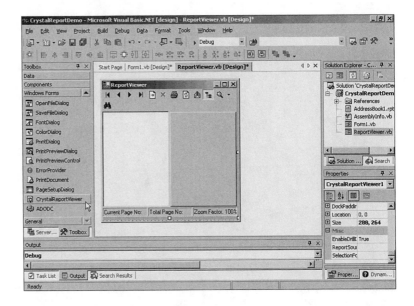

To use this control, simply select it from the Toolbox and place it on the form where you will access the reports. After it's on the form, you can then move and resize it as needed. The Crystal Report Viewer provides the following capabilities:

- Go to first page
- Page Backward
- Page Forward
- Go to last page
- Go to specified page
- Close current window (for group or subreports only)
- Print
- Refresh report
- Export to another report format
- Toggle group tree display
- Magnify/reduce report
- Search

Tip

If you want the report viewer to fill the entire form no matter what size users make it, set the viewer's Dock property to Fill.

Using the Crystal Report Viewer

The key property that you need to specify is `ReportSource`. This specifies the actual report that you want to run from your program. Although only `ReportSource` is required for a report, you may want to use the `SelectionFormula` property, which enables you to limit the number of records that will be included in the report. The `SelectionFormula` property is similar to the `Where` clause of a SQL statement, but it uses its own particular format to enter the information. To specify the `SelectionFormula`, you must enclose the name of any recordset/field combination used in the formula in braces. The final result is an expression that looks like the following:

```
{AddressBook.State}="NY"
```

Of course, you can also use the `AND` or `OR` operators to create multiple expressions.

> If you've entered a `SelectionFormula` when designing your report, any formulas you enter in the `SelectionFormula` property of the Crystal Reports control are added as additional filters.

Displaying the Crystal Report Viewer

To see how this works, add a button to the main form and the following code in its `Click` routine:

```
Dim rptForm As New WindowsApplication6.Form1()
        rptForm.ShowDialog()
```

Remember that this will display the form that contains the Crystal Report Viewer. Now execute the application and click the button to run the report. The report you entered in the `ReportSource` property is executed and displayed in its own window (see Figure 12.23).

12

FIGURE 12.23

Displaying the original report from within a Visual Basic application.

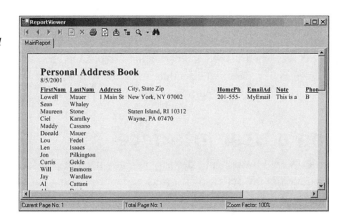

This was just a simple example of displaying a report from an application. You can use many more options, properties, and methods to customize how the report looks when it's displayed, and what data will be retrieved from the database.

What you've just completed is the quickest way of executing a report with Crystal Reports. However, in most applications users usually will need more than one report to display or print, so you will need to change the Crystal Report Viewer properties at run-time. Otherwise, you would need to add a separate form for each report you supply to the users. The two properties, ReportSource and SelectionFormula, are available at run-time. The following sample code sets up the Crystal Report Viewer control for a new report and specifies a selection criteria based on user input:

```
crReport.ReportSource = "AddrList.rpt"
crReport.SelectionFormula = "{EntryList.State}=" & txtStateCd.Text
```

Using the Group Tree

The Group Tree displayed in the Crystal Report Viewer enables you to navigate the report based on the grouping previously defined in the report. Figure 12.24 shows the final report with the last name grouping.

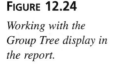
FIGURE 12.24

Working with the Group Tree display in the report.

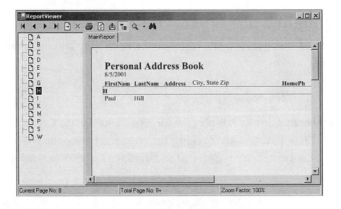

As you can see, when you click a particular group value, the section of the report displayed changes to reflect that selection. Also, the Keep Group Together option forces a page break so that only that particular grouping appears in the viewer.

Creating a User Interface

In complex Visual Basic applications, you really need to give users a good interface to select and modify the options when running reports. In an application that I developed, a

Visual Basic form was used with several controls in conjunction with an input table to create the report manager shown in Figure 12.25.

FIGURE 12.25

The complete report manager from a Visual Basic application.

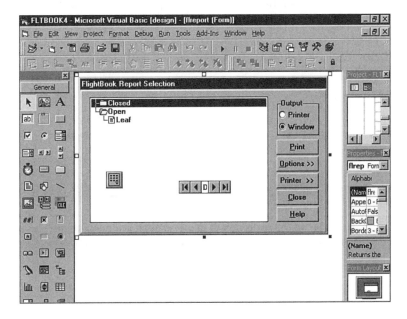

This particular report manager displays report descriptions in a Treeview control with headings for each group of reports added to the list. It also uses the Print Dialog control (see Day 2, "The Face of a Windows Application") to display the Printer dialog box. Using a Treeview control requires copious amounts of code to populate and control it. Instead, you could create a simpler version of this interface, replacing the Treeview control with a ListBox control (see Figure 12.26). For the purposes of today's lesson, you will create a report manager that will give users the following:

- List of reports from which to select
- Printer options

12

FIGURE 12.26

The report manager with the controls in design mode.

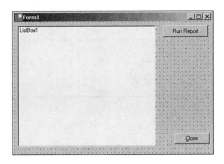

After you complete this example, you can include it in any application for which you need a report manager. To begin this process, start a new project and name it PRTMGR; then name its form frmPrintMgr. Table 12.3 lists the controls and the properties you need to set. Place them on the form as shown in Figure 12.26.

TABLE 12.3 The Report Manager Controls and Property Settings

Control	Property	Value
ListBox	Name	lstReportName
	SelectionMode	One
Button	Name	cmdClose
	Text	Close
Button	Name	cmdReport
	Text	Display

After you add the controls to the form, you are ready to add the necessary code. The first code section that you should always add is the declaration section for the variables used in the code. Add the code in Listing 12.1 to the frmAddress form.

```
Provider=SQLOLEDB.1;Persist Security Info=False;User ID=sa;password=sa;Initial
Catalog=Northwind;Data Source=lbm1;Use Procedure for Prepare=1;Auto
Translate=True;Packet Size=4096;Workstation ID=LBM1;Use Encryption for
Data=False;Tag with column collation when possible=False
```

LISTING 12.1 RPTMGR01.TXT: The Declaration Code for the Report Manager

```
Dim Report_Names() As String
Dim conn1 As New OleDb.OleDbConnection _
("Provider=SQLOLEDB.1;Persist Security Info=False;User ID=sa;
            password=sa;Initial Catalog=AddressBook;Data Source=lbm1;")
Dim cmd1 As New OleDb.OleDbCommand()
Dim MyReader As OleDb.OleDbDataReader
Dim MyReport As String
Dim AppPath As String = "D:\Temp\"
Dim Total_Records As Integer = 0
```

Note The AppPath variable is set to the directory that I was using for the application at the time of development.

The next code section that you must add initializes the form when it's loaded. During the report manager's load routine, you will read the report information from the database table and initialize the list box. Listing 12.2 shows the Form_Load routine for this example.

LISTING 12.2 RPTMGR02.TXT: Initializing the List Box

```
cmd1.CommandText = "Select * from reports order by Reportfilename"
cmd1.Connection = conn1
cmd1.Connection.Open()
lstReportName.Items.Clear()
MyReader = cmd1.ExecuteReader(CommandBehavior.CloseConnection)
'Loop until there are no more reports to add
While MyReader.Read
    lstReportName.Items.Add(MyReader(1))
    Total_Records += 1
    ReDim Preserve Report_Names(Total_Records)
    Report_Names(lstReportName.Items.Count) = MyReader(0)
End While
MyReader.Close()
conn1.Close()
```

In the load routine is a loop that initializes the ListBox control. The data placed in the list box is read from a database table that contains the following information:

Report Description	Description that users see in the list box.
Report File Name	If this record is for an actual report, the filename goes here. If it isn't a report, put spaces here.

This will help you dynamically build the list box data whenever the application is started. The next order of business is to finish the command button code. The code for the Close button is self-explanatory and is as follows:

```
Me.Close()
```

Now, let's add the code for the Report Display button so that you can try out the application. This routine first checks to see whether a report is selected before continuing; if no report is selected, users see an error message. If a report is selected, it checks to see whether the report exists; it obtains the report name from the list box and sets the ReportSource property and finally runs the report. Add the code in Listing 12.3 and try executing the application, selecting a report, and displaying it.

12

LISTING 12.3   RPTMGR03.TXT: The Main Routine in the Report Manager that Displays the Report

```
Private Sub cmdReport_Click(ByVal sender As System.Object,
    ByVal e As System.EventArgs) Handles cmdReport.Click
    If lstReportName.SelectedIndex = -1 Then
        MsgBox("You must first select a Report.", vbCritical, Me.Text)
        Exit Sub
    End If
    MyReport = AppPath & Report_Names(lstReportName.SelectedIndex) & ".rpt"
    If Dir(MyReport) = "" Then
        MsgBox("Report: " & Report_Names(lstReportName.SelectedIndex) & _
        "cannot be found!", vbCritical, Me.Text)
        Exit Sub
    End If

    Dim rptForm As New ReportApp.Form1()
    rptForm.crv1.SelectionFormula = ""
    rptForm.crv1.ReportSource = MyReport
    rptForm.Text = "Address Book Reporting"
    rptForm.ShowDialog()
End Sub
```

 Caution   Remember to select only the report(s) that you've already created; otherwise, you will get an error message that the report file cannot be found. Of course, you should have code that handles this issue.

Now, try running the application, selecting a report, and then clicking the Display button. You now have a working report manager to use in any application that you need to include it in.

Summary

As you can see, designing and displaying reports in a Windows application is not that complicated. In fact, most of what you've just learned can be used when you create a Web application. In Week 3, you will learn how to create a Web application, connect it to your database, and finally incorporate a Crystal Report Viewer in it to display database reports on the Web.

In today's lesson, you saw how to use Crystal Reports to create professional-looking reports with very little effort. You also added the Crystal Reports Viewer Control to a Visual Basic application and used it to run and then display a report in a window. Finally, you saw how to build a report manager to enable the user to select a report to run and then print or display it.

Today's lesson only scratched the surface of the Crystal Reporting Design capabilities and how you can use them in your application. However, it has given you a solid foundation to build on when adding reporting to your application.

Q&A

Q What is Crystal Reports?

A Crystal Reports is a design application included with Visual Basic to enable a developer to add professional reporting directly into her applications.

Q How do I add Crystal Reports to my application?

A You can place a Crystal Report Viewer on an application form for complete access to the properties, events, and methods of the reporting engine, in order to display a report.

Q Can I use it in any application that I create?

A Yes. Crystal Reports can be included in any Windows or Web application.

Workshop

The Workshop provides quiz questions to help solidify your understanding of the material covered, as well as exercises to provide you with experience in using what you've learned. Try to understand the quiz and exercise answers before continuing on to tomorrow's lesson. Answers are provided in Appendix A, "Answers to Quizzes and Exercises."

12

Quiz

1. What databases can I access in a Crystal Report?
2. Do I need to know SQL to build reports using this tool?

Exercise

Take the reporting application that you created in today's lesson and add it to the Address Book application and project. You will need to make some minor changes to the code when you do this.

DAY 13

Coping with Error Handling

In a perfect world the applications you design would work all the time without errors ever occurring. However, we live in an imperfect world where mistakes are made, disk drives stop working, and files are erased. These types of problems and others cause runtime errors. Runtime errors can be separated into two types: those that are found and corrected before the application is released to the users and those that must be handled while the application is being used. Today's lesson spotlights this second group of runtime errors.

To deal with these errors, you must design error handling routines in your application code. Through the years, the process of dealing with errors has become a complex issue. In today's lesson, you will learn what types of errors can occur in your application and how to handle them. You also will see how to use the Visual Basic Error objects, which help you catch any errors that might occur in the application. You also can create a log file that will enable you to see exactly what happened when the error occurred. Additionally, you will learn how a Visual Basic application processes an error.

Understanding the Types of Errors

Before we start discussing error handling, I want to make a blanket statement: *Errors will occur, no matter how good you are! So get over it.* This might sound a bit pretentious, but many programmers think they can't make mistakes—and that's their first mistake. You can create good error handling routines only if you accept that you can make mistakes when designing applications.

Unfortunately, no matter how good your testing is, there will always be errors that you didn't think of or expect in your application. Because the coding of an error routine isn't easy, fun, or exciting, many programmers fall a little short in the anticipation and prevention of any application errors. When this happens, Visual Basic or the new Common Language Runtime (CLR) often takes control and exits your application. This can result in lost data if the error is severe enough.

When the CLR gets involved in handling the error, your application has already been stopped. There is no way at that point for you to undo the damage and allow the application to continue processing. Even more dangerous, if the error doesn't stop your application, it might continue executing with unpredictable results. Like everything else in programming, error handling requires good design skills to create good error handling routines. In a well-designed application, errors are handled by the application and trapped before Visual Basic or the CLR ever sees them.

Errors in General

Before handling any errors, you should understand the types of errors that can occur. The term *error* actually covers a multitude of programming problems that occur during the design, creation, and testing phases of application development. There are four distinct types of errors:

- Syntax
- Compile
- Logic
- Runtime

In previous releases of Visual Basic, the issue of *syntax errors* are dealt with in the Code Editor. If you enter a code line incorrectly, the Code Editor would alert you to the problem before you could continue, and then even display the syntax of the commands you are using along with the valid properties, methods, or events that you could use on a given code line. This enables you to concentrate more on your application's logic than on your typing. However, when you fix a syntax error, it won't occur again.

The next type of error that can occur is a *compile error*, which occurs when your code doesn't adhere to the Visual Basic command structure standards. Again, compile errors are displayed to you when you compile the application, enabling you to fix and then forget them.

Logic errors are the hardest to find in an application because the application will execute without any errors occurring. However, the application probably won't process as you expected. Finding and fixing logic errors will be discussed on Day 14, "Testing and Debugging the Application."

The final error type, *runtime*, occurs while the application is executing and causes it to end abnormally. Today's lesson shows you how to detect and repair runtime errors.

Runtime Error Types

Runtime errors usually occur in one of four similar groups of problems: general file errors, physical errors, code errors, and database errors. Each type of error must be handled differently in your application, and, for each group of errors, you will see what you can and can't do to resolve them.

General File Errors

File errors are one of the oldest types of errors that can occur in your application (see Table 13.1). File errors usually give users a chance to correct the problem. Most general file errors occur because invalid file information is processed by the application. A bad filename or invalid directory path will prevent most applications from continuing to process any information. Usually users can fix these errors, and the application can continue from where the error occurred. The basic error handler for this type of error is to report the problem to users and prompt them for the additional information to complete or retry the operation.

TABLE 13.1 General Visual Basic File Errors

Error Code	Error Message
52	Bad filename or number
53	File not found
54	Bad file mode
55	File already open
58	File already exists
59	Bad record length
61	Disk full
62	Input past end of file

13

TABLE 13.1 continued

Error Code	Error Message
63	Bad record number
64	Bad filename
67	Too many files
74	Can't rename with different drive
75	Path/File access error
76	Path not found

It's important to know that these errors won't occur when you are accessing data within a database. Often you can create a routine that anticipates these errors, prompts users, and then returns the operation that caused the error. In some cases you can't prompt users and retry the operation; you then would display a message giving them the information or at least an error number that will help them identify and hopefully fix the problem.

Physical Errors

Another group of older, common errors is caused by the physical media or hardware on computers. Printers that don't print, disk drives without disks, and disconnected communication ports are the most common examples of physical errors. Users might or might not be able to fix these errors quickly. Usually you can report the error, wait for users to fix the problem, and then either continue with the process or exit the application. For example, if the application is trying to copy a file to a disk and there's no disk in the drive, all you need to do is tell users that they must insert a disk; then wait for them to correct the problem and click OK to continue the process.

Code Errors

A program code error can't be resolved by users. These generally are programming problems caused by unexpected conditions that have occurred in the application code. The best way to deal with these errors is to tell users to report the message to you and exit the program. After you have this information you must find the problem in the application code, fix it, recompile the application, and then send the new executable file to the users.

Database Errors

When you start designing and working with database applications, another type of error that occurs is the *data-related error*. These usually include errors that deal with data type or field size problems: table access restrictions, duplicate or incorrect data added to the database, any SQL-related errors, or an empty recordset that shouldn't be empty. Database access falls into two categories, which you worked with earlier in this book:

Data controls and ActiveX Database Objects (ADO.NET). The way you handle these access errors is unique to the access type. For most errors all you need to do is trap the error, report it to users, and enable users to return to the data entry or display form to fix the problem.

If you use the Data control on your data forms, you can take advantage of the built-in automatic database error reporting. When you try to perform an action that's inherently incorrect for the database the Data control is connected to, the Data control will trap the error and display a message to users. The Data control provides complete database error reporting even if you have no error handling routines in your Visual Basic application. Along with the automatic error handling provided, the Data control also has an Error event that's triggered each time a data-related error occurs. You can add custom code to this event to fix some of the database errors for the user or display a better, more understandable error message.

Note It's usually not a good idea to override the default error routines of a Data control with your own database error code. As long as you use a Data control, you don't need to add database error handling routines to your application. However, if you need to perform special actions when a database error occurs, you must add code to the Data control's Event routine.

On the other hand, if you are using DAO instead of the Data control, you need to add the error handling routine to your project. For example, if you are adding a new record to the database, you must trap for any error that might occur during the add process.

Tip It's a good idea to open database tables in the New procedure so that if any errors occur, you can catch and fix them before any data access really occurs.

13

The Error Handling Process

When you start thinking about creating an error handling routine for your application, realize that error handlers in Visual Basic aren't as straightforward as they might have been in older, more procedure-driven languages such as COBOL or BASIC. This is true for several reasons:

- Visual Basic is *event driven*, meaning that every event that occurs will trigger some operation or action.

- Visual Basic uses a call stack to track the routines being processed and to isolate local variables within a routine. When your application exits a routine, it can lose track of the values of any internal variables it might have been using. This makes resuming execution after the error has been resolved very difficult.

- All errors are local. If an error occurs, it should be handled in the routine where it occurred, which means you must write an error handler for each routine you've included in the application.

Because of the way Visual Basic handles errors, you need to understand how Visual Basic searches application code for an active error routine. You also need to know how to enable an error routine or, as Visual Basic calls it, an *error trap*. Before looking at the hierarchy of the error processing flow, let's look at the two different types of error handling now supported by Visual Basic .NET.

Nonstructured Error Processing

Nonstructured error processing is a new name for an old process. The original way of checking for errors in Visual Basic is by using the On Error and Resume statements. The On Error statement turns on error checking for a procedure or module and then transfers execution of the program to the error code specified in the On Error statement. The error code then checks to see what the error is and processes it accordingly.

The On Error Statement

With the On Error statement you can enable and disable error traps within the application and specify the location of the error handling routine to execute for a given routine or form. The On Error statement comes in three different flavors:

- On Error GoTo [Label] enables the error handling routine that begins at the label specified in the statement. If an error occurs while this error routine is enabled, control will jump to the first code line in the error routine. This is the most common way of using the On Error statement.

- On Error Resume Next sends control to the statement immediately following the one where the error occurred. This way you can trap an error and the application will simply ignore it. Of course, this works only if the code line with the error won't affect any of the subsequent code because of the error.

- On Error GoTo 0 disables the error handling routine in the current procedure. You can use this statement to temporarily disable an error routine in a procedure. You then would need to execute the first or second version of the statement to re-enable the error routine. When you add an error routine to an event procedure or to a subroutine or function you create, it should be placed at the bottom of the routine. You also need to place an `Exit Sub` statement immediately preceding the error routine label to enable the routine to exit normally if execution flows to the bottom of the routine.

The `Resume` Statement

If an error is trapped by an error handling routine and control is passed to the error routine, the only way to deactivate and return from the routine is to execute one of the three forms of the `Resume` statement:

- `Resume [Label]` specifies the label where you want control of the application execution to be returned.

- `Resume Next` causes execution to continue from the statement immediately following the one that caused the error.

- `Resume [0]` re-executes the statement with the error.

If the error routine has resolved the reason the error occurred, you can use `Resume [0]` to retry the operation. The best example of this would be when users try to save a file to a disk but no disk is in the drive. An error will occur and the error routine will be executed. In the error routine, users are told to insert a disk and click OK in the MessageBox; when this is done the application will retry the save operation. Of course, you should enable users to cancel the operation altogether.

The Built-in Error Objects

Among the many objects included in Visual Basic, you can use two to track and report errors that occur during execution of your application. The `Err` and `Error` objects provide useful information about the error that has just occurred.

The `Err` object can be accessed anywhere in a Visual Basic application. Each time an error occurs in the application, the `Err` object's properties are populated with the information about the current error. The object contains several properties and two methods (in Table 13.2) that you can use in the process.

13

TABLE 13.2   The `Err` Object's Methods and Properties

Type	Description
Properties	
Number	The Visual Basic error number
Source	Name of the current Visual Basic file where the error occurred
Description	The description of the error number found in the Number property
HelpFile	The full path and filename of the help file that supports the reported error

TABLE 13.2   continued

Type	Description
HelpContext	The Help topic ID in the help file indicated in the preceding property
LastDLLError	The error code of the last call to a DLL
Clear	Clears all property settings of the Err object

In addition to these properties and methods, you can use one other Visual Basic variable when processing errors. ERL is an undocumented global Visual Basic variable that enables you to access the line number of the code that caused the error. By using both the archaic line numbers in your application code and the ERL variable, you can pinpoint the offending line of code.

 Note

> You don't need to use line numbers in the On Error and Resume statements even if you use them as a numbering scheme for your code. Also, each module in which you use line numbers should have its own unique numbering scheme to enable you to find the offending line.

The Error object and its related Errors collection are available only when the application is using one of the DAO libraries. The Error object is a child of the Connection object and is used to obtain additional information about any database error that might occur in your application. The advantage the Error object has over the Err object is that it contains many more properties directly related to the database server to which it's connected. Because in database servers several errors can occur related to one problem, the Error object can return each error number in the order it is raised. The Err object returns only the last error that occurred. Although the Errors object will be used only when working with older Visual Basic 6 ActiveX controls, it is still important to understand the usage of the Errors object.

When an Error Occurs

When an error occurs in your application, the first question you want answered is, "What process should be performed?" However, the second question is more important: "Which error routine will handle the error?" Every time an On Error statement is executed, another error handling routine is enabled. The only way an On Error statement is disabled is by executing the On Error GoTo 0 statement or by exiting the procedure where the routine was enabled. The active error handler is the one in which code execution is currently taking place.

Now the fun begins! When an error occurs within a procedure without an enabled error handling routine, or an error occurs within the error handling routine itself, Visual Basic will search the calls stack for another enabled error handling routine. The calls stack is the sequence of calls that leads to the currently executing procedure. To display the calls stack yourself (see Figure 13.1), choose Call Stack from the Debug menu.

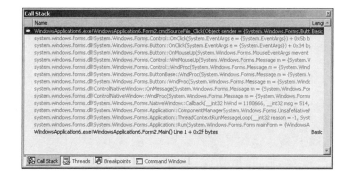

FIGURE 13.1

Viewing the list of procedures in the call stack when an error occurs.

Note   The call stack is available only when the program is halted because of an error or break point.

To understand how this all works, suppose the following sequence of calls has been made in your application as shown in Figure 13.2. The order of execution is listed here:

1. A command button click event calls subroutine A.

2. Subroutine A then makes a call to function B.

3. Function B calls subroutine C.

Whichever routine is currently processing, the routines that precede it are pending—waiting for control to be returned to them. Now if an error occurs in subroutine C and an error handler isn't enabled or none is coded for the routine, Visual Basic will search backward through the pending procedures in the calls stack. First it will look at Function B, then Subroutine A, then the initial Click event, looking for an enabled error handling routine. The search will go no further back than the top of the current calls stack.

If it doesn't find any enabled error handler, Visual Basic will present the default error message and halt the application's execution. If an enabled error handling routine is found, execution will continue in that routine as if the error occurred in the same procedure that contains the error handler itself. If you haven't caught up to the error yet, here's the problem with all this: If a Resume or Resume Next statement is executed in the error handling routine, control will be returned as follows:

13

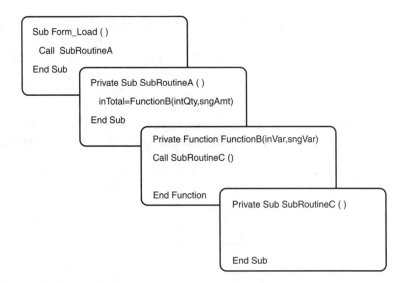

FIGURE **13.2**

A visual diagram of a call stack list.

```
Sub Form_Load ( )
   Call  SubRoutineA
End Sub
      Private Sub SubRoutineA ( )
         inTotal=FunctionB(intQty,sngAmt)
      End Sub
            Private Function FunctionB(inVar,sngVar)
            Call SubRoutineC ()

            End Function
                  Private Sub SubRoutineC ( )



                  End Sub
```

- Resume—The call to the procedure that was just *executed* is re-executed.
- Resume Next—Execution returns to the statement following the last statement executed in the current routine (the one containing the error handling routine).

The common thread here is that the statement to be executed is in the routine in which the error handling routine was found; not necessarily in the routine where the error occurred. If you don't remember this, and don't code an error handler in every routine you create, your code might perform in ways you didn't intend. Also, if the error routine can't handle the error that occurred, use the Raise method to generate an error that will be handled by the error handling routine in the calling procedure.

Introducing Structured Exception Handling

Now that you've reviewed the old standard of global error handling in Visual Basic, let's look at the new way of doing things, because the global error handling lacked the control really needed for your application—and didn't help the readability of the code, either. Also, the global On Error processing required you to do an awful lot of work to get it right. In Visual Basic. NET you can use the new structured error handling features. These features respond to the two issues mentioned in the preceding. They provide you with the control you need to deal with errors and keep the readability of the code in control.

Note

You can use either of the two error handling methods in your application's procedures. However, you can't use both methods in the same procedure.

Structured exception handling enables you to define code blocks that are marked as protected. Protected code is a section or block that's being checked by one or more associated error handlers. Each handler specifies some form of condition for the type of exception it handles. When an exception is raised by code in a protected block, the set of corresponding handlers is searched in order, and the first one with a matching condition is executed. You can add structured error handling to your application by using the `Try...Catch...Finally` statement.

The `Try...Catch...Finally` Process

The `Try...Catch...Finally` syntax is similar to the syntax you are familiar with in the `Select Case` or `While` statement, with exceptions, protected blocks of code, and conditions. Before you see how to use this new error process, look at the statement's syntax and what the different parts really do. The syntax of this statement is shown here with a description of the arguments in Table 13.3:

```
Try
    tryStatements
[Catch₁ [exception [As type]] [When expression]
    CatchStatements₁
[Exit Try]
[Catch₂ [exception [As type]] [When expression]
    CatchStatements₂
[Exit Try]
[Catchₙ [exception [As type]] [When expression]
    CatchStatementsₙ
[Exit Try]
[Finally]
    finallyStatements
End Try
```

TABLE 13.3 Arguments of the `Try...Catch...Finally` Statement

Argument	Description
tryStatements	Block of code where the error can occur.
exception	Any variable name. The initial value is that of the error that occurred.
type	Specifies the type of condition.
expression	Any expression that describes the condition.
CatchStatements	The block of code that will handle the errors that have occurred in the associated `Try` block.
Exit Try	Statement that breaks out of the `Try...Catch...Finally` process. Execution will resume immediately following the `End Try` statement.
finallyStatements	Block of code executed after all other error processing is done.

13

Note   If an error occurs that you haven't handled, Visual Basic still will provide the normal error message to users, as if no error handling process was in place.

The *tryStatements* argument contains the protected code where an error can occur, whereas *catchStatements* contain the code to handle any error that does occur. If an error occurs in *tryStatements*, program control is passed to the appropriate *catchStatement* for disposition. The *exception* is an instance of the Exception class corresponding to the error that occurred in *tryStatements*. The Exception class instance contains information about the error including, among other things, its number and message. You can use the Exception object in the error handling process the same way you would use the ERR object in the unstructured error processing.

The Try Block

The Try block contains the code section you want your error handler to monitor. If an error occurs during execution of any of the code in this section, Visual Basic then examines each Catch statement within Try...Catch...Finally until it finds one whose condition matches that error. If one is found, control transfers to the first line of code in the Catch block. This process continues through the all Catch statements until a matching Catch block is found. If none is found, an error is produced.

 In this new method of error handling, errors are said to be *thrown* and then *caught* in the Catch block.

The Catch Block

If an exception occurs while processing the Try block, each Catch statement is examined in order to determine whether it handles the occurring exception. The identifier specified in a Catch clause represents the thrown exception. A Catch clause with no condition will catch all exceptions derived from System.Exception object. A Catch clause with a condition will catch only exceptions whose types are the same as the type of the condition. The type must be System.Exception or a type derived from it. A Catch clause with a When clause will catch exceptions only when the expression evaluates to True. A When clause is applied only after checking the type of the exception; the expression can refer to the identifier representing the exception.

If a Catch clause handles the exception, execution transfers to that block. At the end of the block, execution will transfer to the Finally block, if it exists; otherwise, execution will be transferred to the first statement following the Try statement.

The `Try` statement won't handle any exceptions thrown in a `Catch` block.

An example of a `Catch` block that traps an overflow exception is as follows:

```
Catch e As OverflowException
         MsgBox("An overflow exception has occurred!")
```

You can trap many different exceptions and find them in the drop-down list displayed when you are entering the `Catch` code (see Figure 13.3).

FIGURE 13.3

Selecting an exception to trap in a Catch *statement.*

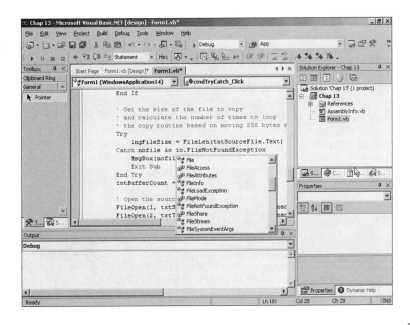

The `Finally` Block

A `Finally` block is always executed when execution leaves any part of the `Try` statement. No explicit action is required to execute the `Finally` block. When the execution of the code leaves the `Try` statement, the system will automatically execute the `Finally` block and transfer execution to its intended destination.

Note The `Finally` block is executed regardless of how execution leaves the `Try` statement.

13

Raising Exceptions

A program indicates that an exception condition has occurred by executing a `Throw` statement. In addition to the system errors that generate a `Throw` statement, you also can issue your own throw to force an error to occur, as in the following example:

```
Sub ForceError()
    Throw New Exception("Your File Cannot Be Found")
End Sub

Private Sub Button1_Click(ByVal sender As Object, _
        ByVal e As System.EventArgs) Handles Button1.Click
    Try
        ForceError()
        Catch myErr As Exception
            MsgBox("Exception in Code: " + myErr.Message, _
                    MsgBoxStyle.Critical)
    End Try
End Sub
```

If you execute this code, the result would resemble Figure 13.4.

FIGURE 13.4

Throwing an exception in your code.

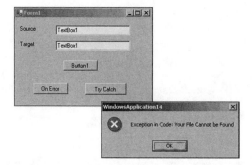

Converting from an `On Error Goto... Resume`

Because there's no equivalent for the `Resume` statement in the `Try...Catch...Finally` statement, converting your code from the standard `On Error` with a `Resume` gets a little tricky. Here is an example of code using the `On Error` and `Resume` statements:

```
Private Sub Procedure_1()
    On Error Goto ErrorHandler
    ' your processing code goes here
    ' this code can also be considered
    ' protected code.
    Exit Sub
ErrorHandler:
    'Your Error handling code goes here
    Resume
End Sub
```

The `Resume` statement enables you to rerun the line that originally caused the error. This functionality does not exist within a `Try` block. To perform the same process, you would use nested `Try` statements as follows:

```
Private Sub Procedure_1()
   Try
   ' your protected code goes here
   Try
   ' the line or lines of code that you might need
   ' to do a resume on.
      Catch
         'code that fixes the problem
   End Try
   ' More protected code goes here
   Catch
      ' Error handling code goes here
   End Try
End Sub
```

However, this code will not repeat endlessly without adding a lot of extra code to perform this repeating. You can try fixing it once and then produce an error message to the user.

Handling Errors

When you've decided how you want to handle the errors you are anticipating in the routines of your application, you must decide whether to use the old `On Error` or the new `Try...Catch...Finally` processing. After you make that decision you can start writing the actual error handling process.

If you use the `On Error` process you first need to add a line label to mark the beginning of the error handling routine. Use a descriptive name for the label and follow it with a colon (`:`). Now code the body of the error handling routine. This code actually handles the error, usually by using a `Select` statement to check for the error codes likely to occur in this procedure and specifying the action to be taken for each of them. You also should add the `else` statement to the `Select` statement, just in case an error has occurred that you didn't anticipate.

If you use the `Try...Catch...Finally` process, you first must decide what you want included in the `Try` block. Now code all `Catch` statements for the errors you want to trap; remember that this is the code that actually handles the error. Code a `Catch` statement without a condition, just in case an error has occurred that you didn't anticipate. Finally, code a `Finally` statement for any process that you want finished before leaving the `Try...Catch...Finally` process.

13

The biggest difference between the two types of error handling methods is that with `Try...Catch...Finally`, you know exactly where the error is being trapped. The `On Error` method, just turns on trapping, so then if an error occurs anywhere within the current scope, you will be transferred to the error routines. Of course, knowing the exact section of code that caused the error makes more sense.

Abort, Retry, or Cancel

The hardest part of the error handling process is deciding what you want the application to do when the error occurs. Some errors can be fixed and the application can continue; others require that you close the application to fix it. Other errors can be ignored if they aren't detrimental to the application process.

Before getting into the process of creating an error handler, let's look at an example for the `Try...Catch...Finally` error handler in Visual Basic. You also will see a comparison of the `On Error` process and how the error handling example would look in using it. To see how to use the basic structure of an error handling routine, start a new project in Visual Basic and add two textbox, label, and button controls to the default form, as shown in Figure 13.5. We will add code to both buttons—one for the `On Error` process and the other for the `Try...Catch...Finally` process.

FIGURE 13.5

Creating a demo application to test the error handling concepts.

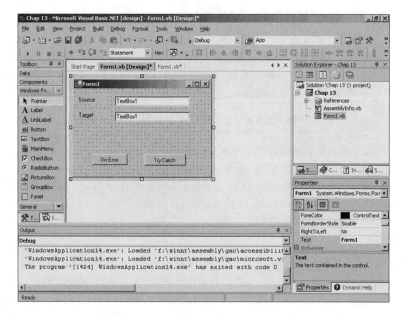

Using the On Error Process

For the On Error button, use the code in Listing 13.1, which you created in the FileCopy project on Day 1. You might notice that the code is simplified so that you can concentrate on the error handling process.

LISTING 13.1   FILECOPY.TXT: A Subset of the File Copy Code from Day 1

```
Private Sub cmdOnError_Click(ByVal sender As System.Object, _
  ByVal e As System.EventArgs) Handles cmdOnError.Click

    Dim lngFileSize As Long
    Dim intLoopCtr As Integer
    Dim intBufferCount As Integer
    Dim strInByte As String
    'Set the length of the strInbyte string
    strInByte = Space(256)
    ' If the destination file exists, ask the user if they
    ' want to continue
    If Dir(txtTargetFile.Text) <> "" Then
        If MsgBox(txtTargetFile.Text & vbCrLf & _
            " already exists. Copy over old file?", _
              MsgBoxStyle.OKCancel) = MsgBoxResult.Cancel Then
        End If
    End If

    ' Get the size of the file to copy
    ' and calculate the number of times to loop
    ' the copy routine based on moving 256 bytes at a time
    lngFileSize = FileLen(txtTargetFile.Text)
    intBufferCount = lngFileSize / 256

    ' Open the source and destination files
    FileOpen(1, txtSourceFile.Text, OpenMode.Binary)
    FileOpen(2, txtTargetFile.Text, OpenMode.Binary)

    ' This routine loops until the entire file is copied
    For intLoopCtr = 1 To intBufferCount + 1
        FileGet(1, strInByte)
        FilePut(2, strInByte)
    Next intLoopCtr

    ' After the copy is complete close both files
    FileClose(1)    ' Close file.
    FileClose(2)    ' Close file.
    ' Inform the user that the function is complete
    MsgBox("Copy function complete", MsgBoxStyle.Information)
End Sub
```

13

For a file copy process, some the errors that could occur are

- File not found

- Device I/O error

- Disk full

To handle these errors, create a routine that resembles the one in Listing 13.2.

LISTING 13.2   ERROREX1.TXT: A Sample Error Routine for a File Copy Process

```
FileCopyError:
    On Error Goto 0
    Select Case Err().Number
        Case 53 'File not found
            MsgBox(CStr(Err().Number) & " — " & Err().Description, _
                vbOKOnly, Me.Text)
        Case 57 'Device I/O error
            MsgBox(CStr(Err().Number) & " — " & Err().Description, _
                vbOKOnly, Me.Text)
        Case 61 'Disk full
            MsgBox(CStr(Err().Number) & " — " & Err().Description, _
                vbOKOnly, Me.Text)
        Case Else 'For unanticipated Errors
            MsgBox(CStr(Err().Number) & " — " & Err().Description, _
                vbOKOnly, Me.Text)
    End Select
```

Note   This error routine will only report what the error was; not correct it. If you want to add code to correct one or more of these errors, simply include that code in the Case statement for that error. You then can decide whether the solution enables you to continue the operation; if it does, you also must add a Resume statement.

This routine is added to the cmdOnError_Click event routine along with the On Error statement at the beginning of the routine, as shown in Listing 13.3.

LISTING 13.3   OnErrorTest.Txt: Enhancing the Error Handling Procedure

```
Private Sub cmdOnError_Click(ByVal sender As System.Object, _
  ByVal e As System.EventArgs) Handles cmdOnError.Click

Dim lngFileSize As Long
Dim intLoopCtr As Integer
Dim intBufferCount As Integer
```

LISTING 13.3   continued

```
Dim strInByte As String * 256

On Error GoTo FileCopyError
'
'BODY OF ROUTINE GOES HERE
'
Exit Sub
'
FileCopyError:
'
'ERROR HANDLING ROUTINE GOES HERE (use code from Listing 13.2)
'
End Sub
```

In addition to handling the anticipated errors, you also should add code that will handle any unexpected errors. You usually can do this by adding the `Case Else` statement to the `Select...End Select` statement group:

```
Case Else 'Unexpected
    MsgBox(CStr(Err.Number) & "—" & _
        Err.Description, vbOKCancel, App.Title)
```

Add the error handling routine to the file copy code in Listing 13.1 and enter an incorrect filename. This will generate an error message telling you that the filename isn't found. You then can re-enter the name and try again. Also notice that this error routine doesn't use the `Resume` statement to exit the error handler. This is because any of the errors that have occurred are all related to the copy operation; after the error occurs, there's no easy way to continue the copy. It's better to just start over.

Using the `Try...Catch...Finally` Process

For the `Try Catch` button we will start with the same code shown in Listing 13.1. However, the error processing will look very different. Listing 13.4 shows how to use the `Try...Catch...Finally` statements in an example.

13

LISTING 13.4   TRYCATCH.TXT: Using `Try...Catch...Finally` to Trap Errors

```
Private Sub cmdTryCatch_Click(ByVal sender As System.Object, _
   ByVal e As System.EventArgs) Handles cmdTryCatch.Click
    Dim lngFileSize As Long
    Dim intLoopCtr As Integer
    Dim intBufferCount As Integer
    Dim strInByte As String
    'Set the length of the strInbyte string
    strInByte = Space(256)
```

LISTING 13.4   continued

```
    ' If the destination file exists, ask the user if they
    ' want to continue
    If Dir(txtTargetFile.Text) <> "" Then
        If MsgBox(txtTargetFile.Text & vbCrLf & _
            " already exists. Copy over old file?", _
                MsgBoxStyle.OKCancel) = MsgBoxResult.Cancel Then
        End If
    End If

    ' Get the size of the file to copy
    ' and calculate the number of times to loop
    ' the copy routine based on moving 256 bytes at a time
    Try
        lngFileSize = FileLen(txtSourceFile.Text)
        catch nofile as io.FileNotFoundException
        MsgBox(nofile.Message)
        Exit Sub
    End Try
    intBufferCount = lngFileSize / 256

    ' Open the source and destination files
    FileOpen(1, txtSourceFile.Text, OpenMode.Binary)
    FileOpen(2, txtTargetFile.Text, OpenMode.Binary)

    ' This routine loops until the entire file is copied
    Try
        For intLoopCtr = 1 To intBufferCount + 1
            FileGet(1, strInByte)
            FilePut(2, strInByte)
        Next intLoopCtr
    catch DiskFull as IO.FileLoadException
        MsgBox("Disk is Full, Cannot complete copy", MsgBoxStyle.Critical)
    Catch IOError As IO.IOException
        MsgBox("An IO error has occurred", MsgBoxStyle.Critical)
    Catch
        MsgBox("An unexpected Error has occurred", MsgBoxStyle.Critical)
    Finally
        FileClose(1)     ' Close file.
        FileClose(2)     ' Close file.
    End Try

    ' After the copy is complete close both files
    ' Inform the user that the function is complete
    MsgBox("Copy function complete", MsgBoxStyle.Information)
End Sub
```

Try running the application again and use the Try Catch button instead. You should see the appropriate message displayed.

Whenever you start adding the error handling routines to your application, you will quickly see that some code is being repeated over and over again. This will cause problems when you have to change the way a particular error is being handled. Also, the more code you add to the application, the more complex it will become. With some careful planning, you can reduce the amount of code you add for error handling by writing a few procedures that the error routines will call to handle the more common error situations.

Testing the Error Routine

When you are creating and testing your application, it's very important to test every error routine you add to the application. One way to do this is to change the code to produce each error that might happen. An easier way, depending on the error handling process you are using, is to make the error happen by using the `Raise` method. This enables you to generate any error that you want from within your code. The syntax of the `Raise` method is

```
Err.Raise number, source, description, helpfile, helpcontext
```

Or, you can call the method by passing the name of each argument and its value:

```
Err.Raise Number:=53 ' File not found
```

To see how this statement works, add it immediately after the first `Try` statement in the `TryCatch` routine; then run the application to see what happens. You should get the message box you coded in the error handling routine.

The `Raise` method of the `Err` object also can be used to create custom errors for your application. Some conditions that you consider errors can occur in your application but Visual Basic considers "legal" code processing. For these types of problems you can create your own error numbers; when they occur, you can `raise` them and deal with them as you see fit. You also can use the other properties of the `Raise` method to set a topic in a help file that users can view.

There's also a new statement that you can use to force errors or to create custom errors in a `Try...Catch...Finally` process. The `Throw` statement syntax is as follows:

```
Throw New Exception(Expression)
```

By using this statement in a `Try` block, you can test your `Catch` processing. Add the following statement to the first `Try...Catch` process:

```
Throw New io.FileNotFoundException()
```

This will cause the `Catch` block to display the message box as coded.

13

Summary

Today, you saw what goes into making your application error free. However, as you well know, there's no such thing as an error-free application. The errors that can occur in the application—and how you handle them—are major design issues that you must deal with for your application. When designing the error handling routines, the more time you spend anticipating errors that might occur, the better your application will be. It all depends on how good you want the application to appear to users. If an error occurs, do you want users to possibly lose hours of work or important data? Hopefully the answer to both is no.

By coding routines that handle any error that might happen, you are making the application easier to use. You have seen how to use the statements and objects provided by Visual Basic to process the errors and maintain the error handling routines. You also learned how to force an error to occur to test the error routines you have created. Finally, by using the Visual Basic methods to force an error, you can create your own errors in the application to process any logic errors that you want to handle as an error.

Q&A

Q What types of errors can be fixed for the program to continue?

A The errors that can be fixed during execution of the application usually are nondestructive. This means that the error hasn't caused any data problems. An example of a fixable error is `Disk Not Ready`.

Q What does an `On Error` command do?

A The `On Error` statement enables you to control the error handling process.

Q What's an `Err` object?

A The `Err` object contains information about an error that has just occurred.

Q What does the `Try...Catch...Finally` statement do?

A The `Try...Catch...Finally` statement allows you to execute a particular block of statements; then, if a specified exception occurs, the code is said to *throw* the exception, and you *catch* it with the appropriate `Catch` statement

Q How would you use a `Throw` statement?

A The `Throw` statement is used to create an exception that can be handled by your application code using either the `Try...Catch...Finally` statement or the `On Error Goto` statement. The syntax of the `Throw` statement is

```
Throw New System.Exception()
```

Q What information does the Calls Stack dialog box give you?

A The Calls Stack dialog box displays all the active procedures that are not yet completed. It can be used to trace the history of calls that got you to the current statement in the application.

Workshop

The Workshop provides quiz questions to solidify your understanding of the material covered and exercises so you can use what you've learned. Try to understand the quiz and exercise answers before continuing on to the tomorrow's lesson. Answers are provided in Appendix A, "Answers to Quizzes and Exercises."

Quiz

1. What's an error trap?

2. What are the two types of runtime errors?

3. What's the difference between structured and unstructured error handling?

Exercise

Open the Address Book application that you have been creating, and determine where you might want to add some error handling. Then design and add the `Try...Catch...Finally` statements and include them in the application. Finally, using the `Throw` method, test each of the errors that you chose to trap.

13

DAY 14

Testing and Debugging the Application

Designing and creating your application is only part of the total process you must perform to fully complete the application. When you've finished writing the application, you must test it to make sure that it works correctly; then if there are any problems, debug it and fix those problems. The problem with testing and debugging is that it takes lots of time and effort to do it properly. Unfortunately, most programmers don't want to take the time to do it properly. This will cause problems for users when bugs make themselves known.

Today's lesson will provide some ideas and tips on testing and debugging your application. You also will explore the tools that Visual Basic .NET has included to assist you in the process. Finally, you will see how to use some of the Visual Basic features that have been added to identify where a problem exists even after the application is in use. What's new in this release of Visual Basic is that the testing and debugging environment has been moved to the Visual Studio environment. This enables you to use the same tools to debug a Web application or use any other language included in Visual Studio .NET.

Understanding What Bugs Are

Before jumping into the tools and techniques of debugging your application, it's a good idea to understand what bugs are and how a user would see a bug. We also will discuss the differences between testing and debugging, and how they are tightly related. Someone once said that testing is a never-ending process, or, to put it another way, there will always be one more bug. But what are bugs? How do we find and then fix them? Back when computers took up whole rooms and used hot vacuum tubes, finding bugs really was quite simple; all you had to do was walk into the computer and remove the dead bugs that were preventing the computer's physical switches from closing. Thus, the term *debugging* was born. Unfortunately, it isn't that simple anymore.

NEW TERM The debugging process is much more complicated, both in terms of what's considered a bug and how bugs are found. Programmers now must test and then debug their application code using time, logic, and the tools available from the development system. But what is *testing* and what is debugging? Testing is the process by which applications are put through every possible keystroke, mouse click, and input; these test cases hopefully exercise every line of code in the application. It's during this process that any indication of an application error should be located.

After a problem is found, the debugging process starts. Debugging is a multipart process that determines the problem and its location in the code and then fixes it. When the problem is fixed, you must go back and rerun the test that caused the error to see whether you really fixed it. If the problem is resolved you can move on to the next test.

The word *bug* can mean different things to different people. Bugs range from the annoying (misspellings) to the serious (Windows terminates), to the deadly (load data). To your application's users, a bug is anything that doesn't conform to their expected results. To programmers a bug is something that produces unexpected results or prevents the application from executing.

These two definitions might sound similar; however, if you take a closer look you will find that they are very different. If an application is executing properly but doesn't perform the tasks or actions that initially were required of it, users could consider it a bug. However, the programmer would say that it's performing as designed; thus to users a bug is anything unexpected (even bad answers, as opposed to incorrect answers), whereas programmers define a bug as a mistake in the technical design and execution of the application.

When testing and debugging your application, you will face many problems that relate to finding and fixing the bugs. Although this will sound a little trite, the best way to debug the application is to take the time to carefully plan and design the application before you begin coding. Beyond that, you should create a physical list of the tests you want to perform on the application during the testing and debugging process. This will prevent you from bouncing from one test to another without any plan. Test the application in a logical sequence so that after you test a portion of the code you can be confident that it will work.

Finding the Problems

Finding where a problem happened in a computer program isn't as easy as it sounds. The fact that you are trying to accomplish it in a Windows environment makes it that much more difficult. Because Visual Basic stops application execution when a problem occurs, this enables you to at least identify the section of code to look at. Often Visual Basic displays an error message, like the one shown in Figure 14.1, which tells you the error. However, it doesn't tell you where it happened or how to fix it.

FIGURE 14.1

A typical error message from Visual Basic during the testing process.

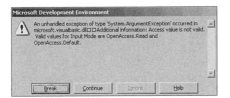

Even more confusing is that the actual problem or error might have occurred earlier—in an entirely different area of the program—but has manifested at this time. What this means in English is that you will have to work backward from the point of the problem to find the real culprit—almost like solving a crime. You have clues, but you have to look carefully for the guilty line of code.

Luckily for us, Visual Basic provides some very good tools to assist you when testing and debugging your application. These tools enable you to look at how the application logic flows from one routine to another. It also enables you to observe how variables and property settings change during the execution of the application. What you're really doing is lifting the hood of your application and looking at the engine.

You can make the testing and debugging process much simpler by adhering to the following concepts and techniques:

- Make sure that the `Option Explicit` parameter is set (it's usually the default) to prevent misspelled variable and object names.
- Include well-designed error handling routines (making use of the new `Try...Catch` process, as discussed on Day 13) to trap many of the problems that can occur.

14

- Keep your routines fairly short and easy to follow.

- Visual Basic .NET now formats your code automatically, indenting where needed.

- Name your forms, objects, and variables logically so that you can instantly know what they are or what they do.

These suggestions will help you resolve many of the problems that can pop up. These are the syntax, compile, or runtime errors. However, the problems you are checking for when you test and debug the application are the logic errors in your code. Logic errors are the toughest type of problem to find and fix because usually they occur further down the execution path in the application.

For example, an incorrect result could be produced at the conclusion of a long series of calculations. In debugging, the task is to determine what and where something went wrong. It could be that you forgot to initialize a variable, chose the wrong operator or function, or used an incorrect formula. Making matters worse, logic problems can be caused by bad data input, which means a particular problem might not always happen.

NEW TERM Sometimes, these problems generate a runtime error that prevents the application from continuing. These bugs usually are found only by checking the results that the application returns against what the results should have been. This means we have to perform the same functions and operations by hand that the application would do on the computer, which enables us to check the answers. This is known as *desk checking* the application. This technique got its name because programmers sat at their desks reading the application code and performing the actions of the application on paper. These days, automated debugging tools have taken the place of the pencil and paper in the desk checking process, although it still should be done.

Unfortunately, there are no magic tricks in the debugging process and there is no specific sequence of steps that will work every time you try them. Basically, debugging helps you understand what's going on during application execution. The Visual Basic–supplied debugging tools give you a snapshot of your application at any given moment in the process. The better you understand how your application works, the faster you can find the bugs.

The Debugging Environment

Visual Basic offers several very good tools for testing and debugging your application. These tools include breakpoint processing, Watch expressions, single-step processing, and the capability to display the contents of variables and properties. You also can modify code and change variable or property values during application execution, and specify the next statement to be executed. To test and debug an application, you must understand the three unique modes that you will be working in. You should already be somewhat familiar with two of these modes.

When you are in the process of creating or coding your application, you are in Visual Basic's Design mode. When you are running the application, you are in Run mode. During the debugging process, you will be working in the third mode, called *Break mode*, which suspends application execution so that you can examine and alter any data or code. To know which mode you are in requires you to look only as far as the Visual Basic title bar, which will always display the current mode (see Figure 14.2). Table 14.1 describes each of these three modes and the actions you can take.

Current mode displayed

Figure 14.2

The Visual Basic title bar will always display the current mode enclosed in square brackets.

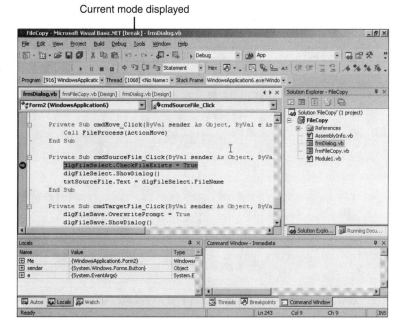

Table 14.1   The Actions of the Three Visual Basic Operating Modes

Mode	Description
Design	Most of the work of creating an application is done at design time. You can design forms, draw controls, write code, and use the Properties window to set or view any property settings. However, you can't execute any code or use the available debugging tools, except for setting breakpoints and creating watch expressions.
Run	When you execute the application, you interact with the application the same as the users. You can view code but you can't change it.
Break	Application execution is suspended. You can view and edit code, examine or modify data, restart the application, stop execution, or continue execution from the same point.

14

The Debugging Toolbars

On the standard toolbar, Visual Basic provides three buttons that enable you to quickly change from one mode to another (see Figure 14.3).

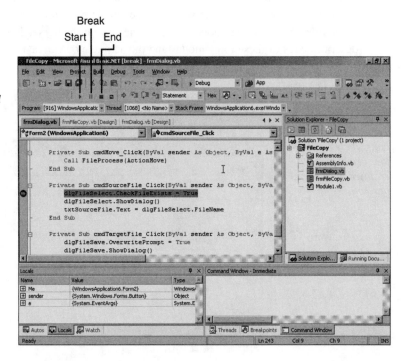

FIGURE 14.3

The three mode buttons—Start, Break, and End—on the standard toolbar offer quick access to control the testing process of the application.

One or more of these buttons will be available depending on whether Visual Basic is in Run, Design, or Break mode. Table 14.2 lists the different modes each button is available in.

TABLE 14.2 The Three Modes and the Available Buttons

Mode	Buttons Available
Design time	Start
Runtime	Break All, Stop Debugging
Break	Continue (when in Break mode, the Start button becomes the Continue button), Stop Debugging

In addition to the mode buttons, Visual Basic provides a Debug toolbar (see Figure 14.4) that you can optionally display; alternatively, you can use the Debug menu instead. Table 14.3 describes each function.

FIGURE 14.4

The optional Debug toolbar provides many of Visual Basic's debugging functions.

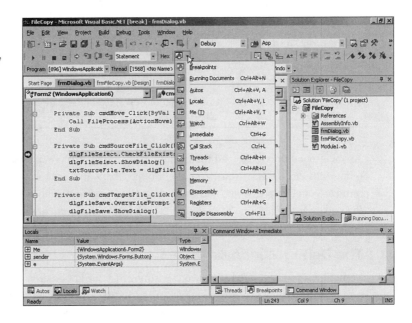

TABLE 14.3   The Available Debugging Functions and Their Purposes

Debugging Feature	Purpose
Insert Breakpoint	Sets a line in the code where Visual Basic suspends application execution
Step Into	Executes the next executable line of code in the application and steps into any procedure
Step Over	Executes the next executable line of code in the application without stepping into any procedure
Step Out	Executes the remainder of the current procedure and breaks at the next line in the calling procedure
Locals Window	Displays the current value of any local variables
Immediate Window	Enables you to execute code or display any values while the application is in Break mode
Watch Window	Displays the values of selected expressions
Quick Watch	Lists the current value of an expression while the application is in Break mode
Call Stack	While in Break mode, presents a dialog box that displays all the called procedures that haven't yet run to completion
Breakpoints	Displays all breakpoints that exist in the application

14

TABLE 14.3   continued

Debugging Feature	Purpose
Modules	Displays all the modules (exe, dll, and so forth) that the application has called
Threads	Allows you to view thread information and manipulate threads when you are testing a multithreaded program

As mentioned previously, all these toolbar functions also are available on the Debug menu. Besides the functions from the toolbar, there also are the options to add and remove Watch expressions, and show the next executable statement. Also, after you place the cursor at a given line of code, you can execute the application until it hits the line with the cursor on it.

The Debug Windows

Sometimes you will need to execute portions of your application code to find the cause of a problem. In most cases you also will have to analyze what's happening to the data. You might find that the problem is in a variable or a property with an invalid value in it. You must find out how and why the value was incorrect. With the different debugging windows, you can monitor the values of expressions and variables while stepping through the statements in your application. You will use three different debugging windows during this process:

- Immediate window
- Watch window
- Locals window

Working in conjunction with the code window, you will use these three windows to fully test and debug your application. The Immediate window displays information from one of two possible areas. By using the Debug object (discussed later in today's lesson), you can have any value or expression printed in this window during the execution of the application. When in Break mode, you also can use the Print command variant to display the contents of any variable, property, or calculation, as shown in Figure 14.5.

On the other hand, the Watch window will display the values of any variable or expression that you've chosen to track (see Figure 14.6).

FIGURE 14.5

Using the Immediate window to visually check the contents of any variable or property value in the application.

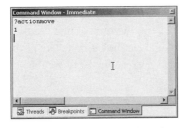

FIGURE 14.6

Using the Watch window to track expressions in the application.

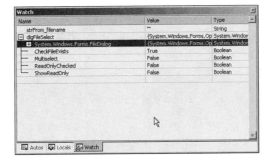

If the statement at which the application is currently stopped is within the specified context of the Watch expression, the value for that expression is displayed. Otherwise, the value column will display a message that the statement isn't in context. Finally, the Locals window displays the value of any variables that are within the scope of the current procedure. As the execution of the application flows from one procedure to another, the Locals window (see Figure 14.7) changes to reflect only those variables applicable to the current procedure.

FIGURE 14.7

The Locals window displays all local variables and all properties associated with the current form.

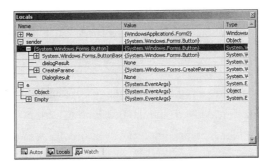

At design time you can modify the design or code of the application; however, you can't see how the changes will affect the way the application will execute. At runtime you can watch how the application will execute; however, you can't change the code or any of the values being processed. By using the Break mode, you can halt the execution of the application and look at a snapshot of its condition at that moment. Variable and property values are retained so that you can analyze the current state of the application and enter changes that affect how the application executes. Here are the actions that you can take while the application is in Break mode:

- Modify application code
- View any changes to the user interface (form changes)
- Determine the procedures that have been called
- Track and display the values of any variables, properties, and statements
- Modify any values necessary
- Specify the next statement you want to be executed
- Execute Visual Basic statements in the Immediate window

When testing and debugging the application, you might want to halt the application at certain places in the code where you think the problem might have started. This is one of the main reasons Visual Basic enables you to set breakpoints. A *breakpoint* defines a statement or set of conditions at which Visual Basic will automatically stop the execution of the application and put it into Break mode without running the statement containing the breakpoint. You can enter Break mode by doing any of the following operations while the application is executing:

- Press the Ctrl+Break keys
- Choose Break from the Run menu
- Click Break on the toolbar

It's possible to suspend execution when the application is between processing of events. When this happens, execution doesn't stop at a specific line but Visual Basic switches to Break mode anyway. You also can enter Break mode automatically whenever one of the following conditions occurs:

- A statement generates a runtime error that wasn't handled by an error handler.
- A runtime error is generated, and the Break on All Errors option is selected.
- A defined conditional breakpoint changes or becomes True, depending on how you defined it.
- Execution encounters a line that contains an unconditional breakpoint.
- Execution reaches a Stop statement.

Setting a Breakpoint

Because there are several types of breakpoints, there are different ways of adding them to your code:

- An *unconditional* breakpoint causes execution to stop at a statement any time the statement is executed.
- A *conditional* breakpoint causes execution to stop at a statement only when a defined condition occurs.

Adding unconditional breakpoints to your application can be done in one of the following ways:

- Click in the border to the left of the statement.
- Select the statement and press F9.
- Select the statement and then right-click it. From the pop-up menu, choose Insert Breakpoint.
- Select the statement and then choose Insert Breakpoint from the Debug menu.

Condition breakpoints require a little understanding before you use them. A conditional breakpoint really is an unconditional breakpoint with an expression of some type attached to it. Such breakpoints enable you to stop at a selected statement if a defined expression is True or if a variable's value has changed. To set a conditional breakpoint, you can do one of the following to display the Breakpoint Properties dialog box:

- Select the statement, right-click, and choose New Breakpoint from the pop-up menu.
- Select an existing breakpoint, right-click, and choose Breakpoint Properties.
- Select the statement and choose New Breakpoint from the Debug menu.
- Select the statement and choose the New Breakpoint button from the toolbar.

When the New Breakpoint dialog box is displayed (see Figure 14.8), the Function tab is shown by default.

This tab displays the default break information that will be used for the breakpoint. Depending on the location of the mouse cursor when you right-click, the breakpoint will display the associated function, variable, or expression. The second tab, File, displays the position of the new breakpoint in relation to the file it's in (see Figure 14.9).

14

FIGURE **14.8**

Setting a new break-point using the New Breakpoint dialog box.

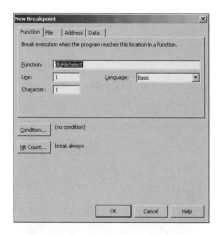

FIGURE **14.9**

Working with the filename and line number for setting a breakpoint.

At any time you can set a condition on the breakpoint by clicking the Condition button to display the Breakpoint Condition dialog box (see Figure 14.10). On this dialog box, you can specify whether to break when a variable or expression changes, or evaluates to True.

FIGURE **14.10**

Setting a condition for a breakpoint.

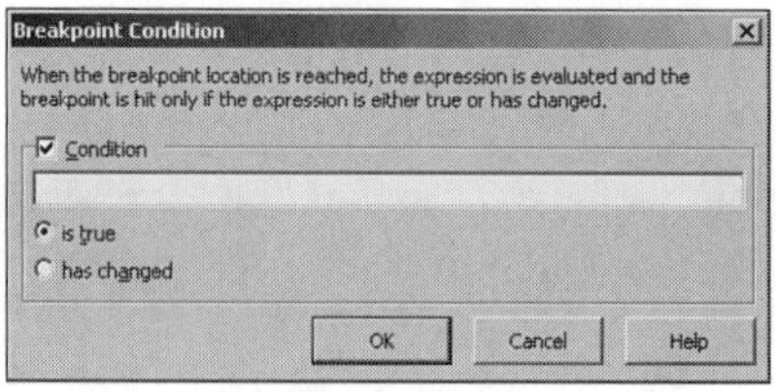

The Reset Hit Count button (see Figure 14.11) enables you to set a breakpoint depending on how many times a statement has been executed.

FIGURE 14.11

Choosing to stop when a statement executes a specified number of times.

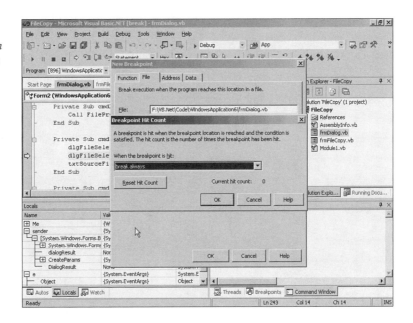

> **Note**
>
> The Hit Count display feature is helpful when you need to know how many times a loop is processed before an error occurs; if so, you can stop after a certain statement is executed a set number of times.

Finally, when a breakpoint is set, Visual Basic will highlight the selected line in bold, using the colors specified in the Editor Format tab on the Options dialog box from the Tools menu. Visual Basic also will highlight the current statement in the code window. Both highlights also are shown in Figure 14.12 with the associated margin indicators.

Another feature has been added to Visual Basic .NET to enhance breakpoint processing: Place the mouse over a breakpoint, and the breakpoint information is displayed in a ToolTip (see Figure 14.13).

14

FIGURE 14.12

Breakpoints and the current statement displayed in the Code Editor.

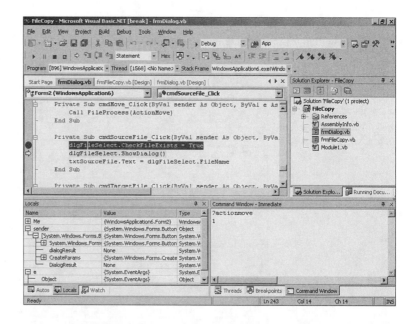

FIGURE 14.13

Display the information for a breakpoint by placing the mouse pointer on the breakpoint itself.

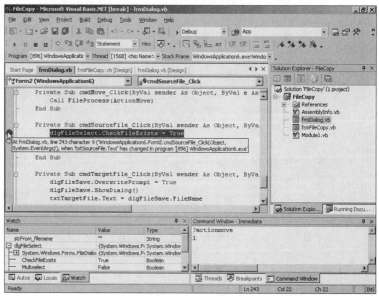

After you reach a breakpoint and the application stops, you can examine the application's current condition by moving the focus among the forms and modules of your application, the Code window, and the debugging windows. A breakpoint stops the application just before executing the line that contains the breakpoint.

Breakpoints are saved with the project and are automatically reconfigured when you open the project the next time. This enables you to stop testing, close the project, and come back to it later without having to remember what breakpoints you had.

Stepping Through the Code

If you want to observe what happens when that line is executed, you must use Step Into or Step Over commands to execute that statement. To see how this works, open the Address Book project and set a breakpoint on the statement that displays the Address Entry form in the Toolbar click event. Now run the application and display a book entry. Visual Basic will stop the application at the selected statement, as shown in Figure 14.14.

FIGURE 14.14

Using breakpoints to stop the execution of an application at a selected statement.

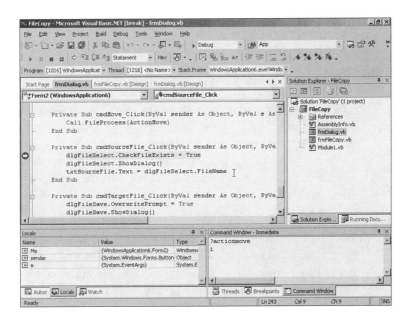

At this point you can display the variables or set any of the other debugging options. If you can identify the statement that caused the error, a single breakpoint might help you locate the problem. More often than not, you know only the general section of code that caused the error. A breakpoint will help you isolate the problem area. By using breakpoints you can step through the logic of your application to see which line or section of code is executed depending on the data being processed.

The Step Into and Step Over commands are used to observe the effect each statement has on the overall process. You also can skip over statements or back up by specifying the line of code to execute. The three step commands that you can use are listed in Table 14.4.

14

TABLE 14.4 The Available Step Commands in Visual Basic

Command	Description
Step Into	Executes the current statement and then stops at the next line, even if it's in another procedure.
Step Over	Executes the entire procedure called by the current statement and then stops at the statement following the current statement.
Step Out	Executes the remainder of the current procedure and stops at the statement following the one that called the procedure.

Note

These commands are available only when the application is in Break mode.

 The Step Into command executes the application code one statement at a time. This process, also known as *single stepping* through the code, enables you to view the effects each statement has on the overall application. When you click the Step Into button or press F8, Visual Basic temporarily switches to runtime, executes the current statement, moves to the next statement, and then switches back to Break mode. Try this in the Address Book project. You still should be at a breakpoint; if you press F8, the application will execute the statement at which you are stopped and then stop at the next executable statement.

The Step Over command is identical to the Step Into command, except when the current statement contains a call to a procedure. Unlike the Step Into command, which will follow the execution into the called procedure, Step Over will execute the procedure as a unit and then stop at the next statement in the current procedure. For example, if the current statement calls the procedure `VerifyZipCode` and you use Step Into,

```
InZipCode = txZipCode.Text
If Not VerifyZipCode(InZipCode) Then
    MsgBox("Invalid Zip Code entered")
End If
MsgBox("Zip Code is Valid")
```

the Code window would jump to the procedure and set the first executable statement in that procedure to the current statement. This enables you to analyze the code with the `VerifyZipCode` procedure.

However, when using the Step Over command, the Code window continues to display the current procedure. Execution then moves to the statement immediately after the call to `VerifyZipCode`, unless the procedure contains a breakpoint or Stop statement. Step

Over is used if you don't need to analyze the `VerifyZipCode` procedure but want to continue single stepping though the code.

Using the Step Into and Step Over commands together, you can single step through the application. When you arrive at a procedure call you can either follow the execution into the call, or step over it and stop at the statement after the procedure is processed. To see the difference between the commands, try them in your application during a debug session. Of course the Step Over process will work only if you have procedures being called in your code.

Now execute the application; when you are stopped at the breakpoint, single-step the code by pressing F8 until you get to a call to a procedure. First try stepping into the procedure and then quit the application and restart it. This time when you get to the breakpoint, single-step to the procedure call and then try the Step Over command by pressing the appropriate key combination. (If you have not modified the default settings, this combination would be Shift+F11; however, if you have changed the settings to reflect Visual Basic 6, then Shift+F8 is the combination.) See how Visual Basic processes these commands.

The third step command is the Step Out command. This is similar to the Step Into and Step Over commands, except that it will execute the remainder of the code in the current procedure. If the procedure is called from another procedure, it will continue execution until it gets to the statement immediately following the one that called the procedure.

While you are stepping through the application code, undoubtedly you will encounter process loops or long sections of plain, boring code that you don't want to step through. To dynamically step over this code you can use the Run To Cursor command to select a statement further down in your code where you want to stop the execution. In the Address Book application, place the cursor on a statement a few lines further down from where you are stopped. By pressing the Ctrl+F8 (Visual Basic 6 setting) keys, you will bypass the code between the cursor and the statement where the code was stopped.

Last but not least is the capability to change the pointer to the next executable statement. Visual Basic enables you to set a different line of code to execute, provided it falls within the current procedure. The effect is similar to using Step Into, except Step Into executes only the next line of code in the procedure. By setting the next statement to execute, you choose which line executes next. To set the next statement to be executed, move the insertion point (cursor) to the line of code you want to execute as shown in Figure 14.15 and then choose Continue from the Run menu.

14

FIGURE 14.15

Moving the current statement pointer to set the next executable statement in the code.

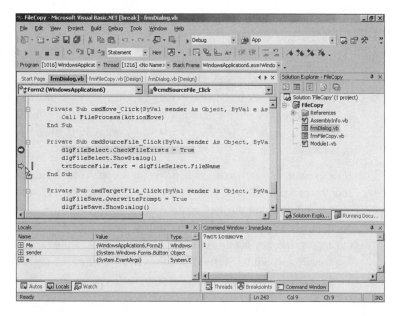

Also, if you've lost track of which statement will be executed next, you can choose Show Next Statement from the Debug toolbar to place the cursor on the line that will execute next. Another Debug option you can use is Set Next Statement. This allows you to specifically set which statement you want Visual Basic to execute next. In effect, you can choose not to execute one or more statements just by using this option.

Watching Your Variables

During the debugging process you might find that a calculation isn't producing the results you want, or problems might be occurring when a certain variable or property contains a particular value. As you've seen, many of the debugging problems aren't immediately traceable to a single statement; this requires you to observe the behavior of the variable or expression throughout a procedure or the entire application. The Watch expression tools enable you to automatically monitor these variables and expressions in your application. When the application enters the Break mode, the Watch expressions you specified will appear in the Watch window where you can observe their values.

For example, if you want to see the contents of a variable at a certain point in a loop, you can single step through the loop until you reach the appropriate counter value. Alternatively, you could put a Break expression on the loop counter for the values at which you want to stop and then run the application. You can add Watch expressions only when the application is in Break mode. When you are in Break mode, you also can check the value of a property, variable, or expression quickly using the QuickWatch dialog box shown in Figure 14.16.

FIGURE **14.16**

The Quick Watch dialog box showing the value of an expression.

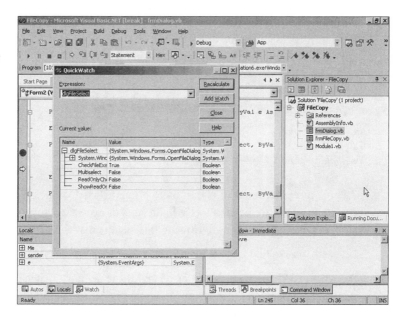

If you need to continue watching this expression, you can add it to the watch window by clicking Add. This expression will appear in the Watch window. The fastest way to access the Quick Watch function is by selecting the variable or expression and pressing the Shift+F9 (Visual Basic settings).

Using the Immediate Window

When you are debugging your application, sometimes you might need to execute individual procedures, evaluate expressions, or assign a new value to a variable or property. The Immediate window is the location where you can accomplish any of these tasks. One of the oldest methods of debugging is to print the contents of variables after each calculation. You can

- Use MsgBox statements to display these values.
- Use the Debug object to print the values directly to the Immediate window.
- When the application is in Break mode, you can enter Print (or ? for short) commands directly in the Immediate window.

When you are in Break mode, you can use the Immediate window to execute almost any Visual Basic command you might need. You can print any variable or expression. Also, if

14

the execution of the application halts within the code that's attached to a form or class, you also can refer to the properties of that form. When doing this, the List Properties/Methods quick list is displayed the same way as when you are entering code during design time. Aside from printing values in the Immediate window, you also can assign values to a variable or property to isolate the possible cause of an error in the application. Any of these commands are entered as standard Visual Basic code, as shown in Figure 14.17.

FIGURE 14.17

Entering standard Visual Basic code in the Immediate window.

After you set the values of one or more properties and variables, you can continue the execution of the application to see the results or even execute any procedure that's accessible in your application. After typing this statement:

```
SaveSetting Me.Text, "Settings", "MainHeight", Me.Height
```

Press Enter. When you press Enter, Visual Basic actually switches to Run mode to execute the statement and then returns to Break mode. At that point you can see the results of the procedure call and test any possible effects it might have had on the variables or properties.

Caution

If the `Option Explicit` parameter is on, any variable you enter in the Immediate window must have been previously defined in the application.

Note

Although most statements are supported in the Immediate window, you can execute only a single line of basic code. To execute multiple statements, you must use colons to separate the statements as shown in the following code:

```
For J = 1 to 5 : txtColor(J).Text = VbRed : Next J
```

Other Debugging Tools to Use

In addition to all the tools you can use when debugging your application, there are several other features that you can use that aren't so much tools as methods and statements in the Visual Basic language. These enable you to build debugging code into the application and control these statements by using the command-line arguments.

Conditional Compiling and Code

You can use command-line arguments to make the application execute certain sections of code only when a particular argument is passed to the application at startup. To enter them, choose Run from the Start menu and then enter the application name, followed by one or more arguments (see Figure 14.18).

FIGURE 14.18

Running the application from the Windows Start menu's Run option, passing debugging arguments on the command line.

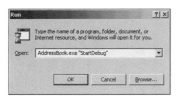

This enables you to have debugging code embedded in your application that won't be executed until you give users the correct argument to enter on the command line. This is one way of obtaining information from your application when a bug occurs after the application is in use. This also helps you get the information as users work with the application.

Note

It is difficult to reproduce an error that a user has reported; without reproducing the error, it's almost impossible to fix the problem.

You also can pass command-line arguments to the application by using the Debugging page on the project's Property Pages dialog box, as shown in Figure 14.19.

FIGURE 14.19

Passing command-line arguments in the project's Property Pages dialog box.

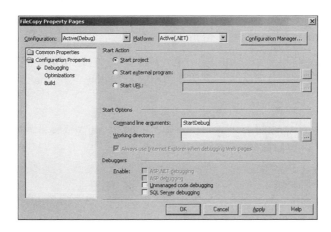

14

In addition to command-line arguments, you can pass conditional compilation arguments to the application. By using the conditional compilation arguments, you can include whole sections of code in the application only if you specify certain arguments when you compile the application. This enables you to remove any debugging statements from your application when you distribute the application. An example of conditional code is shown in the following code:

```
#If conFrenchVersion Then
    ' <code specific to the French language version>.
#ElseIf conGermanVersion then
    ' <code specific to the German language version>.
#Else
    ' <code specific to other versions>.
#End If
```

This enables you to add code to your application that can be used in different versions of the application, such as different languages.

The Debug Object

The Debug object is used during the testing and debugging of an application to send output directly to the Immediate window or to force an *assertion* in the code when a specified condition is either True or False. An assertion is a convenient way to test for conditions that should exist at a given point in your application. In Visual Basic, assertions are created using the Debug object and the Assert method using the syntax shown in the following code:

```
Debug.Assert (boolean_expression)
```

When you are testing your application, this statement will cause the application to enter Break mode with the line containing the statement highlighted (that assumes that the expression evaluates to False). The Debug.Assert statement is very similar to setting a Watch expression with the Break When Value Is True option selected, with the exception that it will break when the expression is False.

The other method of the Debug object also is very useful. The WriteLine method is used to print information directly into the Output window using the following syntax:

```
Debug.WriteLine(String)
```

In fact, you can add If statement logic to the Debug Write statement. Using either WriteIf or WriteLineIf methods as shown:

```
Debug.WriteLineIf(x = 2, "got a 2")
```

This statement will print got a 2 only when the variable x equals 2.

```
Debug.WriteIf(x = 2, "got a 2")
```

This statement works the same as the previous one. The only difference between the `Write` and `WriteLine` methods is that adding `Line` to the method forces the output specified to the next line.

> **Tip**
>
> The easiest way to display the Output window is by pressing Ctrl+Alt+O.

> **Note**
>
> When debugging your application, you can have as much information as you need printed to the Output window to help you track down the problem you are trying to fix.

> **Note**
>
> Don't worry about having the `Debug` methods in your application; when you compile your application, the compiler ignores all references to the `Debug` object.

Summary

Today you've seen all the tools, tips, techniques, and Visual Basic statements you have available when debugging your application. By using all of these together, you will be able to test your application and fix almost every problem there might be. Of course, I said *almost* every problem; you will never get your application to a point where problems will never happen again. Debugging can be a very daunting task once you finally complete your application; however, there are several ways to simplify this task. The following lists just some of the tips you can use when debugging applications:

- When the application doesn't produce correct results, browse through your code looking for statements that might have caused the problem and then set breakpoints at one or more of these statements and restart the application.

- When the program breaks, display the values of any important variables and properties by using the Immediate window.

- Step through your code, using Watch expressions and the Locals window to monitor how values change during the process.

- If an error occurs in a loop, define a conditional breakpoint to determine where the problem occurs.

- If you determine that a variable or property is causing problems in your application, use a `Debug.Assert` statement to halt execution when the wrong value is assigned to the variable or property.

14

As you've seen, debugging is something that's learned, not necessarily taught. There is an art to the debugging process; the fact that you know how to use the tools doesn't imply that you will do a good job when debugging the application. You should strive to understand the process and think of the application code as whole units instead of statements. This will help you understand and discover where things might go wrong.

Q&A

Q **What is a breakpoint?**

A A *breakpoint* is a method of setting automatic stops within the application code to halt the execution of the application at a particular statement to debug a problem.

Q **What are the different ways of setting a breakpoint?**

A There are many different ways to set a breakpoint when in a Visual Basic application. Depending on whether you are setting a conditional or unconditional breakpoint, you can set breakpoints by using the mouse, the Debug menu, or toolbar.

Q **What is a Watch expression?**

A A Watch expression enables you to define a particular variable or an expression that Visual Basic will watch. In this case, *watch* means displaying any changes to the value of the variable or expression in the Watch window when in Break mode.

Q **What is the Immediate window used for?**

A The Immediate window is used to execute any Visual Basic statement or procedure while testing the application. You also can display the value of any variable, property, or expression by using the `Print` command.

Workshop

The Workshop provides quiz questions to solidify your understanding of the material covered and exercises to help you use what you've learned. The answers to the quiz questions and exercises are provided in Appendix A, "Answers to Quizzes and Exercises."

Quiz

1. What's the difference between a Watch expression and a conditional breakpoint?
2. How can you set a Watch expression?
3. What information does the Locals window provide you?

Exercise

In the Address Book application, place several breakpoints to follow the flow of execution when you select a book entry to display. Choose a variable or expression and set a Watch expression for it. Finally, while at a breakpoint change the value of the `AddressID` variable to see how it affects the execution of the application.

WEEK 2

In Review

The second week took you through the steps to add database access to your application by covering design, creation, SQL programming, and actual building of the database. Then, you saw how to use the ActiveX data control and objects to connect to the database. Week 2 also looked at the new ADO.NET capabilities to access data. You learned how to use Crystal Reports to create a professional-looking report for your application. The final two days of this week were spent learning how to use the new capabilities for error processing and how to test and debug the application.

Database Design and Access

Day 8, "Designing a Database Application," took you through what you should consider when designing a new database. The different types of databases to be accessed from within Visual Basic were discussed, including how to use the functional specifications of your application design to help with the design of the database. At the end of Day 8, you saw how to use the Data Form Wizard to have Visual Basic create the database access forms for your application by using the database table design. Over Days 9, "Processing Data," and 10, "Accessing the Database,"), you saw how to design a database and what it takes to actually build the database using SQL Server 2000 as an example. In addition to the design and creation of the database, you took a short look at the SQL programming language that is used to access the data in a relational database. Finally, ActiveX Data Control and Data Objects were covered.

Enhancing the Application

On Day 11, "Enhancing the Application with Custom Objects," you saw how to use many of the newest controls and features in Visual Basic .NET. Using Visual Basic, you can now create data-aware controls to use in your application to enhance the user interface. By using these techniques, you can now include a form within an application as a control to fully integrate it into the application.

Using Crystal Reports

One of the more important features needed to create a professional Windows application is the ability to create reports from the data entered into the application. Day 12, "Working with Crystal Reports," introduced you to Crystal Reports, which is a separate application tool distributed with Visual Basic. Crystal Reports gives you the ability to create any type of report from the simple to the complex. You also saw how to incorporate Crystal Reports directly into your application by making use of the Crystal Reports Control that is included with the product.

Tuning the Application

Days 13, "Coping with Error Handling," and 14, "Testing and Debugging the Application," covered all the issues that help you to create an application that handles errors that might occur when the application is being used, including the new error-handling functions and methods provided in Visual Basic .NET. You also saw how to use the debugging tools that are included with Visual Basic to test and fix any errors that might be found.

WEEK 3

At a Glance

Week 3 will cover some of the newer, hotter topics in
Windows programming today—that is, the Internet- and Web-
enabled applications. This week will discuss creating Help
files and performance tuning. In addition, it will introduce
you to the concepts and information involved in getting a
product to market. Finally, Week 3 will teach you what a Web
service is and how to create one.

- Day 15, "Programming for the Internet," will discuss
  the latest craze in computer programming—Internet
  access. This day's lesson will not discuss how to create
  Internet or Web applications (that will be covered in the
  following two lessons); it will, however, show you how
  to include Internet access to the desktop application that
  you are creating. This will give users a way to browse
  the Web, but will also give them a way to upgrade the
  application software directly from your Web site (if you
  have one). Day 15 will show you how to use the new
  HTML Page Designer to create Web pages directly
  within Visual Basic. Finally, it will present a brief lesson in what HTML is and how it works with a subset of
  Visual Basic called VBScript.

- Day 16, "Creating a Web Application," will show you
  how to create a Web-based application. A Web-based
  application is an application that is executed across
  the Internet, as opposed to running on the desktop.
  This day will also show you how to give a Web user
  the same interface capabilities that a desktop user
  would get.

15

16

17

18

19

20

21

- Day 17, "Adding Data Access to the Web," will take the Web application discussed on Day 16 and show you how to connect to a database within a Web application. This will use the new ADO.NET data connection capabilities.

- Day 18, "Building Online Help," will introduce you to the Windows Help system. You will learn how to design and create a working Help system. It will also show you how to incorporate Help into your application using the different functions, controls, and features available in Visual Basic.

- Day 19, "Tuning and Tweaking Performance," will cover the concepts and techniques that you can use to make your application run more quickly and use fewer resources on the computer. You will see different techniques that can be used to enhance the performance of an application.

- Day 20, "Finishing the Application," will cover the information you will need to package the application you have written. Besides teaching you the actual creation of the distribution software, Day 20 will teach you other topics and issues that you will have to deal with if you want to sell the application you have created.

- Day 21, "Working with Web Services," will cover the topic of Web Services, including what they are and how they affect you. Day 21 will also introduce you to one of the new concepts in the .NET Framework: Simple Object Access Protocol, or SOAP. Finally, it will teach you to create a simple Web service and then a Web service client that will use the service you created.

WEEK 3

DAY 15

Programming for the Internet

Internet programming has become one of the hottest skills in computer programming. With the wide acceptance of the Internet and the World Wide Web, almost every company or group and many individuals have their own Web sites. One capability that you can include in your desktop applications is Internet access from within your application.

In the past, Web programming was done in either Visual InterDev or Visual Basic by creating HTML pages and then publishing them out to the Web. Of course, these pages included some type of scripting code, such as VBScript. With the release of Visual Studio .NET, you now can use the Visual Studio design environment to create professional Web-based applications, which will be discussed on Days 16, "Creating a Web Application," and 17, "Adding Data Access to the Web."

Today, you will see how to use the Internet Browser control, which is a component of the Microsoft Internet Explorer that you can use in your application. You will also get a glimpse of what HTML is all about and how to code a simple HTML page that you can view with your own application. You will see how to use your Visual Basic programming skills when creating Web pages by using VBScript, a subset of the full Visual Basic programming language. Then on Day 16 and Day 17 you will see how to create a Web application by using the new ADO.NET capabilities along with standard Visual Basic code instead of VBScript.

Adding Internet Control Access

Among the many tools, controls, and features that you can use in a Visual Basic application is the Internet Browser control. This control enables you to give your application's users the ability to access the Internet from within the application.

Adding the browser control to your application from scratch isn't an easy proposition; however, you will see how to add this control with minimum effort.

To test or use the Internet browser tool, you need to be connected to the Internet or a local network with an intranet or have Personal Web Server running on your PC while you're developing those functions.

In the following section, you will learn how to add an Internet browser to an application that will use the Microsoft Web site as its default home page. You will also see how to let users download files from the Web. The browser itself supports file downloads specified in an HTML page, but the File Transfer control lets you code a direct download of a file without having the browser open.

The best way to develop an application that uses the Internet tools is by using the Windows Personal Web Server that runs locally on your PC and is available as a free download from the Microsoft Products Web site (www.microsoft.com/products).

Adding the Browser Control to the Toolbox

Although the control isn't automatically included and displayed in the Visual Basic toolbox, you can add it to the toolbox yourself. In fact, if you want to use the control, you must add it to the toolbox in order to access and place it on a form.

Adding the Browser control to the toolbox is a pretty simple task. With a project open, follow these steps:

1. Right-click the toolbox and select Customize Toolbox from the pop-up menu.

2. In the Customize Toolbox dialog box (see Figure 15.1), you can select .NET components or older COM components to add to the toolbox. In this dialog box, locate the Microsoft Web Browser controls.

15

FIGURE 15.1

Adding the Browser control to the toolbox using the Customize Toolbox dialog box.

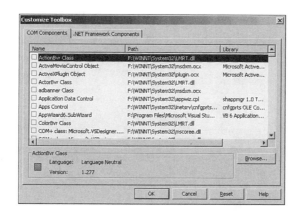

3. Select the check box for the control and then click OK to add it. The Browser control should now appear at the bottom of the Windows Forms list (see Figure 15.2).

FIGURE 15.2

Accessing the new control on the toolbox.

 Note

After you add the Browser control to the toolbox, it will be available to any project opened within the Visual Basic .NET IDE.

Internet Browser

The Internet Browser control enables you to attach to the Internet by using your PC's default Internet connection and to browse the World Wide Web. If you look at a browser application such as Internet Explorer, however, you will see that it contains more than just the browser itself (see Figure 15.3).

FIGURE 15.3

Browsing the Internet requires many more controls than the browser itself.

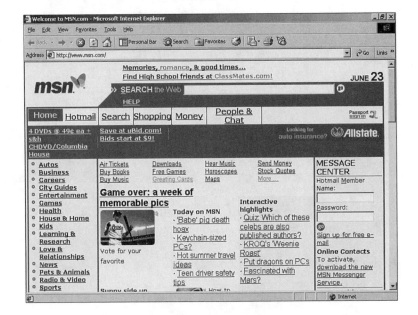

The Browser control is nothing more than a frame used to view Web pages. Although it contains the methods, properties, and events needed to perform all the required browser functions, no user interface objects are built into it. Therefore, it's up to you to design and create the necessary form for users to interact with. Because a browser can be and is an application by itself, creating a browser form for your application can be just as complicated as creating the application.

Depending on what capabilities you want to provide users, the amount of work you will need to do to include a browser in your application will vary. The following sections will discuss the minimal code additions that you must make for a functioning browser along the lines of Internet Explorer.

The Browser control provides several properties, methods, and events that you will make consistent use of, as described in Table 15.1. Table 15.1 by no means lists the entire set of elements for the Browser control; however, very little documentation can be found on how to use this control.

TABLE 15.1 The Internet Browser's Most Used Elements

Name	Description
LocationURL	Contains the URL for the displayed or requested Web page
LocationName	Contains the defined name of the displayed Web page
Busy	Returns if the browser engine is busy retrieving a Web page
Events	
DownloadComplete	Triggered whenever a Web page retrieval is completed
NavigateComplete	Triggered whenever a new URL is entered
Methods	
Navigate	Informs the browser to go to the specified URL
Stop	Stops the current browser action
GoBack	Navigates to the previously displayed Web page
GoForward	Navigates to the next Web page that was already displayed
GoHome	Navigates to the defined home page
GoSearch	Uses the Microsoft search engine to initiate an Internet search
Refresh	Refreshes the Web page now displayed

NEW TERM A *URL (uniform resource locator)* is an Internet Web site address. Every Web site, if registered properly, has a unique URL assigned to it. If you add the Internet-access capability to your application, you can supply a default URL Web page for the application's browser. When users start the browser in the application, the browser connects to the URL specified in the StartingAddress variable.

Tip Although every URL should begin with http://, many Internet browsers no longer require you to add this text; the browser will insert it for you. In fact, the browser that you create will also work without your having to include http:// at the beginning of the URL.

Adding the Browser

To see how this works, start a new project and name it BrowserApp. Next, add the following controls to the form in the order they are listed in Table 15.2 (see Figure 15.4).

TABLE 15.2   Controls Needed for the Internet Browser Form

Control	Name
Toolbar	tbToolbar
Image List	imgButtons
Picture box	picFrame
Label	Label
ComboBox	cboAddress
Browser	AxWebBrowser1 (can't be changed)
Timer	timTimer

FIGURE 15.4

The initial browser form with all the controls added.

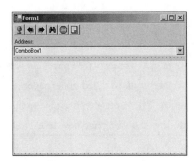

 Note

When you add the Browser control, you can't change its name. This is due to a limitation of using the older ActiveX technology in Visual Basic .NET.

Caution

For this to work properly, you must add the Picture box control first, and then select it before adding the Label and ComboBox controls to the form. This will place these controls within the Picture box control instead of directly on the form.

The first step in the process is to populate the image list with the button icons for the toolbar buttons that will help navigate the browser. For these icons, you can choose any images you want to use for the following functions:

- Home
- Back
- Forward

15

- Refresh
- Search
- Stop

Now that you've defined the images, create the same number of buttons in the toolbar and associate each button with the correct image, placing the name of the button in the `ItemData` property for each button as you go.

 Note

> You will use the `ItemData` values to identify which button was clicked in the Toolbar `buttonclick` routine.

Table 15.3 lists the event routines that you will need, along with a brief description of each routine's function.

TABLE 15.3 Adding the Routines for the Browser Functionality

Control	Routine Name	Description
AxWebBrowser1	NavigateComplete	Places the new URL in the ComboBox drop-down list, ensuring that there are no duplicate entries.
cboAddress	KeyPress	Calls the `SelectedIndexChanged` routine for the ComboBox only when Enter is pressed.
	SelectedIndexChanged	Enables the timer and then instructs the browser to navigate to the new URL entered or selected in the ComboBox.
TimTimer	Tick	Places the text `Working...` in the form title bar until the browser returns the URL. It then places the name of the Web page in the title bar.
TbToolbar	ButtonClick	Checks to see which button was clicked using a `Select` statement, and then executes the correct browser method depending on the button.
Form	Load	Shows the form, calls the form's resize routine, and then navigates to the starting address specified in the code.
	ReSize	Resizes the Browser control to fill the entire form except for the toolbar and picture frame areas.

Listing 15.1 shows the completed code for the Browser application. Place the code in the respective routines and then execute the application and see how the browser works.

LISTING 15.1   INTERNETBROWSER.TXT: Navigating and Controlling the Internet Browser

```
Private Sub AxWebBrowser1_NavigateComplete2(ByVal sender As Object,
      ByVal e As AxSHDocVw.DWebBrowserEvents2_NavigateComplete2Event)
      Handles AxWebBrowser1.NavigateComplete2
   Dim i As Short
   Dim bFound As Boolean
   If cboAddress.Items.Count > 0 Then
      For i = 0 To cboAddress.Items.Count - 1
         If InStr(AxWebBrowser1.LocationURL, _
            cboAddress.Items.Item(i).ToString) > 0 Then
            bFound = True
            cboAddress.Items.RemoveAt(i)
            Exit For
         End If
      Next i
      mbDontNavigateNow = True
   End If
   cboAddress.Items.Insert(0, AxWebBrowser1.LocationURL)
   cboAddress.SelectedIndex = 0
   mbDontNavigateNow = False

End Sub

Private Sub Timer1_Tick(ByVal sender As Object,
      ByVal e As System.EventArgs) Handles Timer1.Tick
   If AxWebBrowser1.Busy = False Then
      Timer1.Enabled = False
      Me.Text = AxWebBrowser1.LocationName
   Else
      Me.Text = "Working..."
   End If

End Sub

Private Sub tbToolBar_ButtonClick(ByVal sender As System.Object,
      ByVal e As System.Windows.Forms.ToolBarButtonClickEventArgs)
      Handles tbToolBar.ButtonClick
   Timer1.Enabled = True

   Select Case e.Button.ItemData
      Case "Back"
         AxWebBrowser1.GoBack()
      Case "Fwd"
         AxWebBrowser1.GoForward()
      Case "Refresh"
         AxWebBrowser1.Refresh()
```

LISTING 15.1   continued

```
            Case "Home"
                AxWebBrowser1.GoHome()
            Case "Search"
                AxWebBrowser1.GoSearch()
            Case "Stop"
                Timer1.Enabled = False
                AxWebBrowser1.Stop()
                Me.Text = AxWebBrowser1.LocationName
        End Select
End Sub

Private Sub cboAddress_KeyPress(ByVal sender As Object,
        ByVal e As System.Windows.Forms.KeyPressEventArgs)
        Handles cboAddress.KeyPress
    Dim KeyAscii As Short = Asc(e.KeyChar)
    If KeyAscii = System.Windows.Forms.Keys.Return Then
        cboAddress_SelectedIndexChanged(cboAddress, New System.EventArgs())
    End If
    If KeyAscii = 0 Then
        e.Handled = True
    End If

End Sub

Private Sub cboAddress_SelectedIndexChanged(ByVal sender As Object,
        ByVal e As System.EventArgs) Handles cboAddress.SelectedIndexChanged
    If mbDontNavigateNow Then Exit Sub
    Timer1.Enabled = True
    AxWebBrowser1.Navigate(cboAddress.Text)

End Sub

Private Sub Form1_Load(ByVal sender As Object,
        ByVal e As System.EventArgs) Handles MyBase.Load
    Me.Show()

    Form1_Resize(Me.ActiveForm, New System.EventArgs())
    If Len(StartingAddress) > 0 Then
        cboAddress.Text = StartingAddress
        Timer1.Enabled = True
        AxWebBrowser1.Navigate(StartingAddress)
    End If

End Sub

Private Sub Form1_Resize(ByVal sender As Object,
        ByVal e As System.EventArgs) Handles MyBase.Resize
    cboAddress.Width = Me.ClientRectangle.Width
    AxWebBrowser1.Width = Me.ClientRectangle.Width
```

LISTING 15.1   continued

```
AxWebBrowser1.Height = Me.ClientRectangle.Height - _
                (picAddress.Top + picAddress.Height)
picAddress.Top = tbToolBar.Top + tbToolBar.Height
picAddress.Left = 0
```

```
End Sub
```

Now, run the application and maximize the form. You should see something similar to Figure 15.5. You can see that the Browser control fills up the form, and you can enter Internet URLs into the ComboBox or select one already in the drop-down list. Finally, the toolbar allows you to navigate around the Web pages you've displayed.

FIGURE 15.5

Working with the final Web Browser form.

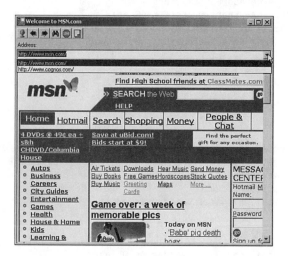

> **Note**
>
> If you aren't already connected to the Internet, when you display browser form, it will use the default connection information on your PC to attempt to connect to the Internet.

Compare Figure 15.5 with Figure 15.3 and notice that they look very much alike. At this point, you're connected to the Internet and can browse any Web site that you want.

> **Note**   The Web Browser control provides a simpler version of the full Internet Explorer application. The browser methods supply all the common features needed, such as a page previous, next page, and home page buttons. If you click the Search button, Internet Explorer uses Microsoft's search Web site to initiate a search request.

15

You now have a working Internet browser in your application. If you decide to enhance the browser with more features, you can use more of the elements supported by the control.

Coding in HTML

Although Visual Basic provides you with everything you need to access the Internet, to fully understand and use the Internet, you should learn some of the other languages that bring things together: Hypertext Markup Language (HTML) and VBScript. HTML, the formatting language behind Web pages, is designed for two purposes:

- Format Web pages in columns with graphics and appropriate titles
- Allow the integration of additional Internet service programs, such as VB ActiveX documents and Java (a programming language that activates Web pages)

NEW TERM   HTML is known as a *scripting language*, which isn't compiled like Visual Basic programs are. Instead, HTML formats Web pages, specifies where graphics and frames go, and allows you to embed activated applications, such as ActiveX documents and Java programs.

VBScript is another scripting language designed by Microsoft to be a subset of the Visual Basic programming language. This means that you'll feel right at home with VBScript. It becomes very useful when you want to add key Visual Basic features to a Web page, such as pop-up messages, input boxes, and loop-through calculations.

HTML Basics

NEW TERM   HTML isn't complex to learn. Coding in HTML is just as easy as the early word processors that used codes instead of mouse clicks to perform actions. Unfortunately, it's also just as tedious when you forget the closing code of a matched pair. The codes to control the look of a page are always surrounded by a pair of angle brackets (<>). These commands or codes are called *tags*. Some HTML tags are paired, whereas others aren't.

All browsers support HTML, which is why the Web works the way it does. Even an all-text browser can understand the simplest HTML text tags; however, when you start using complex tags such as frames, you require a browser that supports these features.

Because every Web page is created with HTML code, you can view the HTML source code for any Web page that you can see in your Web browser. In Internet Explorer, choose Source from the View menu to see the HTML source code for the current Web page (see Figure 15.6).

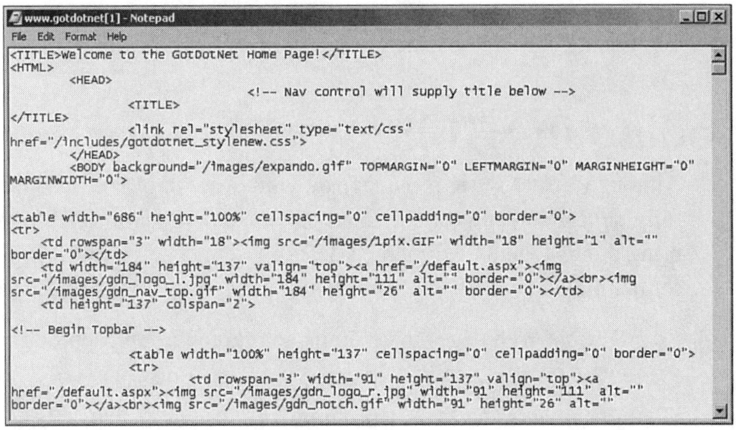

FIGURE 15.6

Displaying the HTML source of a Web page in Internet Explorer.

If you look at enough Web pages, you'll see that they have several common elements. Every Web page is made of essentially the following lines of HTML code:

```
<html>
  <head>
    <title>Demo Home Page</title>
  </head>
  <body>
  </body>
</html>
```

This is the basic structure of every HTML file that you'll work with, no matter how complex they get. The tags <head>, <body>, and <html> start sections, which are closed with </head>, </body>, and </html>, respectively. Remember, not all HTML tags have to be closed.

Understanding HTML Tags

HTML pages have their instructions or tags enclosed in brackets, as discussed in the preceding section. These tags aren't displayed in the browser window; they serve to tell the browser how to display the text.

Most tags are closed by duplicating the tag instruction with a slash (/) placed at the beginning of the tag name. Every HTML page begins with an <HTML> tag and ends with an </HTML> tag. These two tags tell the browser where the Web page begins and ends. Between these HTML tags, every page has two sections: the head and the body, both of which must be defined for the browser to display the page properly. The head is everything between the <head> and </head> tags, whereas the body is anything between the <body> and </body> tags.

 Tip   It doesn't matter whether the tags are uppercase, but consider capitalizing them to make them easier to find when making changes to the Web page later.

In the head section of Figure 15.6, notice that one line is

```
<title>Welcome to the GotDotNet Home Page</title>
```

The browser will display the words between those title tags on the title bar of the browser window. Although the average visitor won't pay much attention to the title bar while viewing the Web page, text within the title tag is what browsers usually save with a bookmark or as Favorites in Internet Explorer.

Other codes can also appear in the head section of an HTML document. For example, you could use a link tag here to define a relationship between the Web page and yourself as the owner or manager of the Web page. Your link could look like this:

```
<LINK rev=made href="mailto:yourid@youraddress">
```

Another tag you may want to put in the head section is <meta>, a generic tag that you can use to embed information about your document that doesn't fit in the other HTML tags. It's usually used to give the page keywords for indexing in catalogs and Web crawlers. An example would be the following:

```
<meta keywords= Ski, Snow, Winter>
```

Everything else in the HTML code is part of the body, which is enclosed in the <body> and </body> tags.

HTML tags allow you to create some very fancy-looking forms. Some must be paired and are listed in Table 15.4; others don't use an ending tag, as shown in Table 15.5.

TABLE 15.4 Paired HTML Tags That You Can Use on a Web Page

Code Pair	Description
`<I>...</I>`	Begins and ends italicized text
`<B>...</B>`	Begins and ends boldfaced text
`<BIG>...</BIG>`	Displays large type
`<A HREF=xxxx>...</A>`	Creates a hypertext link to another file or a bookmark within this file
`<Address>...</Address>`	Begins and ends a formatted section for contact information
`<ul>...</ul>`	Displays unnumbered lists
`<dl>...</dl>`	Displays definition lists
`<dt>...</dt>`	Displays defined terms in a definition list
`<dd>...</dd>`	Displays definitions in definition list
`<em>...</em>`	Displays emphasized text
`<strong>...</strong>`	Displays boldfaced text
`<Hn>...</Hn>`	Displays headlines, usually from H1 (the largest) to H6 (the smallest)

TABLE 15.5 Non-Paired HTML Tags That You Can Use on a Web Page

Tag	Description
`<IMG SRC=xxxxx>`	Places an image on a Web page
`<li>`	Displays a list of items
`<P>`	Creates a paragraph break, a line break, and a blank line
` `	Adds a line break, but no blank line
`<HR>`	Adds a rule between sections

Many more tags are available but aren't covered today. If you want a best-selling book on HTML coding, read Laura Lemay's *Sams Teach Yourself Web Publishing with HTML and XHTML in 21 Days* (Sams Publishing, ISBN 0-672-32077-0).

Creating an HTML Page

Let's start the process by creating a very simple Web page and then browse it to see how it works. Many HTML editors available, including Microsoft FrontPage 2000, can help you create the Web pages you need. In this section, you can use Notepad to create your HTML code. Open Notepad and enter the following code to create the simple HTML page:

```
<HTML>
  <HEAD>
    <TITLE>Demo Page 1</TITLE>
  </HEAD>
```

```
<BODY>This is a sample web page</BODY>
</HTML>
```

The title element is always inserted in the head of your HTML page, indicated by the <HEAD> and </HEAD> commands. The first few lines of your HTML code won't appear in your actual page—they act as extra information. Any actual page content is inserted in the file's body section. After you finish, save the file as HTMLDEMO.HTM.

> The .HTM and .HTML file extensions are used to signify a standard HTML file.

To view your first Web page, start your Web browser, choose Open from the File menu, and select the file you just saved. The Web page should look like the one in Figure 15.7.

FIGURE 15.7

The first Web page created by using HTML scripting code.

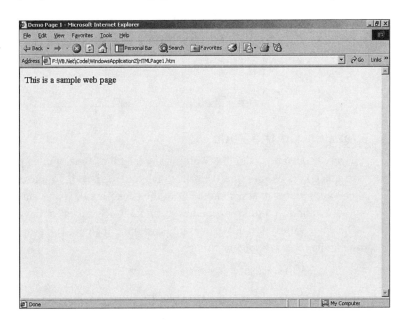

The first thing that you'll probably put on your Web page is a heading. It's also the first thing that you insert into the page's body section. After the beginning body tag, add the following line of code to produce the largest sized text heading on the Web page:

```
<H1>My Demo HTML Page</H1>
```

You also can center the text on the page. You must enclose the heading line with this tag pair as follows:

```
<CENTER><H1>My Demo HTML Page</H1></CENTER>
```

Add this line of code to the HTMLDEMO file and save it. Now, in Internet Explorer, refresh the page to see the changes you made (see Figure 15.8).

FIGURE 15.8

Adding a heading to the simple Web page.

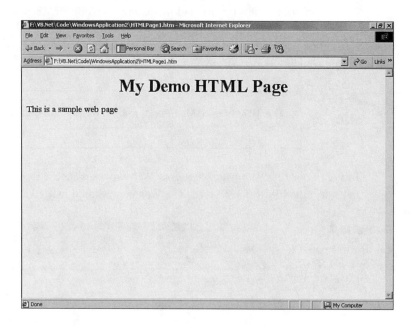

Jazzing Up the Page

If you've been browsing the Web for any length of time, you've probably seen nice background colors used on the Web sites that you've visited. To make your Web page more pleasant to look at, add some color to the background. Using tags to set the background color requires you to know the hexadecimal RGB values for the color you want to use. The color value is usually entered by assigning the bgcolor property of the <body> tag, using the form #*rrggbb* as follows:

```
<body bgcolor="#C0C0C0"> </body>
```

This will change the background color to silver.

Next, you could add an image to the Web page by modifying the Web page's <body> tag. The following is an example that adds the background image shown in Figure 15.9 to the page:

```
<body background=file:///C:/temp/CDROM.gif bgcolor="#C0C0C0"> </body>
```

Of course, you have to make sure that the path you specify matches the machine where the Web page will execute from. The background colors and images usually appear as the first item inserted after the <body> tag.

FIGURE 15.9

Displaying images as a background on a Web page.

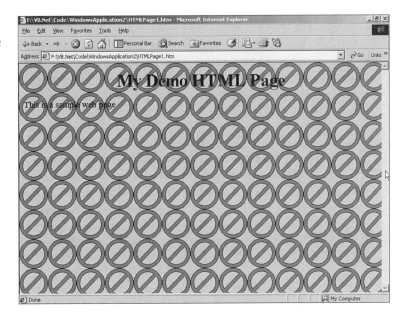

Tip

Internet Explorer users can borrow the background images used in any Web page by right-clicking the background and choosing Save Background Image from the pop-up menu.

Linking to Other Pages

Linking to other pages requires nothing more than coding a hyperlink in your Web page. Hyperlinks are probably the first thing you used when you started browsing the Internet. Used correctly, hyperlinks transport users to interesting and related Web sites.

To create an external link in the HTML code, you would use the `<A>...</A>` tags. The HTML code that links to Microsoft's home page is shown as follows:

```
<A HREF=http://www.microsoft.com>Microsoft HomePage</A>
```

Using VBScript

VBScript, a scaled-down version of Visual Basic, uses fundamental VB syntax but is intended as a scripting language, similar to a DOS batch file. VBScript code is usually found embedded directly in a Web page, as is JavaScript. The following sections give you a brief overview of VBScript and how to use it, as well as some notes on how it varies from the standard Visual Basic language.

VBScript Overview

VBScript was designed to be a subset of the full Visual Basic language, because its code is interpreted as the Web page is displayed. As you already know, the HTML code behind a Web page can also include scripting code to enhance the Web page. Before the introduction of VBScript, JavaScript had established itself as the industry standard for Web page scripting; however, JavaScript is very similar to C++, which made it difficult for VB programmers to use.

The main purpose for Microsoft's developing VBScript was to provide a Web scripting language compatible with Microsoft's industry standard for Windows development, Visual Basic. Because this new language would be embedded into Web pages, it needed to be simple enough that it could be interpreted as quickly as JavaScript. To accomplish this, the Visual Basic language needed to be simplified.

VBScript also was scaled down from Visual Basic for security concerns. If VBScript programmers could call the Windows API or perform file I/O, hackers could easily write a virus in VBScript to crash every system that executed their VBScript Web page. To reduce the chances of this happening, all features of Visual Basic that potentially could be abused were removed.

Perhaps the biggest difference (and source of frustration) between VBScript and standard Visual Basic is that VBScript supports only the `Variant` data type. This means that a statement such as

```
Dim x As Integer
```

would trigger an error in VBScript, because the `Integer` data type isn't supported. Using just the `Variant` data type simplifies the code for the interpreter, thus making execution much faster.

When you start working with VBScript, knowing what commands and features of Visual Basic aren't supported is a good idea. This keeps you from designing a function that can't be coded in VBScript. Table 15.6 lists the features that you can't use in VBScript code.

TABLE 15.6 Visual Basic Features Not Supported in VBScript

Category	Feature or Keyword
Collection	Add, Count, Item, Remove, access to collections by using ! character
Conditional compilation	#Const, #If...Then...#Else
Control flow	DoEvents, GoSub...Return, GoTo, On Error GoTo, On...GoSub, On...GoTo, line numbers, line labels, With...End With

TABLE 15.6   continued

Category	Feature or Keyword
Conversion	CVar, CVDate, Str, Val
Data types	All intrinsic data types except Variant, Type...End Type
Date/time	Date statement, Time statement, Timer
Debugging	Debug.Write, End, Stop
Declaration	Declare (for declaring DLLs), Property Set, Public, Private, Static, ParamArray, Optional, New
Error handling	Erl, Error, On Error...Resume, Resume, Resume Next
File input/output	All
Financial	All financial functions
Object manipulation	TypeOf
Operators	Like
Strings	Fixed-length strings, Mid statement, StrConv

Don't worry if the list seems long. The most important features of Visual Basic are included in VBScript, so you still can write powerful scripts. The only difference is that now you have to be more inventive when designing the code. You may find that some tricks you invent to overcome these limitations are so good that you want to use them in your normal Visual Basic applications.

Adding VBScript to an HTML Page

To see how VBScript works, look at what you have to add to a Web page to make it perform some processing. To use VBScript in your Web page, you must add some HTML code that tells the browser that your Web page contains script code. VBScript also doesn't support the forms you're accustomed to using in Visual Basic, meaning that your code must include information about which controls to use and where they should be placed on the page.

To begin using VBScript in an HTML page, you must tell the browser which scripting language you'll be using. This is done by using the <Script...></Script> tags, which define the script block in the Web page. For VBScript, the syntax in a Web page would start out as follows:

```
<Script Language="VBScript">
   ...
</Script>
```

Immediately after the <Script> statement, your VBScript code is added in an HTML comment block (<!-- and --> tags) so that your code isn't displayed by browsers that don't support VBScript. At the end of the comment block, the closing </Script> tag tells the browser that there's no more code. Listing 15.2 shows a simple Web page that displays a message box every time the page is accessed.

LISTING 15.2   HTMLDEMO1.HTM: A Simple Web Page That Displays a Visual Basic Message Box

```
<HTML>
  <HEAD>
    <SCRIPT LANGUAGE="VBScript">
      <!--
        MsgBox "Hello World!"
      -->
    </SCRIPT>
  </HEAD>
<BODY>
</BODY>
</HTML>
```

Although you can have code executed when the page is loaded, typically you would want to execute your code in response to an event, the same way as in Visual Basic. To do this, you need a control on the page that users can interact with and an event routine for that control. In Visual Basic, this is done for you when you place a command button on the form, and a Click event is created when you double-click the control. In VBScript, you must do everything yourself, but it isn't as difficult as it sounds. Listing 15.3 shows you how to create a command button on the Web page and display a message box in response to the Click event.

LISTING 15.3   CMDBTN.HTM: Adding and Then Using a Command Button on a Web Page

```
<HTML>
  <HEAD>
    <meta name=vs_defaultClientScript content="JavaScript">
    <meta name=vs_targetSchema content="Internet Explorer 5.0">
    <meta name="GENERATOR" content="Microsoft Visual Studio.NET 7.0">
    <meta name=ProgId content=VisualStudio.HTML>
    <meta name=Originator content="Microsoft Visual Studio.NET 7.0">
    <SCRIPT LANGUAGE="VBScript">
      <!--
        Sub Command1_OnClick()
          MsgBox "Hello World!"
        End Sub
      -->
    </SCRIPT>
  </HEAD>
```

15

LISTING 15.3   continued

```
<BODY>
    <INPUT NAME="Command1" TYPE="BUTTON" VALUE="Say Hello!" ID="Command1">
</BODY>
</HTML>
```

Now that you've seen how to work with a simple VBScript Web page, you need to modify the HTML page you just created. The code in Listing 15.4 shows you how to add a text box and command button to the Web page and then have a subroutine executed whenever users click the command button.

LISTING 15.4   HTMLCODE.HTM: A Complete VBScript Application on a Web Page

```
<html>
<head>
<title>HTML Code Demo</title>
    <meta name=vs_defaultClientScript content="JavaScript">
    <meta name=vs_targetSchema content="Internet Explorer 5.0">
    <meta name="GENERATOR" content="Microsoft Visual Studio.NET 7.0">
    <meta name=ProgId content=VisualStudio.HTML>
    <meta name=Originator content="Microsoft Visual Studio.NET 7.0">
    <SCRIPT LANGUAGE="VBScript">
      <!--

        Sub SayHello(InputName)
          Dim Reply

          Reply = MsgBox("Hello " & InputName & ", _
                   are you ready to compute?", 36)

          If Reply = 6 Then
              MsgBox "Okay, Let's see what we can do!", 64
          Else
              MsgBox "This function has been canceled", 64
          End If
        End Sub

        Sub Command1_OnClick()
          SayHello Text1.Value
        End Sub
        -->
    </SCRIPT>
      </head>
      <body MS_POSITIONING="GridLayout">
        <BR>
        <H3>Enter your name:</H3>
        <P>
```

LISTING 15.4   continued

```
    <HR>
    <INPUT NAME="Text1" TYPE="TEXT" VALUE="" ID="Text1">
    <INPUT NAME="Command1" TYPE="BUTTON" VALUE="Say Hello!" ID="Command1">
</body>
</html>
```

As you can see, VBScript allows you to add complex processing code to your Web-based applications.

Note

Don't try to use any of the included Visual Basic constants that you've probably become used to. VBScript doesn't support them, which means that you have to code the numeric values for such constants as vbInformation.

If you start Internet Explorer or Netscape and open this Web page, the resulting display should look like Figure 15.10.

FIGURE 15.10

Displaying the demo HTML/VBScript Web page in Internet Explorer.

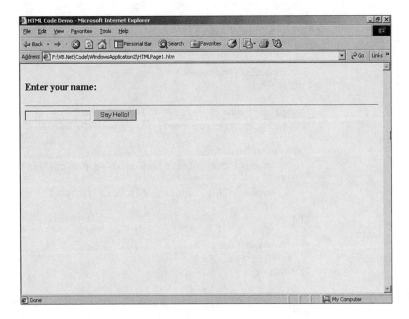

Summary

Today you looked at how to add the hottest thing in computers today. With the Browser control, your users can browse the Internet without having to open any other application. Also, if you have your own Web site, you can point users directly to it and have your application automatically download upgrades for itself. You also saw a little of what it takes to create Web pages and add processing code in the form of VBScript to the HTML page. Unless you're creating a full Internet Web application, these concepts and controls will serve only to add enhancements to any application that you create.

In the next two days, you will learn how to create a true Web-based application using the new Web Forms package included in Visual Basic .NET. You will also learn how to connect to a database in a Web application.

Q&A

Q What does the Web-browsing application that I create using the Browser control do with the URL I supply?

A The application uses the URL to set the starting or default URL page when the browser is opened.

Q What's the difference between an intranet and the Internet?

A An *intranet* is a Web server that's local to the computer you're using (a network or a personal server). The *Internet* is a worldwide system of linked computer networks that facilitates data communication services such as remote logons, file transfer, electronic mail, and newsgroups. The World Wide Web is a major part of the Internet.

Q Which scripting languages work with HTML to enhance the Web page?

A VBScript and JavaScript are two of several languages used to enhance HTML Web pages.

Workshop

The Workshop provides quiz questions to help you solidify your understanding of the material covered and exercises to provide you with experience in using what you've learned. The answers are provided in Appendix A, "Answers to Quizzes and Exercises."

15

Quiz

1. What different Internet objects can you use in your applications?

2. What's the difference between Visual Basic and VBScript?

Exercise

Create a Web page with three separate headings on it that asks users to input their first and last names in different text boxes. Then add two command buttons: one to put a message box onscreen saying hello to users and one to reset the text boxes.

DAY 16

Creating a Web Application

Over the last two weeks you've been introduced to many of the more advanced features and functions that are available in Visual Basic .NET when creating a Windows application. This includes the capability to access any database and to produce professional reports with minimal effort using the Crystal Report Designer. At the beginning of this week you learned how to use the `LinkLabel` control to provide Internet access in your application using the installed browser on the computer. You also learned how to add a browser directly inside your application. Finally, you had a brief lesson in HTML programming and how to use it to create Web pages.

In the next two days you will see how you can apply almost everything you've learned so far to the creation process of a Web-based application. Today we will take a brief look at the basic concepts of ASP.NET. We also will create a very simple Web application, just to get your feet wet; then, we will re-create a portion of the Address Book application that was created earlier. This will be done using some extra Web controls that Microsoft provides on its Web site. Along the way you will learn what does and doesn't make the transition to the Web from the Visual Basic .NET tools.

Tomorrow you will add the database access to the application, as well as a Crystal Report for the Web user to display. By the time you reach the end of these lessons, you will see that working with a Web application is as easy as working with a Windows application.

Introducing ASP.NET

ASP.NET is much more than the next version of the Active Server Pages (ASP) technology. You now can develop enterprise-wide Web applications with the same ease as a Windows application. Even though ASP.NET is compatible with ASP, it provides a new programming model that enables a very powerful class of applications to be designed. In fact, if you are familiar and comfortable with ASP, you can work your way into ASP.NET slowly by incorporating it into your existing applications. Because ASP.NET is a compiled .NET-based environment, rather than interpreted every time it's executed, you can author an application in any of the .NET-compatible languages—including, of course, Visual Basic.

When creating an ASP.NET application, you choose from two unique models:

- *Web Forms* allow you to build very powerful forms-based Web pages. When working with Web Forms you can use ASP.NET server–based controls to create a common interface that's familiar to a user.

- *Web Service* (discussed on Day 21, "Working with Web Services") is a way to access server functionality from any application, Windows or Web.

One big change that ASP.NET has endured is that the Web pages are compiled. You no longer are required to code the Web logic in a scripting language. This provides a comfortable environment in which to develop your Web application. Also, one of the biggest impacts to Web performance is with data access (connecting and querying the database). ASP.NET comes with a data-caching module that allows you to specify what data on an ASP page to cache, and when to flush that cache and requery the database.

You might be asking yourself, "So, what is ASP.NET?" Well, there really isn't a single answer to that question. What you will learn are the different components, concepts, and programming changes that comprise the new ASP.NET.

The Different Stages of Web Programming

There have been several different attempts to provide an easy-to-use Web programming environment. On Day 15, you learned about the basic Web programming language, HTML, and how to create Web pages using this language. The next step in the process was the addition of scripting languages that you could use to add logic to the Web page. For this, you learned a little about VBScript and how to incorporate it into a Web page.

In the previous release of Visual Basic, Microsoft provided a Web interface called Dynamic HTML (DHTML) for your use when creating a Web-based application. Although this provided a more sophisticated way of adding logic to a Web page, there actually were two versions of DHTML: one that ran in Internet Explorer and another that ran in Netscape Navigator. DHTML was a client-side scripting technology that offered browser interaction. By using DHTML, you could add effects to the Web page, such as drop-down menus, without the need for the server to refresh and resend the Web page.

16

Defining the Execution Side

Most browsers available today support the capability for a Web page to have some type of script embedded within it, as you saw on Day 15, "Programming for the Internet." The most widely used scripting languages are JavaScript and VBScript, both of which are subsets of their respective "real language" counterparts, Java and Visual Basic. Scripting is most commonly used to provide user input validation, executing before a page is posted back to the server and informing the user that something was missing or input incorrectly.

Client-side scripting should be clearly distinguished from server-side scripting. A server-side script actually is executed as the Web page is being built by the server to be sent and displayed on the user's browser. A page that has been built and sent to the browser won't contain any server-side scripting by the time it's displayed.

What this separation provides you with is the capability to perform certain actions on the client browser (as in data input validation) while performing more complex data retrieval and updating on the server. This creates a much faster application that doesn't require a transmission back to the server if any user input was incorrect.

The Components of a Web Application

When you create a new Web application using the New ASP.NET Web Application template, it creates a project that contains many different component files. These are used by the application project for the proper execution on the Web (see Figure 16.1).

The files added to your project are the standard ones used in most Web applications, including

- Namespace references
- web.config
- global.asax
- A default .aspx Web Forms page

FIGURE 16.1

*The different files used
by a Web application
listed in the Solution
Explorer.*

The full application project actually builds a project file structure both on your computer
and the Web server where you are executing the application. In contrast, if you create an
empty Web project, none of these files are added to the project. Creating an empty Web
project is useful when

- Working only with HTML files, and possibly ASP, instead of ASP.NET files. If
  you aren't using ASP.NET, you don't need the support for it.
- The application project will need only a few of the files normally added to the Web
  project.
- You intend to add the files needed manually.

When a Web project is created, Visual Basic .NET creates the following on the server:

- A physical directory structure under the default Web site (such as
  `Inetpub/wwwroot`) of the Web server computer you specify
- An identity for the directory as an IIS application
- A FrontPage Web page (if FrontPage Server Extensions are installed)

In the solution on your computer, additional files (listed in Table 16.1) are added.

TABLE 16.1   Files Added for an ASP.NET Web Application Project

File	Description
WebForm1.aspx, WebForm1.aspx.vb	These two files together make up a single Web Form. The aspx file contains the visual elements of the page; the aspx.vb class file is a hidden file that contains the code associated with the Web form.
AssemblyInfo.vb	Project information file.
Web.Config	An XML-based file that contains the configuration data on each unique URL resource used in the project.
Global.asax, Global.vb	Optional files for handling application-level events.

TABLE 16.1   continued

File	Description
Styles.css	Support files for cascading style sheet styles to be used within the project.
.vsdisco	An XML-based file that contains links to resources that provide discovery information for a Web Service.

This is a brief overview; entire books have been written about ASP.NET. If you want more detailed information about ASP.NET, several good books are available, including *Sams Teach Yourself ASP.NET in 21 Days* by Chris Payne and Scott Mitchell (Sams Publishing, ISBN 0-672-32168-8).

16

Creating a Simple Web Application

The first step in understanding how a Web application actually works is to create one. Follow these steps:

1. From the File menu, choose New and then Project to open the New Project dialog box.

2. From the Visual Basic Projects folder, select ASP.NET Web Application (see Figure 16.2) and specify the following:

   • **Name.** The name for your project.

   • **Location.** The IIS server computer on which you want the project's Web files to be created.

FIGURE 16.2

Starting a New ASP.NET Web Application Project.

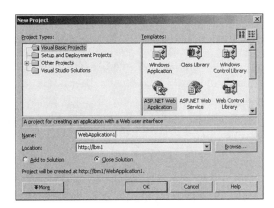

3. Click OK to create the new Web project.

You should see a blank Web Form displayed in the Design Editor (see Figure 16.3). You are now ready to start adding controls and code logic to this Web page.

FIGURE 16.3

The new Web Form displayed in the Design Editor for the ASP.NET Web application.

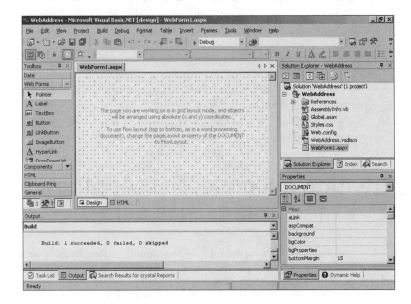

Working with Web Forms

The Web Form provided by ASP.NET fills the gap between the techniques used to build a desktop application and those used to create a Web application. With Web Forms, developers can rapidly develop platform and browser independent Web applications using the very same techniques previously utilized to create Windows applications.

The Web Form divides the user interface of a Web application into two distinct areas:

- The *User Interface Element* consists of a file containing HTML server controls and Web Server controls (both will be discussed later in this section).

- The *User Interface Logic* consists of code that you create to interact with the form. This program code remains in a separate file from the user interface file and normally is referred to as the *code-behind* file.

A Web Forms page acts as a container for the static text and controls you want to display. Using the Visual Studio HTML Editor with the Web Forms controls, you can design the form just like any other Visual Basic application.

Designing the Web Form

To create a Web application that uses Web Forms, you would simply add a Web Form to your project, drag a control to the page, and then double-click the control to add the code required for that control. For this simple demo, add the controls listed in Table 16.2 to the Web Form as shown in Figure 16.4.

TABLE 16.2 Building the First Web Forms Page

Control Type	Control	Property	Value
Web Forms	Label	Text	Enter your Name:
Web Forms	Textbox	ID	txtNameIn
Web Forms	Button	ID	cmdProcess
		Text	Process
Web Forms	Label	ID	lblMessage
		Text	Leave blank
HTML	Horizontal Rule		

FIGURE 16.4

The Simple Web Application with the controls placed on the form.

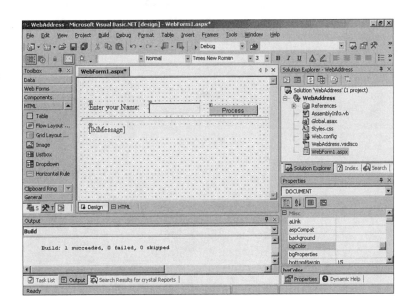

After you add these controls, try executing the application by performing the following tasks:

- Enter your name and click the button.
- Leave the name field empty and click the button.

Nothing should happen either time, because we need to add the following code to the button click routine:

```
lblMessage.Text = ""
lblMessage.Text = "Hello there, " & txtNameIn.Text
txtNameIn.Text = ""
```

ANALYSIS   The first line will blank out the output message if one was displayed. Next, the message label is initialized to the message with the name concatenated. Finally, the input textbox is blanked out.

Now try the same tasks as before to see what happens. The first test—entering a name and clicking the button—produces the expected results (see Figure 16.5). However, when you click the button without entering a name, you get a result that you probably didn't want (see Figure 16.6).

FIGURE 16.5

Having the Web Application redisplay the entered name with a string constant attached to it.

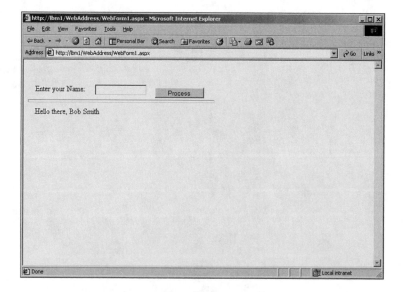

In the next section, you will be introduced to some the different controls that you have access to when designing a Web Forms application. These include a Validation control, which will assist you in determining if the input is correct.

FIGURE 16.6

Without a name being entered, the code still displays the string constant, which is incorrect.

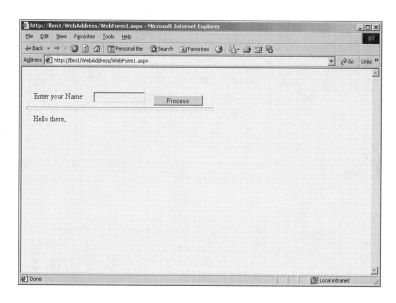

16

Introducing the Web Forms Controls

As you've seen in the previous section, when designing a Web Form you have access to several different types of server controls, which you can add to the form. These server control types are as follows:

- *HTML server controls* are HTML elements exposed to the server so you can program them.

- *Web server controls* contain more built-in features than HTML server controls. They include not only form-type controls such as buttons and textboxes, but also special-purpose controls such as a calendar.

- *Validation controls* incorporate logic to allow you to test user input. A validation control is attached to an input control to test what the user enters for that control.

- *User controls* are custom controls you can create to use on a Web Form.

HTML server controls contain attributes that make them visible to and programmable on the server. By default, HTML elements on a Web Form aren't available to the server; they are just passed through to the browser. However, you can convert these elements to an HTML server control by adding the following attribute to the controls' definition:

```
RUNAT="SERVER"
```

The complete statement for an HTML button converted to a server control is

```
<INPUT type="button" value="Button" runat="server" >
```

These HTML controls aren't really that sophisticated compared to the ASP.NET controls. These controls have their own area in the Toolbox named HTML in the design environment. To access any of these controls, simply click the HTML tab in the Toolbox, and select and drag the control you want to the Web Design editor. Finally, to enable it as a server control, right-click the control and select Run as Server Control from the pop-up menu.

> **Caution**   If you don't set this parameter for the HTML control, it will continue to act like a standard HTML client control with no server code associated with it.

The Web Server controls are a newer, second set of controls that provide you with much more sophisticated features for your Web application. These include the traditional controls such as buttons and textboxes, and complex controls such as tables, calendars, and repeater controls. They also include controls that assist in the display and manipulation of data from a database.

Using Validation Controls

Validation controls are used to provide various kinds of validation of user data from other controls. The validation scripts are generated based on which browser is executing the application. For some browser types, the validation is executed on the server; for others, it will be executed on the client. If the validation is executed on the server, it will be performed only after the entire form is submitted. Also, for browsers such as Internet Explorer, the validation will be processed on both client and server. Although the validation process is normally performed when an attempt is made to post a page to the server, it also can be set to execute when the user leaves the control.

For the validation process to work, the validation control must reference an input control. The property `ControlToValidate` provides the reference to the control that needs the validation performed. Table 16.3 lists the different validation controls available along with the type of validation they perform.

TABLE 16.3   The Different Validation Controls and Their Actions

Control	Description
RequiredFieldValidator	Tests to see whether data was entered into an input control, such as a textbox
RangeValidator	Ensures that a user entry falls into a valid range as specified

TABLE 16.3 continued

Control	Description
CompareValidator	Compares the input value in one control with the input in another control
RegularExpressionValidator	Checks the input against a regular expression
CustomValidator	Provides the capability to code a custom validation routine
ValidationSummary	Displays a summary of error messages produced by all validation controls on a form

16

To see how this works, add a RequiredFieldValidator control to the form as shown in Figure 16.7, modifying its properties as follows:

Property	Value
ControlToValidate	txtNameIn
ErrorMessage	"You must enter your name to continue"

FIGURE 16.7

Adding a Validation control to the simple Web Application.

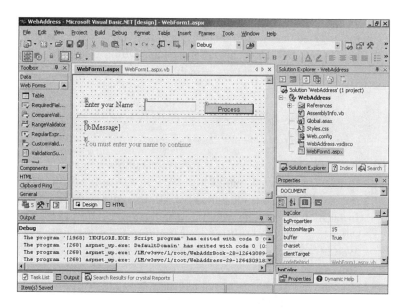

The key is that the text in each control isn't visible unless the validation process produces an error. Now try executing the application again and clicking the button without entering a name. Figure 16.8 shows the result of this process.

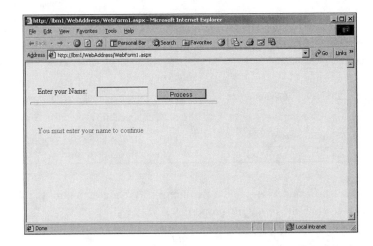

Figure 16.8

Causing a validation error to appear.

Adding Functionality to the Application

Now that you have a working Web application, let's change it. Adding functionality to the application requires adding one or more controls to a form, or one or more forms to the application. You also might need to add some code to perform the task required in the application. Besides the controls available within Visual Basic .NET, Microsoft also has made several other controls available to download from the Web site www.asp.net:

- Treeview
- Toolbar
- Tabcontrol

After you download the Microsoft Web controls, you still need to run the downloaded installation file, Webcontrols.Msi, before you can use them. This installation will install the controls on the computer and create several directories on the Web server. When the installation is complete, you must add the new controls to the Toolbox in Visual Basic .NET by displaying the Customize Toolbox dialog and selecting Microsoft Web.UI.WebControls.dll. You then need to exit Visual Basic .NET and restart it before you can use them.

Starting the Address Book Project

You are now ready to create a Web application that provides some of the capabilities of the Address Book application you created earlier in this book. This application will consist of a

- *Login Form,* which asks the user for a name and password before displaying the Address Book. This allows each user to have a unique address book.

- *Address Book display,* which displays the address book names in a tree structure and detail information when requested.

To start, we will create the Address Book form, because this is the most complex of the three. Start a new ASP.NET Web application and add the following Web controls (listed in Table 16.4) to the form as shown in Figure 16.9.

TABLE 16.4 Creating the Web Address Book Application

Control	Property	Value
Label	Text	"Web-based Address Book Application"
	Font-Bold	True
	Font-Size	Larger
Label	Text	"For: "
	ID	lblOwner
TreeView	ID	tvTreeView
	SelectExpands	True
	BorderStyle	Inset
	Height	450
Button	ID	cmdLoad
	Text	Load Address Book

FIGURE 16.9

Running the new Web Application displaying the Treeview Structure for a phone book.

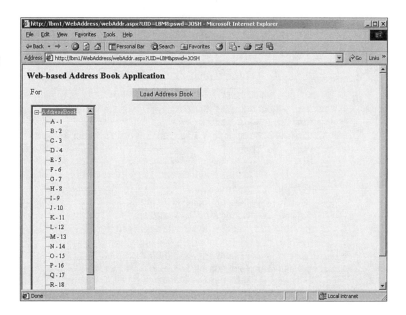

16

When you have this form designed, add the logic that will build the initial tree structure. To perform this task, we are going to "borrow" some of the code you created earlier for the Windows version of the Address Book application. Listing 16.1 shows the original Set_NewTree subroutine used to initialize the tree structure.

LISTING 16.1   WINTREEINIT.TXT: The Original Initialization Code from the Windows Application

```
Public Sub Set_NewTree()
        Dim node_letter As String
        tvTreeView.Nodes.Clear()
'Set the Document Type
        tvTreeView.Nodes.Add("PhoneBook")
'Set the Documents
        tvTreeView.SelectedNode = tvTreeView.Nodes.Item(0)
        tvTreeView.ExpandAll()
        tvTreeView.ShowLines = True
        tvTreeView.ShowPlusMinus = True
        For I = 1 To 26
            node_letter = Chr(64 + I)
            tvTreeView.SelectedNode.Nodes.Add(node_letter)
        Next I
End Sub
```

However, if you try to execute this routine as is, it will fail. The Web version of the Treeview control requires a few modifications, as shown in Listing 16.2.

LISTING 16.2   WEBTREEINIT.TXT: The Web Version of the Tree Structure Initialization Logic

```
Public Sub Set_NewTree()
        Dim myRootNode As Object
        Dim ChildNode As Object
        Dim myNewNode = New Microsoft.Web.UI.WebControls.TreeNode()
        Dim I As Integer
        Dim node_letter As String

        tvTreeView.Nodes.Clear()
        'Set the Document Type
        tvTreeView.Nodes.Add(myNewNode)
        myRootNode = tvTreeView.Nodes.Item(0)
        myRootNode.text = "AddressBook"
        'Set the Documents
        tvTreeView.ExpandLevel = 1
        tvTreeView.ShowLines = True
        tvTreeView.ShowPlus = True
        For I = 1 To 26
```

LISTING 16.2   continued

```
        Dim myNewChildNode As New Microsoft.Web.UI.WebControls.TreeNode()
        node_letter = Chr(64 + I)
        myRootNode.Nodes.Add(myNewChildNode)
        ChildNode = myRootNode.nodes.item(myRootNode.nodes.count - 1)
        ChildNode.text = node_letter
    Next I
End Sub
```

16

ANALYSIS   Notice how the root and child nodes are identified in Listing 16.2 after being created. Each individual node will contain its own level of methods to add new child nodes to it. Hence, a child can be added to a root node by using the following statement:

```
tvTreeView.Nodes.Item(0).Nodes.Add(myNewChildNode)
```

However, to add a child to the newly created child would require the following:

```
tvTreeView.Nodes.Item(0).nodes.item(21).nodes.add(myNode2)
```

As you can see, for each new level added to the structure, the statement reference will get longer and more difficult to follow. This is why I've declared objects to be assigned portions of this structure as follows:

```
'Set the Root Node
myRootNode = tvTreeView.Nodes.Item(0)
'Add the Child Node
myRootNode.Nodes.Add(myNewChildNode)
'Set the Child Node
ChildNode = myRootNode.nodes.item(myRootNode.nodes.count - 1)
```

By having objects point to sections of the reference, you can keep the statement short and readable. Now, to activate this code, place a call to the new subroutine in the Page_Load routine for the Web Form. Try running the application to see how the code is processed. Figure 16.9 shows the initial tree structure when displayed.

Note

> In tomorrow's lesson you will learn how to access the database and populate the tree structure, much as you did in the Windows application.

Using the TreeView Designer

If the structure of the tree you are adding to the form is more static than an address book, which can expand and contract as you add and subtract names, you could initialize it at design time by using the TreeView Designer included with the control. After selecting the TreeView control on the form, you can open the TreeNodeEditor (see Figure 16.10) by clicking the button on the Nodes property in the TreeView's properties list.

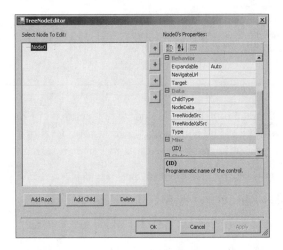

 Tip

To ensure that the entire tree is displayed on the initial form, add all the main children (such as Letters in the address book) and size the tree accordingly. Then you can see what the height was set to and use it in future code assignments.

Redirecting the User

The redirection of the user is a fancy way of changing what is displayed to the user, which can be done in two different ways:

- A Hyperlink Label displays a hyperlink that the user can click to go to a new page.
- The Redirect method is a code statement that will automatically go to a new page.

Using hyperlinks allows users to select what they want to display in a Web application. Almost every Web site you visit uses hyperlinks to display other forms or pages in the browser.

The other method is the automatic redirection of the display in the code. The user doesn't have control of this process, which is used to direct the user to another page when an event occurs on the current form, such as the user clicking a button. In the next section you will see how to use this method to allow users to sign into the address book application and pass their names to the main address book Web form.

Adding More Features to the Application

Before displaying the Address Book Web form to users, they should enter their name and password into a Web page to validate that they are allowed to use the application. Also, the name will be used to read the appropriate address book information from the database, as you will see in tomorrow's lesson. To do this, add a new Web Form to the project and name it WebLogin. Next add the controls listed in Table 16.5 to the form as shown in Figure 16.11.

16

TABLE 16.5   Creating the Login Form for the Application

Control	Property	Value
Label	Text	Welcome to the Address Book Application
	Font-Bold	True
	Font-Size	Larger
Label	Text	Please Sign in
Label	Text	User ID
Label	Text	Password
Textbox	ID	txtUserId
Textbox	ID	txtPswd
Button	ID	cmdLogin
	Text	Continue
Label	ID	lblErrMsg
	Forecolor	Red

The code for this page is pretty simple—when the user enters the userid/password combination and clicks the Continue button, the code will validate the userid/password. If the entry is correct, the user will be redirected to the main address book page. If the entry is invalid, an error message will be displayed. Today we won't validate the entry; we'll do that tomorrow when access to the database is added. For now, we will just add the redirection code to the button's click routine, which will pass the userid and password to the address book form where the name will be displayed.

To redirect the user to the next page, add the following line of code to the button's click routine:

```
Response.Redirect("WebAddr.aspx")
```

Although this statement will take the user to the next form, it doesn't pass the userid/password with it. To do this, you will add a `Query/String` pair parameter to the end of the URL. The syntax of this parameter is

```
?Variable_Name=Value  |  &variable_name=value  |...
```

The first character must be a question mark, which signifies that what follows is a `Query/String` pair to be passed to the next ASP.NET form. You can add pairs by separating them with an ampersand. For this example, the final statement would be as shown:

```
Response.Redirect("WebAddr.aspx?UID=" & txtUserId.Text & _
    "&pswd=" & txtPswd.Text)
```

Of course, unless you add code to the WebAddr.aspx form, these variables won't be used. To access these variables in the form, you would use the `Request` method to retrieve the values. The following code shows how this is done:

```
Dim uid As String
Dim pswd As String

        uid = Request.QueryString("uid")
        pswd = Request.QueryString("pswd")

'Add database access here to get the users name to display

        lblOwner.Text = "Welcome " & uid
```

For the moment, this code will display the userid instead of the name.

Caution

Remember to change the starting Web page from the `addrbook` to the `weblogin` page in the project's properties dialog. Otherwise, the login form won't be displayed first.

When you run the application, the first form displayed should be the Login form as shown in Figure 16.11. After you enter the ID and password, click the Continue button. This will display the Address Book form along with the user ID you entered, as shown in Figure 16.12.

FIGURE **16.11**

*Using the Login form
to start the Address
Book application on
the Web.*

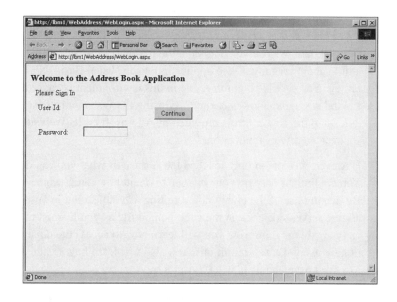

16

FIGURE **16.12**

*Once the login is vali-
dated, the user's name
is displayed at the top
of the Address Book
form.*

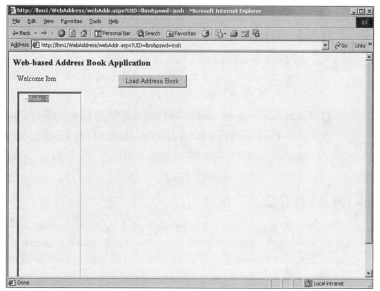

Summary

Congratulations! You've completed the first half of a Web application. Today you learned a little about creating a Web application using Visual Basic .NET and the ASP.NET capabilities. You should be comfortable in this environment because it's very close to the way a Windows application is created. By using the Web controls included with Visual Basic .NET and the new controls provided by Microsoft on its Web site, you can create very sophisticated Web applications.

However, this lesson only touched the surface of what you can do in a Web application. You are limited only by your imagination and how much work you want to put into it. By making use of the client-side scripting as you learned in yesterday's lesson or by adding server-side code in the code-behind file as you learned today, you can do practically anything. Tomorrow you will learn how to access the database from a Web application by using dataset definitions. You also will learn how to add a Crystal Reports Viewer to a Web page and display a Crystal Report.

Q&A

Q What is ASP.NET?

A ASP.NET is the next version of the Web programming environment that Microsoft has made available in the new Visual Studio .NET product. It allows a more powerful class of Web applications to be created.

Q Can a Web application still use VBScript to perform its processing?

A Yes it can; however, the recommendation is to use standard Visual Basic code in the code-behind form for a Web Form.

Workshop

The Workshop provides quiz questions to help solidify your understanding of the material covered, and exercises so you can use what you've learned. Try to understand the quiz and exercise answers before continuing on to tomorrow's lesson. Answers are provided in Appendix A, "Answers to Quizzes and Exercises."

Quiz

1. What's the difference between server-side and client-side processing?
2. When should client-side processing be used?
3. What type of control is provided to validate data on a Web form?

Exercise

As an exercise, try modifying the Address Book application to reflect how you might want the display to appear to users.

16

DAY 17

Adding Data Access to the Web

Yesterday you had your first glance into Web programming using Visual Basic .NET and ASP.NET. As you've probably noticed, Microsoft has made it very easy to create Web applications with the latest release of Visual Studio. Although now you can create some very sophisticated Web applications, they still require access to some data that might be stored in a database.

Today you will learn how to attach a database to the application to provide users with a more useful application. In the process you will see that most of the processing is identical to how databases are accessed in a Windows application. You also will see how to use Crystal Reports in a Web application. You will discover that most of what you've learned about data access and Visual Basic programming in a Windows environment now can be directly applied to a Web application.

Reviewing ADO.NET

As you should remember from Day 10, "Accessing the Database," ADO access has been redesigned to provide enhanced capabilities to Web-based applications. ADO.NET uses the same access methods for local, client/server, or Internet applications that access a database. Although the new ADO.NET data access methods resemble the older ADO methods, there are some significant differences.

ADO.NET provides access to data sources such as Oracle, Microsoft Access, and Microsoft SQL Server. With the release of Visual Basic .NET, there is now a separate data connection to directly connect to Microsoft SQL Server without using an OLEDB connection. All the other databases (that is, Oracle, Sybase, and so on) are still available by using an OLEDB connection. ADO.NET also separates database processing into data access and data manipulation, using the `DataSet` object and .NET data providers. This new structure provides data access to an application, either on the client or on the Web, while being completely disconnected from the database. This allows larger numbers of users to access the data without the need to handle the resources required by everyone being directly connected the entire time.

As a review, the `DataSet` is one of the two components of this disconnected architecture. The `DataSet` is designed to provide independent data access of any data source. As a result, multiple and various data sources can be used at the same time. The .NET data provider works with the `DataSet` defined to access data and is designed to provide fast, efficient data manipulation.

Adding Database Access to the Application

Now that you've taken a quick look back at the definition of ADO.NET and its components, you will see how to add database access to the Address Book Web application you created yesterday. Actually, we will add access to both the Login and AddressBook forms, passing the User ID information from the Login form to the AddressBook form. In the process, you will see how to add the following to a Web form:

- Data Adapter
- Database Connection (either SQL or OLEDB)
- Database Command
- Data Grid

Finally, we will add the actual code to fetch, and display the data. In the process, you will see how to allow additions, updates, and deletions from the Web application.

Note | The actual concepts of the Data Adapter, connection, and command all were covered on Day 10.

Finishing the Login Form

For this Login form to work properly, you will need to add a new table, named Logins, to the database as listed in Table 17.1. This table will contain the names of users who can access the Address Book application.

TABLE 17.1 Adding a Login Information Table to the Database

Column	Data Type	Length
UID	String	5
Pswd	String	4
Fname	String	15
Lname	String	15

17

The first step is to add a SqlAdapter to the Web form by dragging it onto the form from the toolbox. This will automatically add a database connection to the form by prompting you to define a SqlConnection object to the Web form (see Figure 17.1). Select the connection for the Address Book application that you created for Day 10.

FIGURE 17.1

Adding SqlAdapter *and* SqlConnection *objects to the Login Web form.*

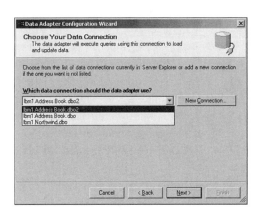

After clicking OK to select the connection, you are ready to define the SQL command you want to use to retrieve the data. For the Login form, the SQL statement should include a parameter for selecting the entered UID and Password. The following SQL statement is an example of what this should look like:

```
Select * from Logins Where UID=@UID And PSWD=@PSWD
```

After you finish entering and testing the SQL statement, click OK to complete the process. Don't forget to create the dataset object from the `SqlAdapter` before continuing. When the form is executed, if no record is returned by the query, users can't access the Address Book application. If a record is retrieved, we will close the command and pass the UID to the Address Book form. Listing 17.1 shows the final code to process a login for the Address Book form.

LISTING 17.1   LOGIN.TXT: Querying the Database for the UID Entered

```
 1: Dim LoginTbl As New LoginDS()
 2: SqlDataAdapter1.SelectCommand.Parameters("@UID").Value = txtUserId.Text
 3: SqlDataAdapter1.SelectCommand.Parameters("@PSWD").Value = txtPswd.Text
 4: LoginTbl.Clear()
 5: SqlDataAdapter1.Fill(LoginTbl)
 6: If LoginTbl.Logins.Count = 0 Then
 7:     lblErrMsg.Text = "User Id or password entered was invalid!"
 8:     SqlConnection1.Close()
 9: Else
10:     Response.Redirect("webform1.aspx?UID=" & txtUserId.Text & _
11:        "&pswd=" & txtPswd.Text)
12:     SqlConnection1.Close()
13: End If
```

ANALYSIS   Let's take a quick look at the code used to validate the login information. Line 1 declares a dataset object named `LoginTbl`, into which the data from the query will placed. Lines 2–3 set the parameters for the SQL query that you defined to pass the user ID and password to the query. Line 4 empties the new dataset to ensure that you are starting with an empty object; then line 5 opens the data connection and fills the `LoginTbl` object with data from the query. Line 6 checks to see whether the user was found in the table; if he isn't found, lines 7–8 display an error message and then close the data connection. If the user exists, line 10 redirects him or her to the Address Book form, passing the user ID. It then closes the data connection. The user ID passed to the Address Book form will be used to display only the address book information that this particular user can view.

Enhancing the Address Book Form

When getting the data, we will be using the UID passed from the Login form to filter the database for only the entries allowed for that user. This requires that you add a new column to the address table to hold the UID value for each record that will be used for the filter.

For the next section, where we will be accessing the database to retrieve the name of each address entry, we'll be using sqlConnection and sqlCommand objects. To populate the tree, you will need to perform the following tasks:

1. Open the database connection.
2. Create a SQL command that includes a filter for the user ID.
3. Initialize the data reader.
4. Get the first letter of each last name.
5. Place the name at the proper position in the tree.
6. Close the connection.

Before you can access the database in code, add sqlConnection and sqlCommand by dragging them onto the main Address Book form. Set the connection to the address book database and then build the SQL command, adding a parameter to filter on the UID field in the table. Listing 17.2 contains the code to perform these tasks. You should place this code in the Page_Load routine to have the tree populated when the page is displayed.

17

LISTING 17.2 TREE_POPULATE.TXT: Populating the Tree Structure by Using a DataReader

```
Sub populate_Tree()
    Dim node_key As String
    Dim entry_letter As String
    Dim node_name As String
    Dim myRootNode As Object
    Dim ChildNode As Object
    Dim NameNode As Object
    Dim I As Integer
    Dim myrdr As SqlClient.SqlDataReader
    Dim myNewNode = New Microsoft.Web.UI.WebControls.TreeNode()
    SqlCommand1.Parameters("@UID").Value = uid
    SqlCommand1.Connection.Open()
    myrdr = SqlCommand1.ExecuteReader(CommandBehavior.CloseConnection)
    myRootNode = tvTreeView.Nodes.Item(0)
    Do While myrdr.Read
        node_key = myrdr.GetString(1)
        entry_letter = myrdr.Substring(0, 1)
        Dim myNameNode = New Microsoft.Web.UI.WebControls.TreeNode()
        node_name = myrdr.GetString(1) & ", " & myrdr.GetString(2)
        For Each myNewNode In myRootNode.Nodes
            If myNewNode.Text = entry_letter Then
                I = Mid(myNewNode.getnodeindex, 3)
                ChildNode = myRootNode.nodes.item(I)
                ChildNode.nodes.add(myNameNode)
                NameNode = ChildNode.nodes.item(ChildNode.nodes.count - 1)
                NameNode.text = node_name
```

LISTING 17.2   continued

```
            End If
        Next
    Loop
    myrdr.Close()

    End Sub
```

ANALYSIS   Most of the code shown in Listing 17.2 should be familiar to you, as it's very similar to the code you created on Day 10, which populated the Treeview structure in the Windows application. The only real changes are for the Web methods as discussed yesterday. The only interesting line of code in the tree population routine is the statement that assigns the variable I to the index value. Because the `GetNodeIndex` method returns the node index in the form of

```
parent_Index.Child_Index
```

To get the actual index value of the node letter, you need to get the child index using the statement that follows:

```
I = Mid(myNewNode.getnodeindex, 3)
```

 Note   Before running this Web application, add at least two users to the logins table. You also should update the Address Book table with user ID values for some of the entries (for each user ID) to allow you to test the query filter process you are creating.

Execute the application and login using the name you entered in the logins table to see the Address Book form, as shown in Figure 17.2.

Adding the Data Grid

The final step is to display the detail information in a Data Grid when a letter folder is selected in the tree. To add the Data Grid to the Web form, select it in the toolbox and drag it to the form, resizing it as shown in Figure 17.3.

When the user clicks a letter folder in the tree structure, you want to open a new connection to the database using both the user ID and the selected letter as parameters to filter the data being returned. You would use the same SQL statement as the one that populated the tree structure, with the additional columns that provide the detail for each name. To actually perform the action of displaying the detail information in the grid, you would need to add the code in Listing 17.3, which

FIGURE 17.2

The Address Book application with the tree structure populated using the database query.

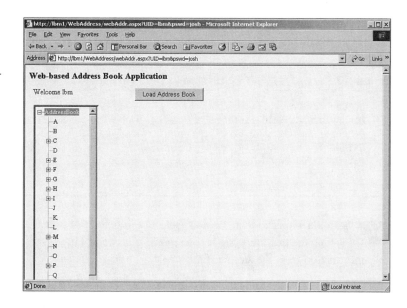

FIGURE 17.3

Adding the Web Data Grid to the Web form.

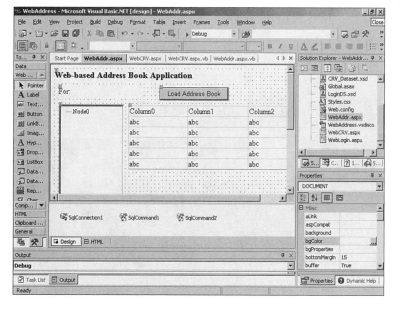

1. Opens a data connection.
2. Initializes a data reader.
3. Sets the DataSource property of the data grid to the data reader.
4. Binds the data grid to the data source.

5. Closes the reader.

6. Closes the connection.

LISTING 17.3 DATAGRID.TXT: Displaying Detail Information in the Data Grid

```
SqlConnection1.Open()
Dim Reader As SqlClient.SqlDataReader
Reader = SqlCommand2.ExecuteReader(CommandBehavior.CloseConnection)
DataGrid1.DataSource = Reader
DataGrid1.DataBind()
Reader.Close()
SqlConnection1.Close()
```

 ANALYSIS Place this code in the node selection routine, SelectedIndexChanged. Also notice that this code is referencing a second SqlCommand object that returns more information from the AddressEntry table.

Note

Closing the connection is important because the connection remains open while the data is being fetched from the database. When you no longer need the connection, close it and free the resources it uses.

When you execute the Address Book application, log in as a valid user, and select a letter folder that contains names; you should see a Data Grid displayed with the detail information for these names (see Figure 17.4).

FIGURE 17.4

The final Address Book display with information in the Data Grid.

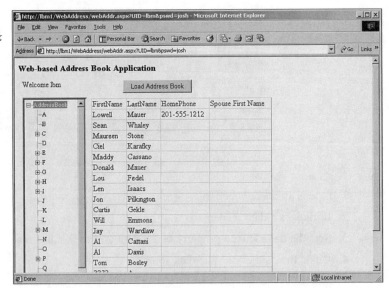

Using Crystal Reports

The next phase of the Web application creation process is to add the ability to view reports over the Web. Adding a Crystal Report Viewer to a Web application requires the same set of tasks as it did in a Windows application. The only difference is how to connect to the database. As you will see, Crystal Reports requires an ADO.NET dataset connection to present data in a report.

Adding the Report Viewer Form

To add the Crystal Report Viewer to your Web application, follow these steps:

1. Add a new Web form to the project and name it WebCRV.

2. Add a button to the main Address Book form that will redirect users to this new form to display the report.

3. Add the actual Crystal Report Viewer to the form by selecting it in the toolbox and dragging it to the form.

4. Resize the viewer so that it fills the entire page (see Figure 17.5), allowing the user the most visible area for the report to display in.

5. Create a DataSet definition and a report to be displayed in the report.

17

FIGURE 17.5

The Web version of the Crystal Report Viewer added to a Web form page.

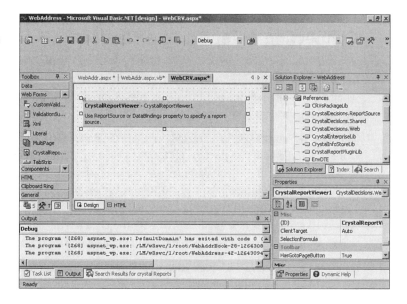

Creating the Dataset Connection

Although you created a dataset on Day 10 and earlier today, we will create one more dataset during the process of creating the Crystal Report to access the information required for the report. Using a SqlDataAdapter control, create a dataset called AddrCr. During the creation process, select the following information from the AddressEntry table:

- First Name
- Last Name
- Address
- City
- State
- Zip
- Home Phone

 Note

Remember to generate the dataset from the SqlDataAdapter control's property before continuing.

Connecting a Report to a DataSet

You might be asking yourself, "Why can't I just use the report that I created earlier for the Windows version of this application?" You can; however, creating a new report and using an old one require the same data connection settings. For the purpose of today's lesson, let's create a new report.

The DataSet object you just created provides the data description that you can select from to add the tables to the Crystal Report Designer. Start by adding a new Crystal Report Item to your project, naming it AddrBkRpt. Remember, when you add a Crystal Report item to the project, the Crystal Report Expert opens. Select Using the Report Expert and the Standard Expert options, and then click OK to continue. The Standard Report Expert opens (see Figure 17.6) with the Data tab displayed. You will select a data source from the Project Data sources, using the new dataset schema you just created.

Select the new dataset and click Next to complete the report creation process, producing the report shown in Figure 17.7.

FIGURE 17.6

Selecting data from a Dataset Schema defined in the project.

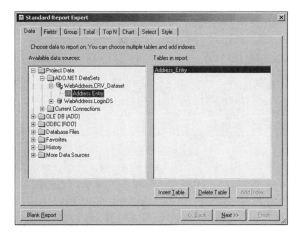

FIGURE 17.7

The final Crystal Report template for the Address Book report.

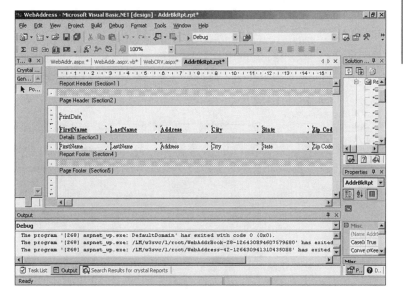

17

Executing the Report

The final step in the process is to add the required code filling the dataset, attaching to the report, and running the report. This code will be added after the `InitializeComponent()` call in the `Page_Init()` routine in the `AddrCR` Web form. Listing 17.4 shows the code required to perform these tasks.

LISTING 17.4   CRYSTALREPORTS.TXT: Initializing the Crystal Report Viewer and Displaying the Report

```
Dim myRpt As Object
Dim CR_Dataset As New addcr()
myRpt = New AddrBkRpt()
SqlDataAdapter1.Fill(CR_Dataset)
myRpt.setdatasource(CR_Dataset)
WebCRV.ReportSource = myRpt
```

ANALYSIS   The code in Listing 17.4 defines a new report object called myRpt, and a new reference to the AddrCr dataset called CR_Dataset. Next, the report object myRpt is set to a new copy of the Crystal Reports object AddrBkRpt. The next step is to fill the dataset using the SqlDataAdapter control's Fill method. Finally, the datasource is set for the report and the Crystal Reports Viewer ReportSource property is set to the report object.

Now try running the Address Book application, clicking the Show Report button to display the final report in the Crystal Report Viewer. You should see the report displayed in the browser (see Figure 17.8) along with several buttons that you can use to modify the display of the report.

FIGURE 17.8

The final Crystal Report displayed in the browser.

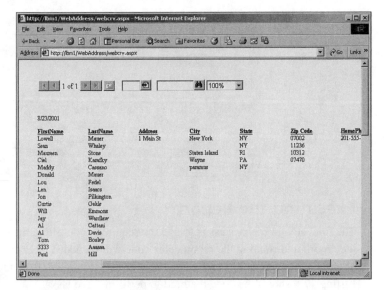

Summary

Today you've learned what it takes to connect your Web application to a database. In the process, you saw how to have several different Web forms relate to each other—either by passing parameters to another form, or by simply redirecting users to a new form to display a report. What you've really seen today is that Web programming in Visual Basic .NET is similar to that of a Windows application. Finally, you learned the differences between coding the Crystal Reports access in a Windows application and what is required for a professional-looking report on the Web. On Day 21, "Working with Web Services," you will see the final piece of the Web programming puzzle.

Q&A

17

Q **What's the difference between accessing data from a Web application versus a Windows application?**

A When accessing data from a Web application, the user shouldn't stay connected to the database while viewing or modifying the data. When using a dataset connection with ADO.NET, the data is retrieved and the connection closed, releasing the connection resources.

Q **What is the function of the `Redirect` method?**

A The `Redirect` method allows you to specify where the user will jump to when a button or hyperlink is clicked on a form.

Q **Why does the Crystal Reports Viewer display phony data in design mode?**

A The Crystal Reports Viewer displays phony data to allow you to resize the viewer control and to show you how the finished report format will appear to users.

Workshop

The Workshop provides quiz questions to solidify your understanding of the material covered and exercises so you can use what you've learned. Try to understand the quiz and exercise answers before continuing on to tomorrow's lesson. Answers are provided in Appendix A, "Answers to Quizzes and Exercises."

Quiz

1. How can you send data from one Web form to another?
2. Can a Web application access a database by using ADO connections instead of a dataset?

Exercise

Add a new form to the application that allows users to add new entries to their address book database. This should include a button on the main form allowing users to select this option.

DAY **18**

Building Online Help

Every Windows application that you've ever used has included some type of help system. Help systems can be as simple or as complex as the application can support. If you've assumed that creating a help system to your application is an impossible task, you're wrong. However, it's a task that requires design time to decide what should be included in the help system and which available features you should use.

Thankfully, Windows has a built-in help engine that almost every application uses. This allows you to concentrate on the content of the help system, not on how to display it. Today's lesson shows how to design, build, and test the help files you'll need to add to your Visual Basic application. You also will learn several different techniques that will give your application's users easy access to the application's help information.

What today's lesson won't teach you is what you should put into the help system. The content of your application's help system depends entirely on the application and the level of help you want to provide.

Designing a Help System

A Help system used to be a help file that could be displayed by itself or from within a computer program. These help files were text files displayed as a scrolling page, with very little in the way of advanced options. These days, a help system is much more complex, including video, pictures, sound, and links to Internet Web sites. Thanks to these additions, creating a help system takes a great deal of thought and effort.

A Help system consists of several different help files that in turn are made up of many different text or topic files. Some of these files will contain the text, graphics, or both that appear in the finished Help system, whereas other files will contain the information that specifies how your Help system will be displayed and how it will perform. In the compile process, you'll take all these files and turn them into one or more finished help files. The best part of this process is that if you don't like any part of the finished system, you can quickly modify the text and recompile it.

To design and create a Help system, you need to know what features are available for you to use in the process. If you've used help at all, you already know some capabilities that you can include in your own help system. Figure 18.1 shows what a Windows Help System display really looks like.

FIGURE 18.1

Windows Help provides users with sophisticated navigation.

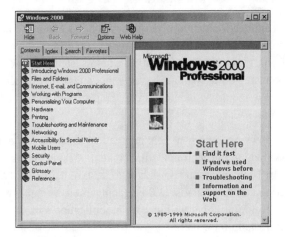

As you can see, the help display is an explorer-style interface that displays HTML-based documents on the right side. Visual Basic .NET comes with an HTML Help Workshop that provides the tools and information that you need to create professional-looking help systems for Windows applications.

> **Note**
>
> The Workshop is included on the Visual Basic product CD-ROM and must be installed manually.

To create your own custom Help system, you will need to follow these general steps:

1. Create the help topic files in HTML format by using Microsoft Word or any other text entry program.
2. Create the project file for this help system.
3. Create the content file to display the table of contents.
4. Attach your finished Help system to your Visual Basic application, where needed.

Help files can be as simple or as complex as you want them to be. To create a topic file, you'll need to perform the following actions:

- Save files in HTML format
- Insert HTML links
- Insert graphics into the documents

The help text or topic files contain topics linked together via hypertext links or special hypergraphics. If the topics weren't linked, they would be isolated sections of information, and your users couldn't move from one topic to another. The way to link topics together is to create hypertext fields that can jump between topics or display a pop-up window. These jumps consist of coded text or graphics that tell the WinHelp engine when to display a different topic in the help window.

Defining the Files

NEW TERM A *topic file* is nothing more than a word processing file saved in HTML format. A completed help file is a combination of topics that provide users with information. When designing and creating topic files, you want to decide what the flow will be from one topic to another. Each topic is directly related to a single document file. Also, because there are no size restrictions, each topic can be as long as you need it to be.

There are many ways to create HTML files; however, as noted previously, I find it very easy to use Microsoft Word to create and format my documents and then save them as HTML.

A topic file contains the words and graphics that make up your help file. To create most topic files, all you need to do is the following:

18

- Type text for the topics
- Add graphics
- Format characters

When entering text for a topic file, hypertext links are added to define links to other topics or for pop-up phrases.

Open your word processor to start a new topic file. To understand how the process works, see how small text files are used to create a help system that will contain hyperlinks, pop-ups, and other help features. (Actually, sections of previous lessons will be used as the sample text for the help topics.) While the first file you can create is a Contents file that lists all the major topics, with the Windows Help system, you no longer need to create your own. The Help Workshop assists in the creation of the Table of Contents.

For this lesson, we will create a main Table of Contents page listing the three main topics in the help file, as shown in HTML in Figure 18.2. Create this file and save it as TOC.HTML.

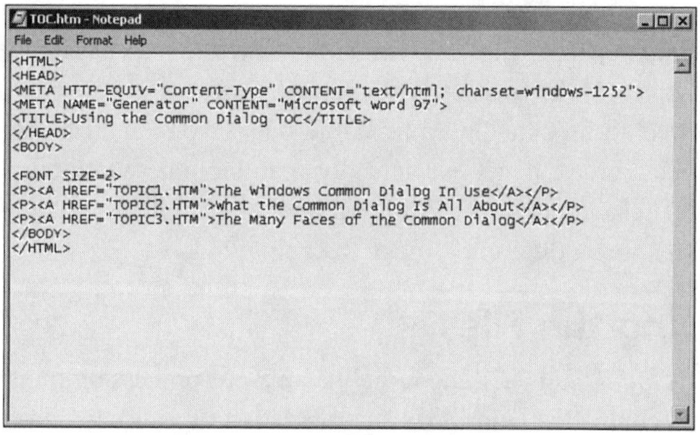

FIGURE **18.2**

The Table of Contents page showing the HTML links inserted for each main topic listed.

Now, let's create the four topic files using the text in Listings 18.1 through 18.4. Create a new document for each listing and then save them as HTML files.

LISTING **18.1**   TOPIC1.HTM: Topic One of the Example Help Topic File

```
The Windows dialog box allows the application to interact with the user with
the same forms that Windows 95 uses. This chapter will review the different
options available in the Common Dialog control and how to use it. Now, you
may be asking yourself, "Why do I need to review this again?" Well, if you
want to create an application that closely resembles the Windows 95 standard,
you want to understand and use as many of the common features that are
```

LISTING 18.1   continued

available in Visual Basic as possible. In addition to the review, you will
also get an understanding of why to use the Common Dialog control and more
importantly, when to use it. Finally, you will be shown another way of
accessing the Common Dialog through the use of the Dialog Automation object,
which comes with the Visual Basic product CD. This object can be included in
your application instead of the Common Dialog control.

LISTING 18.2   TOPIC2.HTM: Text File for Topic 2

When your old DOS-based computers underwent the change from black & white
to color displays, many new commands had to be created for the user to change
these new properties. Then, when Windows was introduced, the developer knew
that there would be many activities that would be performed over and over by
the user. The outcome of this knowledge led to the creation of a 'set' of
Windows dialogs that interfaced with the user. As more and more programs were
written for Windows, the dialogs in this set were copied by many programmers.
It was around this time that developers started calling them the Common
Dialogs.

18

LISTING 18.3   TOPIC3.HTM: Text File for Topic 3

One of the most commonly used functions of the Common Dialog control is the
ability to select a file to open or specify a filename to save. Both the Open
and Save As dialog boxes allow the user to specify a drive, directory,
filename extension, and a filename. If you have been using older versions of
Visual Basic, then you probably think that the code to display the Open dialog
is the following:

```
DlgGetFile.Action =1
```

LISTING 18.4   TOPIC4.HTM: Text File for Topic 4

The actual Common Dialog routines are distributed in a dynamic-link library
file call Commdlg.dll. The way in which you as the developer interact with
this library is by using the Common Dialog control. Even though this control
is used in almost every application that you may create, it is not one of the
default controls that is displayed in the Visual Basic toolbox.

After you create these files, you will see how to add links, pop-ups, and indexes and
search information to the files. After you complete it, you will have a fully functioning
Help system.

Creating HTML Help

HTML Help is the next generation of online help authoring systems that have been created by Microsoft. It uses the underlying components of Microsoft's Internet Explorer to display the Help information, supporting HTML, ActiveX, Java, XML, scripting (both JavaScript and VBScript), and HTML image formats such as .JPEG and .GIF. If you've ever used Windows before, you will be very familiar with many of the features of HTML Help and its associated workshop.

The HTML Help system uses a project file to combine help topics, contents, index, image, and other source files into one compressed help file. HTML Help also provides you with a workshop that helps you create the Help file. HTML Help has no limits to the size of the Help file you can create or to the size of any of the other features in the Help file. The only limitations that you have are those that the computer and the Hypertext Markup Language (HTML) might have.

When using the HTML Help system, navigation is done with HTML tags and ActiveX controls that instruct the Help browser to locate and display another Help topic file. The interface provides ease of movement and a clean interface for users.

When using the new HTML Help system, the documents you design are created using Hypertext Markup Language or HTML. Each topic you create has a corresponding HTML file. Although each Help topic you create appears to be a document with text, graphics, or images on it, the HTML files are actually text documents that contain the HTML formatting codes. The codes tell the Help browser how to display each page and the locations of any files that are referenced on that page.

Your first task when creating an HTML Help system is to design the overall look of your topic pages. Only then can you continue on and actually create the topic files. By using the Table of Contents tab, users can select an item to view and then navigate from one topic to another, based on what they need to find out.

When you've finished creating the HTML Help system, you only need to distribute the actual Help file (.CHM) with your application. To create the topics files, you either need to have a working knowledge of HTML programming to design fancy Help topics or you can use any of the word processors that can save a document in HTML format.

The Help text or topics files are linked together by adding HTML <A> tags to the files. These tags include the reference to the next topic file, or you can use a special ActiveX control that comes with the HTML Help Workshop to enable users to click a button and jump to another topic. To review, most topic files are created by performing the following:

- Enter the text for each topic.
- Add the HTML tags to support the included features (Links, Images, and so on).

Tip

When saving these files as HTML, you should use the names that allow you to understand what's in the file. This is because the HTML tags in the topics will reference the filenames.

A link for a topic requires that you know the name of the HTML file that you want to jump to. You should create most of the topic files before you start adding links and pop-ups to the topic files themselves. A link is added to the file using the HTML <A> tag, as shown in the following example:

```
<A HREF="TOPIC1.HTM">The Windows Common Dialog in Use</A>
```

As you can see, the file that you want to jump to is inserted into the <A> (anchor) tag.

Note

If you aren't sure what tags you can use, refer to the section on HTML tags on Day 15, "Programming for the Internet."

18

At this point, you've created several HTML files for your Help system, but there is nothing that actually makes it into a Help system yet. The best you can do with it is display the files in a Web browser. In the next section, you will see how to use the new HTML Help Workshop to take these files and create the actual help file for you to use.

Using the HTML Help Workshop

The HTML Help Workshop gives you the tools to create an easy-to-use Help system that performs much like an Internet Web site. You need to build a project file used by the compiler to create the final HTML Help file. The best way of producing the project file is by using the new HTML Help Workshop:

1. Start the HTML Help Workshop from the Start menu.
2. Choose File, New from the Workshop's menu.
3. In the New dialog box, select Project and click OK.

A New Project Wizard opens and asks whether you want to convert an older WinHelp project. Leave the option unchecked and click Next. Enter **VBDemoHTML** as the project name and click Next to continue. The next dialog box (see Figure 18.3) asks whether you have any files already created that you want to add to the project.

FIGURE 18.3

Adding existing files to the new HTML Help project.

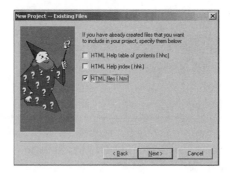

If you check any of these, you are asked to enter the location and name of the file(s). Because you've already created the HTML topic files, select the third check box and click Next. In this dialog box (see Figure 18.4), add the topic files you previously created by clicking Add to select them.

FIGURE 18.4

Adding the topic files you've already created.

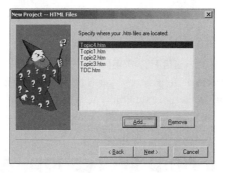

Select all your HTML topic files and click Finish to complete the project's creation. The last step is to set the default topic for the Help file. The easiest way to change a project setting is by double-clicking the setting you want to change in the Options list.

Next, set the default topic file to TOC.HTM. The project file now has enough information to compile your topic files into a working Help file, including the default options set by the Help Workshop when you start a new project (see Figure 18.5).

The Workshop toolbar in Figure 18.5 contains two buttons that you'll be using to compile and test your Help file. To compile your Help project, click the Compile HTML File button; the Create a Compiled File dialog box appears (see Figure 18.6). This dialog box lets you set the Help project filename to compile.

Compile HTML File
View Compiled File

FIGURE **18.5**

The finished project file contains several added parameter sections.

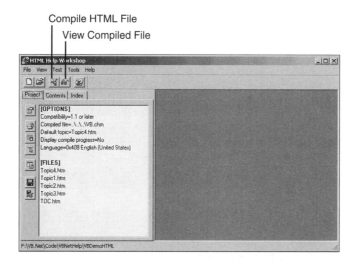

FIGURE **18.6**

Compiling the Help project with the Create a Compiled File dialog box.

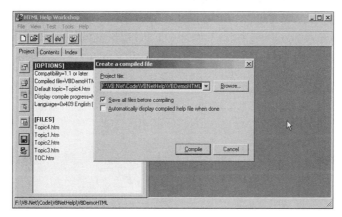

18

Click the Compile button in the Create and Compiled File dialog box to complete the process of compiling the topic files into a Help system file. When the compile is completed, click the View Compiled File button to display the Table of Contents topic from the new Help file (see Figure 18.7).

You now have a completed Help system; however, you can see that there's no Tab frame to the left of the Help information window. This is because you haven't created the Contents or Index files. If you want a Contents tab to appear, you must define a contents file within the Help project. If you want the Index tab to appear, you must define an Index file that contains keywords for your topics. Finally, the Search tab will appear only if you specify that you want it.

FIGURE 18.7

*The compiled table of
contents as users will
see it.*

Building the Contents Tab

In the HTML Help Workshop, click the Contents tab to display the Contents window.
When you do this for the first time, a dialog box will appear asking whether you are creating a new Contents file or using an existing one. Leave the default to create a new one
and click OK. The Windows Save As dialog box is displayed for you to enter the new
filename. Again, leave the default name and click Save. An empty Contents window
appears in the Help Workshop (see Figure 18.8). This is where you'll create the contents
file.

FIGURE 18.8

*The Contents tab
displays the Contents
list as you work.*

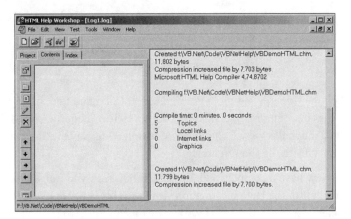

You can add two types of entries to the contents file, each entry giving users the ability
to perform a particular function:

Option	Description
Heading	Used to define a category level shown as a Book or Folder icon
Topic	Defines each main page of the Help system

When adding items, remember that headings are identified by book or folder icons that can be double-clicked to display the topics that they contain. To add the first entry to the list, you can click the Insert a Heading or Insert a Page button, it doesn't matter. The Table of Contents Entry dialog box appears (see Figure 18.9).

FIGURE 18.9

Adding entries to the Contents tab is done with the Table of Contents Entry dialog box.

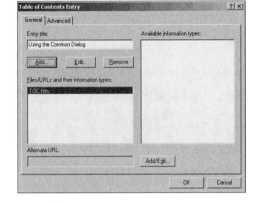

The Table of Contents Entry dialog box is where you specify the entry's title and its associated page or Web link. In fact, headings can now have a topic page associated with them. When you click the Add button, the Path or URL dialog box appears (see Figure 18.10), listing the available HTML file titles (not the filenames) to select from.

FIGURE 18.10

Selecting the HTML topic files for the Contents file.

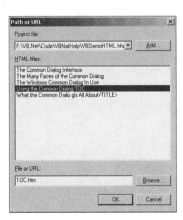

Add the items in Table 18.1 to the contents file.

TABLE 18.1 Topic Items Added to the Content File

Entry Type	Title	Topic File
Heading	Using the Common Dialog	TOC
Page	The Common Dialog in Use	TOPIC1
Page	What it is all About	TOPIC2
Heading	The Many Faces of the Common Dialog	
Page	The Common Dialog Interface	TOPIC3

After you add these entries, the Contents tab should look like the one shown in Figure 18.11.

FIGURE 18.11

The finished Contents tab displayed in the Help Workshop.

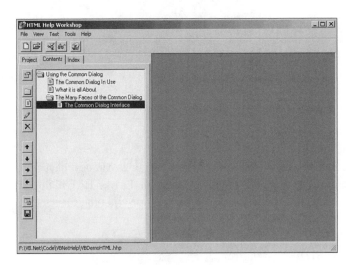

After saving the changes to the contents file, test it by compiling the Help file and viewing it. To test the Contents file, click the View Compiled File button to see the new Help system, shown in Figure 18.12. Try clicking the book icons and then the item icons to see what happens.

FIGURE **18.12**

*The finished Help file,
including a Contents
tab.*

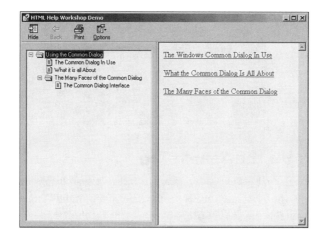

Adding Keywords to the Index Tab

If you recall, the Index tab appears only if you have keywords defined for your topic
pages. Then, by double-clicking a keyword displayed on the Index tab, users can display
the related topic. You add keywords to the Index the same way you added items to the
Contents tab. By clicking the Index tab in the HTML Help Workshop, you are prompted
for the name of the new Index file to create. You also can add multiple topic pages to a
keyword definition (see Figure 18.13).

FIGURE **18.13**

*Adding multiple topic
pages to an Index
keyword.*

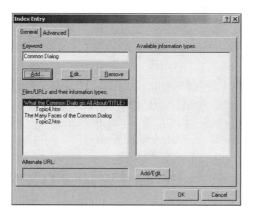

Then, when you are in the Help system and click that topic, a selection dialog box opens,
as shown in Figure 18.14.

FIGURE **18.14**

*Getting a Topics Found
dialog box from the
Index tab.*

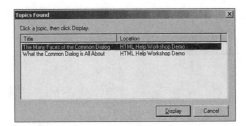

Setting Up the Search Tab

The Search tab enables users to perform a full-text search for every word in a Help file.
For example, if users enter OPEN on the Search tab in the Windows Help browser, every
topic that contains the word **OPEN** is listed. If you choose to have the project compile in
a full-text search file (.CHG), you must distribute it with the Help file. To enable this
option, simply click the Compile Full-Text Search Information check box on the
Compiler tab of the project's Options dialog, as shown in Figure 18.15. This will add
Full-text search=Yes to the Options list in the project (as also shown in Figure 18.15).

FIGURE **18.15**

*Enabling the Full-Text
Search option.*

Converting from Older Help Projects

If you are a Visual Basic developer who has already created help systems for your applications, don't panic—the HTML Help Workshop has a conversion feature that enables
you to easily create an HTML Help project from an existing WinHelp project. The New
Project Wizard will convert the WinHelp project file (.HPJ) to an HTML Help project
file (.HHP), the topic files (.RTF) to HTML topic files (.HTM), the contents file (.CNT)
to the HTML Help contents file (.HHC), and any index files to the new format (.HHK).

Any bitmap images you may have in the files will be converted to either .GIF, .JPEG, or .PNG depending on your target browser. If you want, see how this works by converting the Standard Help project that you created earlier today.

Using Advanced HTML Help Features

You can add many different components to your Help system by using the different HTML code tags. HTML tags support everything from adding images to an HTML page to having animations or movie clips displayed on the HTML page. Also, by using the HTML Help Workshop, you can define different window formats so that you can have certain topics displayed differently than others. The types of windows that you can create or customize are as follows:

- The *default window* is where topics will automatically appear. You never have to create the default Help window, but you can customize them.

- A *secondary window* is a custom window in which you can assign topics to display.

- An *embedded window* is also a secondary window, but rather than stay on top of the Help display, embedded windows are nested into the software program.

To define a new window, go to the Project tab and click the Add/Modify Windows Definition button. Now enter the name for the new window and click OK to go to the Window Types dialog box (see Figure 18.16).

18

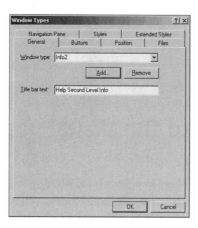

FIGURE 18.16

Defining a new window to be used by the Help system.

This dialog box enables you to customize almost every aspect of a window frame. Then to use a custom window, you would change the Window property for a given Contents item, as shown in Figure 18.17.

FIGURE **18.17**

Setting the Window property of a Content item to display the information in a custom window.

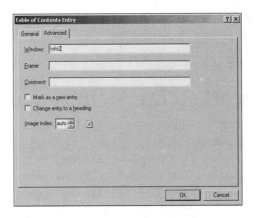

Linking to the Internet

Many newer applications, such as Microsoft Office 2000, use jumps in their Help systems to take users to specific pages on the Web. When creating your Help system, you can also provide users with a way to locate your Web site or any other Internet Web site. You do so by setting a URL Web address instead of a local Help filename.

Adding Multimedia

Another way to enhance your Help system is by adding video and sound clips to it. Video can be useful and fun to include in your Help system. Windows uses it in its *Online User's Guide*. Several topics include animation to explain how to perform a particular function. You add any video or audio features to your Help system by using standard HTML tag commands. The following code line will add a video to a topic page:

```
<A href="../Images/File.avi"> Click here to see a movie.</A>
```

This will be played using the registered media player on the users' computers.

Connecting Help to the Visual Basic Application

After you design and create the help system, which probably includes many of the features discussed, you're ready to add it to your application. You can access help from within your Visual Basic application in one of two ways. You can use the Help Provider control as discussed in Day 2, "The Face of a Windows Application," or by adding items to the Main Menu in your application and then displaying help using the Help Provider control in the menu item code.

Summary

You've seen several different concepts today. First, you saw that the creation process for a professional Windows Help system is really quite easy if you use the HTML Help Workshop. Designing and selecting what you want in the Help system is the hard part of the job, however. You may have figured out that the design of the Help system should be done in parallel with the design and creation of the actual application. This way, you can list what topics you'll need mapped in the Help system and how many topics there should be. Finally, you saw how you could add the help system access directly into the application by using the Help Provider control and other features of the included Visual Basic objects.

Q&A

Q What does it take to create a Help system?

A Creating a Help system requires a word processor and the help compiler or Workshop supplied with the Visual Basic product. You also need an understanding of what you want to put into the help topics and how to access them from an application.

Q How can hypertext links improve a Help system?

A Hypertext links allow users to move from one topic to related topics based on highlighted text defined in the text of the topic they're viewing.

Workshop

The Workshop provides quiz questions to help solidify your understanding of the material covered, as well as exercises to provide you with experience in using what you've learned. Try to understand the quiz and exercise answers before continuing on to tomorrow's lesson. Answers are provided in Appendix A, "Answers to Quizzes and Exercises."

Quiz

1. How do you connect context-sensitive help to the help topics?

2. How do you add the Help button to a form?

3. What are some features of the help project file?

Exercise

Create a small Help system that you can add to the Address Book application. Try making use of as many of the help functions and features as you can. This will enhance the overall usability of the application.

DAY 19

Tuning and Tweaking Performance

Making an application run better and faster is every programmer's goal. Performance is the second most important aspect of any application, right behind the application's usability and features. When anyone talks about performance in an application, however, the answer these days is usually, "Get a faster computer." If things were perfect, your application's users would have a computer with the fastest possible processor, plenty of memory, and unlimited disk space.

Unfortunately, reality dictates that for most users, one or more of the proceeding factors affects the actual performance of an application. In today's world, computer processing speed is quickly passing the 1GHz range, meaning that users have come to expect better performance out of every application they install on their computer. In fact, the connection to the Internet has gone from 28.8K to 512K and higher with DSL and cable modems.

NEW TERM   As your applications become larger and more complex, the amount of memory it
uses and the speed in which it executes becomes very important. To get your
application performing the best it can, you need to understand the different code and techniques that affect performance. This is known as *optimizing and tuning* an application.

When you're optimizing the application code, you can use several techniques to increase
performance. Some techniques will help make your application faster, whereas others
will help make it smaller. One problem that you face when tuning your application is that
the changes you make to the code may not always benefit you in the long run. Changes
made to the application to improve its performance can cause the code to become more
difficult to maintain or change in the future. Sometimes a change can actually decrease
application performance.

What you have to do is weigh and decide what the final performance of the application
will be against the changes that you make to affect it. Today's lesson focuses the different tips and techniques that you can use to enhance the performance of an application.

Creating the Right Impression

You know how first impressions are important. An application that takes a long time to
load can annoy users and appear as though it's not working correctly. The larger and
more complex the first form in the application is, the slower it will load. Any custom
controls in the form also must be loaded at startup. And if the first form calls procedures
in other modules, these modules must be loaded at startup time as well. Even when you
are considering a Web application, you want to make sure that the initial display comes
up (downloads) on the client browser quickly.

As you can see, performance can very quickly become a domino effect. Adding all this
up causes the application to slow down. You can resolve the perceived problem by
changing how the application is started. Rather than have the application's main form be
the first one displayed, use a splash screen instead (see Figure 19.1).

FIGURE 19.1

*Presenting users with
a splash screen to
enhance startup
performance.*

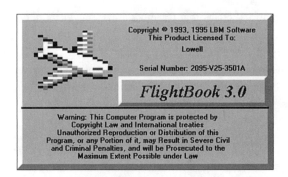

This splash screen should have the minimum amount of processing code in it. While the screen is displayed, the main form is loaded by using the New keyword. Finally, when the main form is ready to appear, the splash screen is unloaded. The code you could use to perform this task is shown here:

```
Sub Main()
Dim fSplash As New frmSplash()
        fSplash.Show()
        fSplash.Refresh()
        Dim fMainForm As New frmMain()
        fSplash.Close()

        fMainForm.Show()

End Sub
```

Giving Windows a Chance

Another reason an application appears to slow down occurs when code routines that are processing large amounts of data don't have any commands that require calls to the Windows engine. This will cause users to think that the computer has frozen or locked up. Windows can't process any user input, such as mouse clicks, unless a Visual Basic control command or Windows call is executed. To prevent this from becoming obvious, you should execute a DoEvents statement within the intensive processing code. This statement passes control to the operating system. After the operating system finishes processing the events in its queue and all keys in the SendKeys queue are sent, control is returned to your application.

 Caution Although the DoEvents statement is an essential and useful tool to allow Windows to do some processing, it has been known to cause some unexpected problems to appear. Use this statement carefully.

19

Distracting the User

Another way to prevent the perceived impression of a slow application is to display the status of a process, which you can accomplish by using a combination of progress bar and a Label (see Figure 19.2). You can create a professional-looking status display that will do several things: tell users that something is definitely being processed and, in most cases, show users that the computer hasn't locked up.

FIGURE 19.2

*Progress bars display
the status of an appli-
cation process.*

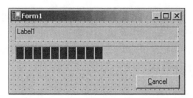

Using Other Tricks to Increase Perceived Speed

In addition to the tips already discussed, you can use other tricks to provide a snappier look and feel to your application. Each tip helps your application perform better, faster, and more efficiently. For example, don't load modules that you don't need. Visual Basic loads code modules on demand, rather than all at once when the application starts. This means that if you never call a procedure in a module, that module will never be loaded. If your startup form or main form calls procedures in several modules, however, all those modules will be loaded as your application starts and before it's displayed.

The following sections discuss other tips and tricks.

Run a Small Visual Basic Application First

Visual Basic spends a large amount of time during the application startup process simply loading the various components used by Visual Basic, ActiveX, and ActiveX controls. If these components are already loaded, however, none of that time would be spent by your application. This means that your application would start up faster if another Visual Basic application were already executing on the computer.

Keep Forms Hidden but Loaded

If you intend to use a form again later in the application process, you might consider hiding instead of unloading it. This will keep all controls and variables in memory so that they don't have to be loaded again when the form is needed. The obvious downside to this technique is the amount of memory used by these forms. If you think your application's users can afford the memory usage, however, this is an excellent way of having forms appear quickly.

Preload Data

Another way to improve the perceived speed of the application is by preloading any data that it might need. For example, if you need to read several files from disk, it's more efficient to read all the files at once rather than read one, read another, then another, and so on. No matter how fast the computer gets, starting disk access always slows down the process. The time spent loading the additional files will probably go unnoticed by users, and you'll have loaded all the required data.

Getting the Application to Perform Better

Tuning or optimizing an application is a combination of some programming techniques and some common sense. When you get past the obvious things that you can change in the way the application is processed (as discussed in the preceding sections), any other changes will take some thought and possibly design time before you can implement them. An important part of the process is understanding what you can and can't optimize. You can optimize Visual Basic code, processing algorithms, and data access. But you can do nothing about any operation that occurs outside your control, such as network file access.

A common misconception is that the optimization process takes place at the end of the application development. To create a truly optimized application, you must be optimizing it at the same time that you're developing it. By choosing your algorithms carefully, weighing speed against size and other constraints, you should be able to tell which parts of the application will be fast or slow, large or compact.

If you don't start with a clear goal in mind, you could waste time optimizing the wrong areas of your application. Everything you do should be based on user needs and expectations. The key to the optimization process is to understand the real problem that optimization will address. If you're like most programmers, you don't want to take the time to optimize everything in your application. Because of time, it's obvious that you should focus on the areas that seem to be the slowest or fattest, but to make the results of your efforts count, you should concentrate on the code where a little work will make a lot of difference.

19

Optimizing the Code

You can modify your code to enhance performance in many different ways. But unless your application is performing tasks like generating fractals, they're unlikely to be limited by the actual speed of your code. Other factors, such as video speed, network delays, or disk activities, are usually the limiting factor for your application. However, you may find areas in your application where your code's speed is the limiting factor, especially for frequently called routines. When that's the case, you can use the following techniques to increase your application's speed:

- Avoid using `Object` variables.
- Use `Long` integer variables and integer math.
- Cache frequently used properties in variables.
- Replace procedure calls with inline procedures.
- Use constants whenever possible.
- Cache control values in variables.

- Use new base classes for more optimized performance (that is, instead of concatenating strings, use the new `StringBuilder` object).

- Create new variables to handle derived objects (that is, `xmlNode = XMLDocument.DocumentElement.ChildNode(0)`).

- Pass arguments `ByVal` instead of `ByRef`.

Even if you're not optimizing your code for speed, being aware of these issues and their underlying concepts helps. As you get into the habit of choosing more efficient methods while you create your code, the gains can add up to a noticeable improvement of your application speed.

Replace Code with Functions

Visual Basic .NET includes several language functions that you can use to replace older, less efficient ways of processing data. By replacing these older multiple function statements with the newer functions, the application will perform better. The following code section was used to search each element of an array for a specific string value and place those elements into a second array:

```
J = 0
For I = 0 To 99
    If Instr(arrInput(I),"Demo") > 0 then
        J = J + 1
        ReDim arrFound(J)
        arrFound(I) = arrInput(I)
    End If
Next I
```

As you can see, although this code works, it does require some processing time for the computer to perform the loop and the `If` statement test. If you use the new `Filter` function, this process would be reduced to one statement:

```
arrFound = Filter(arrInput,"Demo",True,vbTextCompare)
```

By using this statement, you are using an internal function to perform the task instead of standard basic code. Table 19.1 describes some of these functions. Take a few minutes to investigate these commands to see when you can or should use them.

TABLE 19.1 Useful Functions Included with Visual Basic .NET

Function	Description
Filter	Returns a zero-based array containing a subset of the original array based on a specified value
Replace	Returns a string where a specified substring has been replaced with a new substring wherever it was found
Round	Returns a number rounded to a specified number of decimal places

TABLE 19.1   continued

Function	Description
Split	Returns an array containing a specified number of substrings from a single string expression
StrReverse	Reverses the character order of a specified string
Join	Returns a string created by joining all elements in a string array
WeekdayName	Returns the name of the specified day of the week
MonthName	Returns the name of the specified month

In addition to these functions, you can use several functions to format numbers and dates. The name of each function basically explains its function:

- FormatCurrency
- FormatDateTime
- FormatNumber
- FormatPercent

Use Long Integer Variables and Integer Math

If your application performs complex arithmetic operations, you should avoid using Currency, Single, and Double variables. Use Long integer variables whenever you can, particularly in loops; because the Long integer is the 32-bit CPU's native data type, operations that use such integers are very fast. If you can't use Long variables, the Integer or Byte data types are the next best choice.

Cache Frequently Used Properties in Variables

You can get and set values of variables faster than those of properties. If you're frequently getting the value of a property (such as in a loop), your code runs more quickly if you assign the property to a variable outside the loop and then use the variable instead of the property. Variables are generally 10 to 20 times faster than properties of the same type. The following code is very slow:

```
Do Until EOF(F)
    Input #F, nextLine
    Textbox1.Text = Textbox1.Text + nextLine
Loop
```

This version of the code runs much more quickly:

```
Imports System.Text
Dim stbBuffer as New StringBuilder("")

Do Until EOF(F)
    Input #F, nextLine
```

19

```
        stbBuffer.Append(nextLine)
Loop
Textbox1.Text = stbBuffer.ToString()
```

Replace Procedure Calls with Inline Procedures

Although procedures help make your code more modular, every procedure call involves some additional work and time for your application. If you have a loop that calls a procedure several times, you can eliminate this overhead by placing the body of the procedure directly in the loop, or you can place the loop inside the procedure.

Use Constants Whenever Possible

Using constants makes your application run more quickly. Constants also make your code more readable and easier to maintain. If some strings or numbers in your code don't change, declare them as constants. Constants are resolved once at compile time. Because variables must be resolved each time the application runs and finds a variable, the application must access the variable in memory to get the current value.

Pass Arguments `ByVal` Instead of `ByRef`

When writing procedures that include arguments, passing the arguments by value (`ByVal`) than by reference (`ByRef}` is faster. If you don't need to modify the arguments within the procedure, define them as `ByVal`.

Building the Application

When you compile or build your Visual Basic application, you're actually creating a file that will be executed by the computer as an .exe file. With Visual Basic .NET, Microsoft has greatly simplified the compilation process. For any given application, you can display the project properties to see both optimization options (see Figure 19.3) and build options (see Figure 19.4).

FIGURE 19.3

Specifying optimization options for the application.

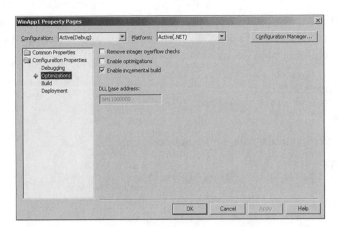

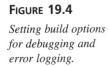

FIGURE **19.4**

Setting build options for debugging and error logging.

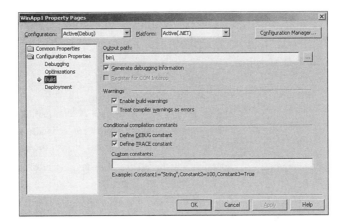

You can open both property pages by displaying the application's Properties and selecting the Configuration node. Table 19.2 describes some of the more common options shown in Figures 19.3 and 19.4. If you're unsure of which options to change, the safest thing to do is to use the default settings.

TABLE 19.2   Configuration Options for Optimization and Builds

Option	Description
Optimizations Dialog Box	
Remove Integer Overflow Checks	Turns on or off overflow error checking for integer operations. This causes the compiler to check all integer calculations for errors such as overflow or division by zero. Turning off this option prevents error checking and can make integer calculations faster. However, without error checking, incorrect results may be stored without raising an error if data type capacities are overflowed.
Enable Optimizations	Turns on or off compiler optimizations. Such optimizations make your output file smaller, faster, and more efficient, but also can make debugging difficult.
Enable Incremental Build	Optimizes the build process by building only those parts of the project that changed since the last compilation. If there are many changes, making it difficult to determine where changes have occurred, a full build will occur.
DLL Base Address	Specifies a default base address when creating a DLL.

19

TABLE 19.2 continued

Option	Description
Build Dialog Box	
Output Path	Specifies the directory in which output generated by the project should be placed. For client-based projects, this can be any valid file or Universal Naming Convention (UNC) path. For Web-based projects, any relative path within the project folder is allowed. By default, this is set to the bin\ directory in the current project directory structure.
Generate Debugging Information	Specifies whether to create debugging information during compilation.
Register for COM Interop	Indicates that your managed application will expose a COM object (a COM-callable wrapper) that allows a COM object to interact with your managed application. The Output Type property of this application must be Class Library for this property to be available.
Enable build warnings	Indicates that build warnings should be displayed to the Task List during compilation.
Treat Warnings as Errors	Indicates that build warnings should be treated as errors during compilation. A warning will cause no output file to be produced.
Conditional Compilation Constants	Determines whether tracing and debugging statements should be compiled into the assembly.

Using Resource Files

One of the easiest things to change in an application that would affect size and speed are the static resources the application uses. Every time you use a string constant for messages or labels, it increases the size of the application, as do picture resources used by the application. If the picture resources are loaded rather than included in the application, the load process also affects the application's speed. All these items are collectively called *application resources* and can be defined in a resource definition file.

NEW TERM *Resources* are the presentation data that your application uses—that is, no matter what your application does, it uses resources to interact with users. You can divide resources into two main groups: string and binary. String resources contain text string data, such as Hello World or (more realistically) Cannot find Name in Address Book! Binary resources can contain icons, bitmaps, cursors, sounds, videos, or any other data that's usually stored as binary information.

Using a resource file allows you to collect into one file all the version-specific text, bitmaps, and sounds for an application. This information is kept separate from the code, allowing better control over them. In addition to the obvious optimization effects, resource files also give the application the capability to change its strings, pictures, fonts, sounds, and so on, depending on user input.

A good example for using resource files is when an application is sold in other countries. When an application is distributed in another country, it should display words and images in that country's language. Rather than rewrite the application for each country, you can have a resource file that contains the different country-specific information and then, depending on an installation prompt, uses the correct file.

 Visual Studio .NET uses two formats for resource files. String resources and serializable objects can be contained in an XML-based format with the file extension .resources. (*Serializable* means you can store the object linearly or sequentially.) Binary information such as pictures, as well as strings, can be contained in a format with the file extension .resX, which contains both binary images and XML code.

By using resource files, you can take most of your memory-intensive resources and define them in a text file and compile them with the actual resource files into a single binary (.resX) file or an XML (.xml) file by using the Resource File Generator.

> **Note**
>
> The Resource File Generator is included with the .NET Framework tools and is installed along with Visual Basic .NET.

Creating a Resource File

Visual Basic automatically generates a .resX file for each form in a Windows Forms application when the `Localizable` property for that form is set to `True`. All resources for localizable properties (Text, Picture, and so on) of the form and any contained controls are written to the .resX file rather than the form file.

Additional .resX files are generated when the `Language` property is set. For these files, the language name for the selected locale is added to the filename. For example, choosing the English (United States) language setting would create a resource file named File1.en-US.resX.

In addition to Visual Basic creating the resource file, you can also create a resource file manually. There are three ways to create additional resource files for resources such as strings:

19

- Create a text file containing string resources, and convert it to a resource file using conversion tools included with Visual Studio .NET.
- Add resources directly to a .resX file using the XML editor.
- Use code to save string resources to a resource file.

Generating Resource Files Automatically

To see how Visual Basic creates the resource files for you, start a new project and then set the default forms `Localizable` property to `True`. Notice that the `Language` property is set to `Default`, which is the language specified for your computer.

Now add a button control to the form and set its `Text` property to `"Good Morning"`. To see the resource file created for the form, click the Show All Files button in the Solution Explorer (see Figure 19.5). You should see the default .resX file for the form.

FIGURE 19.5

Displaying all files in a project.

Now, change the property to Spanish (Spain) and then change the button's `Text` property to `"Buenos Diaz"`. In the Solution Explorer, you should see another resource file appear named Form1.es-ES.resx, the resource file for Spanish as spoken in Spain. The last step is to save and build the application. Depending on the language set for your computer, you will either see the default English or Spanish.

Without changing your computer language specification, you can still test the different resource files that have been created by setting the language for your application within the code. To set the language in your application, perform the following:

- Add the following code before the `Public Class Form1` declaration:
  ```
  Imports System.Globalization
  Imports System.Threading
  ```

- Add the following code in the `New` function, before calling the `InitializeComponent` function.

  ```
  Thread.CurrentThread.CurrentUICulture = New CultureInfo("es")
  ```

This will use the resources for Spanish when the application is executed (see Figure 19.6).

FIGURE 19.6

Accessing the correct language resource file.

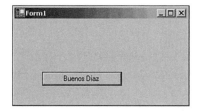

Generating Resource Files Manually

The easiest way to create a resource file manually is by adding an Assembly Resource File to your project. Add a new resource file to your existing project by adding a new item. Name the new resource file Resources1 and click Open to display the Resource Designer. If the XML Designer is displayed, click the Data tab at the bottom of the window, and then select Data in the Data Tables pane (see Figure 19.7).

FIGURE 19.7

Working in the Data Grid for a new resource file.

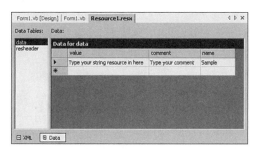

You can now add any number of values and their associated names. Enter the following information into the grid to see how to use a resource file:

Value	Name	Comment
This is a message Test	Message1	This is used to display an error message.
Good Afternoon	Button1Text	This will be used to change the text displayed in the button.

After you create this file, you can use the information in it by making the following changes to your application:

- Add the following code before the Public Class Form1 declaration:
  ```
  Imports System.Resources
  ```

- Define a variable to contain the language setting for your application:
  ```
  Dim LocRm As New ResourceManager("windowsapplication5.DemoRes",
                      GetType(Form1).Module.Assembly)
  ```

19

- To access a string, use the `GetString` method, specifying the name of the string you want to retrieve:

```
Button1.Text = LocRM.GetString("ButtonText")
```

The really neat thing about all this is that if you create a different version of this custom resource file for each language you want to support, Visual Basic will use the correct file depending on the language set for your computer.

Creating a Resource File from Text

If you need to create a resource file that contains a large number of strings to be used in the application, the quickest way is to use a text file to generate the data and then generate a resource file from that. The syntax for a text file is as follows:

```
Name=Value
```

To create the same resource file as the one in the previous example, you would create a text file with the following:

```
Message1="This is a Test Message"
ButtonText="Good Afternoon"
```

After you add all the strings you might need, save the text file.

Generating a Resource File from Text

After you create a text file that contains the strings you want for the application, the last step is to use the resource generator to create the actual resource file. The resource generator is executed from the command prompt window and has the following syntax:

```
Resgen [/compile] inputfilename [outputfilename]
```

Table 19.3 lists the arguments and their descriptions for this utility.

TABLE 19.3 Executing the Resource Generator

Argument	Description
inputfilename	The name of the input file to convert.
outputfilename	Optional when converting from a .txt or .resx file. You can specify the .resources extension when converting a text or .resx file to a .resources file. If you don't specify an outputfilename, Resgen.exe appends a .resources extension to the inputfilename argument and writes the file to the directory that contains inputfilename.
/Compile	Allows you to specify multiple .resx or .txt files to convert to .resources files in a single bulk operation. If you don't specify this option, you can specify only one input file argument.

If you've created a resource file using the Resource Generator, you will then have to add the new file to your application by selecting Add Existing Item from the Project menu and then selecting the resource file you've just created.

Adding Non-String Objects to a Resource File

If you want to create a resource file that contains objects other than strings, the process gets a bit more complicated. A resource file that contains objects such as pictures must be created using code. Listing 19.1 shows how to add both a string and icon to a new resource file.

LISTING 19.1   RESOURCES.TXT: Adding Objects to a Resource File

```
1: Dim rw As ResXResourceWriter = New
2  ResXResourceWriter("d:\temp\strings2.resX")
3: Dim b As Bitmap = New Bitmap("d:\temp\FLGUSA02.ico")
4: Dim amessage As String = "Hello, and welcome!"
5:     rw.AddResource("flag", b)
6:     rw.AddResource("welcome", amessage)
7:     rw.Generate()
```

In addition to the code in Listing 19.1, you must also add the following statement to the form, before the form definition.

```
Imports System.Resources
```

ANALYSIS   Let's take a quick look at what the code actually does. Lines 1 and 2 open a new resource file using the specified name. Lines 3–4 define variables that will contain the information you want to add to the resource file. Then, lines 5–6 use the AddResource method to actually add these objects to the file. Finally, you generate the new resource file by using the Generate method on line 7.

To retrieve an object from the resource file, you would need to use the following code:

```
Dim rm As ResourceManager = New
        ResourceManager("windowsapplication5.strings3",
          GetType(Form1).Module.Assembly)
        Button1.Image = CType(rm.GetObject("flag"), System.Drawing.Bitmap)
```

ANALYSIS   This code will define a new Resource Manager variable that points to the resource file, "Strings3". Then, the GetObject method would retrieve the object specified from the correct language version of the file. To then use these objects, you would simply assign the appropriate property to the object retrieved.

19

Summary

Today, you've seen how an application's performance can be affected by many different changes, Visual Basic commands, and techniques that you've used in the application. However, performance by itself is a very subjective concept. Making very minor changes in the way the application executes can create the impression of a faster application. Anytime you make changes to increase an application's speed, you should always retest the application to ensure that the changes haven't hurt performance rather than help it. You must also test for reliability after such changes. It's not uncommon for the changes you make to "break" working code somewhere else in the application.

Also, putting many of the more size-intensive resources into their own resource file that your application can access reduces application size and increases performance. Finally, you can create executable files that are optimized for the type of computer the application will probably run on.

The suggestions and techniques that you've seen today are by no means the only ones that you can use to enhance your application. You may think that some suggestions appear too simple to really do anything; however, the best changes you can make to an application are those that require more common sense than complex coding changes.

Q&A

Q Why is using an `Integer` data type more efficient?

A Depending on the type of numeric data you are using, the `Integer` data type is processed more efficiently by the computer.

Q What can make my application appear slow?

A An application can appear slow for many different reasons, including very complex forms and large sections of code without any Windows function calls in them.

Q How can I display my first form more quickly?

A If you display a splash screen while the initial form is being loaded, the application will appear to load faster. Also, remove any unnecessary procedure calls in the first form to reduce the amount of procedure calls the application must do before displaying the first form.

Workshop

The Workshop provides quiz questions to help solidify your understanding of the material covered, as well as exercises to provide you with experience in using what you've learned. Try to understand the quiz and exercise answers before continuing on to tomorrow's lesson. Answers are provided in Appendix A, "Answers to Quizzes and Exercises."

Quiz

1. What's a resource file?
2. Name three ways to increase application performance.

Exercise

Open the Address Book application and identify any resources or variables that you can change to optimize the process. Also, locate any sections of code that you can modify to tune the process even more.

DAY 20

Finishing the Application

If you're like most Windows developers, you've spent a lot of time on what type of application to create, and even more time actually creating it. You also must have spent time learning the Visual Basic programming language. Well, you've done it—your application is written, tested, and ready to go. But go where? Today's lesson covers several topics dealing with the packaging and deployment of your application.

Unless you work for a company that sells or uses the software you work on, you'll probably want to sell your application. If this is what you want to do, you need to worry about many more issues in addition to creating a working application, such as advertising, customer support, protection of your creation, and—of course—the actual distribution of the software.

Understanding What Makes Up a Windows Application

Finishing a Windows application is a lot more than just putting your application on disks and selling it. The whole process of what the final application package should be starts right at the beginning. If you're like most programmers, you probably think you have the best application in the world. But if your packaging doesn't look good or the advertising isn't effective, you won't sell many copies. You should start a list of the things you like and don't like about the companies, products, and support that you've dealt with through the years. You also should write down how you think you can improve on these things. The different areas that you must consider when striving for a Windows application package fall into product-related or support-related issues.

Product-Related Issues

When you've decided to create an application, you should realize that you have to consider many topics. Dealing properly with these topics or issues is what eventually will help you create a great application product. Most product-related issues you'll deal with will fall into one of the following categories:

- Program design
- Reporting
- Online help
- Performance
- Error handling
- Printed documentation

Although some of these issues have been discussed to some degree earlier in this book, don't stop here. Make sure that you continue to address each issue as you continue your application's design and development process.

Program Design

Deciding what your application will do and how it should look is the most demanding task in the creation process. Time spent in designing the application will provide you with an easier task when coding the application. Because your application will run in the Windows environment, the overall look of the forms that you design should reflect the type of person who will use them.

Reports

When adding the reporting capability to your application, you have to decide on the type of reporting to give your application's users. Unfortunately, the various reports that might be needed tend to evolve during the creation process. You generally don't know exactly what reports are really needed until the application is completed. However, reports—like weeds—keep popping up, even when you thought you had covered them all.

Online Help

The online Help system included with the final application wasn't a walk in the park to create. As you've already seen, designing and creating the Help system is as difficult to do as the application design and creation was. Designing the Help system after the application is done only delays the final application, as you go back and add the help topic references to the application code and retest the application. What you should really do is design the Help system as you design the application, working with both of them at the same time.

Performance

Performance is a difficult topic to cover because the idea of performance is as fleeting as the most current PC on the market today. No matter how well you design your application, it will run differently on each computer that it's installed on. Because each computer is unique and so many types and speeds of computer exist, the best you can hope for is to get your application to run as fast and efficiently as possible.

Error Handling

If everything worked the way it should, there would be no need for error handling in your application. However, this is an imperfect world where mistakes happen, files are deleted, and hard disks still run out of space. If you have no error handling in your application, Visual Basic must handle any problems that happen. Unfortunately, Visual Basic isn't as forgiving as you might be when it comes to error handling. If an error occurs, Visual Basic will display a simple default error message and then stop the application's execution. It's your job to code enough error-handling routines to deal with any problems that you think might happen.

Printed Documentation

A good manual for your application is difficult to produce. Deciding what to put into it and how detailed to get is a complicated procedure. You not only decide what topics are in the manual, but you also have to decide which forms and examples from the application should be placed in the manual. The starting point of any design is to assume that users won't be at the computer when reading the manual. You need to balance the manual's content between text and figures as users read about what the application will do. A good manual usually contains the following sections:

- Table of contents
- Product introduction
- Getting started
- Using the product

20

- Troubleshooting
- Getting technical support
- Index

Each section of the manual should give users enough information to get started, to figure out some of the simpler questions, and to know where to find technical support.

Again, you should look at other product manuals to see which features you like and which features you don't like. If your manual is well laid out and well written, with the online help file, the amount of support calls you receive from users should be fairly low.

Another way of producing a manual, without incurring the cost of printing, is by using a product such as Adobe Acrobat. Acrobat and products like it allow you to create an electronic format of your manual that you would include on your distribution disks. This way, users can view the manual on their computer or, if they want to, print it.

Support-related Issues

Support means different things to different people. This all depends on what the problem, question, or concern might be. When customers call the software company that created an application they use, they want their answers quickly, and they want the answers to be correct. What happens when you call a company for support? Do you like the response that you get, or can they do better? Providing customers with a way of getting good application support is part of the overall application package that you must create.

No matter how hard you try, you'll never be able to satisfy everyone who buys your software. Don't be upset when someone returns the software because it doesn't do what he needs it to do. (You've returned software for this reason yourself, right?) Most often, users call support only when they run out of all the other options. By the time they call you for support, they're annoyed with the product, and you have to work harder just to calm them down.

When considering the concept of support, there's more to this process then just having someone answer a phone when it rings. You must consider the following issues when developing a plan for supporting your application:

- Easy access
- Questions and problems
- Application upgrades and fixes

You need to plan for each issue when deciding how to give your users support. If you do all this correctly, your product will be well received by the people who use it.

Easy Access

The entire idea of easy access to technical support has changed over the past few years. In the past, technical support was usually provided by telephone, fax, or mail. Now, with the increasing use of the Internet, most software providers (a category to which you now belong) provide access to technical support through a page on their Web site. Depending on the time and money that you want to spend in this area, you can give your users one or all of the following options:

- Direct technical support phone number
- Toll-free technical support
- 24-hour technical support by fax
- Technical support e-mail address
- Interactive Internet support Web page

Every option that you give users comes with its own unique set of problems and—more importantly to you—cost. The best, most used method of offering support to your users is over the phone. However, unless you plan to sit by the phone 24 hours a day, five to seven days a week, you need some type of answering machine or service to take phone messages. Of course, allowing users to fax questions can be useful, but what if you have questions to ask them? That particular resolution process tends to get drawn out and frustrating for users. If you set a standard of getting back to your users within a range of six hours, users will get the impression that you care about the application and their use of it.

The hottest way to offer support these days is by using the World Wide Web. If you decide to use this method, you need to obtain space on a Web server, design and build the Web site, and then set up a method for checking messages that come into the site, in addition to updating the information on the site. Also, you can have any fixes or upgrades to your application available to your users on the Web for them to download when needed.

Deciding on the type of support that you want to supply to the users of your application really depends on your budget. However, you must pick one or more of these options and then implement it before you start distributing the application.

Questions and Problems

Now that you've given users a way of calling, faxing, or e-mailing their questions and problems to you, how will you handle them? You have to develop a way of tracking the user who sent the question or problem. This way, you can keep track of who your users are. It also allows you to know which questions are being repeated, so you can determine what needs to be changed in your application and whether it's part of the interface or the documentation.

Problems and questions should be dealt with a little differently. With questions that deal with how your application works, you can usually answer them quickly, with a simple answer or instructions on how to do something. With problems, however, you need to obtain enough information to allow you to resolve a problem. When taking a problem report, ask the user for every bit of information that you can think of to figure out the problem. You should request some of the following information when users report a problem:

- The version of the application they're using
- The type and speed of their computer
- The amount of memory the computer has on it
- The exact error message that appeared
- Any recent changes made to the PC (hardware, software, or both)
- Precisely what users were doing when the error occurred

The last item listed is by far the most difficult to get from users. You often hear that a user started the application and then it "blew up." This isn't a very specific indication of what happened. You need to know what the user typed, which function keys were pressed, or which command buttons were clicked. These bits of information are important when you're trying to narrow down the possible problem(s).

New Term Sometimes, when a problem is difficult to resolve, you might come up with a way around it. Called a *workaround*, this stop-gap solution doesn't fix a user's problem, but it allows that user to continue working with the application while you're revising it. Workarounds are important because sometimes a problem takes a long time to fix or can't be fixed without major changes to the application.

Application Upgrades and Fixes

When you decide that it's time to create the next version of your application, you have to figure out what new features should be added. You also need to think about how your current users will upgrade to this new version. You must give your users the ability to use the new release without having to input their data all over again. Think of how you would feel if you had spent months learning and entering information into an application, only to receive the next release with no way of moving your preexisting data over to it. Keep this in the back of your mind; otherwise, you'll quickly lose customers.

When designing an upgrade to your application, consider how you want to distribute it. If many things have changed in the application, you might consider creating a new set of distribution disks. If only a few things have changed, you would want to distribute only the changes. Also, you'll want to have two separate sets of distribution disks: one for new users and one for current users who are upgrading to the new release. Generally, upgrades should contain fixes to problems that have occurred, as well as any new features and functions. This gives current users a good reason to buy the upgrade and new users a reason to try the application.

Distributing the Application

After you complete the development of your application and decide that you've tested it enough, you're ready to make copies of it. Before Windows was around, many applications fit on one disk and were easy to distribute to users. You would copy the files onto the disk, and then when users purchased the software, they would copy it onto their computer.

It's not that easy anymore. These days, you have to choose how you want to distribute your application. Of course, the methods you choose depend on the type of application you are deploying (that is, Web versus Windows). Because of the complexity of today's applications, many more files are required for support of your application that need to be included along with your application. You might also need to create a new database when your application is being installed.

Understanding the New Deployment Projects

Visual Basic .NET provides you with four different types of deployment projects (listed in Table 20.1). A Setup Wizard is also provided to help step you through the process of creating deployment projects.

TABLE 20.1   The Different Types of Deployment Projects

Project Type	Description
Merge Module	Allows you to package files or components into a single module for sharing the files between multiple applications
Setup	Creates an installer for a Windows-based application that will install files into a Program Files directory on a computer
Web Setup	Creates an installer for a Web-based application that will install files into a Virtual Root directory on a Web server
Cab	Creates a cabinet file for downloading to a legacy Web browser

20

 Caution

After you create a deployment project, you can't change its type. If you need to deploy the application to different environments, you need to create a new deployment project for each environment.

All these templates can be found under the Setup and Deployment Projects node when you start a new project (see Figure 20.1). So that you can understand which method to use, let's take a closer look at each method.

FIGURE 20.1

*Selecting a
Deployment project
from the Add New
Project dialog box.*

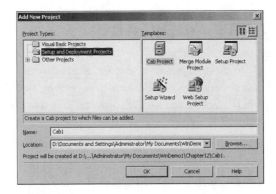

Merge Module Project

This type of project allows you to create reusable setup components that provide the capability to share setup code between Windows Installers. The merge module file (.msm) is a single package that contains all files, resources, Registry entries, and setup logic needed to install a component. These modules can't be installed alone, but must be used with a Windows Installer File (.msi).

Any dependencies for a given component are captured in a merge module. This allows you to ensure that the correct versions are installed. After you create a merge module and distribute it, never modify that module. If changes are required, create a new merge module for the next version of the component.

Setup Projects

A Setup project allows you to create an installer to distribute your application. What's actually created is a Windows Installer (.msi) file, which contains the application, any dependent files, information about the application such as Registry entries, and instructions for installation. When this .msi file is distributed and executed on another computer, it will be installed properly. If you've installed Microsoft products in the past year, including any Microsoft Office release since 2000 or Visual Basic .NET, you've experienced a Windows Installer process. If the installation of your application fails (that is, the target computer doesn't have the required operating system version), the installation will be cancelled and the computer returned to its previous state.

Web Setup Projects

Besides the standard Setup project, you can also create an installation for deploying your application to a Web server. Using deployment to install files on a Web server provides an advantage over simply copying files—deployment handles any issues with registration and configuration automatically. The installer you create for Windows application also can be deployed to a Web server so that users can download and run them from a Web site when needed.

To deploy a Web application to a Web server, you create a Web Setup project, build it, copy it to the Web server computer, and run the installer to install the application on the server using the settings defined in your Web Setup project.

> **Note**
>
> To deploy to a Web server, you must have administrative access privileges for that computer.

To deploy an application from a Web server by downloading it, you must create a Web Setup project and add the project output group for the application to the Web Setup project in the File System Editor. After building the installer, you need to copy it to the Web server computer, where it can then be downloaded via a Web browser.

> **Note**
>
> When an installer is made available for download, there's no guarantee that the Windows Installer runtime files will be available on the user's computer. Always make sure that the runtime files are also available for download.

CAB File Projects

A CAB project allows you to create a package of ActiveX controls that can be downloaded from a Web server to a Web browser. Unlike the other deployment projects you've seen, no editors are provided for working with CAB projects. Files and project outputs can be added to a CAB project in Solution Explorer, and properties can be set in the Properties window or in the Project Property pages. Properties of CAB projects allow you to do the following:

- Specify a level of compression
- Implement Authenticode signing
- Set the display name and version information
- Specify the location of dependent files on the Web

20

> **Note** Dependencies aren't calculated for CAB projects; you must determine and reference any dependencies.

Deploying the Application

A deployment project is used to create the files that the Windows Installer (.msi) can use to distribute and install your application on another computer. The resulting installer files can then be distributed on any media, such as floppy disks or CD-ROMs, or you can put them on a network drive for installation across the network. The process of deploying an application starts with the creation of a Setup project that determines where and how the installer will be created.

To assist you in building the deployment project, Visual Basic .NET includes a Setup Wizard that takes you through the process with the following steps:

1. Choosing a project type to specify the type of project to create. You can create any of the following: a Windows or Web application, a merge module, or a CAB file.

2. Choosing the project outputs to include, which specifies which project outputs you want to add to the deployment project. When an output is selected, the Description field displays a description of that output.

3. Choosing the files to include. Additional files can be included for deployment.

Finally, the wizard displays a summary of the options selected for the deployment project.

> **Note** Projects created via the Setup Wizard place the deployment files on your local computer for later distribution.

Before a solution is deployed, you have to define all the properties of the deployment. You must identify three main items for each deployment you create:

- What you want to deploy
- Where it should be deployed
- The method of deploying the solution

This process is done by adding one or more deployment projects to your solution. Three required and six optional tasks are involved in creating a deployment project for your solution. Each will be discussed in the next few sections.

Adding a Deployment Project

You must add a deployment project to the solution that also contains the project you want to deploy. To add a deployment project, right-click the solution name in the Solution Explorer and choose Add, New Project from the pop-up menu. In the Add New Project dialog box, select the Setup and Deployment Projects node to display the different options (refer to Figure 20.1).

At this point, you can choose to use the Setup Wizard to create the deployment project or add the project manually. You will see how to use the Setup Wizard later, so select the Setup Project icon, give the project a significant name, and click OK. You will see the File System Editor displayed, as shown in Figure 20.2. This is where you can specify where you want the application installed.

FIGURE 20.2

Specifying what files are needed by the application.

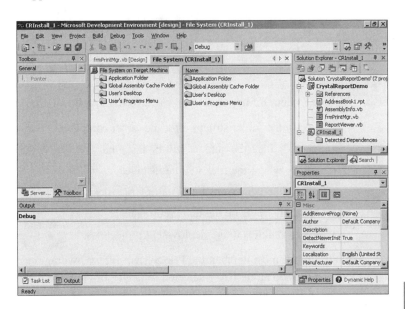

The File System Editor allows you to add project outputs, files, and other items to the deployment project and specify where you want them installed on the target computer. What's displayed when the project is added are the default folders that reflect the standard folders on a target computer. You can also add your own subfolders to this list by right-clicking the File System on Target Machine node in the editor and selecting a folder type from the pop-up menu (see Figure 20.3).

20

FIGURE 20.3

Adding custom folders to the deployment project.

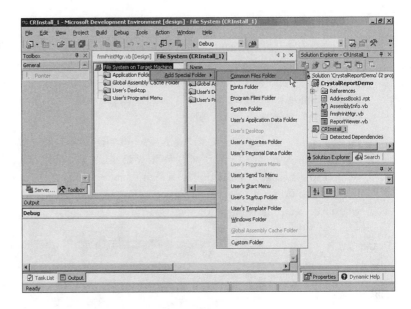

The File System Editor allows you to perform the following tasks:

- Specify the folder structure for the target computer
- Specify where the outputs will be installed
- Specify where the files will be installed
- Specify the conditions for installing the files
- Create shortcuts on the target computer
- Add assemblies to the deployment project

You can move most items in the File System Editor by dragging them to the required location. To add an item to a selected folder, right-click the folder, select Add to display the list of four options (see Figure 20.4), and select the item from this list.

You can use this method to add your own custom folder to the structure. If you choose to add files, the Add Files dialog box appears (see Figure 20.5), allowing you to select a file.

If you choose to add a project output, the Add Project Output Group dialog box appears (see Figure 20.6), allowing you to select the project you want to deploy from the drop-down list. Then you can select one or more of the groups listed and click OK to add them to the File System Editor.

FIGURE 20.4

Adding a new item to a folder in the File System Editor.

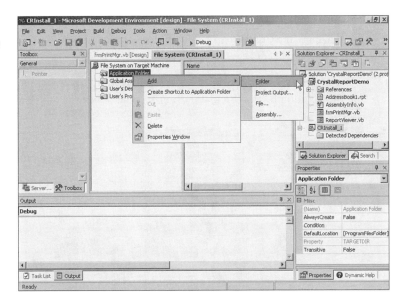

FIGURE 20.5

Selecting files to add to the project.

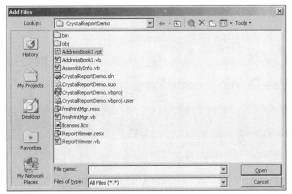

FIGURE 20.6

Selecting a project output group to add to the deployment project.

20

Finally, you can add an assembly by selecting that option from the pop-up menu. This will display the Component Selector to select the system files you want to add along with your application.

Any of the deployment editors can be displayed by right-clicking the deployment project in the Solution Explorer and choosing View and then the editor needed (see Figure 20.7).

FIGURE 20.7

Displaying the correct deployment editor.

Setting the Deployment Properties

Deployment projects have two categories of properties:

- General project properties
- Configuration-dependent properties

General properties are set in the Properties window and apply to all project configurations. To set configuration-dependent properties, use the Deployment Properties dialog box. These properties apply only to the specific project configuration you are working with at that moment.

To view the project properties for the deployment project, right-click the deployment project in the Solution Explorer and select Properties to display the properties, as shown in Figure 20.8.

This property page allows you to set the following properties for a deployment build:

- Output File Name is the location and name of the final .msi Windows installer file that will be created by the deployment project.

- Package Files allows you to specify whether to create a single setup file or create CAB files to contain most of the files in the application. If you choose CAB files, you can then specify the size of the CAB files that will be created.

- Bootstrapper specifies whether you want the Windows or Web installation program to be included with your deployment package.

- Compression specifies whether to compress the final deployment files for speed or for size.

- Authenticode Signature specifies whether the outputs of the deployment project will be signed using Authenticode signing security.

FIGURE 20.8

Modifying the configuration properties for a deployment.

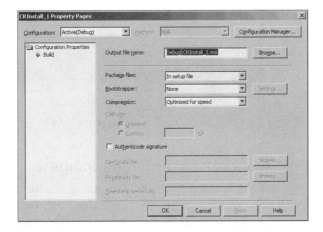

Specifying Registry Settings on Target Computer

By using the Registry Editor, you can specify the Registry keys and values to be added to the Registry of the target computer when your application is installed. By default, the Registry Editor displays a standard set of Registry keys that correspond with the standard Windows Registry keys:

- HKEY_CLASSES_ROOT
- HKEY_CURRENT_USER
- HKEY_LOCAL_MACHINE
- HKEY_USERS
- HKEY_PER_USER

In the editor, you can right-click any of these folders to add the required registry settings (see Figure 20.9).

20

FIGURE 20.9

*Adding Registry set-
tings to the deployment
project.*

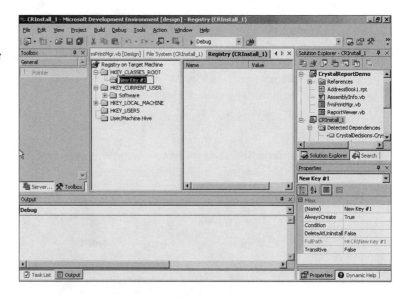

You can add your own keys under any of the Registry keys or sub-keys or import
Registry files.

Setting File Associations on Target Computer

The File Types editor (see Figure 20.10) is used to establish file associations on the target computer. It does this by associating file extensions with your application and specifying the actions allowed for each file type. When you select any file type or action in
the File Types Editor, any related properties are displayed and can be edited in the
Properties window.

A file association allows users to double-click a file with the defined extension to have
the application start up and open that file.

Specifying the User Interface

With the deployment project, you can define any number of dialog boxes that will be displayed to users during the installation process. These forms ask users what tasks, if any,
they might want to perform during the installation. An example of this is the form you
usually see at the end of an installation asking if you want to display the ReadMe file.

The User Interface Editor is used to specify and set properties for predefined dialog
forms displayed during installation on the target computer. When the editor is displayed
(see Figure 20.11), you can add dialog forms to two sections: Install and Administrative
Install.

FIGURE 20.10

Adding file associations to your deployment project.

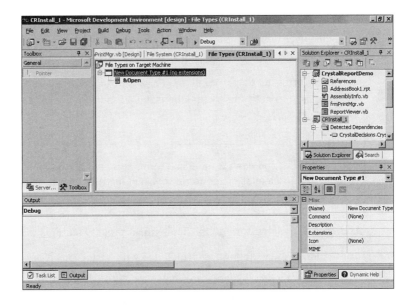

FIGURE 20.11

Working with the UI interface for the deployment project.

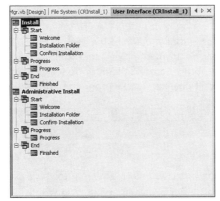

20

The Install section contains dialog forms that will be displayed when the end user runs the installer; the Administrative Install section contains dialog forms that will be displayed when a system administrator uploads the installer to a network location.

A default set of predefined dialog boxes are already included in the deployment project and are displayed in the editor as shown in Figure 20.11. You can choose to rearrange or delete any of these dialog forms. The default set of dialog forms will vary depending on the type of deployment project you are creating. These predefined dialog forms are divided into three categories:

- Start forms are displayed before the installation begins and can be used to gather customer information or to allow users to change the installation directory.
- Progress forms are displayed to provide feedback on the progress of an installation.
- End forms are displayed as soon as the installation has finished successfully. These are used to notify users that the installation is complete or to allow users to launch the application.

Tip   If you don't want dialog forms displayed during the installation process, delete all dialog forms shown in the User Interface Editor.

Adding a new dialog form to the deployment process requires the following tasks:

- Adding a new dialog form (included with Visual Basic or one that you created)
- Modifying the appearance or behavior of the dialog form
- Enabling online registration

Note   Any dialog forms that you add to the default forms require you to make changes to the deployment process that will process the input made by the user on these forms. Some of these forms, such as the registration form, require an additional executable program to run when the form is displayed.

Setting Actions

At the end of the installation process, you might want to run a program that associates a server component with a particular message queue. You would define this action using the Custom Actions Editor (see Figure 20.12). The editor displays four folders that correspond with one phase of the installation process:

- Install
- Commit
- Rollback
- Uninstall

Custom actions must be compiled as a .dll or .exe file, or added to a project as a script or assembly, before they can be added to a deployment project. Actions can be run only at the end of an installation.

FIGURE 20.12

Adding custom actions to the deployment process to be executed at the end of the installation.

Note

Custom actions are run in the same order that they are displayed in the editor.

Specifying Conditions

When creating the deployment project, you can specify conditions that must be met on the target computer for the installation to successfully run. For example, you might want to check for a specific version of an operating system. If the installation is performed on a system that doesn't meet the condition, the installation will be aborted with an error message to the user. The Launch Conditions Editor (see Figure 20.13) allows you to add searches and conditions to the deployment project.

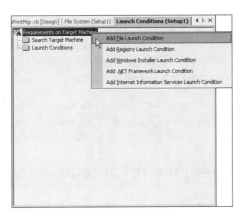

FIGURE 20.13

Adding launch conditions to the deployment project.

20

The three types of searches that you can perform on the target computer are as follows:

- File Search determines whether a file exists on a target computer and aborts the installation if it doesn't.
- Registry Search determines whether a Registry entry exists on a target computer and aborts the installation if it doesn't.
- Windows Installer Search determines whether a Windows Installer component exists on a target computer and aborts the installation if it doesn't.

After you define the search condition, you can then define the condition that will be associated with a search definition and the error message that will be displayed to users if the condition isn't met.

Using the Microsoft Windows Installer

Microsoft provides the final piece of this puzzle with the Microsoft Windows Installer. This tool is included with the following:

- Windows 2000
- Windows Me
- Windows XP
- Windows 95/98
- Windows NT 4.0

The Windows Installer uses a single file that provides all installation data and instructions in a single package. By using the Windows Installer, each computer keeps a database of information about every application that it installs, including files, Registry keys, and components. If an application is uninstalled, the database is checked to make sure that no other applications rely on a file, Registry key, or component before removing it. This prevents the removal of one application from breaking another. It also provides the capability to perform a self-repair. This allows an application to automatically reinstall missing files that users might have accidentally deleted.

Finally, the installer provides the ability to roll back an installation. If a launch condition isn't met during the installation, it would be aborted and the computer returned to its pre-installation state.

Creating the Deployment Package with the Setup Wizard

To see how the deployment process works, let's see how to create a Windows deployment project using the Setup Wizard. Because a standard setup and a Web setup are different in only a couple of ways, today's lesson will look at the differences at the end of the process.

This demo will use the Address Book application designed in the course of this book. You can choose to use the same solution or any other solution that you might have available. The solution that you are deploying isn't as important right now as the process of creating the deployment project. At the end of the process, you will have an installer that will

- Create file associations
- Create shortcuts
- Display a custom dialog box
- Check for the existence of Internet Explorer 5.0

Before you add a deployment project to your solution, build the application so that an executable file exists for the installation process to work with. To start, open the solution for which you want to create the deployment project. Then, add a new project to the solution, using the Setup Wizard in the Add New Project dialog box, as discussed earlier today. Name the new deployment project DemoInstall and click OK to start the wizard. The first dialog box that appears is a Hello form, which you can bypass by clicking Next. The second dialog box (see Figure 20.14) asks you what type of deployment you want to create and what type of distribution package you want.

FIGURE 20.14

Specifying the type of deployment project to create.

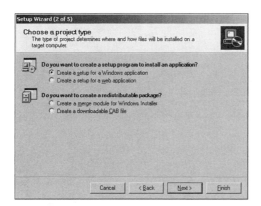

20

For this demo, select a Windows application setup, leaving the redistributable selection blank. Click Next to choose the Project Outputs to include in the deployment project. In this dialog box (see Figure 20.15), you can choose one or more of the output groups listed. If you click on an item, the description of the item will appear at the bottom of the dialog box.

FIGURE **20.15**

Choosing project out-
puts to be installed.

FIGURE **20.15**

Choosing project out-
puts to be installed.

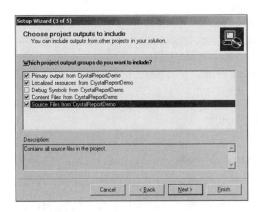

Select all the items listed and click Next to continue. In the next dialog box (see Figure 20.16), specify what additional files you want included in the installation process.

FIGURE **20.16**

Choosing additional
files to include in the
installation process.

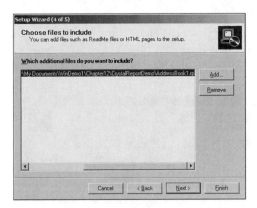

The last dialog box displays a summary (see Figure 20.17) of what tasks the wizard will perform. Click Finish to create the deployment project.

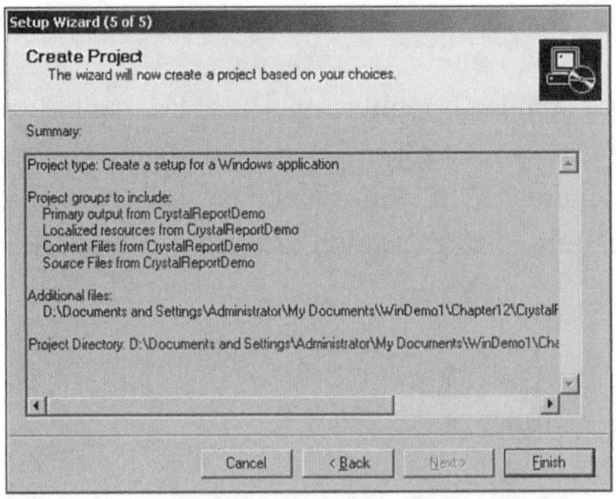

FIGURE **20.17**

Summary listing the
tasks that the Setup
Wizard will perform.

After the wizard completes the process, you should see the deployment project in the Solution Explorer. Open the File System Editor and select the Application Folder to see what items have been added to the project (see Figure 20.18).

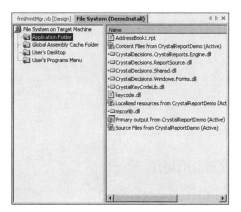

Creating a Shortcut

Next, you will create a shortcut for the program. If you've added the deployment project to an existing solution, you should see the primary output reference in the Application Folder. Right-click this item and choose Create Shortcut to Primary Output from the pop-up menu. This will add a shortcut to the list; rename the shortcut to My Address Book. Now, select the shortcut item and drag it to the User's Desktop folder (if you want the shortcut to appear on the target computer desktop). Create a second shortcut for the application, using the same name, and then drag it to the User's Programs Menu folder. This will place a shortcut for your application in the Start menu's Programs list.

Adding a File Association

If the application you are deploying can open a file based on the file extension, you need to add a file association to the project. To add an association, open the File Types Editor, and add a new file type to the File Types on Target Machine node as shown in Figure 20.19.

Change the New Document Type #1 value to a descriptive value that will be understandable to the user. Next, make the following changes to the properties of this new association:

Property	Value
Extensions	adb
Command	Application executable filename

20

FIGURE 20.19

Adding a file association to the deployment project.

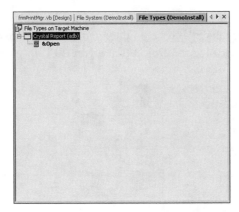

Setting a Launch Condition

The next step is to add the conditions that must be met for the application to be installed. Open the Launch Condition Editor for the deployment project. Right-click the Requirements on Target Machine node and choose Add File Launch Condition from the pop-up menu. This will add a Search for File 1 entry (see Figure 20.20). Rename the new condition to Search for Internet Explorer.

FIGURE 20.20

Adding a launch condition to the deployment project.

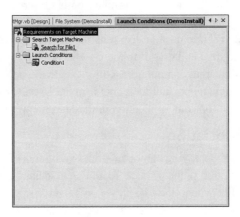

In addition, set the properties for this condition as listed in Table 20.2.

TABLE 20.2   Property Assignments for the File Launch Condition

Property	Value
FileName	Iexplore.exe
Folder	[ProgramFilesFolder]

TABLE 20.2 continued

Property	Value
Depth	2
MinVersion	5.00
Property	IEFILEXISTS

Next, select the Condition1 item in the Launch Condition folder and set the following properties for this condition:

Property	Value
Condition	IEFILEEXISTS<>""
Message	"Microsoft Internet Explorer 5.0 or higher is required. Please install Internet Explorer and rerun the installation."

Inserting a User Interface Dialog

For this demonstration, you will add a dialog box that will use a check box dialog to ask users if the sample files should be installed. To add a new dialog, open the User Interface Editor. Right-click the Start node under the Install node and select Add Dialog from the pop-up menu. This will display the Add dialog (see Figure 20.21), which provides several different types of dialogs from which to choose to add to the installation process.

FIGURE 20.21

Choosing a User Interface dialog from the Add dialog.

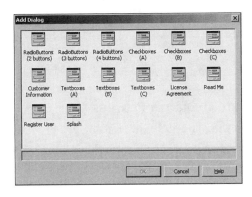

20

Choose CheckBoxes (A) and click OK to add the dialog to the interface list. Modify the properties for this dialog as listed in Table 20.3.

TABLE 20.3 Property Settings for the Custom User Dialog

Property	Value
BannerText	Samples.
BodyText	By selecting this option, the sample address book database will be installed.
CheckBox1Label	Install Sample Address Book?
CheckBox2Visible	False.
CheckBox3Visible	False.
CheckBox4Visible	False.

Now that the new dialog is included in the installation process, you need to define the rules in the File System Editor for this to work properly. When the installation is executed, this custom dialog (see Figure 20.22) will be displayed to the user.

FIGURE 20.22

Asking the user for options during the installation process.

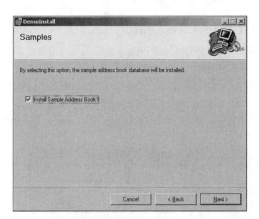

Defining the Custom Dialog Process

To define the rules that will allow the custom dialog you just created to work, you need to associate the selections on the custom dialog with a program or file, depending on what the new dialog is asking the user for. For this example, you will associate a sample file with the check box that asks if the user wants the file installed by following the steps listed:

1. Display the File System Editor.
2. Right-click the Application Folder. Name the folder Samples.
3. Right-click the Samples folder and select Add, File.

4. Browse to select the Samples file. If more than one sample file exists, repeat steps 3 and 4.

5. For each file, select the file and change the Condition property to reference the check box or option in the custom dialog. (For this example, you would enter `Checkboxa1=1`.)

After you complete these steps, you need to build the deployment project. However, you must build the application project before building the deployment project.

Now that you've finished building the deployment process for your application, you should take the time to test the installation process by installing your application on a different PC. The PC that you use to test the install program shouldn't have Visual Basic installed on it; this would invalidate the test because the Visual Basic files would already be on the PC. The purpose of the test is to ensure that all the required files for your application were included in the installation file set.

Ensuring Ownership of Your Code

After working for many weeks, months, or years on designing, creating, and distributing your application, you want to make sure that you own everything about the application. This means dealing with several different legal issues related to the ownership of the application and the source code you've written. This all might sound a bit daunting if you work at home. However, with the right amount of information, these issues aren't all that mysterious. You must consider the following issues:

- User registration of the application
- Software theft
- Trademark
- Application copyright

Having users register the purchase of the application and worrying about software theft are really two sides to the same coin. There's really no foolproof way of preventing someone from copying your application disks and giving them to someone else. However, if you require that users register the application with you to obtain technical support, you'll reduce the possibility of this theft from happening. Another way to help in the prevention of product theft is to have a serial number associated with each copy of the application that you produce. Although the serial number can be given with the disks, it makes it a little easier for you to keep track of who really owns a particular copy of the software.

20

The incentive for users to register the application with you is the availability of support and the notification of any upgrades, fixes, or new versions of the application. When you receive a call from users for support, you should first see if they're already registered; if not, you should ask them for the serial number. If they can't tell you what the serial number is, you must decide whether to refuse to answer their question or to continue with the phone call. At the end of the day, if you do catch someone who doesn't own your software but has a copy of it, you must decide what course of action—legal or otherwise— you want to take.

Protecting Your Application Name

Protecting the name of your application requires you to trademark the name. The decision to trademark the name is the first step in a long legal process, however. Having a trademark for your application prevents someone else from legally using the name. For example, if someone designed a new operating system and wanted to call it Windows, Microsoft would have the legal right to prevent it. However, before you jump into the trademark process, you should know that it takes time and money to get it done. Some developers decide to take a chance and not trademark their application. Unfortunately, if someone decided to trademark the name, the developer would have to change the name of the application wherever it might appear in the application, documentation, and marketing.

As you can probably guess, this decision could be expensive. When applying for a trademark, you need to be aware of many rules. If you can afford it, you should really use a trademark lawyer because this type of lawyer does this type of work daily and knows what to watch for that might cause problems. If you decide to do it yourself, you should know that if the trademark is denied, you don't get your processing fee refunded. To get the information about the trademark process, call or write to the trademark office in Washington, D.C., as soon as you can:

> U.S. Department of Commerce
> Patent and Trademark Office
> Washington, D.C. 20231
> (703) 308-4357

The process can take from three to six months if the trademark submission doesn't run into delays or problems.

Copyrighting Your Work

Another area that you need to protect yourself is the possible theft of your idea, design, or implementation of your application. If you decide to copyright your application, you're protecting it from unauthorized copying. Although you can copyright your source code, help files, and documentation, you can't copyright the actual idea or form design that your application uses. If you decide to copyright your application, however, you should apply for the copyright protection before you start selling your application. The actual protection afforded you by obtaining a copyright is directly proportional to your desire to take legal action against the person who has violated the copyright. For more information about obtaining a copyright, call or write the following:

Publications Section
LM-455
Copyright Office
Library of Congress
Washington, D.C. 20559
(202) 707-3000

A copyright is considered effective on the date the copyright office receives all the required elements. A return receipt should be used when sending the application to the copyright office so that you know when it gets there.

Making the Final Decision: How to Sell Your Product

When choosing the way you want to sell your product, you have only three real choices: sell your product yourself, sell with the help of another company, or place your application into the wonderful world of shareware. Shareware is a different way to "sell" your product. Shareware products aren't sold through the use of advertising, direct mail, or catalogs; in fact, they aren't actually sold. They're instead placed in an area on the Internet or on an accessible download area of a service such as America Online (AOL). Users who want to try your application can just copy it from one of these locations. If they like the application, they're supposed to send you the price of a copy of the software. Unfortunately, there's no real way to actually force anyone to pay for the product. To encourage people to pay for the shareware product if they decide to keep it, most shareware products use one of three methods:

- Use a "Nag" dialog box. Every time the shareware product is started, users are presented with a dialog box reminding them that the product isn't free and that they should pay the specified amount to get a registered copy and upgrades from the company.

- Build in a kill switch. After a shareware product has been used for a preset number of days or occasions, a *kill switch* causes the product to stop working.

20

- Disable several of the application's more interesting features. The only way users can use these features is to purchase the application, at which time you would send them an update of the executable file that would unlock the features.

One of the most successful products on the market today started as a shareware program. PKZIP was originally developed to address the issue of space on a computer disk. It allowed users to compress their files when they weren't needed and to decompress them when they were needed. Because of the way it worked, people who used the program told everyone they knew about it, until the product became a requirement on a computer.

Many online services today, such as AOL, have areas for posting shareware products. And catalogs of shareware products have popped up over the years. Of course, the best part of selling your product as shareware is the small amount of money required to do so.

By comparison, the retail world is more costly and much more confusing. Retailing your application often consists of everything but programming. You can advertise your product through the following mediums:

- Magazines
- Newspapers
- Trade journals
- Direct mail
- Internet/Web
- Television

Each option has its own associated costs and concerns. You should also investigate paying a catalog service to advertise your product for you. If you have a small budget, this is probably one of the best methods of selling a product. The catalog company does all the advertising and order processing for you, at a price. (Generally, the company takes a percentage of the sale price for its services.)

Summary

In today's lesson, you saw the issues that you must resolve before actually distributing your application. You need to think about many different things when you're creating an application you want to sell. Technical support is an area that you want to really think about before you actually have to deliver any. Also, you saw how to use the different deployment projects available in Visual Basic .NET that assist you in the creation of a professional-looking installation program that your users will need to install your application on their computer or Web server. Finally, you learned about the topics of product security and obtaining trademarks and copyrights.

Q&A

Q When you develop an application, what are some things you must consider?

A Besides worrying about the standard programming issues such as error handling and documentation, you must also consider what you need to do to support users after they purchase the application.

Q Why should you protect your software from theft or copying?

A If you don't protect your software by getting a trademark or copyright, someone could steal your application name or your code and create their own version of the software.

Workshop

The Workshop provides quiz questions to help solidify your understanding of the material covered, as well as exercises to provide you with experience in using what you've learned. Try to understand the quiz and exercise answers before continuing on to tomorrow's lesson. Answers are provided in Appendix A, "Answers to Quizzes and Exercises."

Quiz

1. Why is customer support so important?

2. What's the difference between selling your application or releasing it as shareware?

3. What's the difference between a trademark and a copyright?

Exercise

Take one of the applications you created earlier in this book and create a deployment package for it by using the correct deployment project.

20

DAY 21

Working with Web Services

With the increased use of the Internet for business applications and shared utilities, you now require the capability and skill to design and create a shared application process that can be executed as a Web Service. These services are accessible by anyone who can use the Web application from which it's called.

The oldest idea of an application is of a unique piece of software that runs on a single computer, accessing basic operating system services, such as the file system. The next step in the evolution of programming moved toward the client/server design, where some of the base functionality was moved out to other applications, such as a database server. Web Services now represent the latest step to allow the application to access different services, no matter how they were written or on what platform they execute. Web Services allow you to build applications by combining local and remote resources to produce an overall integrated solution.

Today you will learn the basics of a Web Service, how to create a simple service, and how to access that service from a client application. You will see how Visual Basic .NET provides the tools to make this entire process no more difficult than creating a standard Windows application.

What Is a Web Service?

A Web Service is a program module that provides a single element of functionality, such as a unique piece of application logic, and is accessible to any number of different systems through the use of Internet standards (such as XML and HTTP). The use of Web Services depends heavily on the acceptance of XML as the new data transport across the Web. This creates an infrastructure that supports application interaction at a level that resolves many of the problems that previously hampered attempts at this global interaction.

Any Web Service can be used, either internally by a single application or externally over the Internet by any number of applications. Because it's accessible through a standard interface, a Web Service allows different systems to work together as a single Web process. By using XML-based messaging to create and access a Web Service, both the Web Service user, or client, and the Web Service provider need to know only what the input and output should be and where the service is located.

The Uses of a Web Service

Web Services are designed to provide a mechanism for any type of program to communicate over the Internet (using *SOAP*, or *Simple Object Access Protocol*). This is very similar to DCOM (which has been included in the previous releases of Windows and Visual Basic) in that it enables a distributed environment. However, Web Services works in a much broader context; the client no longer cares what type of technology is at the target of the call.

Today, most data is transmitted across the Web embedded in a Web page. By using a Web Service, data can be sent across the Web and used by the consumer program in any way required. Some examples of Web Services that might be used on the Internet are

- Stock quotes
- Current weather
- Best sellers on a retail site
- Employee benefit information
- Product sales information
- Current interest rates

Understanding SOAP

The Simple Object Access Protocol is an XML-based standard for communication using HTTP. Because the protocol is based on XML, it's text based and can go through most

Web server firewalls. Part of this protocol describes how Web Services initially establish a communication with each other.

 The first phase of the communication handshake is called the *discovery phase*. During this phase, a Web Service transmits information about the available component using a SOAP subprotocol called *Service Contract Language* (*SCL*). After this phase is completed, normal component interface calls are performed. These calls look and act like calls to a local component, except the information is being transmitted across the Web in XML.

The final phase of a Web Service call is an XML document that contains all the information returned by the Web Service. The program that called the service then interprets the XML document and extracts the needed information.

> **Note**
>
> When coding in Visual Basic .NET, you don't really need to know what's going on under the covers. The .NET Framework manages the process for you.

Using a Web Service

There are several different ways of using Web Services to enhance your Windows or Web application. Understanding the type of application you are creating and what kinds of computations might be needed will help you to decide what, if any, Web Services you might need. The three main scenarios of Web Service usage follow with brief descriptions of each.

A Simple Service

A *simple service* provides some fundamental piece of functionality for its clients to utilize. As an example, many of the .com e-commerce Web sites need to calculate charges for an assortment of shipping options. That type of an application would require current shipping cost tables from each shipping company to use in these calculations. You would need maintenance codes to download the current tables and update the Web site every time there's a change. The shipping companies also would have to alert the other companies that a change has occurred. There are several points where something could go wrong.

Instead, using HTTP, an application could send a simple XML-based message over the Internet to the shipper's cost calculation Web Service. The message might provide the weight and dimensions of the package, ship from and ship to locations, and other

21

parameters that might be required. The shipper's Web Service then would calculate the shipping charge using the latest cost table and return the correct amount to the calling application, which would use it to calculate the total charge to the customer.

Application Integration

You also can use Web Services to integrate a seemingly unrelated group of existing applications. The wide use of custom software throughout virtually every department of most companies has resulted in a vast array of useful but isolated islands of data and business logic. Due to the varied circumstances under which each was probably developed and the ever-evolving nature of technology, it could be a daunting task to create a functional group from these applications.

By using Web Services it's possible to expose the functionality and data of each existing application as a Web Service. You then could create a composite application that uses this collection of Web Services to enable communications between the individual applications.

Workflow Solutions

Web Services aren't limited to remote procedure calling. They also can be used as a powerful mechanism by which applications that constitute end-to-end workflow solutions can be created. Such solutions are appropriate for long-running scenarios such as those found in business-to-business transactions.

Introducing the Web Service Client

Using a Web Service involves making calls to the service from your application. When accessing a Web Service, you

- Receive information about the service and the access points it offers.
- Reference the service in your project using a typed proxy object. This object provides a view of the Web Service as typed methods, which you can reference in your application code.
- Create an instance of the proxy and use it to call the Web Service methods in the application code.

A Web Service can be accessed by a number of clients. They can be called from any Web-based application, including another Web Service. In fact, you can even call it from a client-based Windows application, although this isn't done very often. Most clients are server-based applications such as Web Forms and Web Services.

Creating a Simple Web Service

Creating a Web Service is much like creating any other type of application project in Visual Basic .NET. You open a new project, add some code that performs some type of function, and finally compile it and reference it from another application. To see how this process works, we will create a Web Service that calculates a tax amount based on three inputs—State, City, and Sale Amount—and then returns the correct tax amount. You actually will start with a simple version of this Web Service by using a constant to calculate the tax amount. Then we will add a database query to get the proper tax amount based on the parameters. Later today you will learn how to access this service from both a Web and Windows client application.

Here are the basic steps to create a Web Service:

1. Create a new Web Service Project.
2. Define one or more public methods in the WebService class.
3. Add the WebMethod attribute to each public method you want to expose on the Web.
4. Build the project.

Creating the Service Project

You can create a Web Service project as part of an existing solution or as its own solution. The ASP.NET Web Service project provides you with the following:

- An .asmx file that represents the service
- A class file associated with the .asmx file, which will contain the code for the service
- The dynamic discovery document for the Web Service project, which will be published with the service and used to generate the *Service Description Language* (*SDL*) file when accessed by client application
- Appropriate references by importing the System.Web.Services library, which creates the namespace for your project

For the example Web Service, start a new solution selecting the ASP.NET Web Service from the New Project dialog box as shown in Figure 21.1, and naming the project TaxCalc.

21

FIGURE 21.1

Starting a new project to create a Web Service.

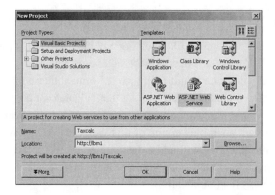

It also will ask you for the location of the Web server where you will be developing this Web Service. By default, the project will use your local machine name, `http://localhost`. By convention, when you develop a Web Service, you are doing it on a development server, which defaults to the local machine you are using. Typically, the project is developed and built on one server and then deployed to another server that will act as the host for the Web Service.

 Note

Having the Web Service developed on the same machine you will use to create the client application will prevent you from having to deploy or install the Web Service before using it. It already exists on your machine.

After you enter the required information, click OK to complete the process. The project template provides all the necessary files and includes the necessary reference to support a Web Service. The window displayed to you is the Component Designer for the default service Service1.asmx (see Figure 21.2).

Although a designer is displayed, you shouldn't place any components on the designer that normally would be displayed to the user, such as a textbox. The wizard adds all the necessary files and references needed to support the Web Service to the project.

Designing the Methods

After you create the Web Service project, design and implement the methods you want exposed in the Web Service. The functionality that you want the client application to access must be coded as functions in the Web Service. To display the code window for the Web Service, click the link labeled <u>click here to switch to code view</u>. This will take you to the Code Editor for the service (see Figure 21.3). You will see a commented sample service function for the "Hello World" example.

FIGURE 21.2

When the project is created, the Component Designer is displayed for you to work with.

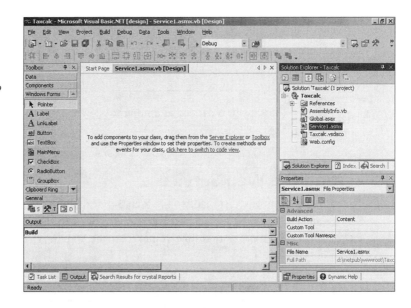

FIGURE 21.3

Working in the Code Editor for the Web Service.

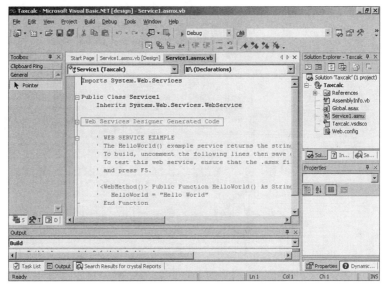

The service will be designed to accept three parameters and return one to calculate the tax amount. To see how this is done, we will build the functionality of this service in pieces, adding each section of functionality as we proceed. The following code should be placed after the commented example. This code is the initial function with a static tax rate amount used to calculate the tax amount to return.

21

```
<WebMethod()> Public Function TaxAmt(ByVal txCity As String,
          ByVal txState As String, ByVal SaleAmt As String) As Double
   TaxAmt = SaleAmt * 0.06
End Function
```

Note   The SaleAmt is defined as a string to allow the function to validate the value
             as a number.

Testing the Web Service

To test the changes you just made to the Web Service, you only need to build the Web
Service and execute it by making the Web Service the starting application in the Project
Properties dialog box. The first time you execute the Web Service, you will see the page
shown in Figure 21.4.

FIGURE 21.4

*Executing the Web
Service from within
Visual Basic .NET for
testing.*

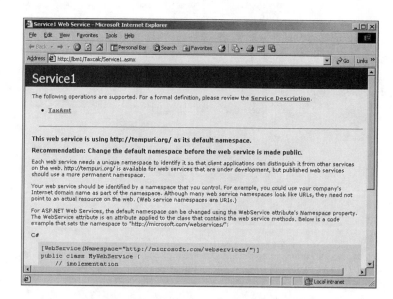

Besides having the exposed functions displayed at the top of the page, you are informed
that the namespace used is the default and that you should change it. To change the
namespace, add the following code to the Public Class definition at the beginning of the
code:

```
<WebService(Namespace:="http://LBM1/Demo",
            Description:="This service will calculate
                          the tax amount based on a tax
                          rate from a database table.")>
            Public Class Service1
```

When you add this statement, rebuild, and then execute the Web Service, you will no longer see the default message, and the description will be displayed (see Figure 21.5).

FIGURE 21.5

Changing the namespace and adding a description.

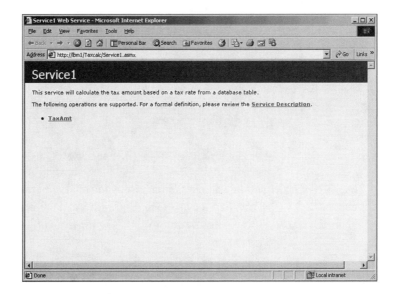

If the function was added properly, you should see the function name displayed. To test the code you added to the function, click the function name to display the test page (see Figure 21.6). This page also contains examples of how to call the Web Service using any of the following methods:

- SOAP
- HTTP Get
- HTTP Post

21

FIGURE 21.6

Testing the Web Service function.

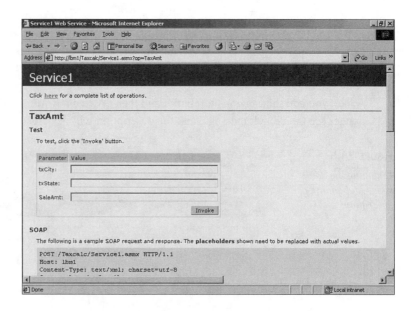

Enter a city, state, and sale amount on this form and click the Invoke button. This will send the data to the Web Service and then display the value returned in a new page (see Figure 21.7). As you can see, the return value is in the form of an XML code segment.

FIGURE 21.7

Displaying the results of the Web Service function call.

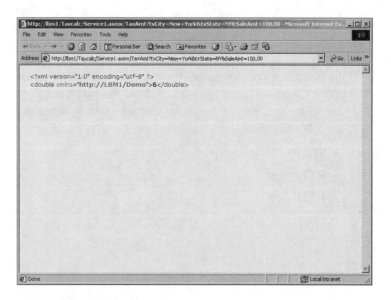

If you enter an invalid value, you will get a very long error message from the Web Service, as shown in Figure 21.8.

FIGURE 21.8

Default error messages from the Web Service.

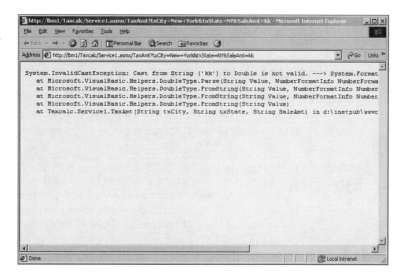

> **Note**
>
> When testing complicated functions, you can use all the debugging techniques covered on Day 14, "Testing and Debugging the Application." You can set breakpoints and step through the code in the functions.

In the next section you will see how to add error handling to the function and add a database call to retrieve the proper tax rate.

Checking for Errors

Now that you have a working Web Service, you need to add a process to inform the calling application if a problem occurred. Depending on what the error was, a different error number would be returned. At the moment, the only errors that could happen are

- No sales amount entered
- Invalid sales amount entered
- No city or state entered

To inform the calling application that these errors occurred, you could use the following code:

```
If Not IsNumeric(SaleAmt) Then
        TaxAmt = -97
        Exit Function
    End If
```

21

Of course, this is a simple error check; depending on what the Web Service method is performing, the error handling might be very complex.

Adding Database Access

The final step in the creation of the tax rate Web Service is to add the database access. This will take the city and state parameters passed to the method and use them in a SQL query to get the current tax rate from the tax table in the database.

Note

For this demo, I've added a TaxRates table to the Northwind database in SQL Server 2000. This table contains only a few city/state combinations. In the real world, this table probably would be very large to contain all the different combinations of tax rates available. The definition of the TaxRates is

```
[City] [varchar] (50),
[State] [char] (2),
[TaxRate] [money] NULL
```

To access this tax table, you will need to use the skills that you learned on Day 10, "Accessing the Database," by using a SqlDataAdapter object with a DataSet in the Web Service. The first step is to drag a SqlDataAdapter to the component designer. Remember, if you aren't using Microsoft SQL Server, you would use the OleDbDataAdapter instead of the SqlDataAdapter.

When you add the adapter, follow the steps in the wizard to create the dataset definition for the tax table you are using. One difference is that when defining the query, you must include criteria, using parameters, for each column on which you want to search. Figure 21.9 shows the query with the parameters included.

FIGURE 21.9

Adding a parameter-driven SQL query to the data adapter.

Data Adapter Configuration Wizard	X
Generate the SQL statements	
The Select statement will be used to create the Insert, Update, and Delete statements.	

Type in your SQL Select statement or use the Query Builder to graphically design the query.

What data should the data adapter load into the dataset?

```
SELECT
   City,
   State,
   TaxRate
FROM
   TaxRates
WHERE
   (City = @City) AND
   (State = @State)
```

Advanced Options...   Query Builder...

Cancel   < Back   Next >   Finish

After you finish adding the `SqlDataAdapter` and `SqlConnection` objects, the component designer should resemble the one in Figure 21.10.

 Caution   Don't forget to create the `DataSet` object after you define the data adapter.

FIGURE 21.10

Adding the SQL connectivity to the Web Service.

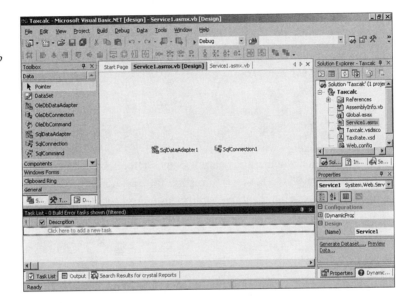

Now you need to add the code to the `TaxRate` method that executes the query you defined, passing it the parameters required to retrieve the correct tax rate. Listing 21.1 shows the code you would need to add to the method to retrieve the correct tax rate.

LISTING 21.1   TAXRATE1.TXT: Accessing the Tax Rate Table in the Database with the City and State Parameters

```
Dim TaxRateTbl As New DataSet1()
Dim tmpTaxRate As Double
SqlDataAdapter1.SelectCommand.Parameters("@City").Value = txCity
SqlDataAdapter1.SelectCommand.Parameters("@State").Value = txState
TaxRateTbl.Clear()
SqlDataAdapter1.Fill(TaxRateTbl)
tmpTaxRate = TaxRateTbl.TaxRates.Item(0).TaxRate
```

21

When the returned tax rate is in the variable `tmpTaxRate`, you can use it to calculate the tax amount to return to the calling application as shown in the following code line:

```
TaxAmt = SaleAmt * tmpTaxRate
```

The only thing still missing from the method is code that will ensure that the query returned a valid row of data. You can do this in two steps:

1. Make sure that the calling application actually passed values in the City and State parameters, as shown in the following code:

```
If txCity = "" Then
   TaxAmt = -98
   Exit Function
End If
If txState = "" Then
   TaxAmt = -99
   Exit Function
End If
```

2. Check whether the query is empty before accessing the data row. You can do this by checking the `Count` property to see if it's zero. The following example shows the code segment that will perform this task:

```
If TaxRateTbl.TaxRates.Count = 0 Then
   TaxAmt = -91
   Exit Function
End If
```

You now have a working tax rate Web Service that can return the calculated tax amount to a calling application. For this Web Service to be accessible, you need to deploy it to a Web server.

Deploying the Service

To deploy a Web Service, use the Web Setup Project to create the setup program. For more information on using the setup projects, check Day 20, "Finishing the Application."

Note The deployment process is needed only when you want the Web Service installed on a production machine, or a development machine other than your local computer.

To create the deployment package, add a new project to the existing solution by right-clicking the solution name in the Solution Explorer and choosing Add, New Project from the pop-up menu. In the Add New Project dialog box, select Web Setup Project from the Setup and Deployment Projects folder. Don't forget to name the project something meaningful for your Web Service, such as `TaxRateInstall`. Now add several files to the project. Right-click the setup project and select Add, Project Output from the menu. This will display the Add Project Output Group dialog box (see Figure 21.11).

FIGURE 21.11

Adding the required Web Service project files to the Setup Project.

From this dialog box, select the following:

- The Primary Output group consists of the project DLL and its dependencies.
- The Debug Symbols group is the project's PDB file.
- The Content Files group references the remaining files for the Web Service, such as the .asmx, .asax, and web.config files.

After selecting these groups, click OK to add them to the Web Application Folder in the File System editor (see Figure 21.12). The final step is to build the setup project.

FIGURE 21.12

The File System editor contains the required files for the deployment of the Web Service.

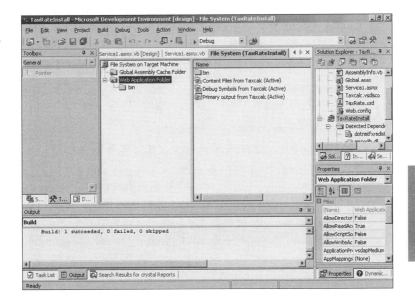

21

This has created the installation package for the new TaxRate Web Service. To actually deploy the Web Service, you must run the installation.

Another way to deploy the Web Service is to copy the project directly to the other machine. To do this, select the Web Service project and then choose Copy Project from the Project menu. This will display the Copy Project dialog box (see Figure 21.13), which will ask for the destination folder for the Web Service and the Web access method you want to use.

FIGURE 21.13

Copying the Web Service to another Web server.

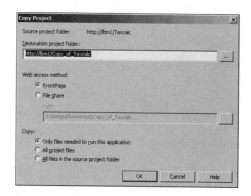

Congratulations! Your Web Service is ready to use.

Creating a Web Service Client

A Web Service client is any component or application that references and uses a Web Service. This can be from either a client-based Windows application or other Web applications. What you will learn in this section is how to access your new Web Service from both a Windows application and a Web application. The process actually is the same for both, so you will see how to add the Web Service reference to your project (Windows or Web) and then access that service in the code.

To see how to access a Web Service, follow these steps:

1. Add a Windows project to the solution.

2. Right-click the project and select Add Web Reference from the pop-up menu.

3. In the Add Web Reference dialog box (see Figure 21.14), you can enter any URL that contains a Web Service, browse to a Microsoft directory of Web Services, or display what's available on the local Web server. When working on your local Web server, you should enter the URL that contains the discovery file for your new Web Service (it should be the Web directory where the solution is located).

Note

A *discovery file* contains the information that describes a particular Web Service using the *Web Services Description Language* (*WSDL*). It's through the discovery file that the client learns where to find the Web Service. For Web Services created in Visual Basic, the discovery file is located in the project with the file extension .vsdisco.

FIGURE 21.14

Adding a Web Reference to the application project.

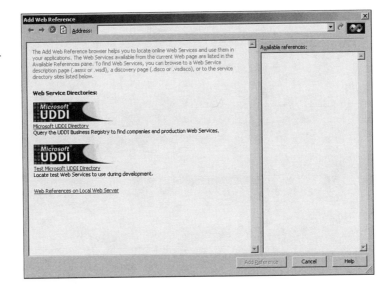

4. The Add Web Reference dialog box displays all the Web Services available in that directory (see Figure 21.15). After confirming that this is the correct Web Service, click the Add Reference button to add the Web Service to your project.

You should see the Web Service in your project, as shown in Figure 21.16.

You are now ready to use the Web Service in your application. Add the controls listed in Table 21.1 to your form as shown in Figure 21.17. This will allow a user to enter the correct information and then request the tax calculation to be performed.

FIGURE 21.15

The Web Service displayed in the Add Web Reference dialog box.

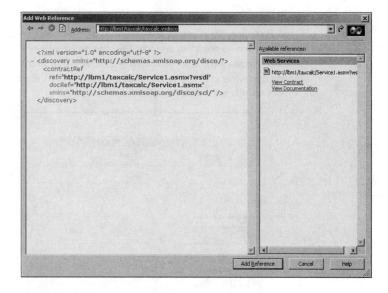

FIGURE 21.16

The referenced Web Service is displayed in the project.

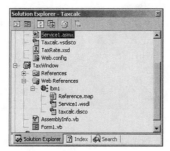

TABLE 21.1 Tax Calculation Windows Form

Control	Property	Value
Textbox	Name	txtCity
Textbox	Name	txtState
Textbox	Name	txtSaleAmt
Textbox	Name	txtTaxAmt
Textbox	Name	txtTotalAmt
Label	Text	City
Label	Text	State
Label	Text	Sale Amount
Label	Text	Tax Amount
Label	Text	Total

TABLE 21.1   continued

Control	Property	Value
Button	Name	cmdCalc
	Text	Calculate

FIGURE 21.17

The Windows form used to interact with the Web Service.

To access the Web Service in your code, you need to add a reference to the service in the code using the following:

```
Dim myTaxCalc As New <web server>.Service1()
```

After you add this statement, you can use the service as `myTaxCalc` anywhere in the application code. For this example, add the following to the Calculate button's click routine:

```
TxtTaxAmt.Text = myTaxCalc.TaxAmt(txtCity.Text, txtState.Text, txtSaleAmt.Text)
        txtTotalAmt.Text = CDbl(txtSaleAmt.Text) + CDbl(txtTaxAmt.Text)
```

This will request the tax amount from the Web Service using the city, state, and sales amount parameters; then it will add the sales amount and tax amount to display in the `txtTotal` textbox. Try executing the application, entering valid and invalid information.

Note

> Remember to set the starting application to the Windows application instead of the Web Service. Otherwise, you can't test the Windows application.

Realize that even though we added error handling in the Web Service, the application isn't checking for it. To do that, add the following as a simple check for errors:

```
If CDbl(txtTaxAmt.Text) < 0 Then
    MsgBox("An error has occurred!")
    Exit Sub
End If
```

21

Another thing you might have noticed is that the first time the Web Service is called, there's a slight delay in the response. Then, for all subsequent requests, the response is almost instantaneous. The reason is that the connection to the database must be opened the first time, which takes a little time.

Now that you know how to use a Web Service in a Windows application, you also know how to use it in a Web application. The process is exactly the same:

1. Add a Web reference to the project.
2. Add a definition to the Web page code.
3. Reference the Web Service in the code.

Summary

Congratulations! You've learned enough about creating Web Services to be a little dangerous. Today's lesson has shown you how to create a Web Service project, add methods to it, and deploy it to a Web server. You also learned how to enhance the methods by adding error handling and database access. Finally, you saw what was required to add this resource to any application.

In addition, you have come to the end of this book. In the past 21 days, you have learned many different and sometimes complex concepts of the Visual Basic .NET language and .NET Framework environment. You have seen how to use the capabilities of Visual Basic .NET to create professional applications for either the Windows environment or for the Web environment. You have also seen many techniques that you can use when designing your applications. Hopefully, you will be able to use this newly acquired knowledge in the near future. Good luck with your programming career.

Q&A

Q What is a Web Service?

A A Web Service is a unique function (program code) that provides a particular element of functionality, such as application logic, to any application that requires that functionality. This functionality can be used either internally by a single application or exposed externally over the Internet for use by any number of applications.

Q Can a Web Service be accessed from a Windows application?

A Yes. A Web Service can be accessed by both Windows and Web-based applications. In fact, the client application can be written in almost any of the accepted languages, such as C++ and Visual Basic.

Q Are any controls associated with a Web Service?

A Because Web Services act more like functions, you can't associate any visible controls with a Web Service, such as a Textbox. However, you can associate controls such as a Data Adapter.

Workshop

The Workshop provides quiz questions to solidify your understanding of the material covered, and exercises so you can use what you've learned. Answers are provided in Appendix A, "Answers to Quizzes and Exercises."

Quiz

1. What type of project is used to create a Web Service?

2. How can you test a Web Service?

3. What method can you use to inform a Web Service client that an error has occurred?

4. What are the two ways of deploying a Web Service?

Exercise

Enhance the tax calculation Web Service by adding a second method that returns the tax percentage used in the calculation.

21

WEEK 3

In Review

Week 3 covered some of the newest topics in the Visual Basic development environment. These included the changes made to Internet programming from within a Windows application, as well as the new Web application development and data access from across the Web. Week 3 also covered many of the topics that are normally forgotten by the average programmer, including performance and tuning of the application, and the creation of a Help system. Week 3 showed what it takes to get a Windows application to market and how to create and work with Web Services.

Internet and the Web

With the release of Visual Basic .NET, you now have the ability to create professional Web-based applications. Days 15, 16, and 17 showed you how to work with these new features. On Day 15, you saw how to add Internet access to your desktop Windows applications. Then in the next two lessons, you learned how to create new Web applications using the new features of Web Forms in the Visual Basic environment.

Help and the Application

On Day 18, "Building Online Help," you learned how to design an application Help system and then create it using the HTML Help Workshop that is included with Visual Basic. Then on Day 19, "Tuning and Tweaking Performance," you were introduced to the concepts, tips, and techniques that you can use to enhance the performance of your application, including using the Resource Editor to compile strings and pictures externally to the application, which reduces the size of the actual application.

Finishing the Application

On Days 20, "Finishing the Application," and 21, "Working with Web Services," the information that you need to know to package and sell your application was presented to you along with the different issues that you should think about when finishing your application. Finally, these days taught you what a Web service is and how to create one. This book covered the different tips, techniques, and skills that you need to design, build, and distribute your application professionally.

APPENDIX A

Answers to Quizzes and Exercises

Day 1, "Writing Professional Visual Basic Applications"

Quiz Answers

1. An application consists of many unique programs combined into one larger related package. This package usually can perform several different functions that all are related to each other.

2. The major steps in a standard life cycle are design, coding, testing, debugging, and documentation.

3. Testing is the process of detecting errors in your application as they occur; debugging is the process of identifying the cause of an error and correcting it.

Exercise Answer

To change the File Copy function to a Move File function, you need to add only one Visual Basic statement to the routine. After you successfully copy the file to the destination, you have to delete it from the source directory. To do so, insert the following line of code immediately after the two `FileClose` statements:

```
Kill (strFrom_filename)
```

This statement deletes the file referenced by the variable.

Day 2, "The Face of a Windows Application"

Quiz Answers

1. The Help Provider doesn't have its own dialog box to display; instead, it displays the specified help topic using the Windows Help engine.

2. You can create an MDSI application by adding a form to your project and then setting the `isMDIParent` property to True.

3. The Explorer interface uses the ListView, TreeView, PictureBox, and Label controls to create the two-pane work area.

Exercise Answer

Any answers or example code that I could provide would match what's already in the lesson. So for these two exercises, you can decide for yourself what the answer is, and it's not even cheating.

Day 3, "Creating Simple Forms"

Quiz Answers

1. A toolbar requires an ImageList and Toolbar control to be on the form; however, if you want to use drop-down menus in the toolbar you must add a ContextMenu control.

2. Yes. A toolbar can display text, images, or both.

3. You can have many top-level menu items as you want; however, too many will make your application very hard to use.

4. No. At any given level of a menu item, only one hotkey can use a particular letter.

Exercise Answer

This project requires the following controls to be added to the form, as shown in Figure A.1:

- ToolBar
- MainMenu
- ImageList
- OpenFileDialog
- TextBox
- SaveFileDialog

FIGURE A.1

The completed form for Day 3's exercise.

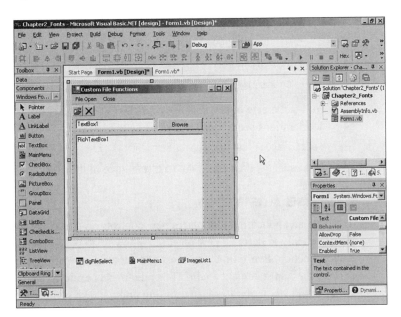

Day 4, "Understanding the .NET Framework"

This lesson didn't have any quiz questions or exercises.

Day 5, "Working with Objects, Collections, and Array Processing"

Quiz Answers

1. Two functions available in Visual Basic determine an object's class: `TypeOf` and `TypeName`.

2. The `With...End With` statements are efficient only when you're working with many properties of a control. When you assign only one or two properties, it's better to just code the full statements.

3. All collections share four objects:

   - `Add` method
   - `Remove` method
   - `Item` method
   - `Count` property

4. You can create a new instance of a class or an object by declaring it in the Declarations section as follows:

   ```
   Public myObj as New [object]
   ```

   The object is created on the first reference in the code.

Exercise Answer

To create an application that places new controls on the form when a button is clicked, you need only to define a new object as a new textbox and then add it to the form's controls collection. Every time you must add another copy of the control to the form, simply execute the `Add` statement again. The code for this exercise uses an existing textbox, which is hidden on the form as a starting point and shown in Listing A.1.

LISTING A.1 CHAP5EXE.TXT: The Finished Code for the Exercise in Day 5

```
Public txtTop As Integer
Public txtLeft As Integer

Private Sub Command1_Click()
    Dim MyText As New TextBox()
        MyText.Location = New Point(txtLeft, txtTop)
        Me.Controls.Add(MyText)

        txtTop = txtTop + 25
        txtLeft = txtLeft + 10
```

LISTING A.1   continued

```
End Sub

Public Sub New()
    MyBase.New()

    'This call is required by the Windows Form Designer.
    InitializeComponent()
    txtTop = 8
    txtLeft = 0

End Sub
```

However, this code will keep adding controls on this form even if there's no longer any room for them to be displayed.

Day 6, "Understanding Procedures, Functions, and Logic"

Quiz Answers

1. A function can return only a single value; however, by using the ByRef keyword, the function can modify any of the variables that were passed to it.

2. The only difference between a subroutine and a function is that a function returns a value, whereas a subroutine doesn't.

3. Using public variables isn't recommended because they can be accessed anywhere in the application code, and you could wind up accidentally modifying a value. This would result in unexpected errors in the application.

4. You can leave any subroutine or object's event routine by using the Exit Sub statement.

5. There's now block scope, which reduces even further the area where a variable is accessible in a procedure.

Exercise Answer

The first part of this exercise will print all the variables because the procedure-level variables are in the routine that will be printing them. However, the second part of the exercise will result in a runtime error because the procedure-level variables aren't accessible. Listing A.2 shows the code to perform the tasks for this exercise. You also will need to add a module to the application as shown in Listing A.3.

LISTING A.2 CHAP6EX1.TXT: Form Module Code for the Exercise

```
Private mVar1 As String
    Private mVar2 As String
    Private pVar1 As String

Private Sub Form1_Load(ByVal sender As System.Object, _
        ByVal e As System.EventArgs) Handles MyBase.Load
    Var1 = "1"
    Var2 = "2"
    mVar1 = "3"
    mVar2 = "this is a string variable"
End Sub

Private Sub myPrint()
    pVar1 = "5"
    MsgBox("Var1=" & Var1)
    MsgBox("Var2=" & Var2)
    MsgBox("mVar1=" & mVar1)
    MsgBox("mVar2=" & mVar2)
    MsgBox(txtInput)
    MsgBox("pVar1=" & pVar1)
End Sub

Private Sub Button1_Click(ByVal sender As System.Object, _
        ByVal e As System.EventArgs) Handles Button1.Click
    Call myPrint()
End Sub

Private Sub Button2_Click(ByVal sender As System.Object, _
        ByVal e As System.EventArgs) Handles Button2.Click
    MsgBox("Var1=" & Var1)
    MsgBox("Var2=" & Var2)
    MsgBox("mVar1=" & mVar1)
    MsgBox("mVar2=" & mVar2)
    MsgBox(txtInput)
    MsgBox("pVar1=" & pVar1)
End Sub
```

LISTING A.3 CHAP6EX2.TXT: Module-Level Code for the Exercise

```
Public Var1 As Integer
Public Var2 As Integer
Public Const txtInput = "Please enter your name"
```

Day 7, "Building Complex Forms"

Quiz Answers

1. The following six design concepts result in well-designed forms:

    *   Make the forms as consistent as possible within an application.

    *   Apply the same standards throughout the application.

    *   Place the command buttons on all forms in the same position and order whenever possible.

    *   Use color to highlight important information.

    *   Don't clutter the forms with too much information.

    *   Keep the data-entry forms simple.

2. No. The only objects that can be placed directly on the MDI parent form are the picture box, menus, and any custom control that supports the Align property, such as the StatusBar control.

3. Although both interface styles use a single form as the main application form, the Explorer interface uses many different controls to create the unique display.

Exercise Answer

To create this application, you need two forms in the new project: the MDI parent and one child form with its visible property set to False.

The MDI parent form will contain a menu, toolbar, and a status bar, and should have the code from Listing A.4 included.

LISTING A.4   CHAP7EXE.TXT: The MDI Parent Code for This Lesson's Exercise

```
Dim intFormCtr As Integer
Private Sub ToolbarButton1_Click()
    Select Case e.itemData
        Case "New"
            Call mnuFileNew_Click
    End Select
End Sub

Private Sub MDIForm_Load()
    intFormCtr = 1
    frmNote.Caption = "NotePad Version " & intFormCtr
End Sub

Private Sub mnuFileNew_Click()
```

LISTING A.4   continued

```
        Dim NewNote As New frmNote
        intFormCtr = intFormCtr + 1
        NewNote.Show
        NewNote.Text = "NotePad Version " & intFormCtr
    End Sub
```

Day 8, "Designing a Database Application"

This lesson didn't have any quiz questions or exercises.

Day 9, "Processing Data"

Quiz Answers

1. When you design a database, you want to meet as many of the following objectives as possible:

   • Allows data to be stored efficiently so that the database doesn't get larger than absolutely necessary

   • Provides for easy data updates

   • Provides a flexible design to allow for the addition of new functions, tables, or data

   • Makes it easy to perform quick searches

2. You can use five main SQL commands to access the data contained within a database: SELECT, INSERT INTO, UPDATE, DELETE FROM, and TRANSFORM.

Exercise Answer

When creating a database design, the first step is to list the tables and columns that will be created. Table A.1 lists the suggested tables and columns for an address book application.

TABLE A.1   Suggested Tables and Columns for the Example Application

Table	Columns
Address Entry	Entry Key
	Date Updated
	First Name
	Middle Initial

TABLE A.1 continued

Table	Columns
	Last Name
	Address
	City
	State
	Zip Code
	Home Phone
Phones	Phone Key
	Entry Fkey
	Phone Type
	Phone Number

Day 10, "Accessing the Database"

Quiz Answers

1. The Data Control provides automatic access to many standard data access features and functions. This way, you can create a data access application without creating any code.

2. The `MoveComplete` event is called whenever the database recordset that's attached to a Data Control is moved to another row.

3. To delete a record, you can use the `Delete` method of the Data Control or recordset.

Exercise Answer

To add a search form to the application, add a new Toolbar button to show the new form; then create the form as shown in Figure A.2. Add the code in Listing A.5 and change the `Name` properties of the different controls to match those in the code.

FIGURE A.2

Adding a search form to the application.

LISTING A.5 CH10EXERCISE.TXT: The Code to Search the Database and Display a List of Found Names

```
Private Sub cmdNew_Click()
lstNames.Visible = False
txtSearch.Text = ""
End Sub

Private Sub cmdQuit_Click()
Me.Close
End Sub

Private Sub cmdSearch_Click()
If optLastName Then
    ADODC1.RecordSource = _
      "Select addressid, LastName, firstname, firstname & "" _
      "" & Lastname as fullname from [address entry] where lastname like '" _
      & txtSearch.Text & "*'"
ElseIf optFirstname Then
    ADODC1.RecordSource = _
      "Select addressid, LastName, firstname, firstname & "" _
      "" & Lastname as fullname from [address entry] where firstname  like '" _
      & txtSearch.Text & "*'"
End If
ADODC1.Requery
lstNames.Refresh
lstNames.Visible = True
End Sub

Private Sub Form_Load()
txtSearch.Text = ""
End Sub

Private Sub lstNames_DblClick()
ADODC1.RecordSet.Find "fullname = '" & _
    lstNames.BoundText & "'", adSearchForward
frmAddressEntry.sqlEntry = _
    "select * from [Address Entry] Where [AddressID] = " _
  & Data1.Recordset.Fields("addressid")
frmAddressEntry.Show

End Sub
```

After adding all the controls, resize the Listbox to fill the area as shown in Figure A.3. Also, set the Listbox's Visible property to False.

FIGURE A.3

The Listbox fills the entire area of the form.

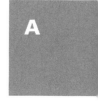

Day 11, "Enhancing the Application with Custom Objects"

Quiz Answers

1. A solution can include several different projects, such as a Windows Forms project and one or more Windows control projects.

2. Custom controls allow you to create any type of functionality you might need by using already existing controls together as a single control in your application. As you've seen in this lesson, you can combine controls to create a function, such as a Filter dialog form. This way, anyone who needs this type of functionality can use this new control rather than have to create it himself.

Exercise Answer

This is an exercise in which only you will know if you found the correct answer.

Day 12, "Working with Crystal Reports"

Quiz Answers

1. Crystal Reports can access any type of database that you might use. It can access most PC local databases directly, although it needs one of the following connections for network or remote databases: ODBC, OLEDB, or ADO.NET.

2. No. Crystal Reports allows you to build reports without any need to learn SQL.

Exercise Answer

First, add a new form named `frmCRViewer` to display the reports. Add a Crystal Reports Viewer to this new form and name it `rptAddress`. Then, in the `frmMain` form, add a button to the toolbar that will display the `frmPrintMgr` form. You also need to add the `frmPrintMgr` form to the project. Finally, change the references in the `frmPrintMgr` form to reference the report viewer in the new form.

Day 13, "Coping with Error Handling"

Quiz Answers

1. An *error trap* is a term that describes the detection of an error during the execution of application code.

2. The first type is one that can be found and corrected during the testing process the other type must be handled during the normal execution of the application.

3. To retrieve the WSDL description, append the string `?WSDL` to the URL for the .asmx page associated with the XML Web service. Place this URL in your favorite browser. ASP.NET generates the WSDL file for the XML Web service automatically and sends the XML file back as a response to the HTTP request from the browser.

Exercise Answer

Because of the nature of error handling, there's no easy way to show an answer to the exercise. How the error processing would look and work is entirely up to you.

Day 14, "Testing and Debugging the Application"

Quiz Answer

1. A Watch expression will track the values of specified variables, properties, or expressions but won't stop the execution of the code. The conditional breakpoint actually will halt the execution of the application when the value of the specified variable, property, or expression has changed or become `True`.

2. A Watch expression is set using the Debug menu's Add Watch option, pressing Shift+F9, or by right-clicking the variable or expression and choosing Add Watch.

A

3. Whenever you are stopped at a breakpoint in a procedure, the Locals window will display the values of all variables and properties now available within that procedure.

Exercise Answer

Because of the way breakpoints work, the only thing I can show you is what it would look like on my computer—not necessarily what you would see on your computer. For that reason, there are no answers for this exercise.

Day 15, "Programming for the Internet"

Quiz Answers

1. The Browser control is the main object you can use to add Internet access to your application.

2. Visual Basic is the programming language used to create Windows applications, whereas VBScript is a subset of the Visual Basic language used to enhance HTML Web pages.

Exercise Answer

This Web page is created by using HTML and VBScript, as shown in Listing A.6.

LISTING A.6 EXERCISE.HTM: Sample Code for Day 15's Exercise

```
<html>
<head>
<title>VBScript/HTML Exercise Page</title>
    <meta name=vs_defaultClientScript content="JavaScript">
    <meta name=vs_targetSchema content="Internet Explorer 5.0">
    <meta name="GENERATOR" content="Microsoft Visual Studio.NET 7.0">
    <meta name=ProgId content=VisualStudio.HTML>
    <meta name=Originator content="Microsoft Visual Studio.NET 7.0">
    <SCRIPT LANGUAGE="VBScript">
<!--

Sub SayHello_OnClick()
    MsgBox "Hello " & fname.value & " " & lname.Value & _
      ", are you ready to compute?", 36
End Sub
Sub Reset_OnClick()
    fname.Value = ""
    lname.Value = ""
    msgbox "Text has been Cleared.",36
End Sub
```

LISTING A.6   continued

```
-->
</SCRIPT>
</head>
body MS_POSITIONING="GridLayout">
    <BR>
    <H1> This is the exercise for Day 15</H1>
    <H2> Please enter your first and last name</H2>
    <H3> A message box will be displayed.</H3>
    <P>
    <HR>
    <INPUT id=fname type=text name=fname>
    <INPUT id=lname type=text name=lname>
    <INPUT id=SayHello type=button value="Say Hello" name=sayhello>
     
    <INPUT id=Reset type=button value=Reset name=Reset>
</body>
</html>
```

Day 16, "Creating a Web Application"

Quiz Answers

1. When a Web application is executed, the server will process any code specified as server-side and add the results to the Web page form sent to the browser. Client-side processing is done on the browser and doesn't require data transmission to the server to perform any action.

2. The best use of client-side processing is the validation of user input before sending it to the server. If the input is invalid, there is no reason to have the server try to process it.

3. ASP.NET provides a group of Validation Controls that provides you with the capabilities to validate different types of input, including ranges of values, empty input areas, and so forth.

Exercise Answer

Without knowing what you might have decided to change, there's no definitive answer that I could show you for this exercise.

Day 17, "Adding Data Access to the Web"

A

Quiz Answers

1. Data can be sent from one Web form to another by using Query/String pairs or by setting Session variables that can then be accessed in the next form.

2. Yes. Although a Web application can access a database using ADO, the recommended access method is using ADO.NET dataset connections.

Exercise Answer

Adding a new entry to the Address Book database from the Web application requires the same basic code and database connection information that you've already learned to create and use in order to read data from the database. The routine in Listing A.7 is an example of the code required to add a new row to the database. It's by no means complete—in fact, you would need to create a Web Form to accept the input for this routine.

LISTING A.7   AddingRecord.txt: Adding a New Row of Data to the Database

```
Sub AddAuthor_Click(Sender As Object, e As EventArgs)
Dim myCommand As SqlCommand
Dim insertCmd As String

'Build a SQL Insert statement string for all the input-form
'field values.
insertCmd = "insert into Authors values (@Id, @LName, @FName," _
        & "@Phone, @Address, @City, @State, @Zip, @Contract);"
'Initialize the SqlCommand with the new SQL string.
myCommand = New SqlCommand(insertCmd, myConnection)

'Create new parameters for the SqlCommand object and
'initialize them to the input-form field values.
myCommand.Parameters.Add(New SqlParameter("@LName", _ SqlDbType.VarChar, 40))
myCommand.Parameters("@LName").Value = au_lname.Value
myCommand.Parameters.Add(New SqlParameter("@FName", _ SqlDbType.VarChar, 20))
myCommand.Parameters("@FName").Value = au_fname.Value
myCommand.Parameters.Add(New SqlParameter("@Phone", _ SqlDbType.Char, 12))
myCommand.Parameters("@Phone").Value = phone.Value
myCommand.Connection.Open()
'Test to see whether the new row can be added and display the
'appropriate message box to the user.
Try
    myCommand.ExecuteNonQuery()
    Message.InnerHtml = "<b>Record Added</b><br>"
Catch ex As SqlException
    If ex.Number = 2627 Then
```

LISTING A.7   continued

```
        Message.InnerHtml = "ERROR: A record already exists with " _
                          & "the same primary key"
    Else
        Message.InnerHtml = "ERROR: Could not add record, please " _
                          & "ensure the fields are correctly filled out"
        Message.Style("color") = "red"
    End If
End Try

myCommand.Connection.Close()

End Sub
```

You can see in the example that a SQL INSERT command is built using the parameters to hold the data you want to add. Also, the new Try...Catch statement is used to check for errors. After you insert a new entry into the address book, you want to rebuild the tree structure. The easiest way to perform this action is to clear out the tree structure and then re-execute the code used to initially build the tree structure.

Day 18, "Building Online Help"

Quiz Answers

1. You connect context-sensitive help to its related topics by using HTML tags within the help topic file.

2. The Help button is added by setting the following properties of a form:

Property	Setting
HelpButton	True
ControlBox	True
MinButton and MaxButton	False
BorderStyle	Fixed, Single, or Sizable

3. The help project file can contain definitions for secondary windows, bitmap references, and topic file references.

Exercise Answer

I can't put any answers here that would match what you would do. The design, creation, and inclusion of a Help system into a Visual Basic application are very unique and personal things. As long as the Help system can be accessed and the information in it makes sense in regards to the application, you did it correctly.

Day 19, "Tuning and Tweaking Performance"

Quiz Answers

1. A resource file contains all the string constants and picture objects that your application will use. It also allows you to quickly change the language of all the application's messages and labels.

2. You can increase the performance of your application in many different ways, including the following:

   - By keeping forms hidden instead of unloading them
   - By using more efficient Visual Basic variables and processing
   - When appropriate, by compiling the application into a native code executable

Exercise Answer

Because you can affect performance so many different ways, there's nothing I can show you that would be the "correct" way of doing things. Only you will know if you got it right.

Day 20, "Finishing the Application"

Quiz Answers

1. If you can't support your application after you sell it, your users won't recommend it to other people they talk to.

2. When selling your application, you need to advertise and set up a process by which customers can purchase your software. By selling as shareware, however, all you need to do is put your application on a shareware server and wait for the money to start coming in.

3. A copyright protects you from someone stealing your code and idea of the application you've created. A trademark protects only the name or symbol that you've chosen for that application.

Exercise Answer

This is an exercise in which only you will know whether you've found the correct answer by testing the setup program after you create it.

Day 21, "Working with Web Services"

Quiz Answers

1. You would use an ASP.NET Web Service project to create an XML Web service.

2. An XML Web service can be tested from within the Visual Basic IDE by making it the startup application. You also can set breakpoints within the code to test the processing.

3. You need to create error numbers that can be recognized by the client application as errors.

4. An XML Web service can be deployed either by using the Copy Project dialog box in Visual Basic or by creating a Web Setup project for the Web Service.

Exercise Answer

This new method is almost identical to the original method. The only change is what is being returned. Listing A.8 is an example of this new method:

LISTING A.8   WebService.txt: Adding Functionality to a Web Service

```
<WebMethod()> Public Function TaxRate(ByVal txCity As String,
                      ByVal txState As String) As Double
    If txCity = "" Then
        TaxRate = -98
        Exit Function
    End If
    If txState = "" Then
        TaxRate = -99
        Exit Function
    End If
    Dim TaxRateTbl As New DataSet1()
    SqlDataAdapter1.SelectCommand.Parameters("@City").Value = txCity
    SqlDataAdapter1.SelectCommand.Parameters("@State").Value = txState
    TaxRateTbl.Clear()
    SqlDataAdapter1.Fill(TaxRateTbl)
    If TaxRateTbl.TaxRates.Count = 0 Then
        TaxRate = -91
        Exit Function
    End If
    TaxRate = TaxRateTbl.TaxRates.Item(0).TaxRate
End Function
```

INDEX